2000-200

BEST COUNTRY SONGS

ISBN-10: 0-7390-4236-X
ISBN-13: 978-0-7390-4236-6

CONTENTS

GOGGLES ON
LIKE WE NEVER LOVED AT ALL
My Give a Damn's Busted
JO DEE MESSINA
Big Time
MISSISSIPPI GIRL
BACK WHEN
TIM McGRAW
Suds In The Bucket
TOUGH LITTLE BOYS
Dixie Chicks

AMERICA WILL ALWAYS STAND

Words and Music by RANDY TRAVIS, YVONNE SANSON, DOC WALLEY, BECKI BLUEFIELD and MIKE CURTIS

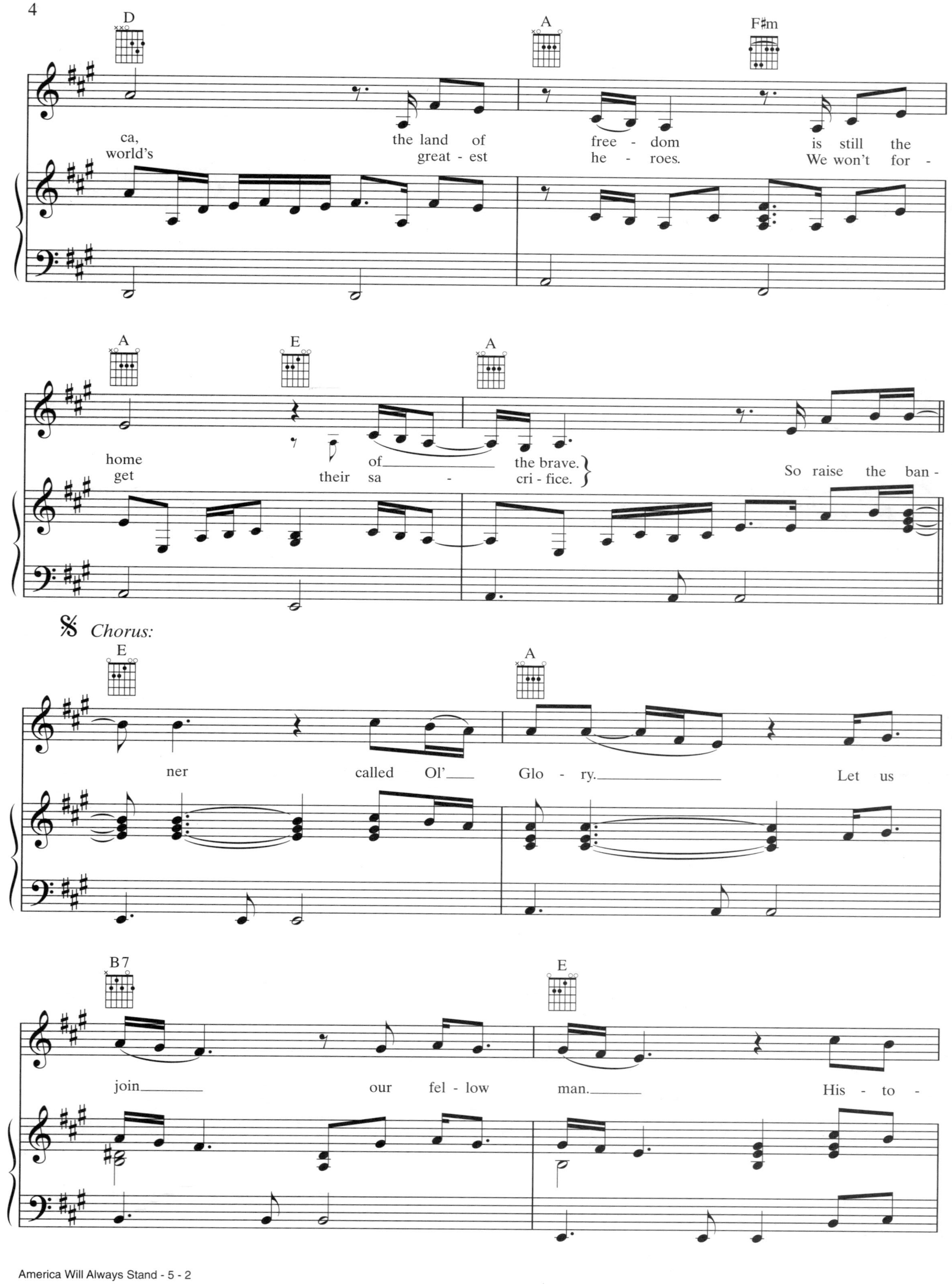
D
A
F♯m
ca, the land of free - dom is still the
world's great - est he - roes. We won't for -
A
E
A
home of the brave.
get their sa - cri - fice.
So raise the ban -
Chorus:
E
A
ner called Ol' Glo - ry. Let us
B7
E
join our fel - low man. His - to -

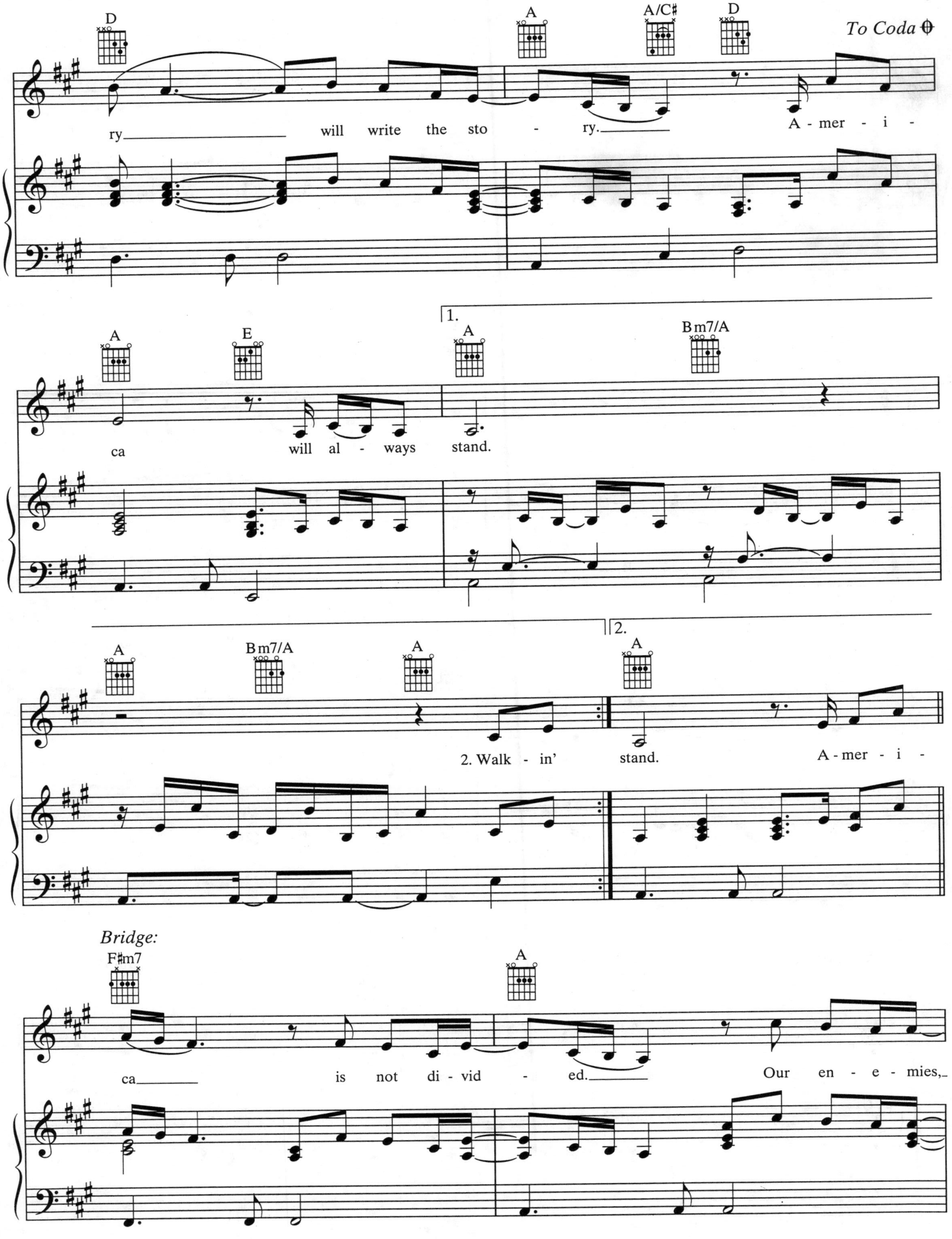
To Coda
D
A
A/C♯
D
ry will write the sto - ry. A - mer - i -
1.
A
E
A
Bm7/A
ca will al - ways stand.
2.
A
Bm7/A
A
A
2. Walk - in' stand. A - mer - i -
Bridge:
F♯m7
A
ca is not di - vid - ed. Our en - e - mies,

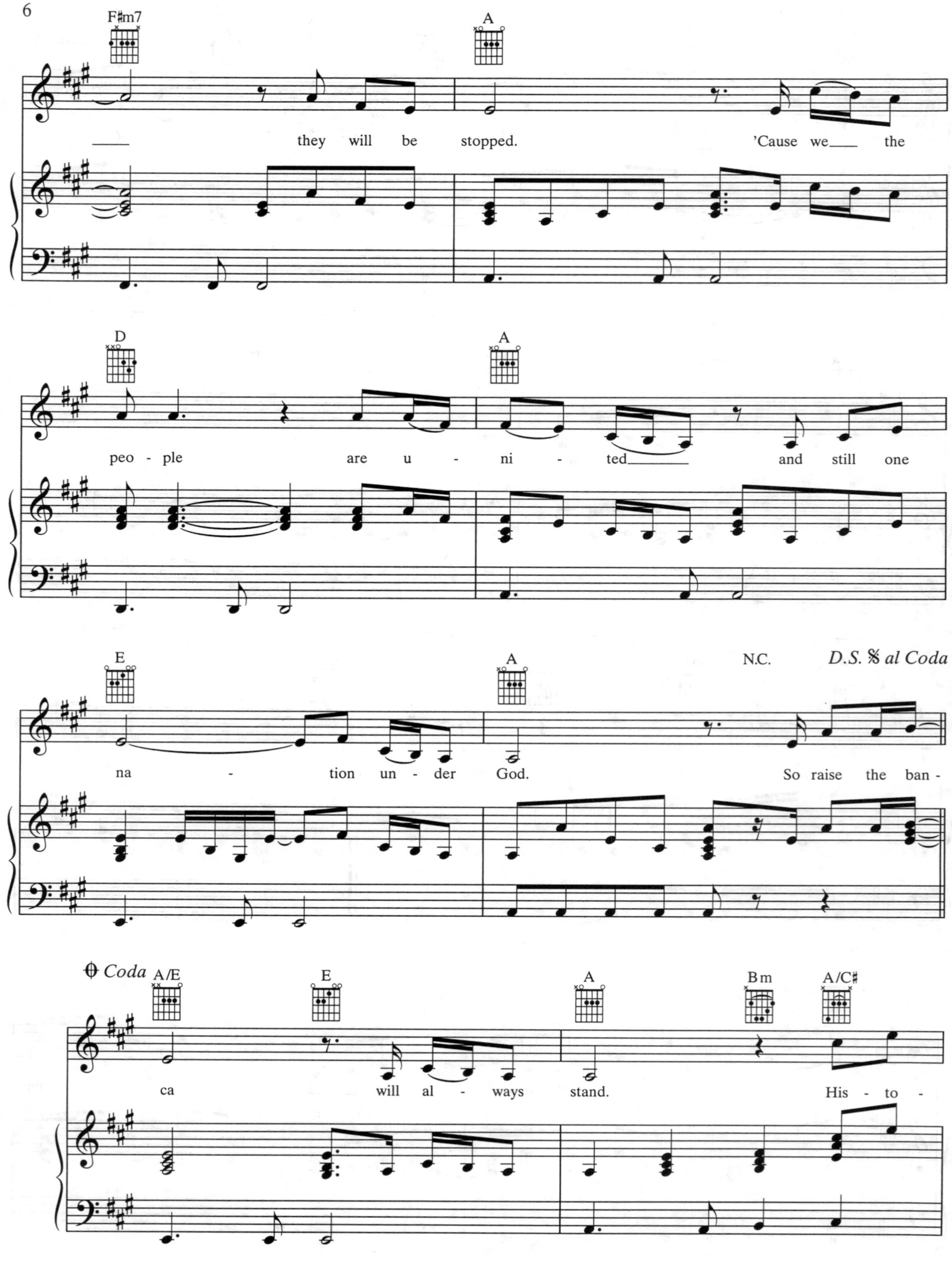
F♯m7
A
they will be stopped.
'Cause we the
D
A
peo - ple are u - ni - ted and still one
E
A
N.C.
D.S. 𝄋 al Coda
na - tion un - der God.
So raise the ban -
𝄌 Coda
A/E
E
A
Bm
A/C♯
ca will al - ways stand.
His - to -

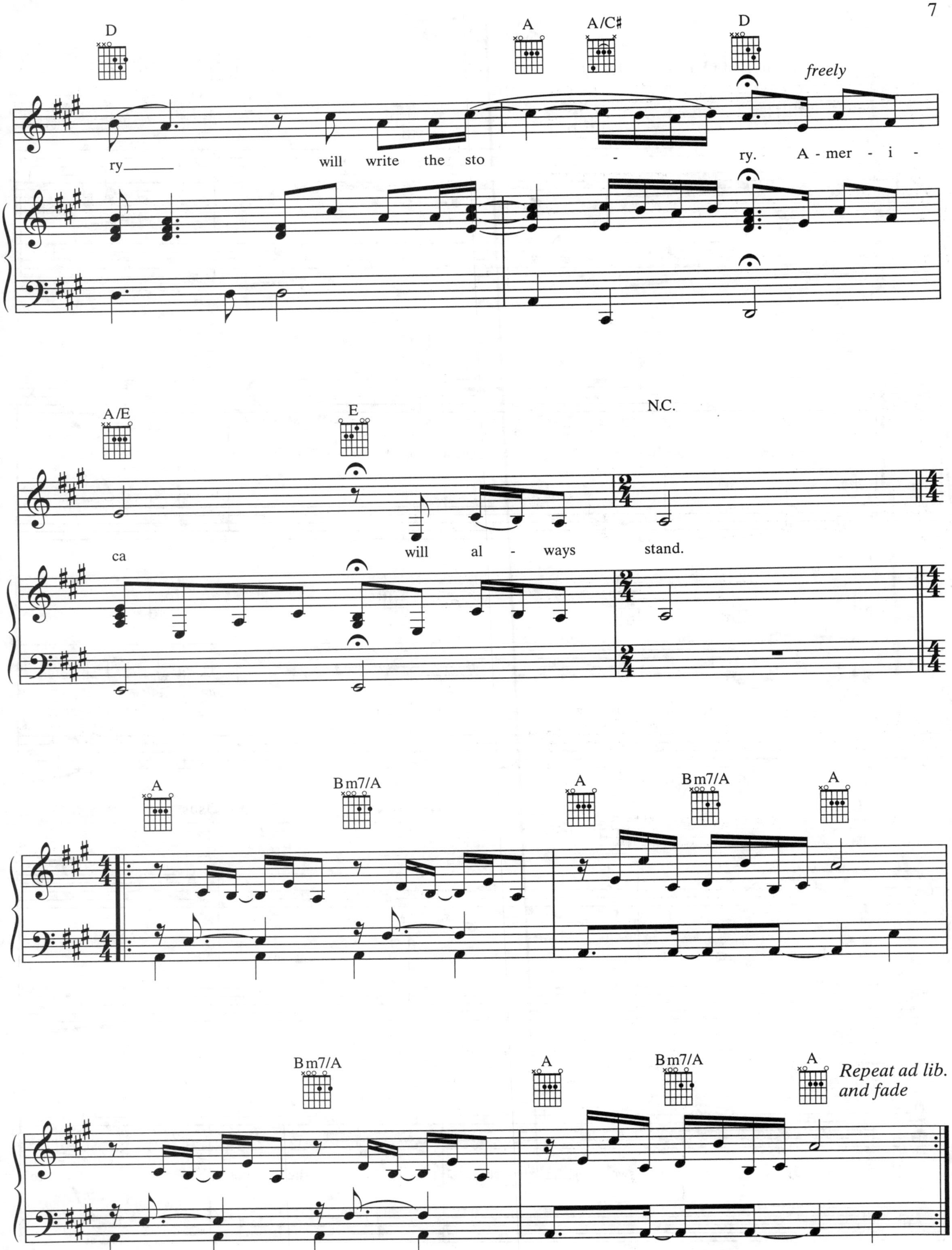
D
A
A/C♯
D
freely
ry___ will write the sto - ry. A - mer - i -
A/E
E
N.C.
ca will al - ways stand.
A
Bm7/A
A
Bm7/A
A
Bm7/A
A
Bm7/A
A
Repeat ad lib.
and fade

AUSTIN

Words and Music by
DAVID KENT and KIRSTI MANNA

Moderately, in half time (𝅗𝅥 = 60)

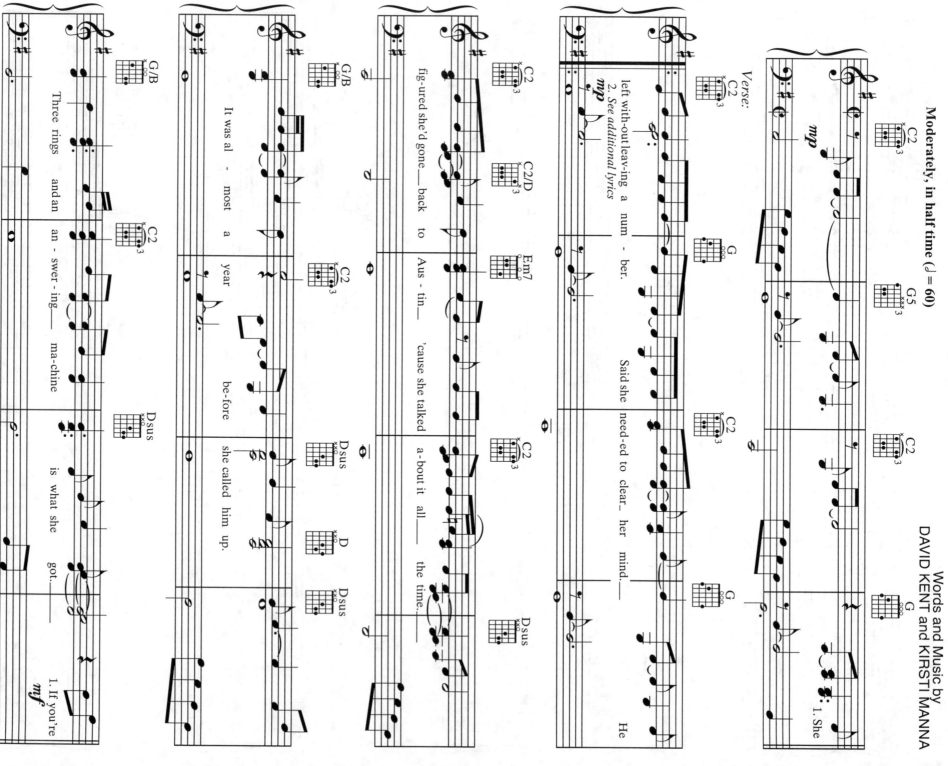

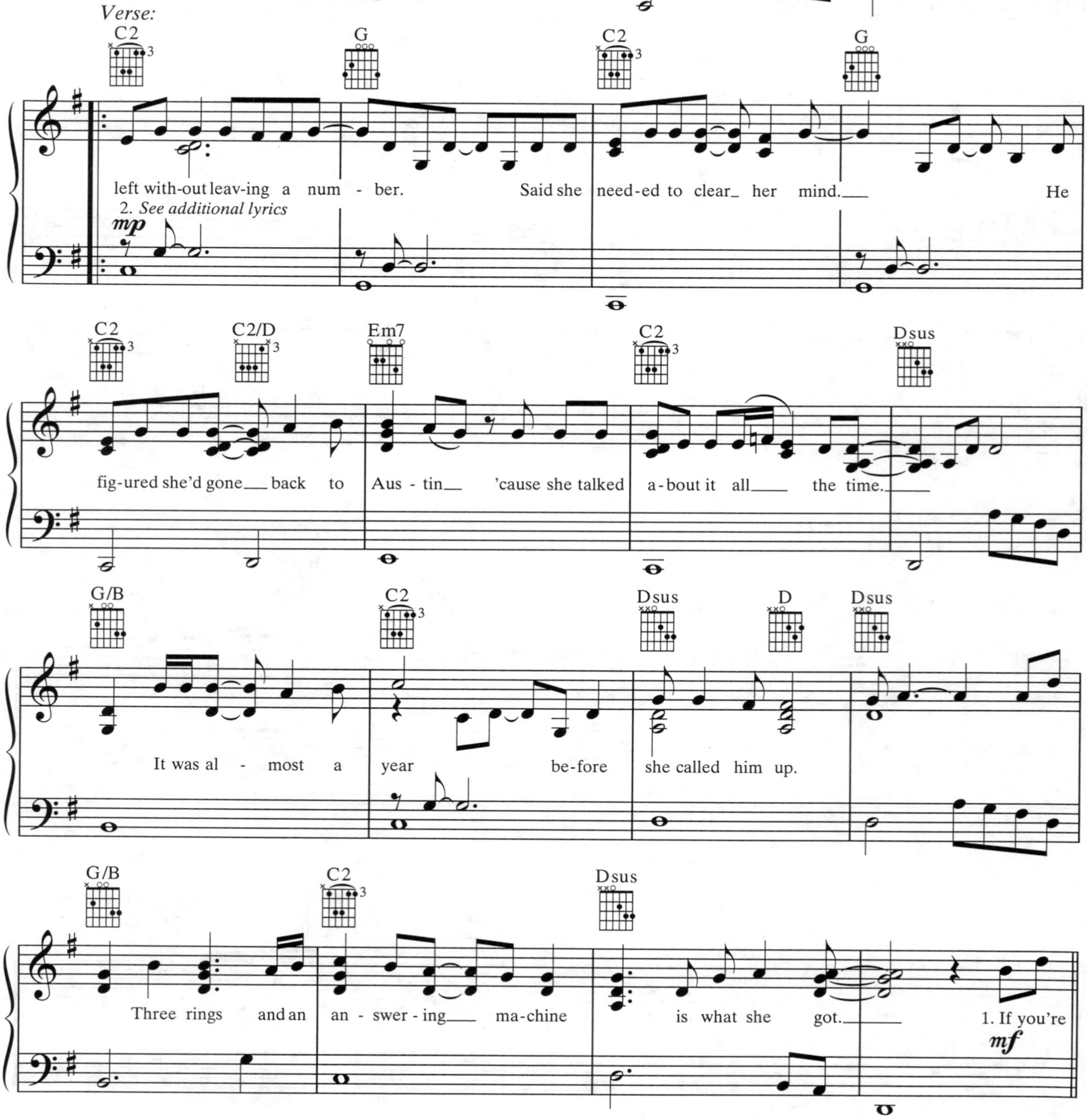

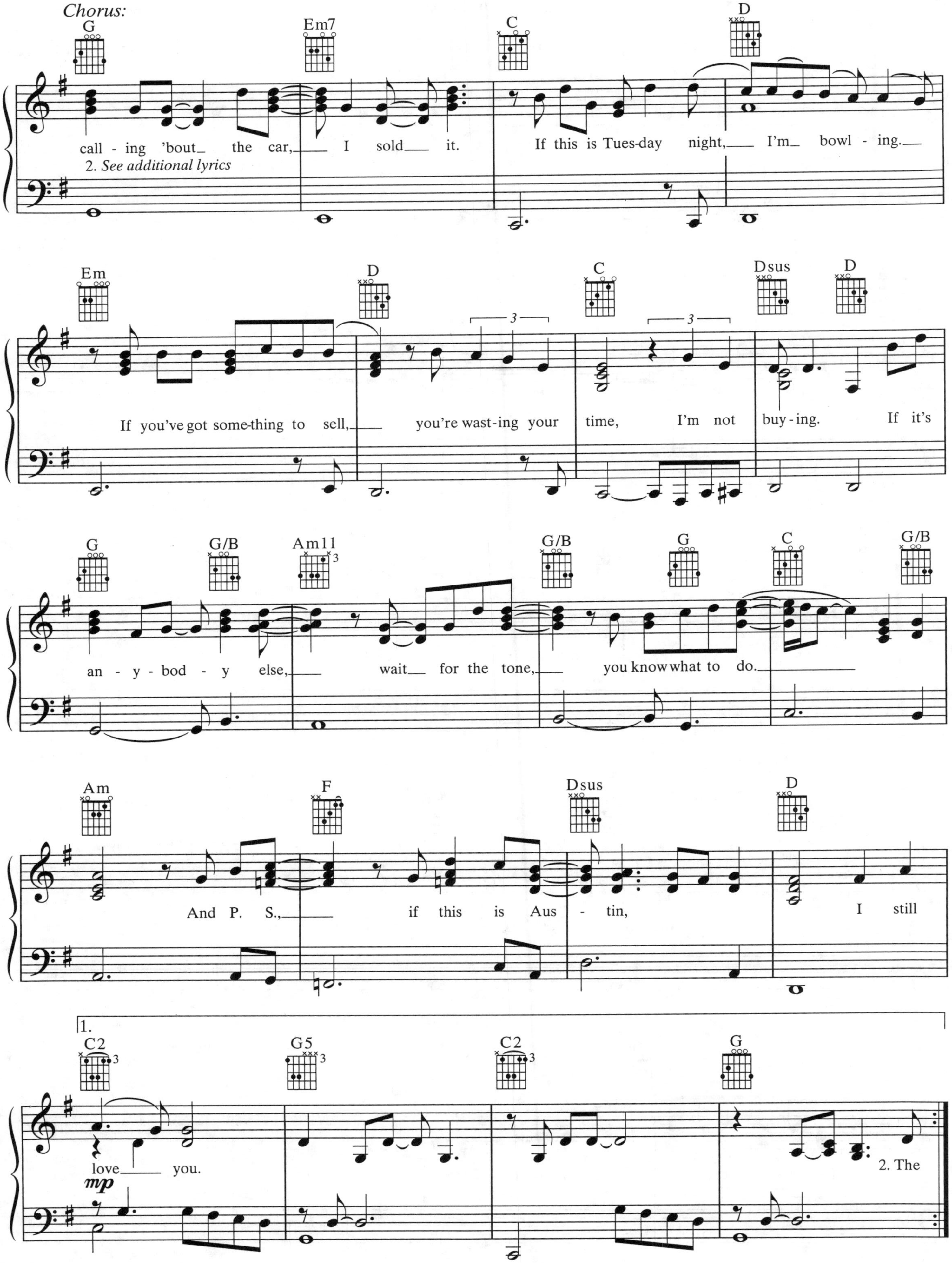
Chorus:
G
Em7
C
D
call - ing 'bout the car, I sold it.
2. See additional lyrics
If this is Tues-day night, I'm bowl - ing.
Em
D
C
Dsus
D
3
If you've got some-thing to sell, you're wast-ing your time, I'm not buy-ing. If it's
G
G/B
Am11
G/B
G
C
G/B
an - y - bod - y else, wait for the tone, you know what to do.
Am
F
Dsus
D
And P. S., if this is Aus - tin, I still
1.
C2
G5
C2
G
love you.
mp
2. The

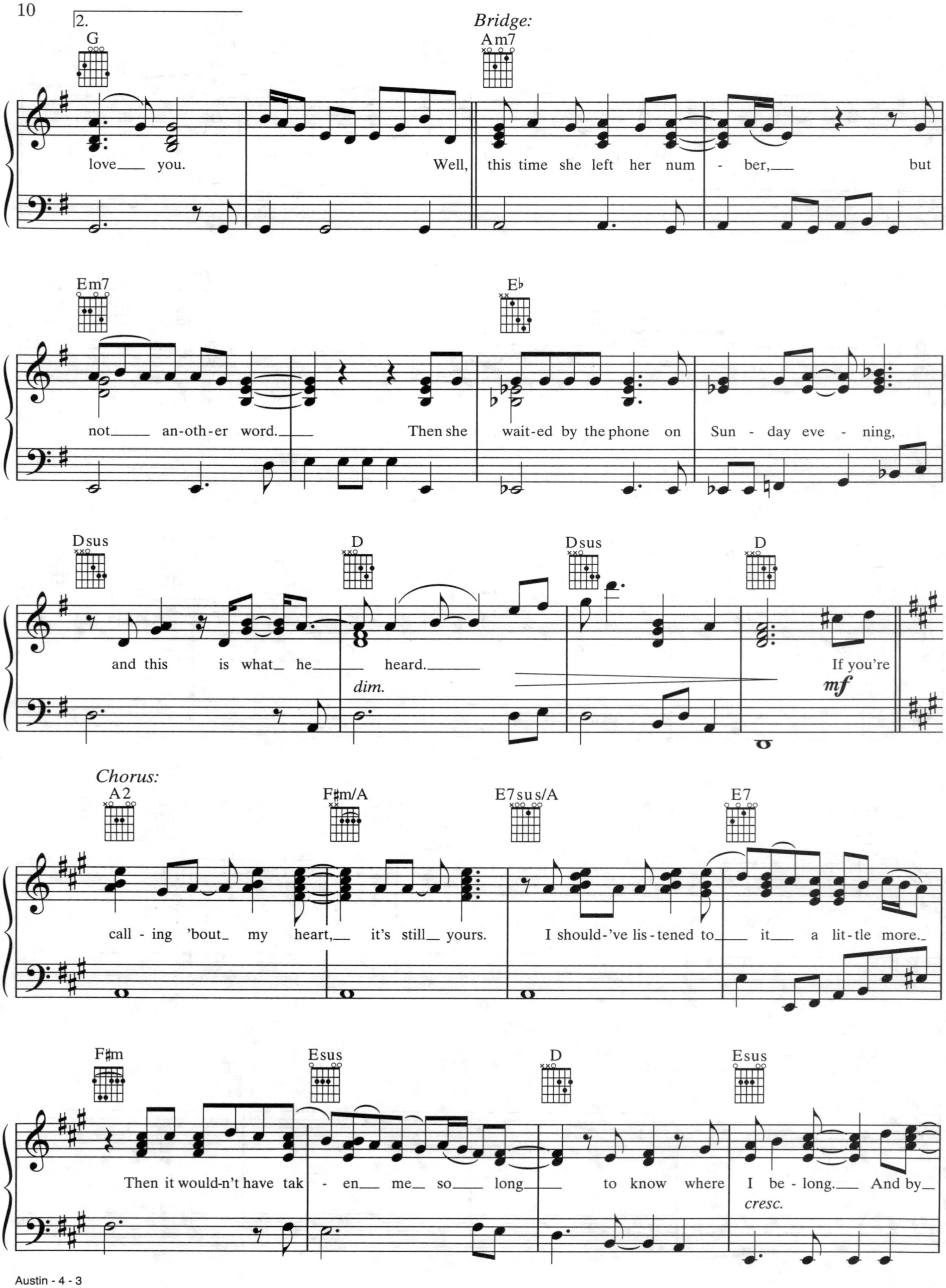
2.
Bridge:
G
love___ you.
Am7
Well, this time she left her num - ber,___ but
Em7
not___ an-oth-er word.___
Then she
E♭
wait-ed by the phone on Sun - day eve - ning,
Dsus
and this is what___ he___ heard.___
D
dim.
Dsus
D
If you're
mf
Chorus:
A2
call - ing 'bout___ my heart,___ it's still___ yours.
F♯m/A
E7sus/A
I should-'ve lis-tened to___ it___ a lit-tle more.___
E7
F♯m
Then it would-n't have tak - en___ me___ so___ long___
Esus
D
to know where
Esus
I be - long.___ And by___
cresc.

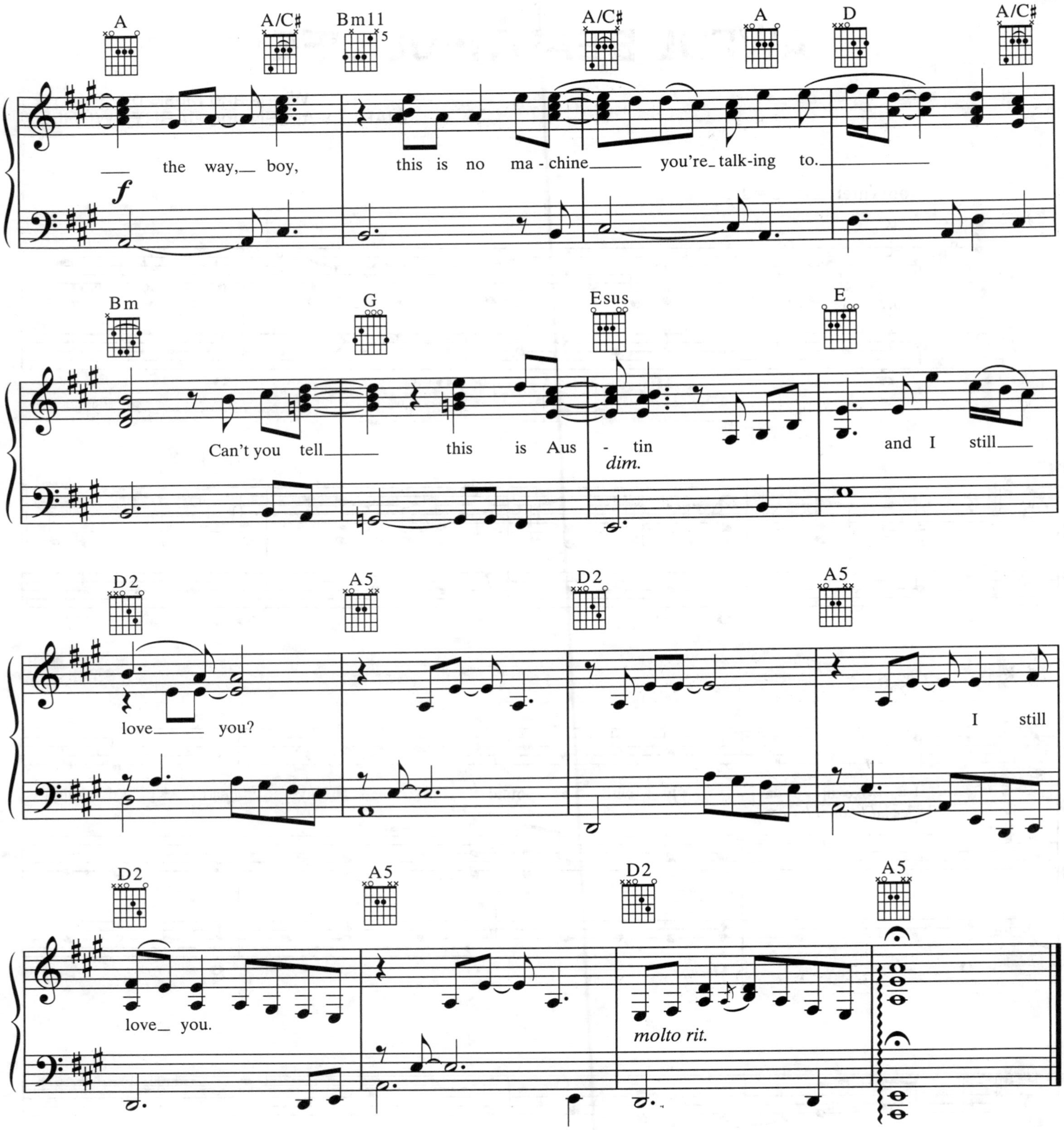

Verse 2:
The telephone fell to the counter.
She heard, but she couldn't believe.
What kind of man would hang on that long?
What kind of love that must be!
She waited three days and then she tried again.
Didn't know what she'd say, but she heard three rings and then...

Chorus 2:
If it's Friday night, I'm at the ballgame.
And first thing Saturday, if it don't rain,
I'm headed out to the lake and I'll be gone all weekend long.
But I'll call you back when I get home on Sunday afternoon.
And P. S., if this is Austin, I still love you.
(To Bridge:)

AWFUL BEAUTIFUL LIFE

Words and Music by
HARLEY ALLEN and DARRYL WORLEY

Moderately fast ♩ = 112
N.C.
mf
Verses 1 & 3:
N.C.
1. I woke up ear - ly with a pound - in' in my head. I'd been
3. See additional lyrics
out the night before with all my friends.

A lit - tle wor - ried, kind - a won - d'rin' what I did. I said,
"Lord, please for - give me for my sins." My
A
G
wife want - ed to kill me, but she tried to save me first.
A
Bm
A
G
D/F♯
"You're go - in' if I have to drag your butt to church."

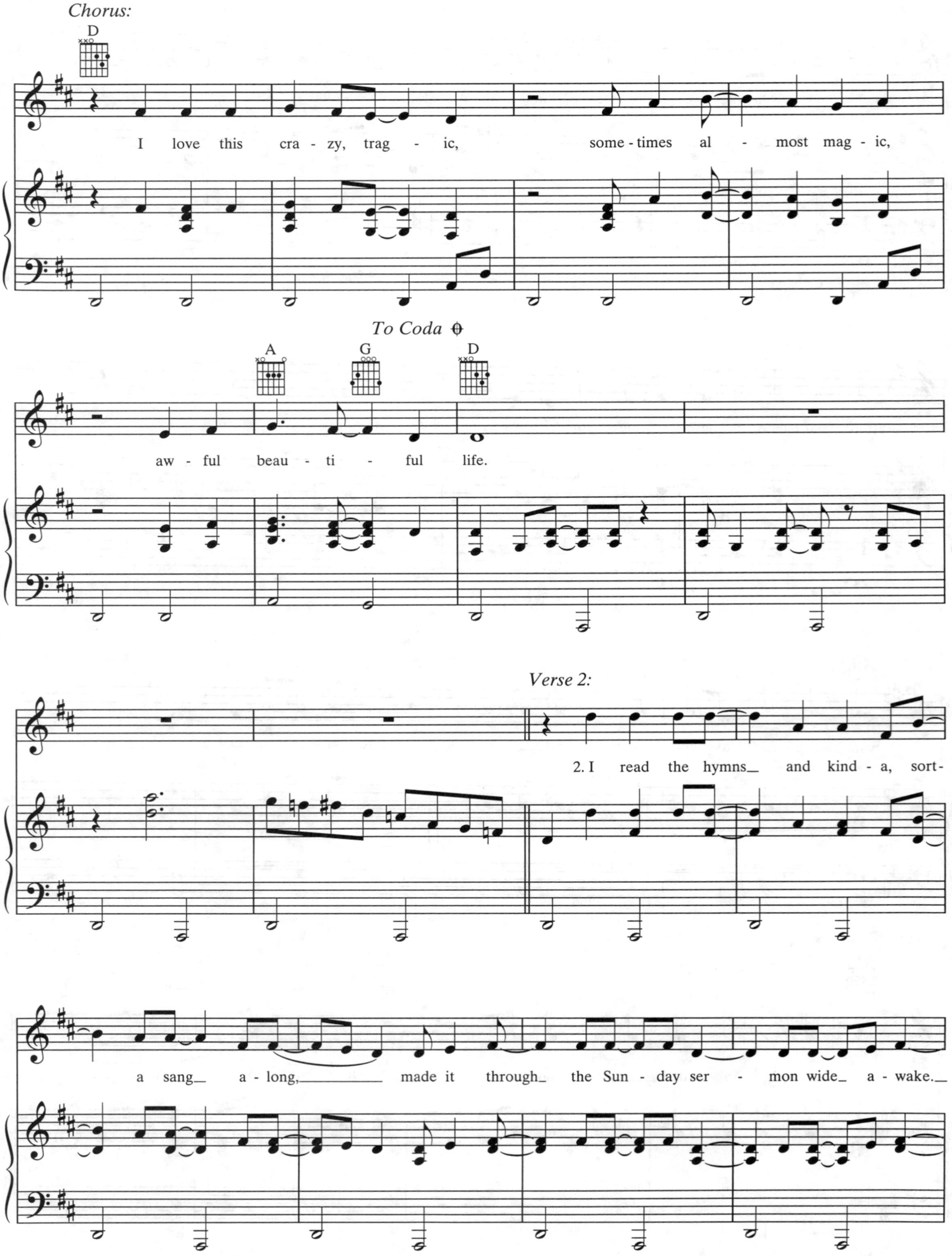
Chorus:
D
I love this cra - zy, trag - ic, some - times al - most mag - ic,
To Coda Φ
A
G
D
aw - ful beau - ti - ful life.
Verse 2:
2. I read the hymns_ and kind - a, sort-
a sang_ a - long,_ made it through_ the Sun - day ser - mon wide_ a - wake._

We met the fam - 'ly for
din - ner at our home, drank some beer and watched a game, and cooked some
steaks.
A
My lit - tle broth - er had a big
G
fight with his wife
A
and my poor moth - er sat be - tween

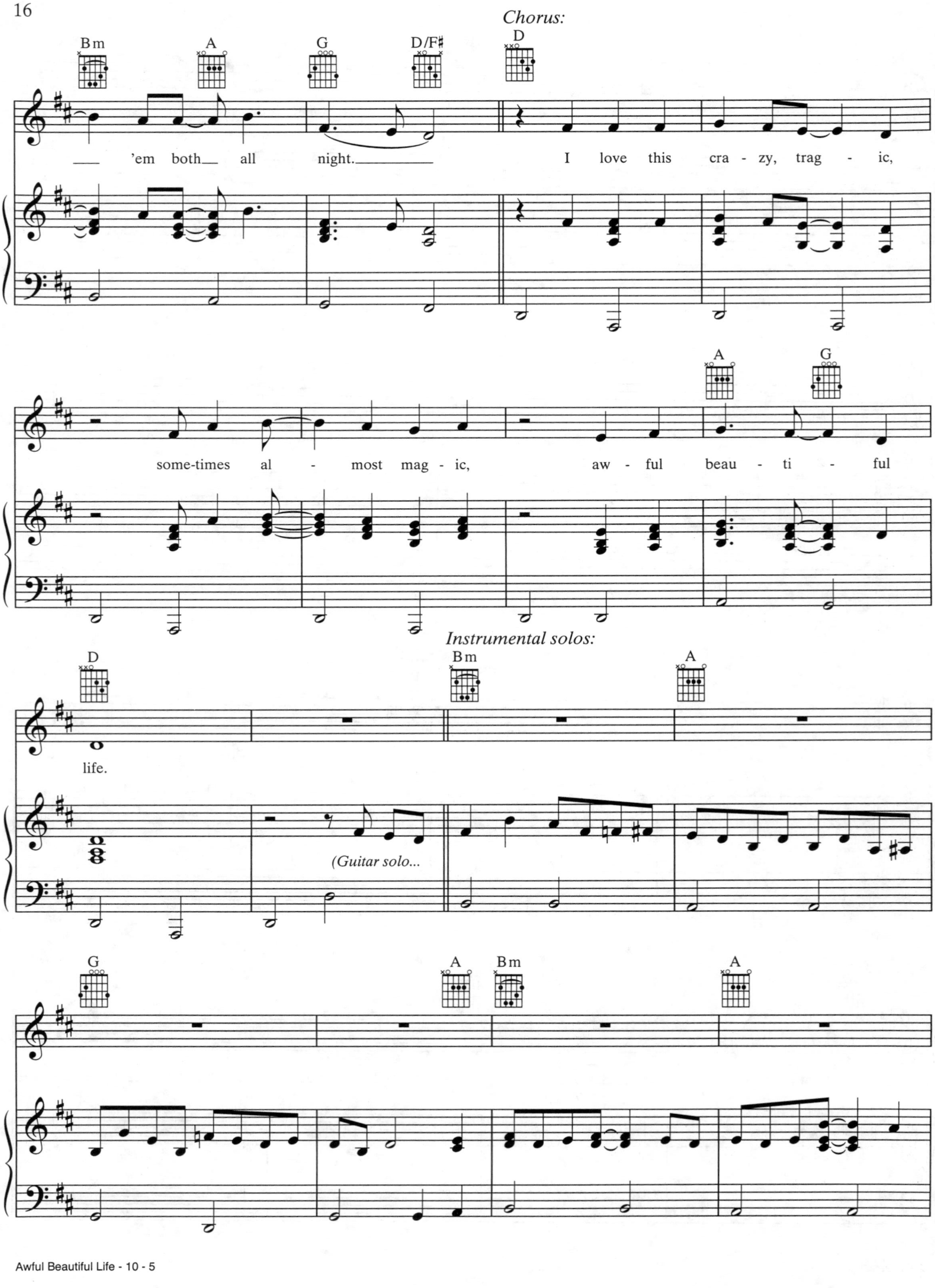
Chorus:
Bm
A
G
D/F♯
D
— 'em both— all night.——
I love this cra - zy, trag - ic,
A
G
some-times al - most mag - ic,
aw - ful beau - ti - ful
Instrumental solos:
D
Bm
A
life.
(Guitar solo...
G
A
Bm
A

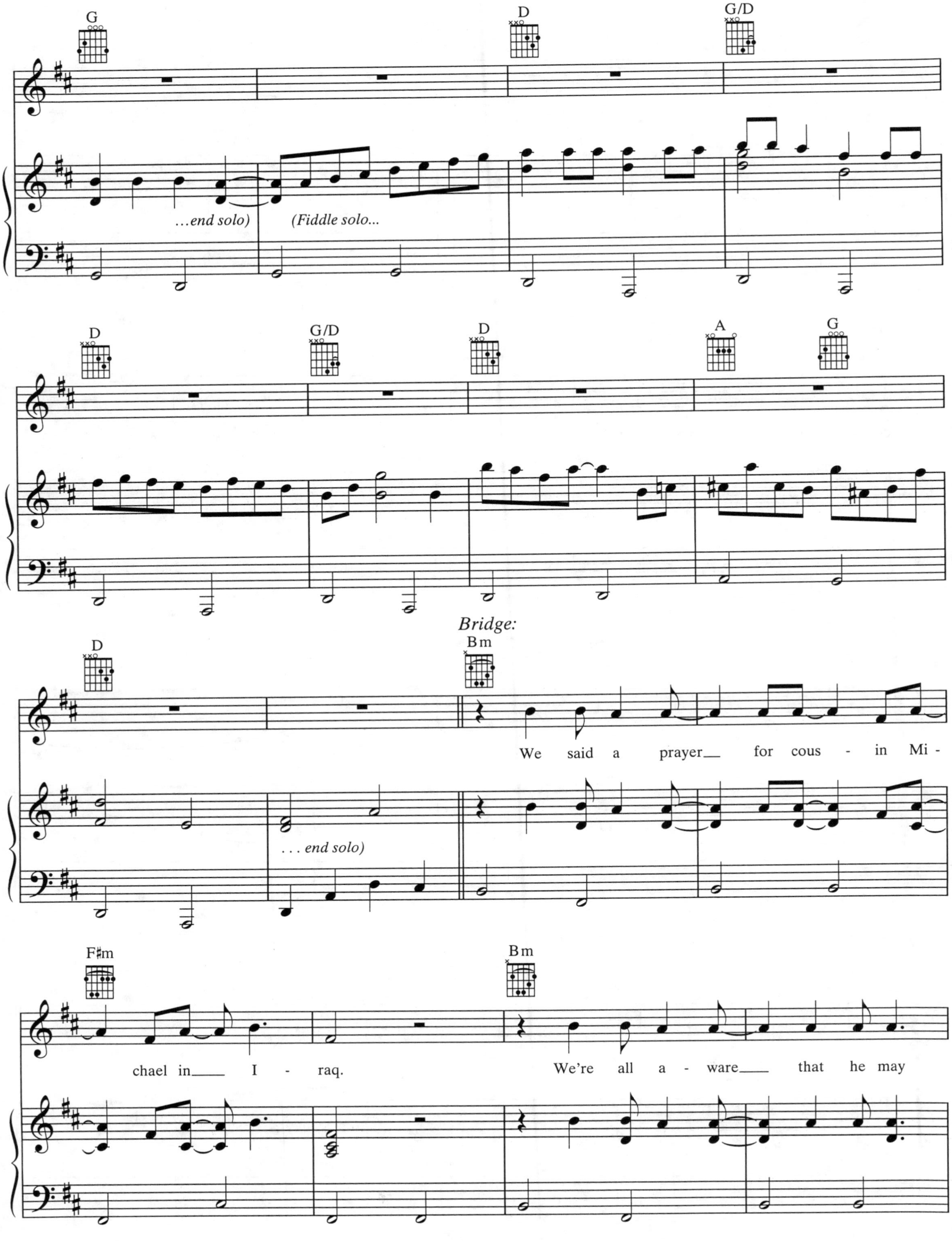
G
D
G/D
...end solo)
(Fiddle solo...
D
G/D
D
A
G
Bridge:
D
Bm
We said a prayer__ for cous - in Mi -
. . . end solo)
F♯m
Bm
chael in__ I - raq.
We're all a - ware__ that he may

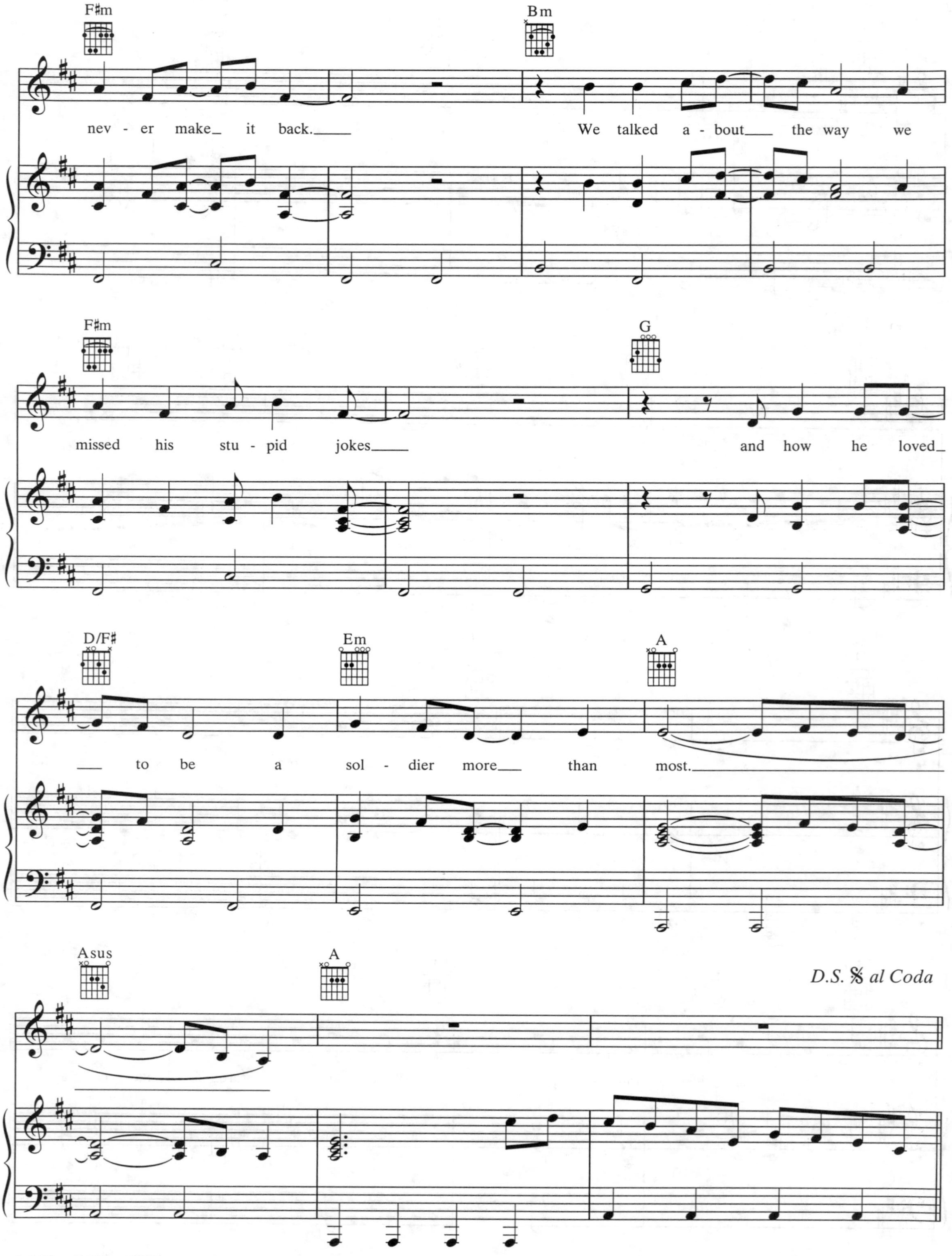
F♯m
Bm
nev - er make it back.
We talked a - bout the way we
F♯m
G
missed his stu - pid jokes
and how he loved
D/F♯
Em
A
to be a sol - dier more than most.
Asus
A
D.S. 𝄋 al Coda

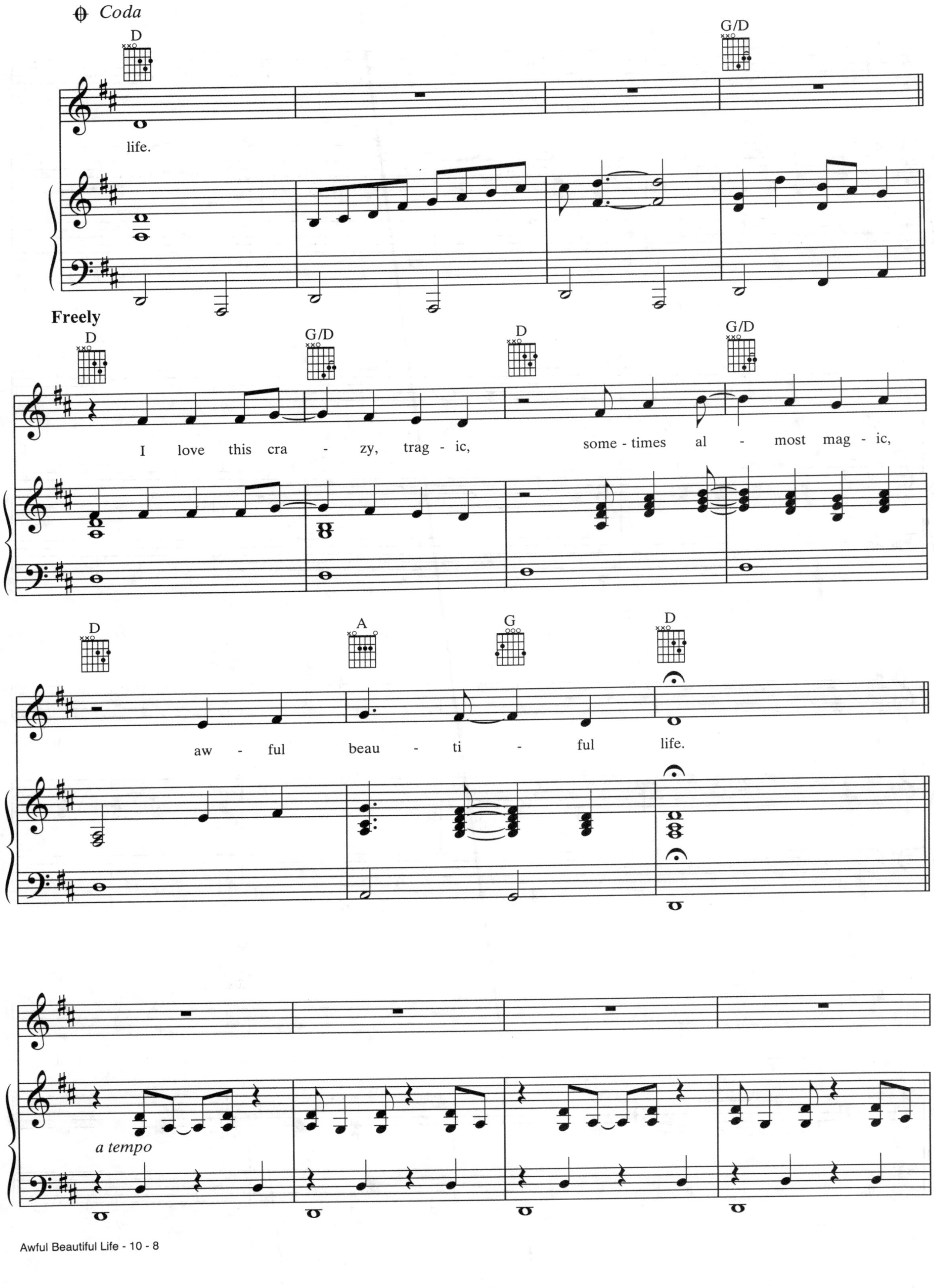
Coda
D
G/D
life.
Freely
D
G/D
D
G/D
I love this cra - zy, trag - ic, some - times al - most mag - ic,
D
A
G
D
aw - ful beau - ti - ful life.
a tempo

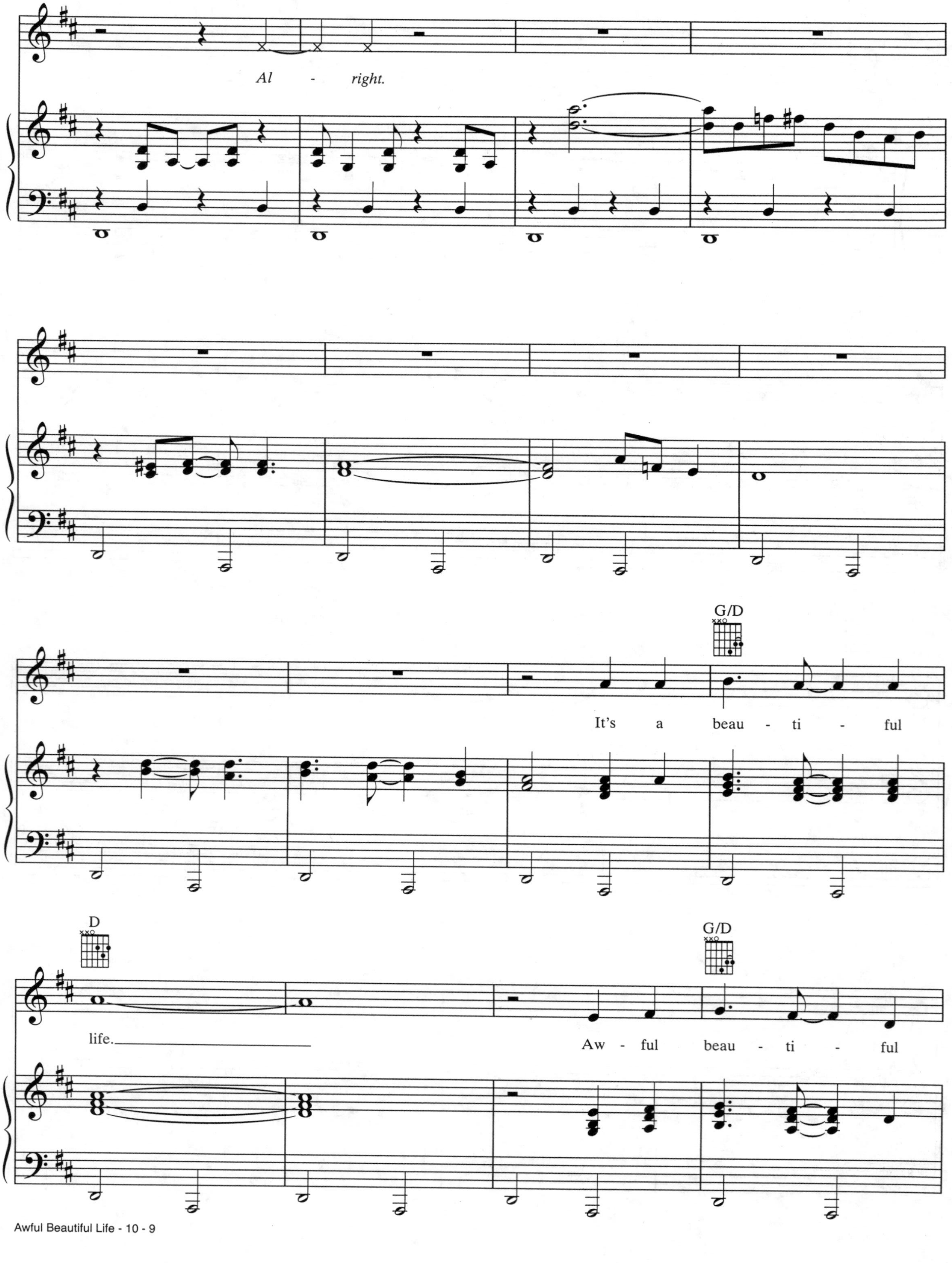
Al - right.
G/D
It's a beau - ti - ful
D
life.
G/D
Aw - ful beau - ti - ful

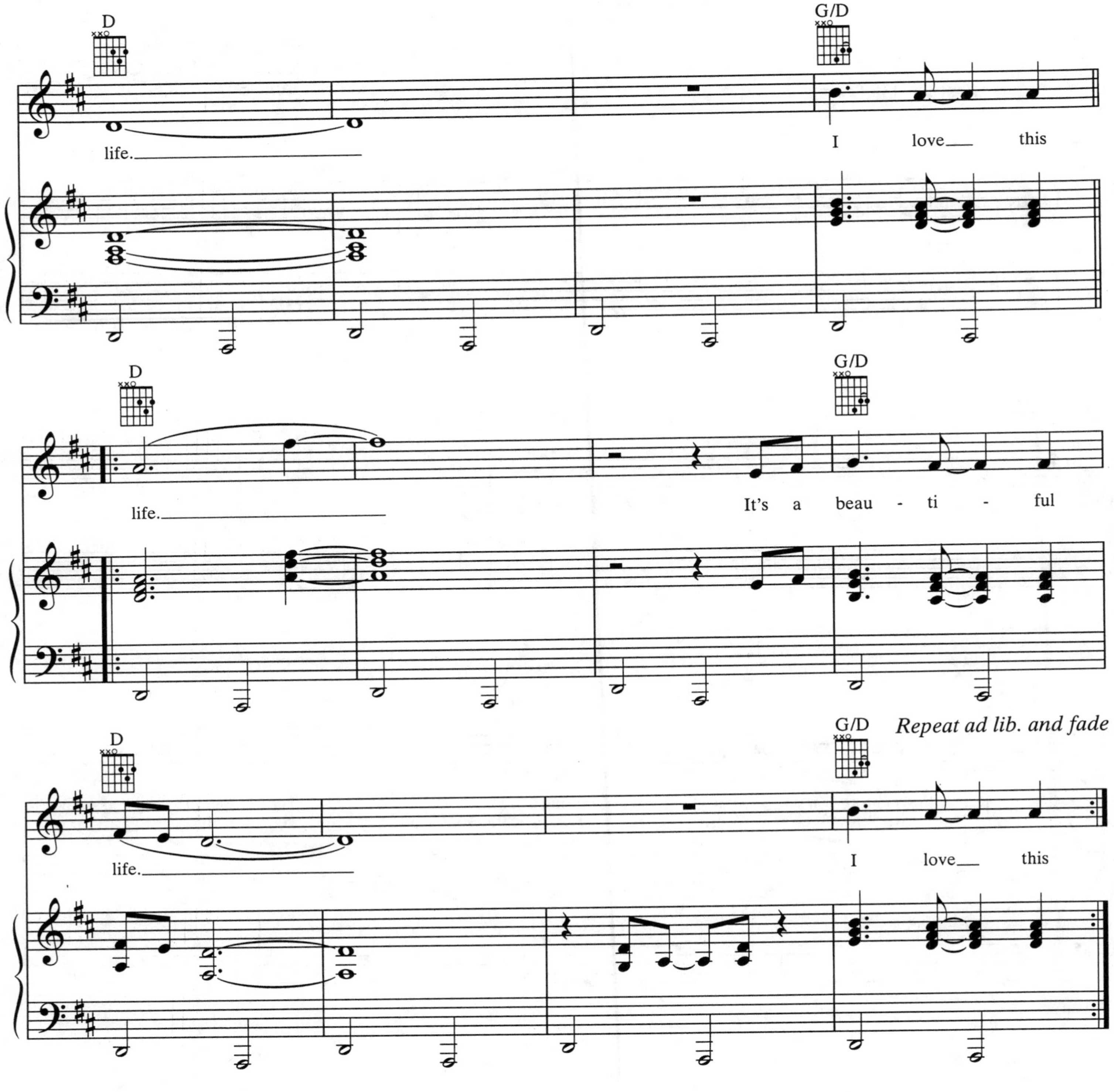

Verse 3:
I laid in bed that night and thought about the day
And how my life is like a roller coaster ride.
The ups and downs and crazy turns along the way.
It'll throw you off if you don't hold on tight
You can't really smile until you've shed some tears.
I could die today or I might live on for years.
(To Chorus:)

BACK WHEN

Words and Music by
JEFF STEVENS, STEPHONY SMITH
and STAN LYNCH

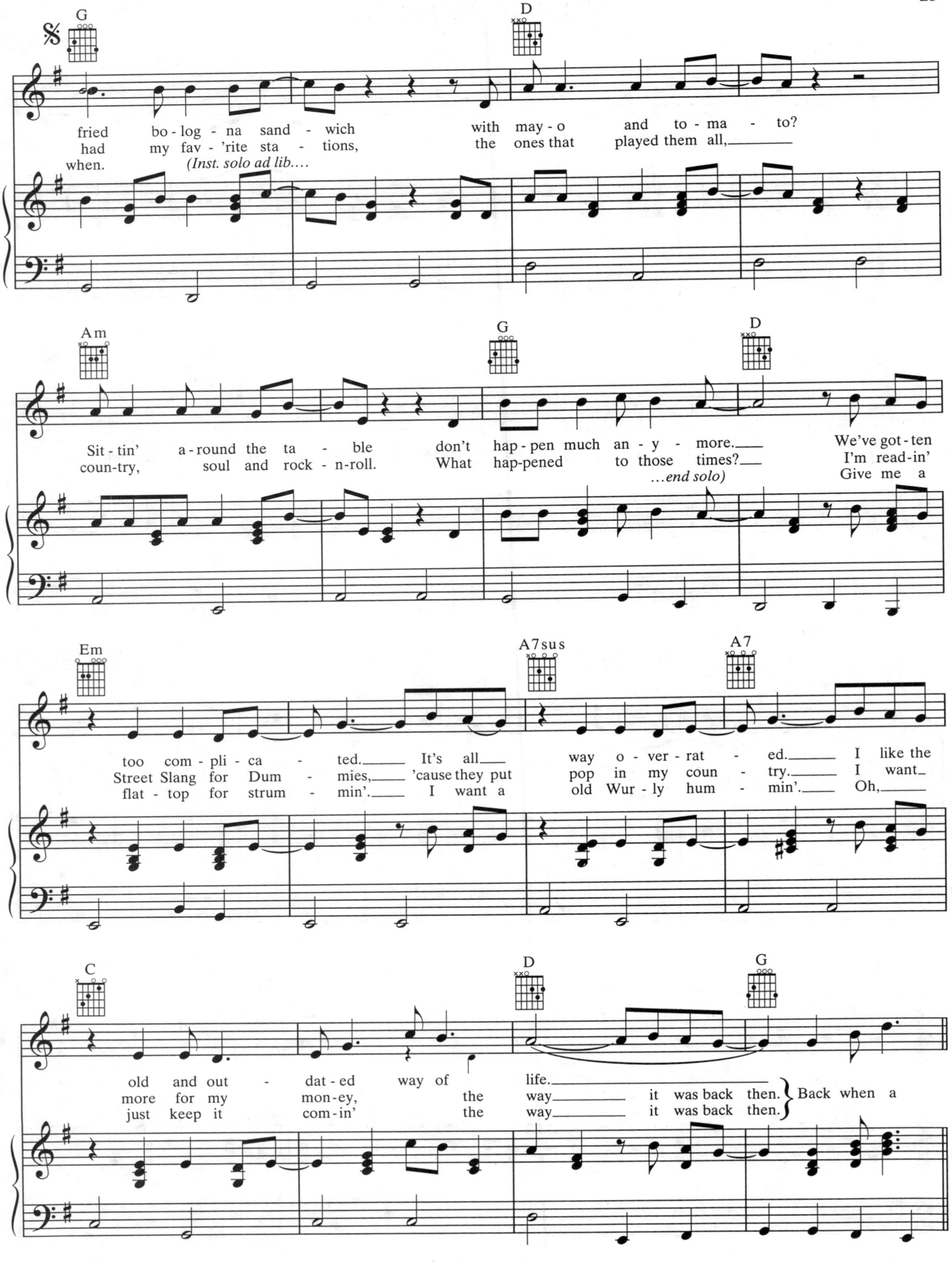
G
D
fried bo-log - na sand - wich with may-o and to-ma - to?
had my fav - 'rite sta - tions, the ones that played them all,
when. (Inst. solo ad lib....
Am
G
D
Sit-tin' a-round the ta - ble don't hap-pen much an - y - more.
coun-try, soul and rock - n-roll. What hap-pened to those times?
...end solo)
We've got-ten
I'm read-in'
Give me a
Em
A7sus
A7
too com-pli-ca - ted. It's all way o - ver-rat - ed. I like the
Street Slang for Dum - mies, 'cause they put pop in my coun - try. I want
flat - top for strum - min'. I want a old Wur-ly hum - min'. Oh,
C
D
G
old and out - dat-ed way of life.
more for my mon-ey, the way it was back then.
just keep it com-in' the way it was back then.
Back when a

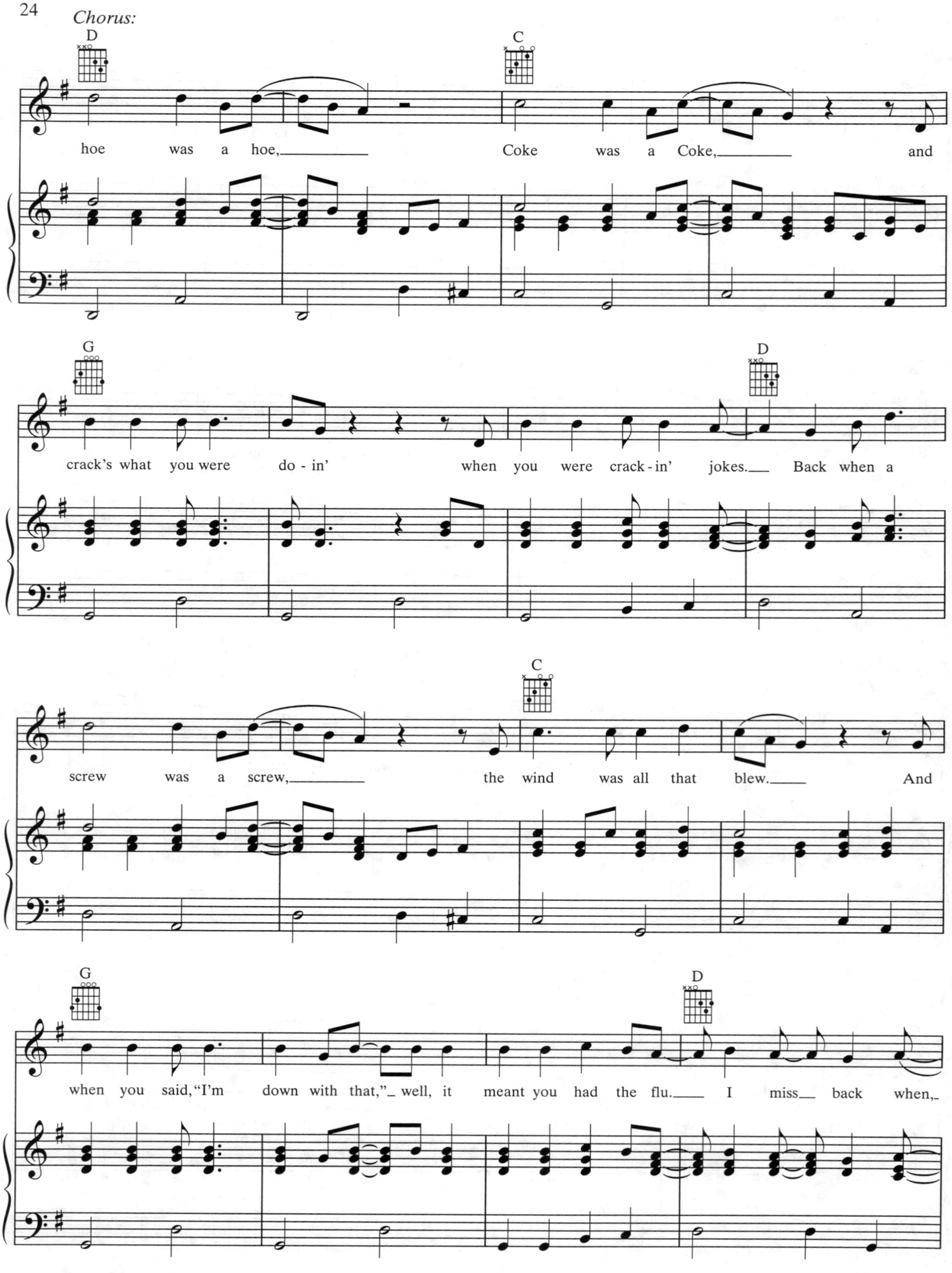
Chorus:
D
C
hoe was a hoe, Coke was a Coke, and
G
D
crack's what you were do - in' when you were crack - in' jokes. Back when a
C
screw was a screw, the wind was all that blew. And
G
D
when you said, "I'm down with that," well, it meant you had the flu. I miss back when,

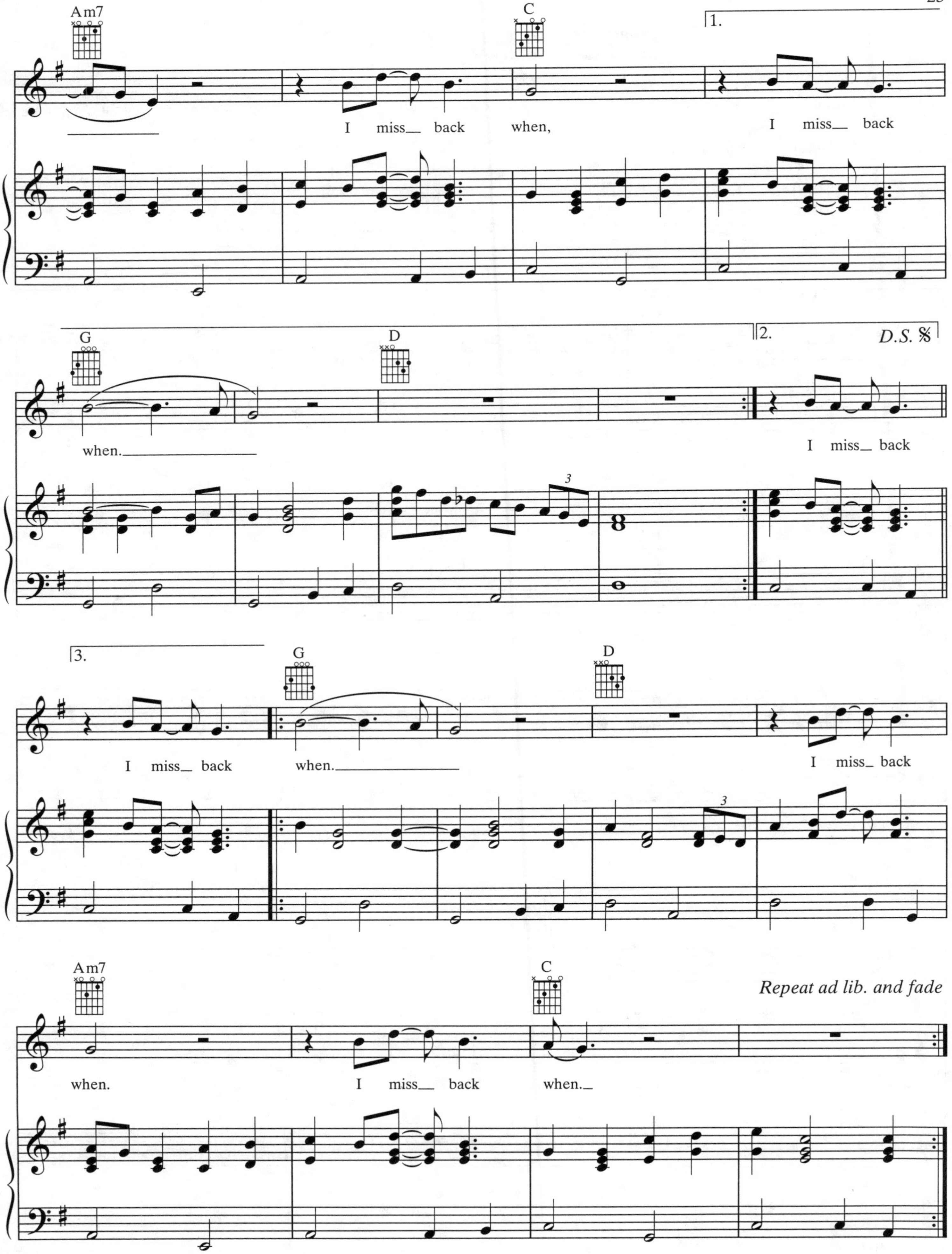

Am7
C
1.
I miss_ back when,
I miss_ back
G
D
2.
D.S. 𝄋
when.
I miss_ back
3
3.
G
D
I miss_ back
when.
I miss_ back
3
Am7
C
Repeat ad lib. and fade
when.
I miss_ back
when._

BEST I EVER HAD

Words and Music by
MATTHEW SCANNELL

*Recorded in F♯ major.

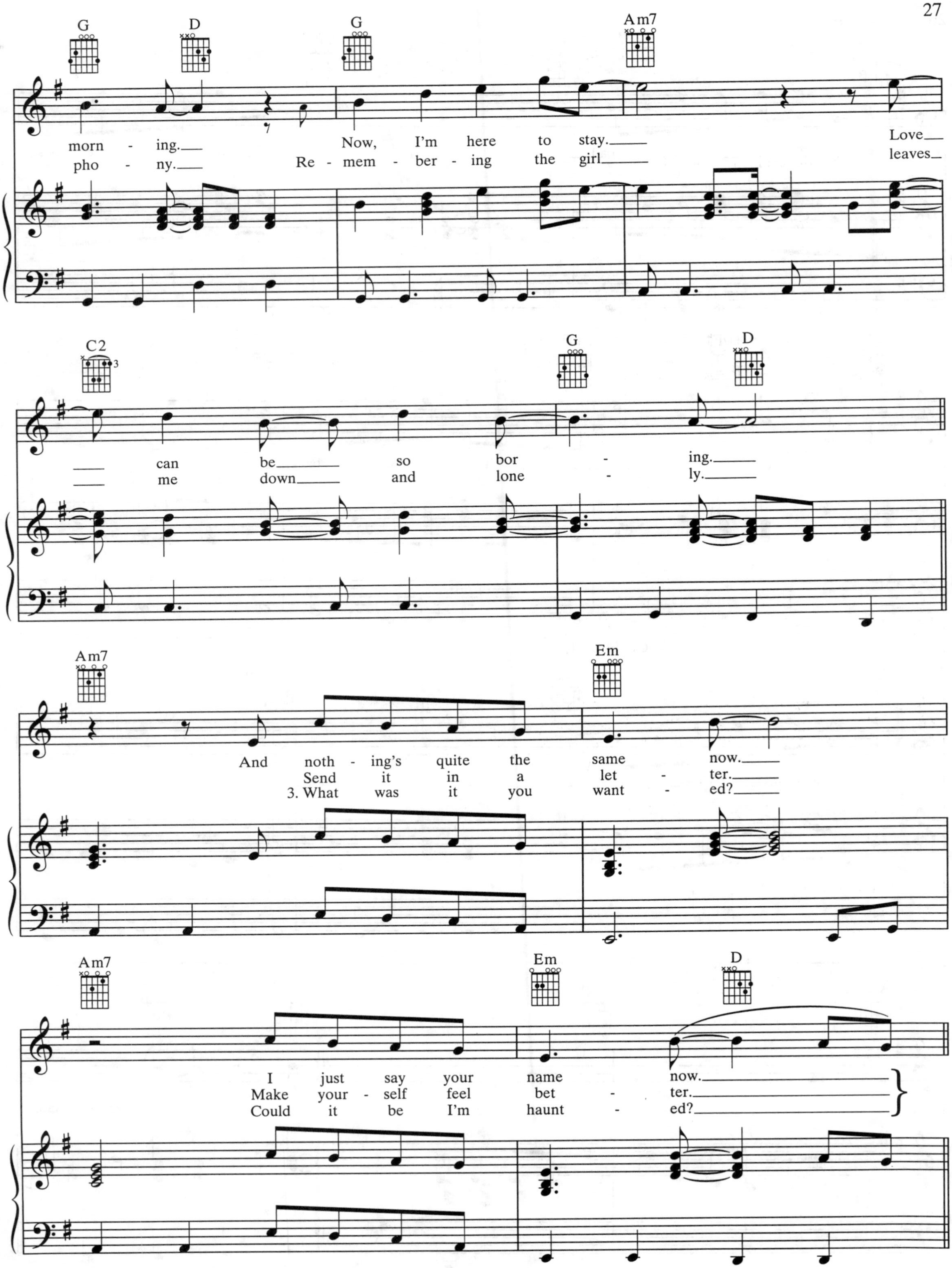
G
D
G
Am7
morn - ing. Now, I'm here to stay. Love
pho - ny. Re - mem - ber - ing the girl leaves
C2
G
D
can be so bor - ing.
me down and lone - ly.
Am7
Em
And noth - ing's quite the same now.
Send it in a let - ter.
3. What was it you want - ed?
Am7
Em
D
I just say your name now.
Make your - self feel bet - ter.
Could it be I'm haunt - ed?

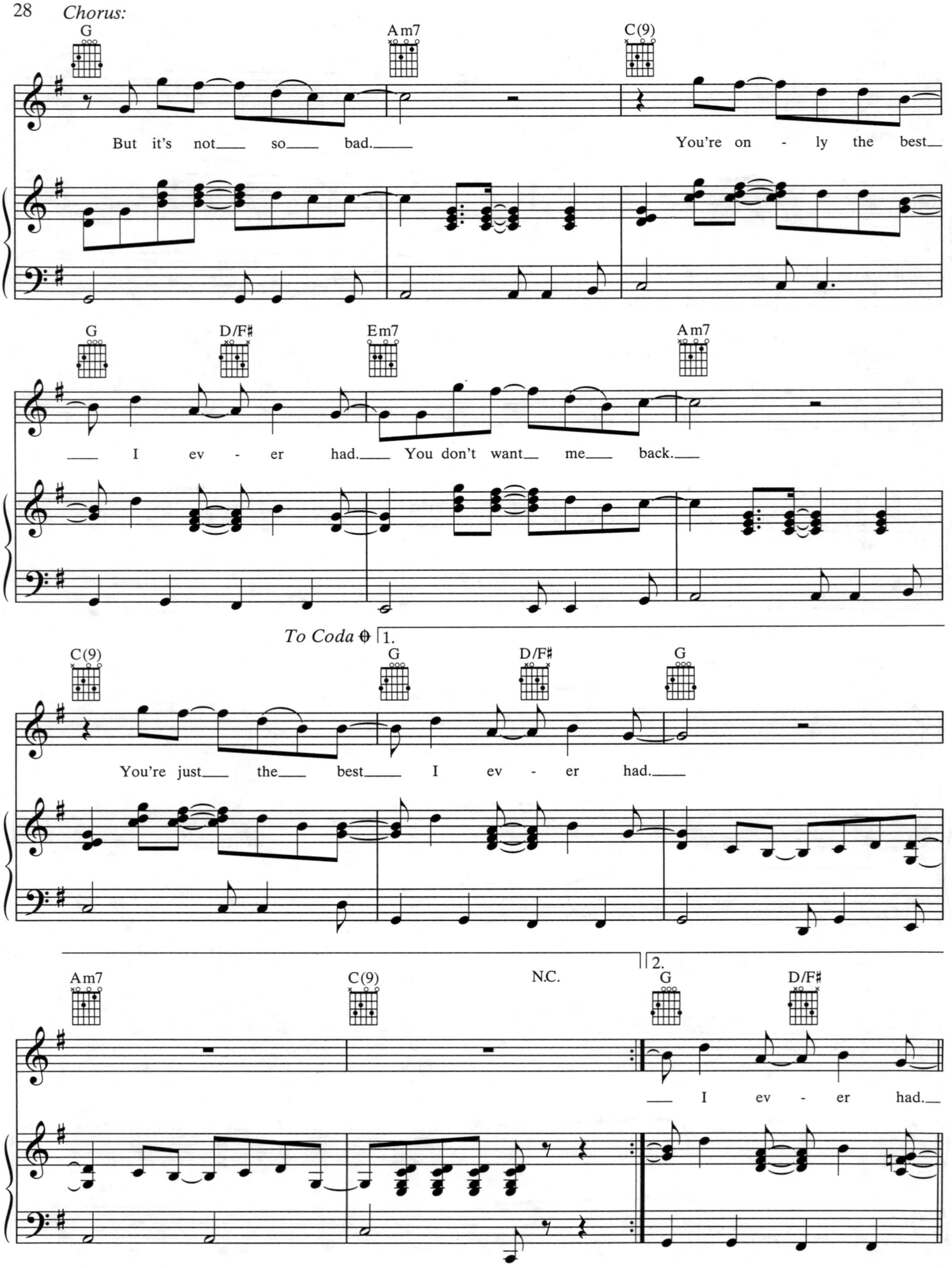
Chorus:
G
Am7
C(9)
But it's not__ so__ bad.__
You're on - ly the best__
G
D/F♯
Em7
Am7
__ I ev - er had.__ You don't want__ me__ back.__
To Coda 𝄌
1.
C(9)
G
D/F♯
G
You're just__ the__ best__ I ev - er had.__
2.
Am7
C(9)
N.C.
G
D/F♯
__ I ev - er had.__

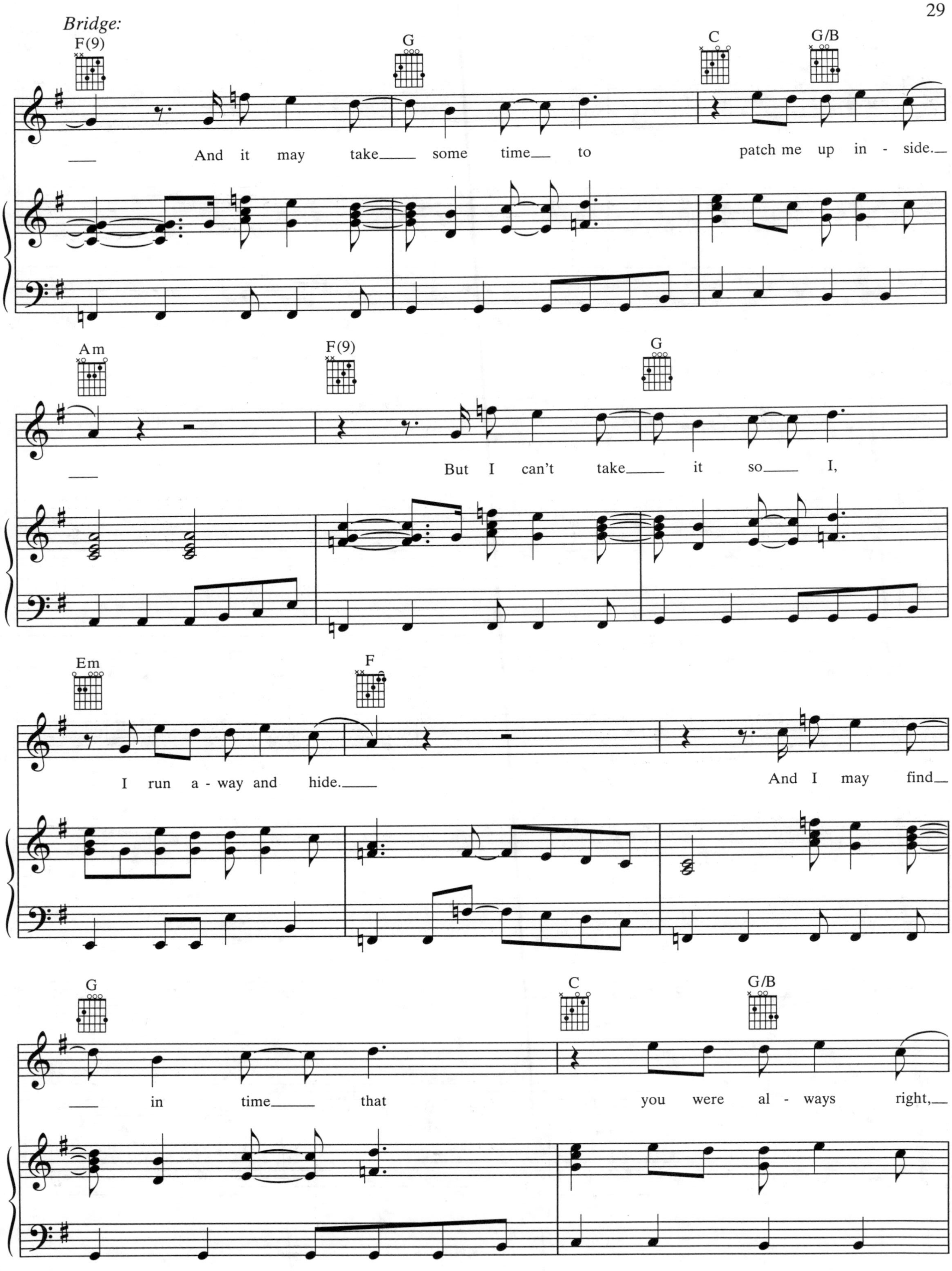
Bridge:
F(9)
G
C
G/B
And it may take some time to patch me up in - side.
Am
F(9)
G
But I can't take it so I,
Em
F
I run a - way and hide.
And I may find
G
C
G/B
in time that you were al - ways right,

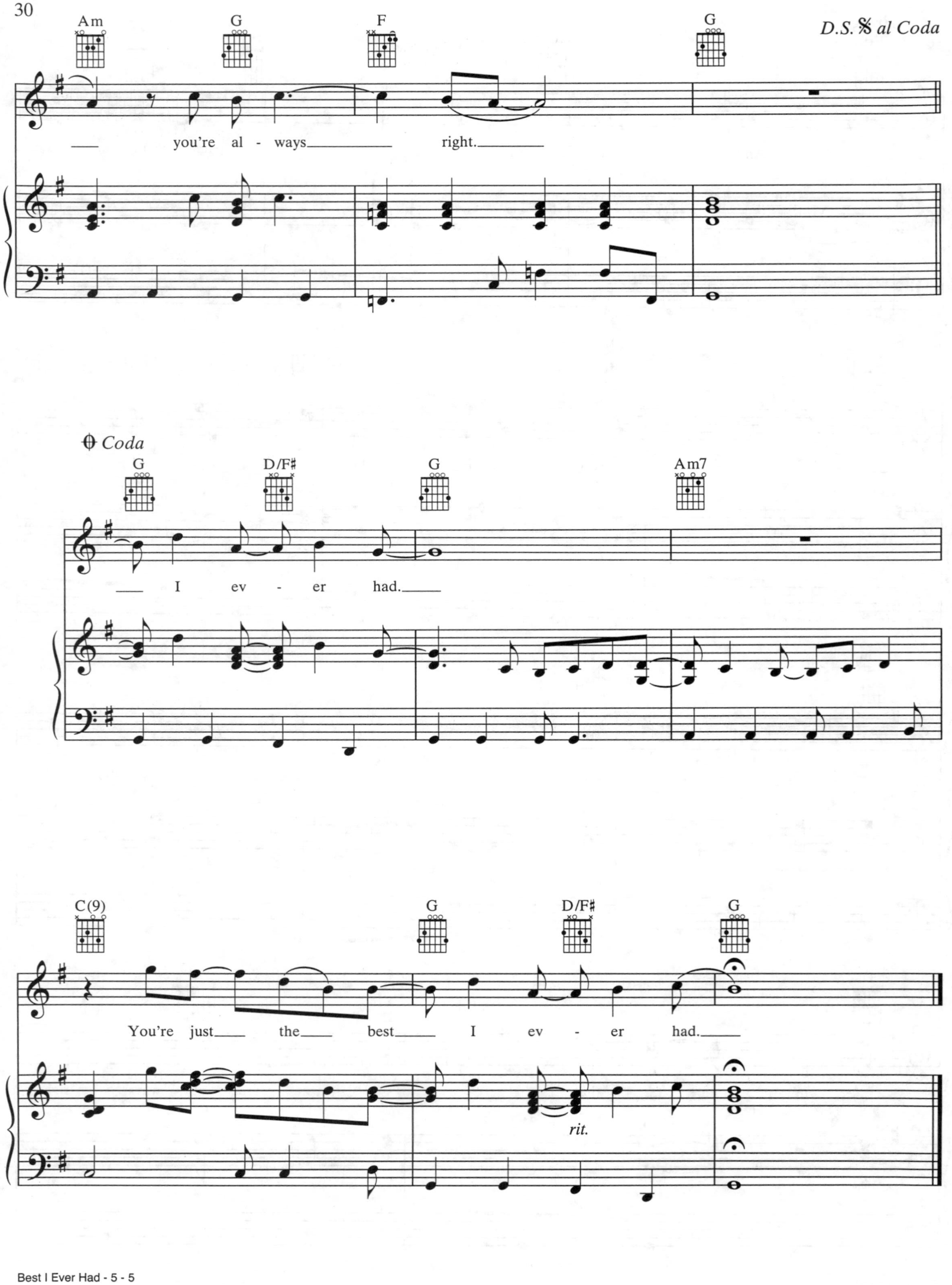
D.S. 𝄋 al Coda
Am
G
F
G
you're al - ways right.
Coda
G
D/F♯
G
Am7
I ev - er had.
C(9)
G
D/F♯
G
You're just the best I ev - er had.
rit.

BIG TIME

Words and Music by
JOHN RICH, KENNY ALPHIN
and ANGIE APARO

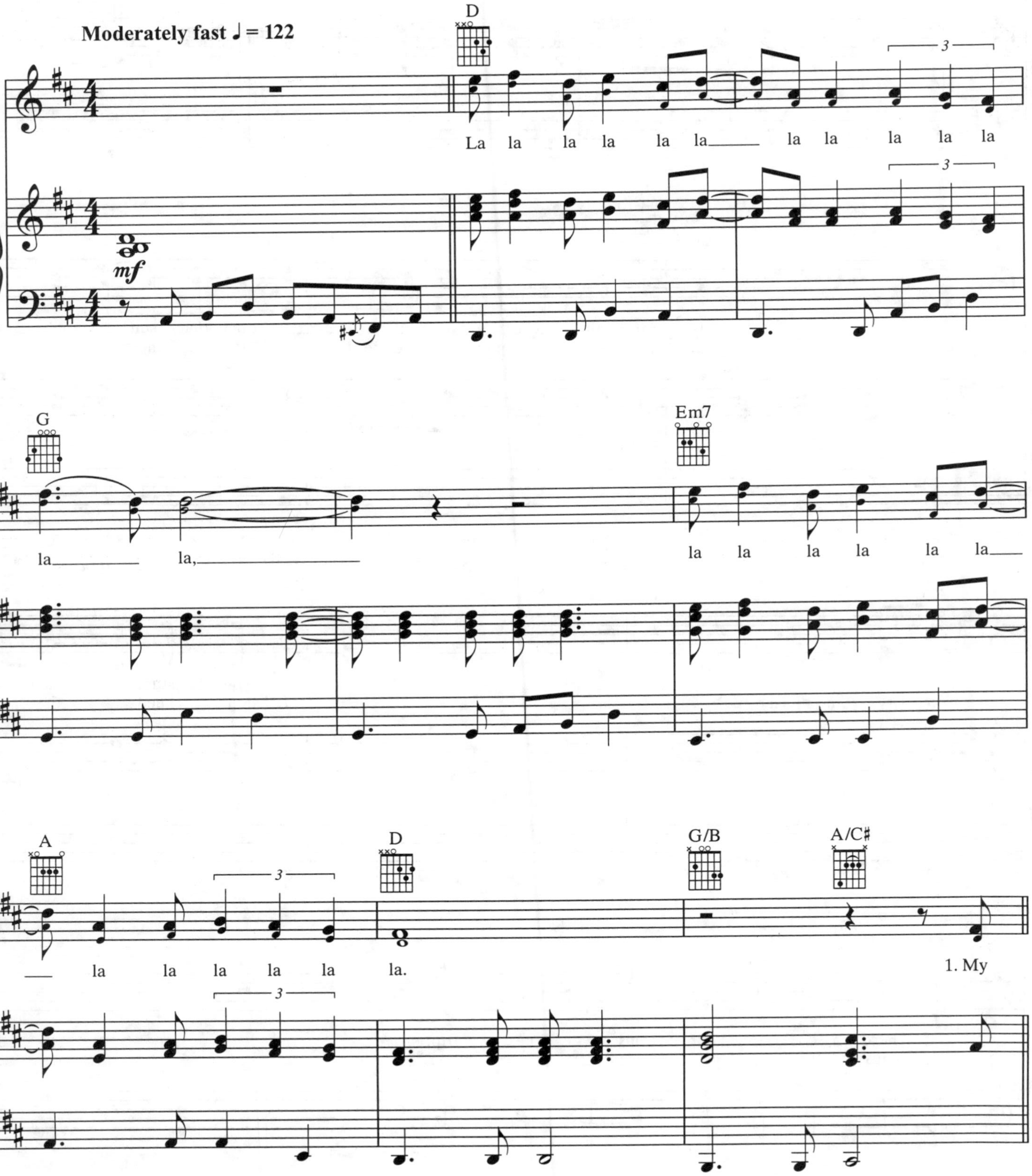

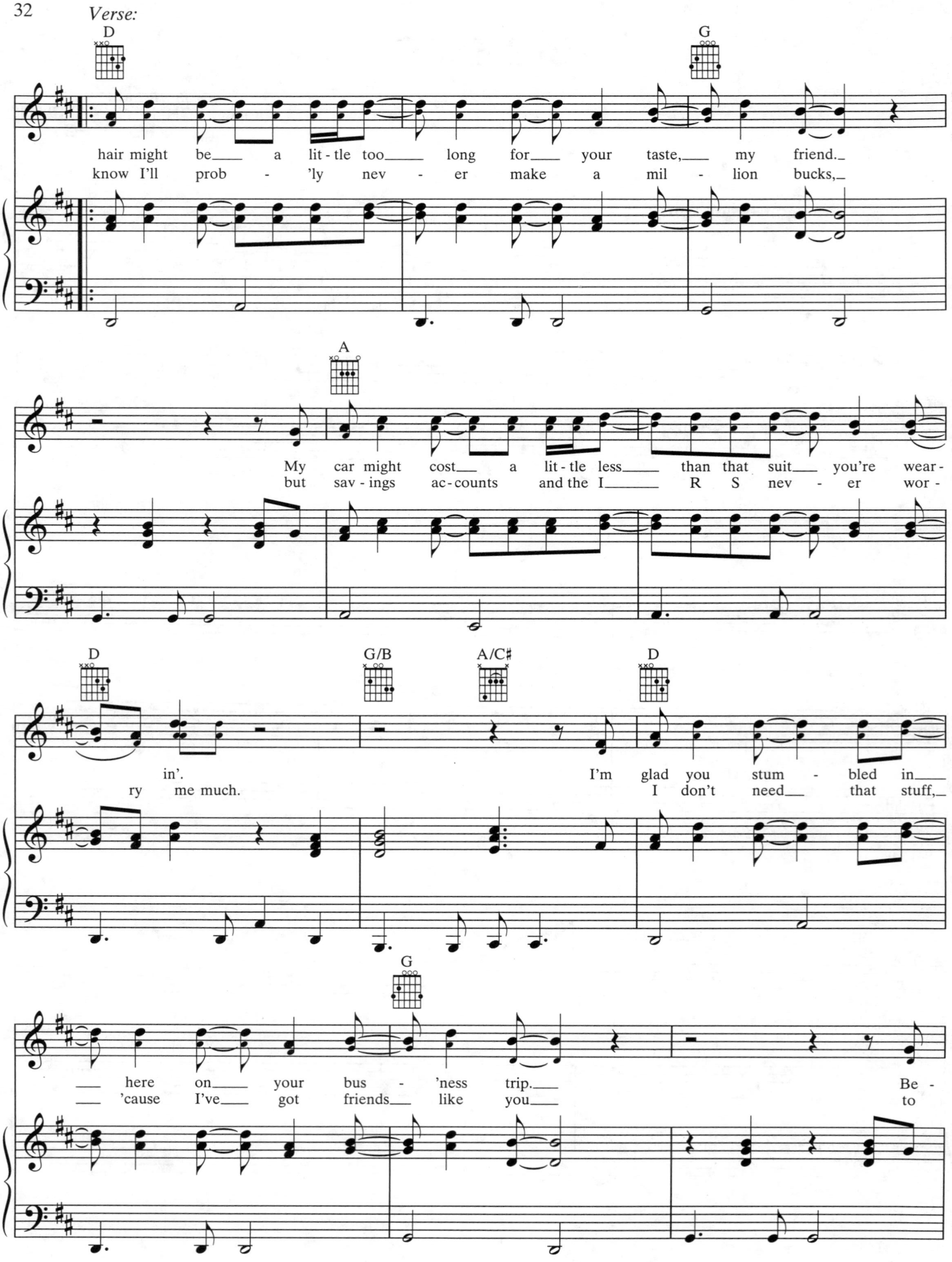
Verse:
D
G
hair might be___ a lit - tle too___ long for___ your taste,___ my friend._
know I'll prob - 'ly nev - er make a mil - lion bucks,_
A
My car might cost___ a lit - tle less___ than that suit___ you're wear -
but sav - ings ac - counts and the I___ R S nev - er wor -
D
G/B
A/C♯
D
in'. I'm glad you stum - bled in___
ry me much. I don't need__ that stuff,_
G
___ here on___ your bus - 'ness trip.___ Be -
___ 'cause I've___ got friends___ like you___ to

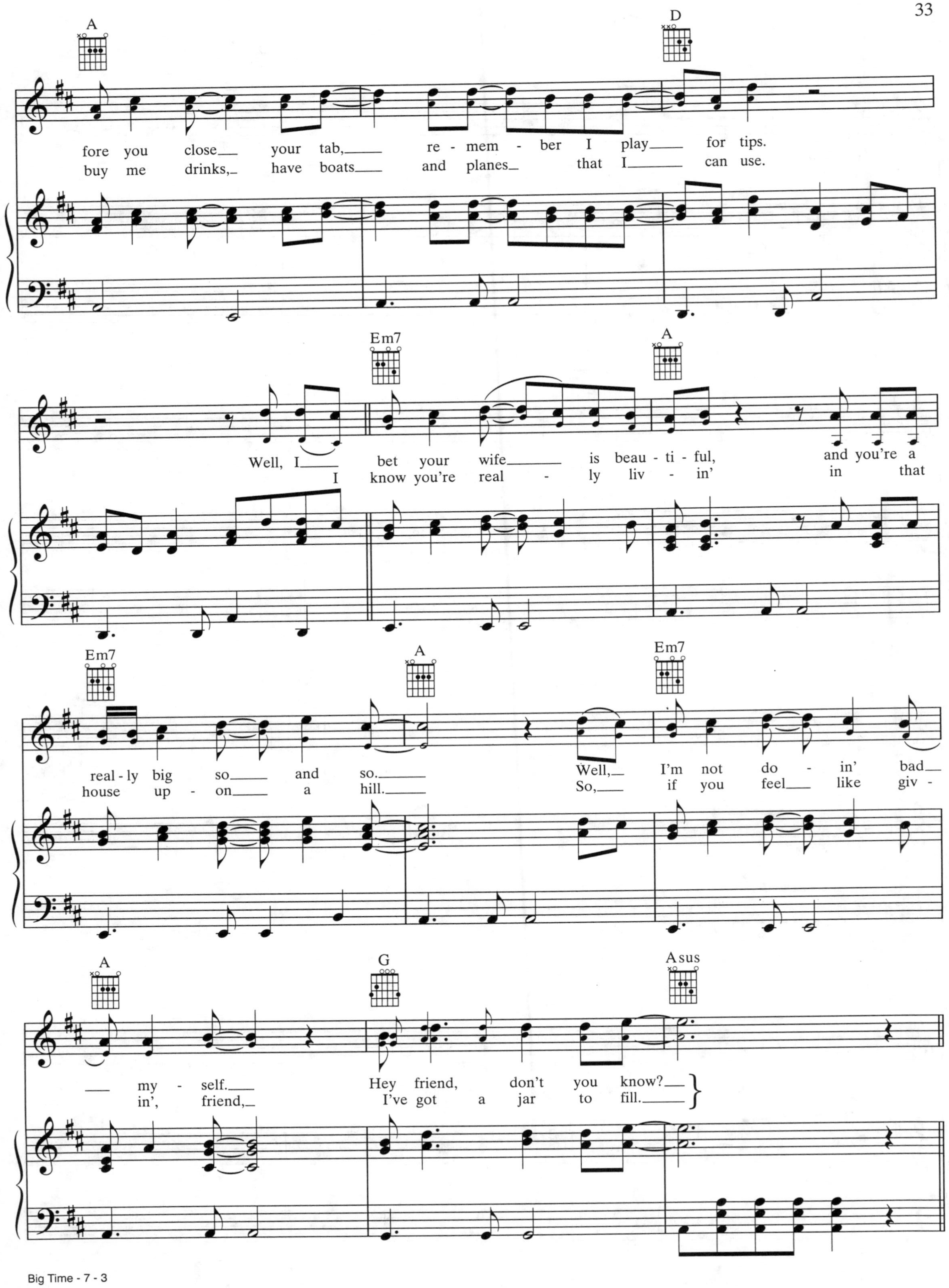
A
D
fore you close your tab, re - mem - ber I play for tips.
buy me drinks, have boats and planes that I can use.
Em7
A
Well, I bet your wife is beau - ti - ful, and you're a
I know you're real - ly liv - in' in that
Em7
A
Em7
real - ly big so and so. Well, I'm not do - in' bad
house up - on a hill. So, if you feel like giv -
A
G
Asus
my - self. Hey friend, don't you know?
in', friend, I've got a jar to fill.

Chorus:

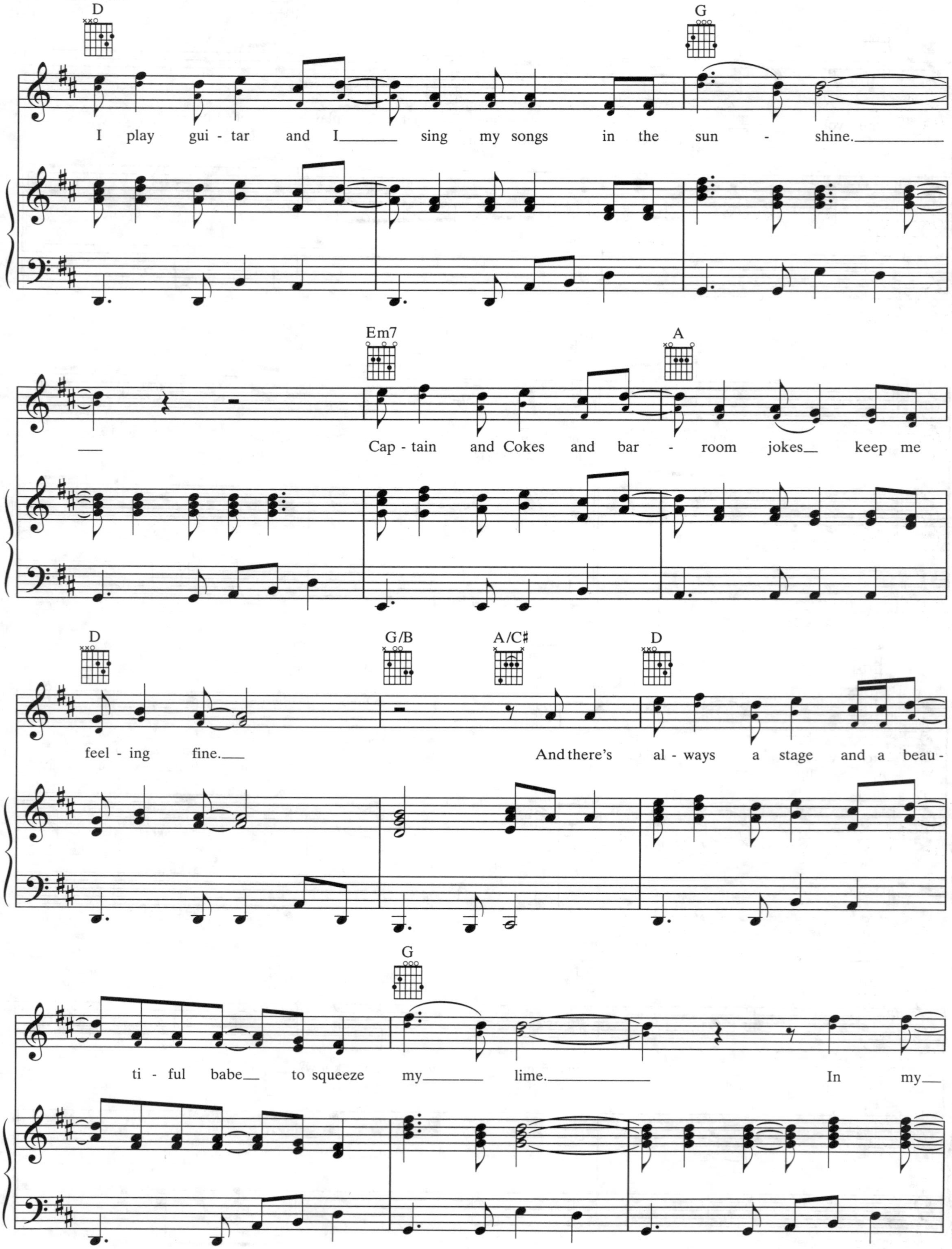
D
G
I play gui - tar and I___ sing my songs in the sun - shine.___
Em7
A
___ Cap - tain and Cokes and bar - room jokes__ keep me
D
G/B
A/C♯
D
feel - ing fine.__ And there's al - ways a stage and a beau -
G
ti - ful babe__ to squeeze my___ lime.___ In my__

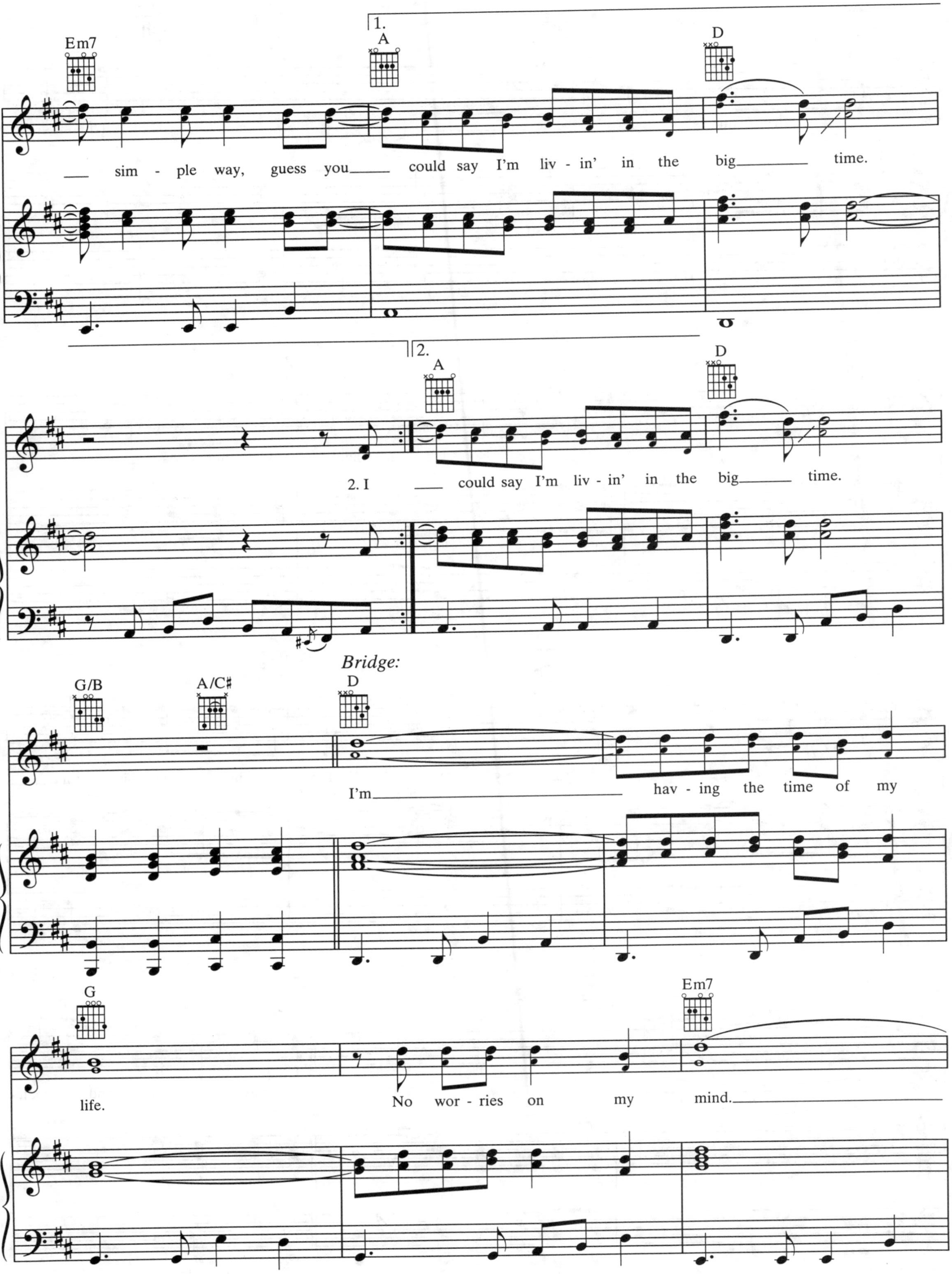
1.
Em7
A
D
— sim - ple way, guess you — could say I'm liv - in' in the big — time.
2.
A
D
2. I — could say I'm liv - in' in the big — time.
Bridge:
G/B
A/C♯
D
I'm — hav - ing the time of my
G
Em7
life. No wor - ries on my mind. —

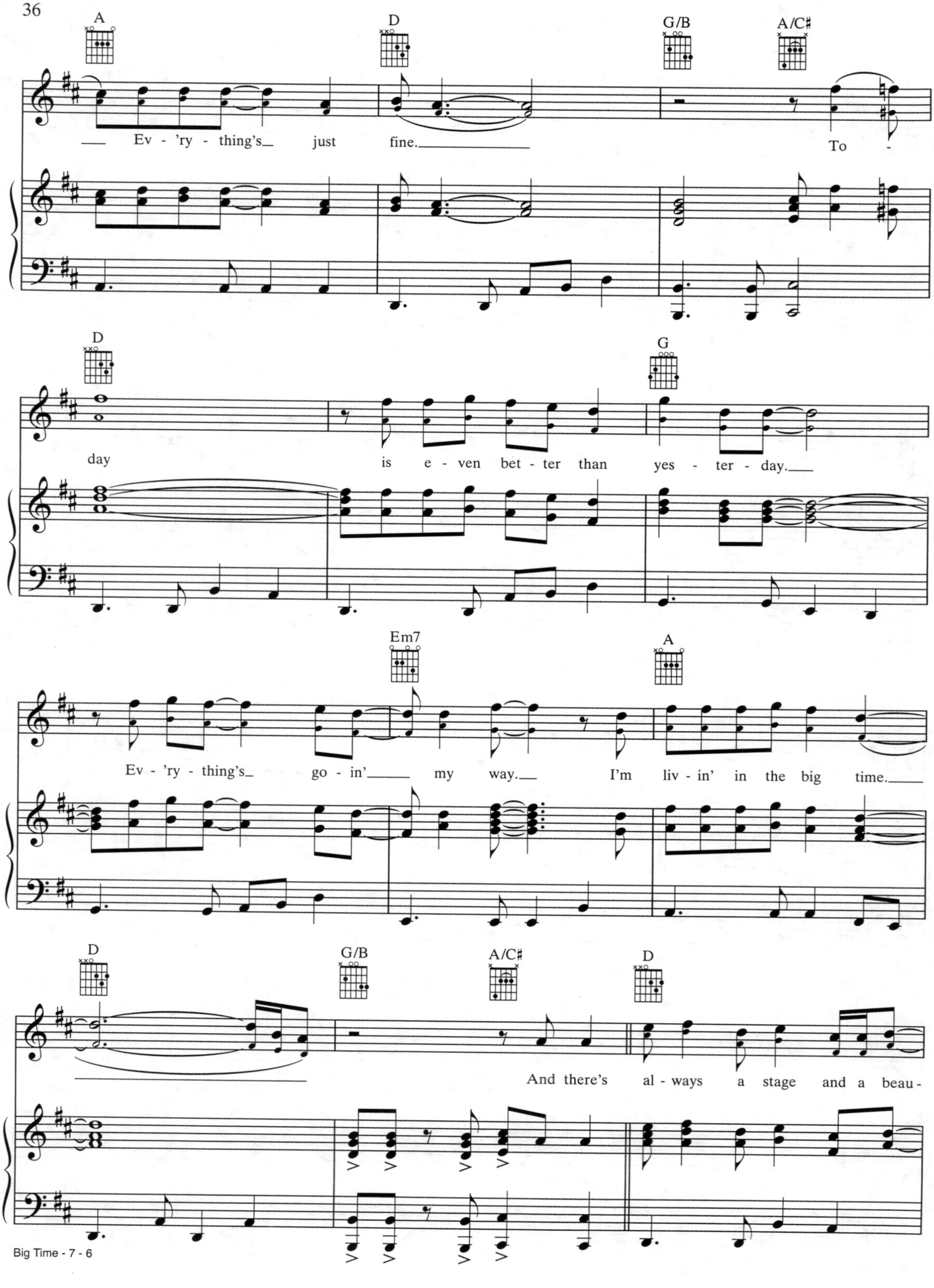
A
D
G/B
A/C♯
Ev - 'ry - thing's just fine. To -
D
G
day is e - ven bet - ter than yes - ter - day.
Em7
A
Ev - 'ry - thing's go - in' my way. I'm liv - in' in the big time.
D
G/B
A/C♯
D
And there's al - ways a stage and a beau -

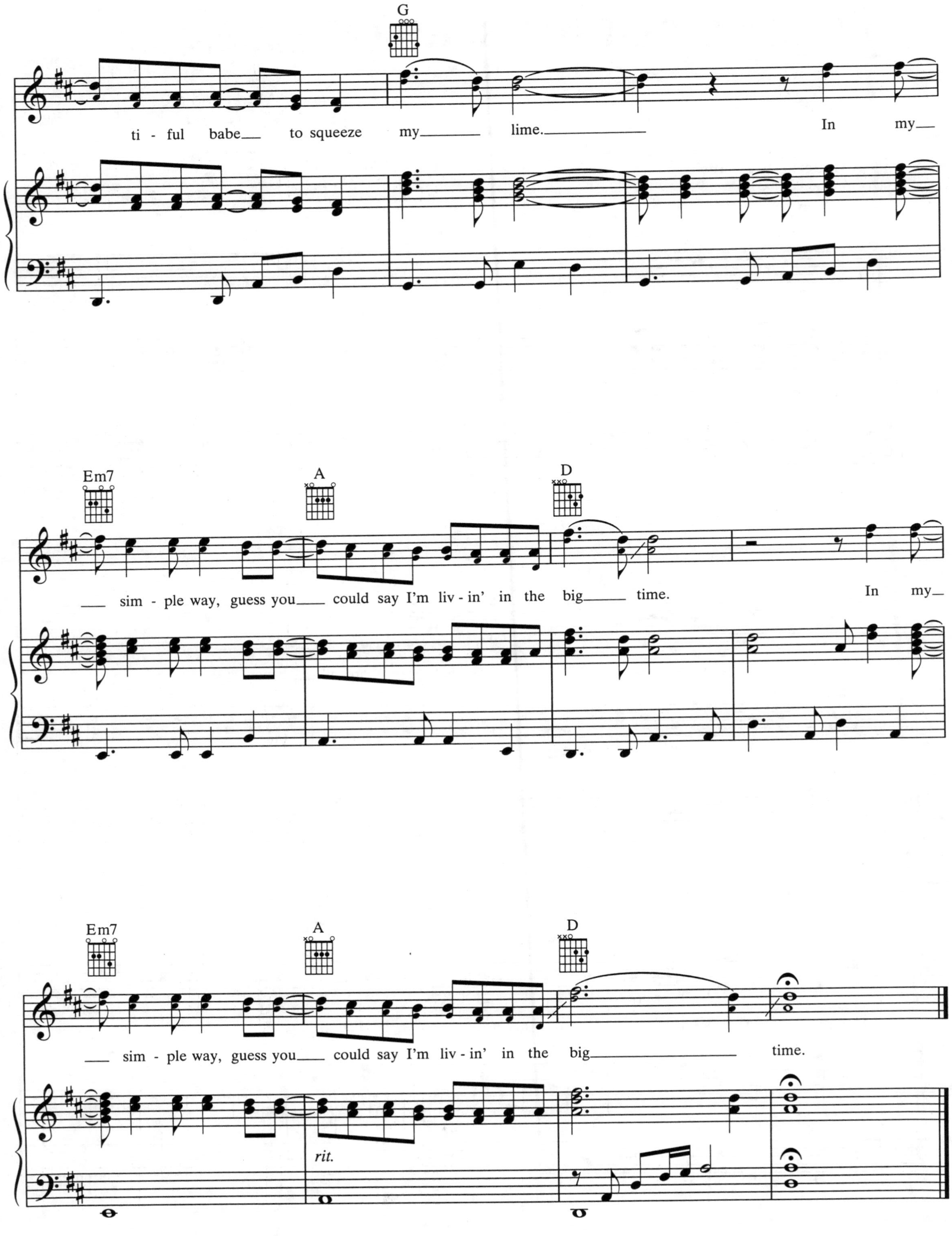
G
ti - ful babe__ to squeeze my______ lime.__________ In my__
Em7
A
D
__ sim - ple way, guess you___ could say I'm liv - in' in the big_____ time. In my__
Em7
A
D
__ sim - ple way, guess you___ could say I'm liv - in' in the big__________ time.
rit.

BILLY'S GOT HIS BEER GOGGLES ON

Words and Music by
PHILLIP B. WHITE and MICHAEL MOBLEY

N.C.
Hey!
2. She left him
Verses 2 & 3:
C
broke in his new truck. He don't smoke, but he lights one up. Tem-po-ra-ry fix for his heart-ache. He's hurt-in' bad, but he's feel-in' great.
drunks get-tin' real mean. They'll pick a fight o-ver an-y-thing. Bil-ly wants to laugh, that's why he's here. You won't see him cry, 'less you spill his beer.
N.C.

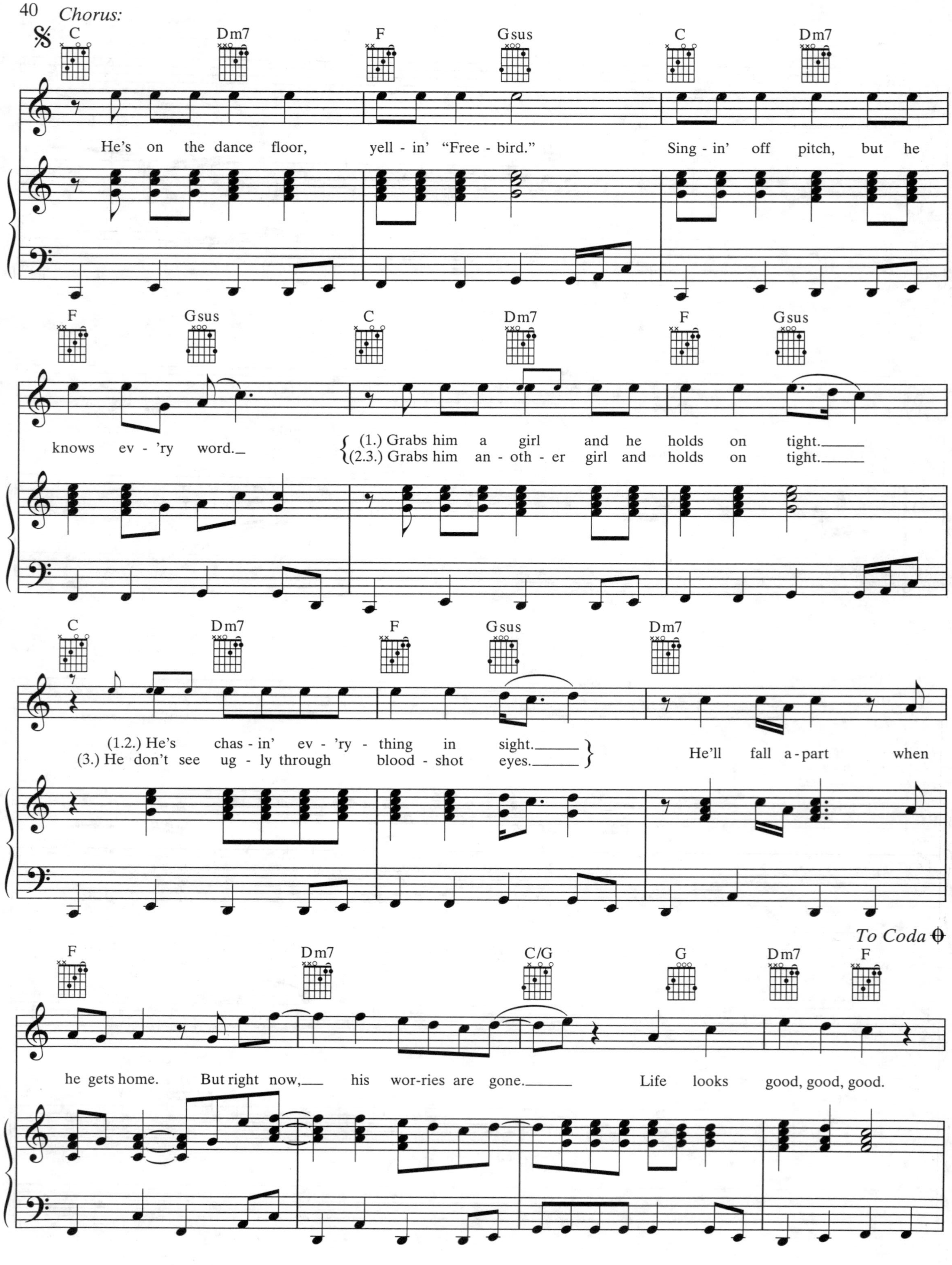
Chorus:
C Dm7 F Gsus C Dm7
He's on the dance floor, yell - in' "Free - bird." Sing - in' off pitch, but he
F Gsus C Dm7 F Gsus
knows ev - 'ry word.
(1.) Grabs him a girl and he holds on tight.
(2.3.) Grabs him an - oth - er girl and holds on tight.
C Dm7 F Gsus Dm7
(1.2.) He's chas - in' ev - 'ry - thing in sight.
(3.) He don't see ug - ly through blood - shot eyes.
He'll fall a - part when
To Coda
F Dm7 C/G G Dm7 F
he gets home. But right now, his wor-ries are gone. Life looks good, good, good.

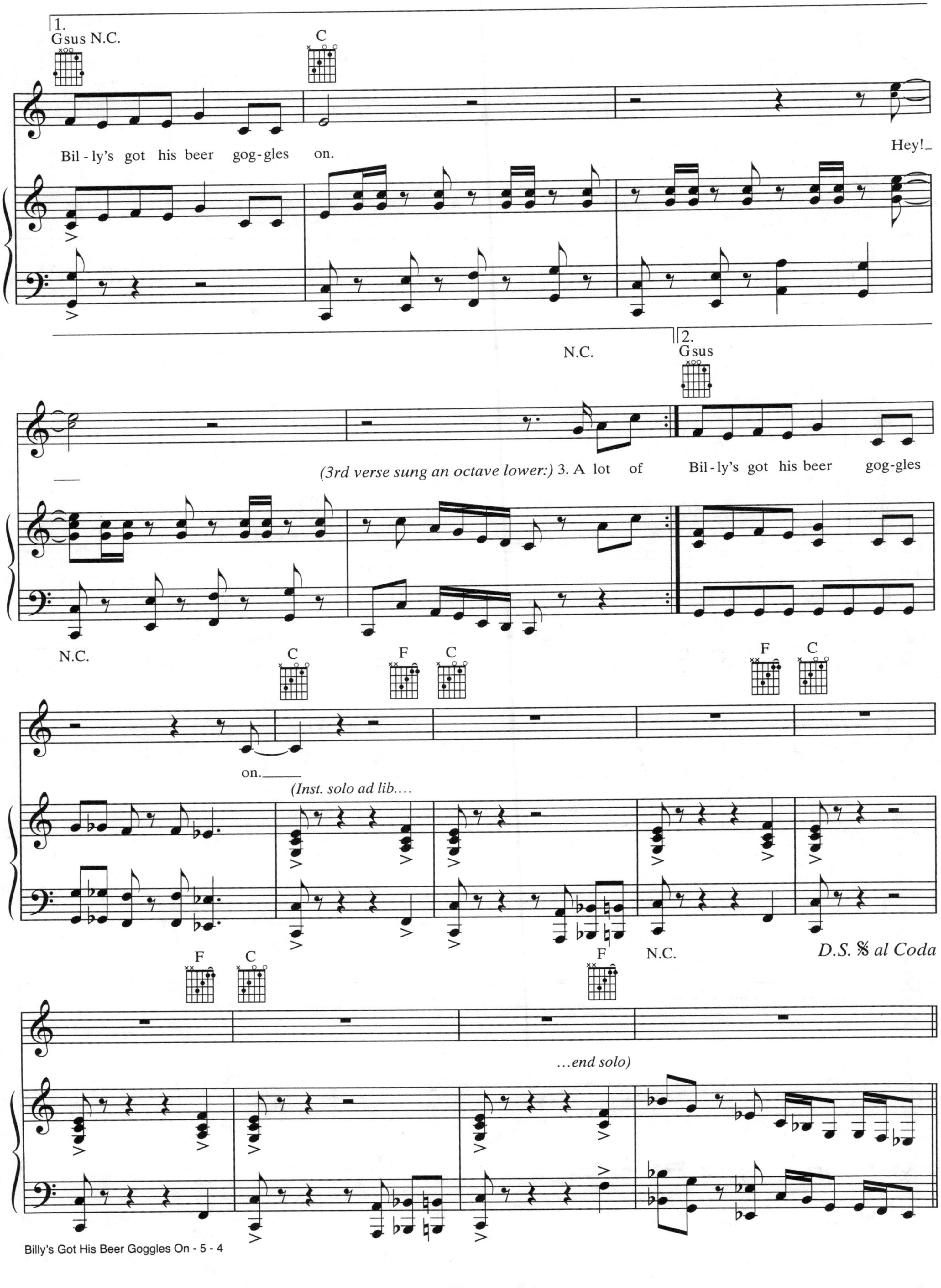
1.
Gsus N.C.
C
Bil - ly's got his beer gog - gles on.
Hey!
N.C.
2.
Gsus
(3rd verse sung an octave lower:) 3. A lot of
Bil - ly's got his beer gog - gles
N.C.
C
F
C
F
C
on.
(Inst. solo ad lib....
D.S. % al Coda
F
C
F
N.C.
...end solo)

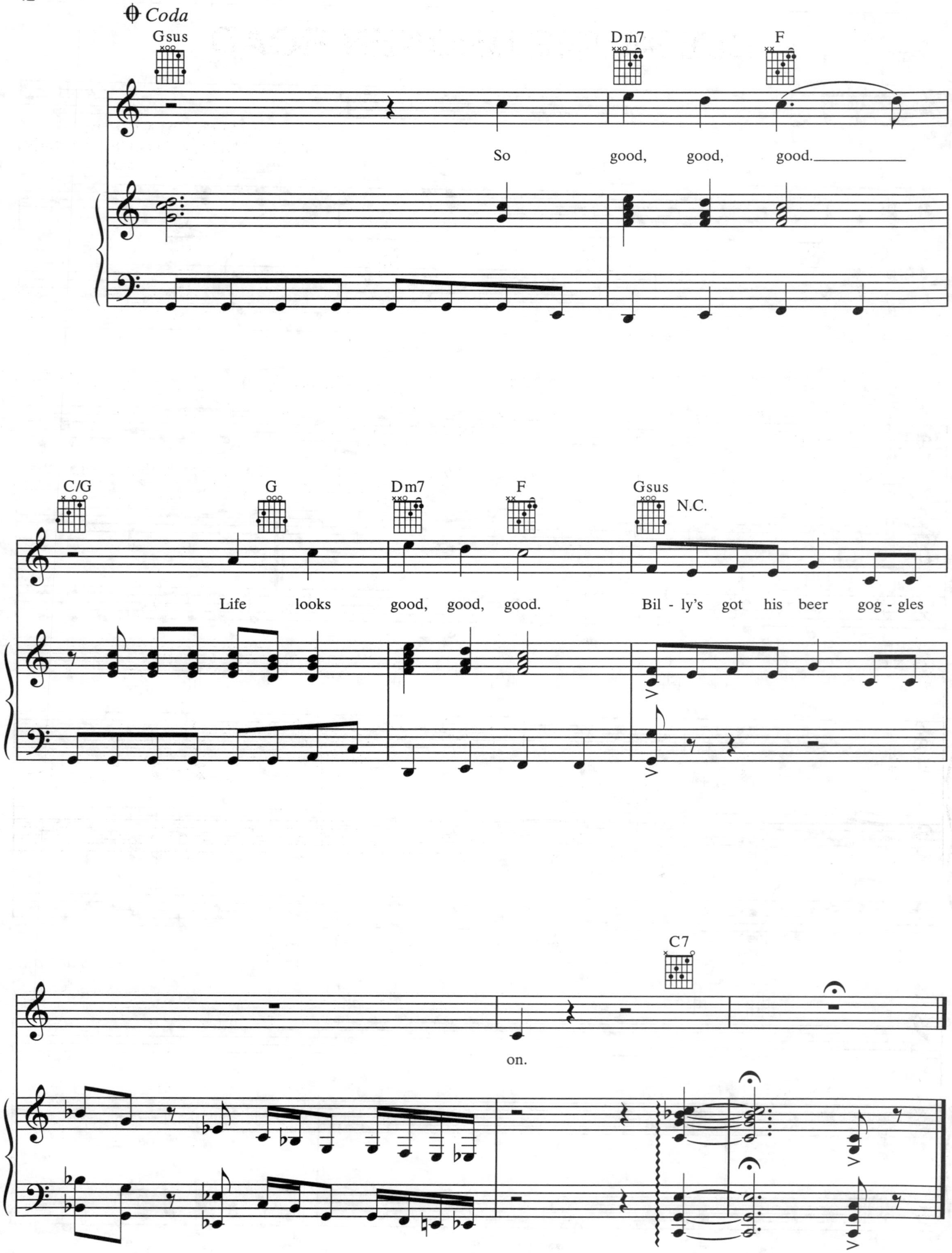
Coda
Gsus
Dm7
F
So good, good, good.
C/G
G
Dm7
F
Gsus
N.C.
Life looks good, good, good. Bil - ly's got his beer gog - gles
C7
on.

BLESS THE BROKEN ROAD

Words and Music by
JEFF HANNA, MARCUS HUMMON
and BOBBY BOYD

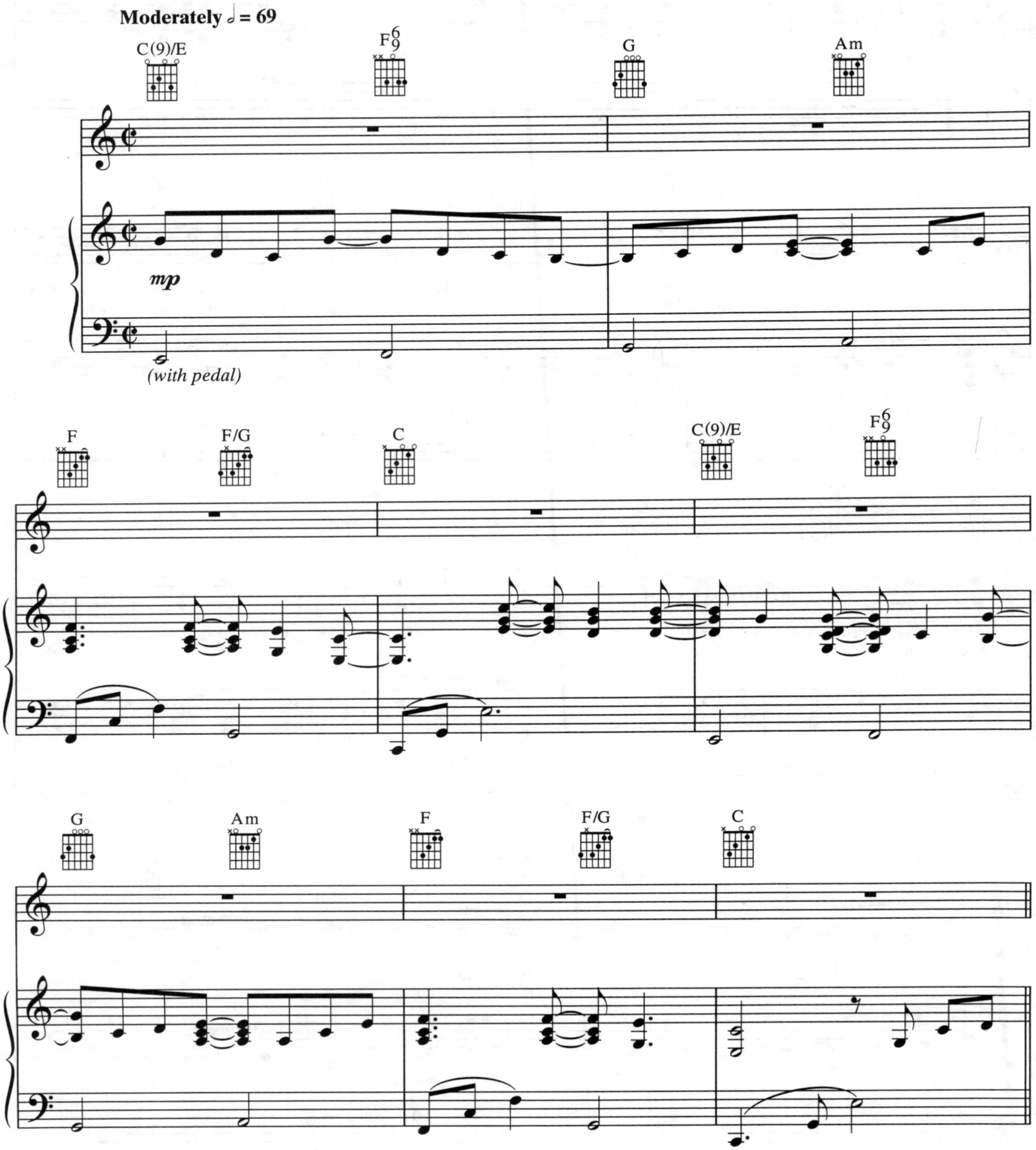

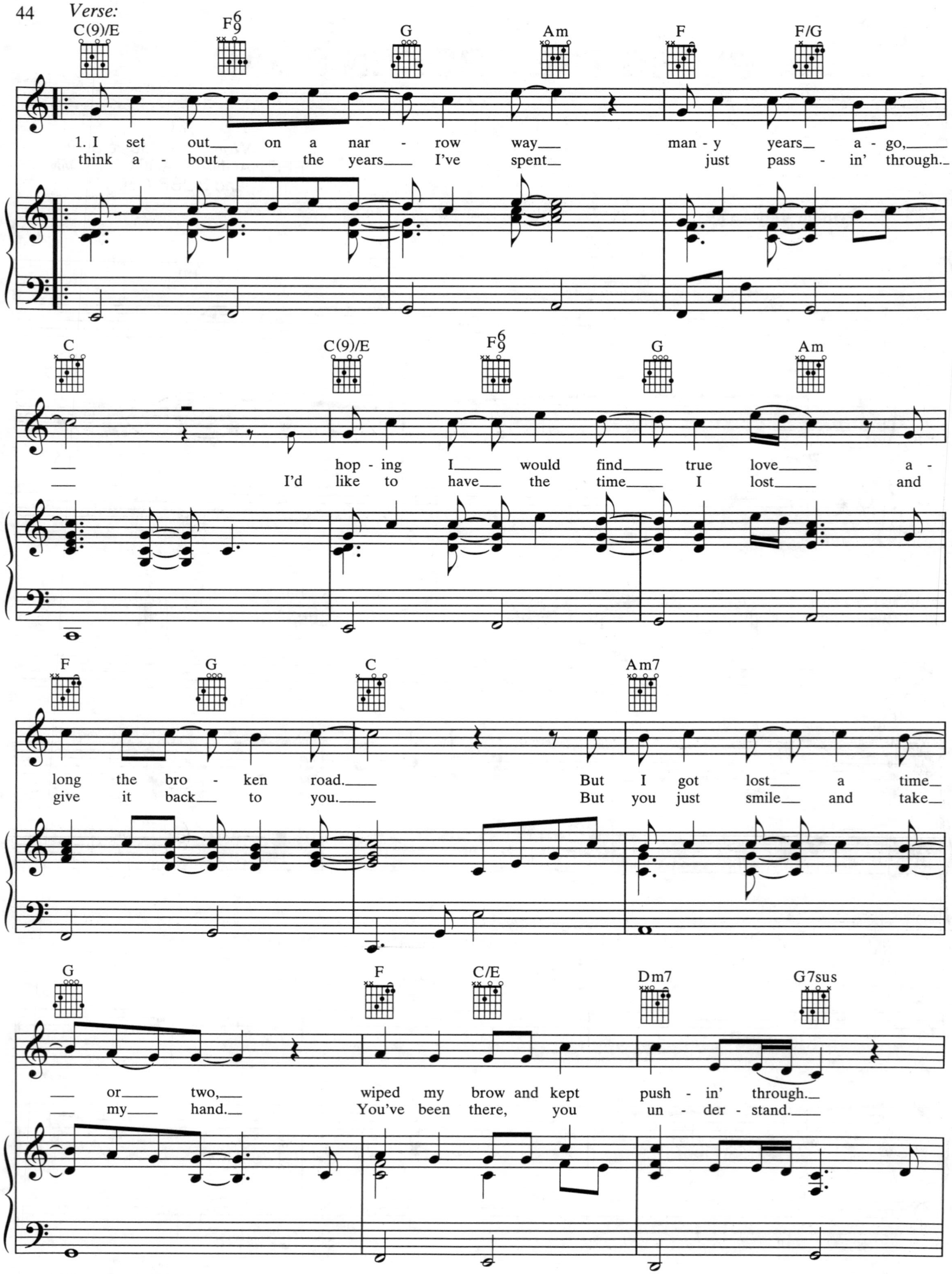
Verse:
C(9)/E F6/9 G Am F F/G
1. I set out on a nar - row way many - y years a - go,
think a - bout the years I've spent just pass - in' through.
C C(9)/E F6/9 G Am
hop - ing I would find true love a -
I'd like to have the time I lost and
F G C Am7
long the bro - ken road. But I got lost a time
give it back to you. But you just smile and take
G F C/E Dm7 G7sus
or two, wiped my brow and kept push - in' through.
my hand. You've been there, you un - der - stand.

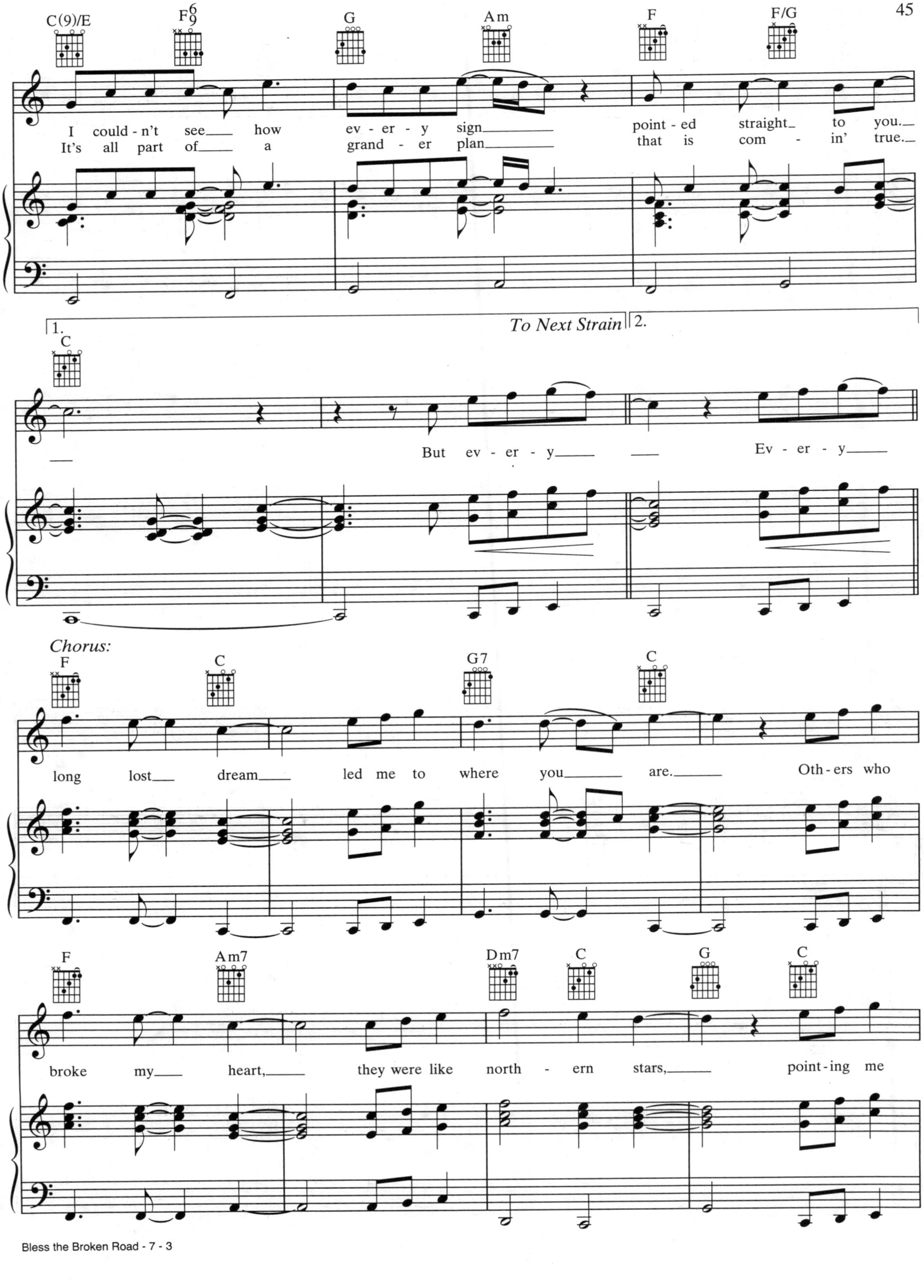
C(9)/E F6/9 G Am F F/G
I could-n't see how ev-er-y sign pointed straight to you.
It's all part of a grand-er plan that is com-in' true.
1. C
To Next Strain
2.
But ev-er-y
Ev-er-y
Chorus:
F C G7 C
long lost dream led me to where you are. Oth-ers who
F Am7 Dm7 C G C
broke my heart, they were like north-ern stars, point-ing me

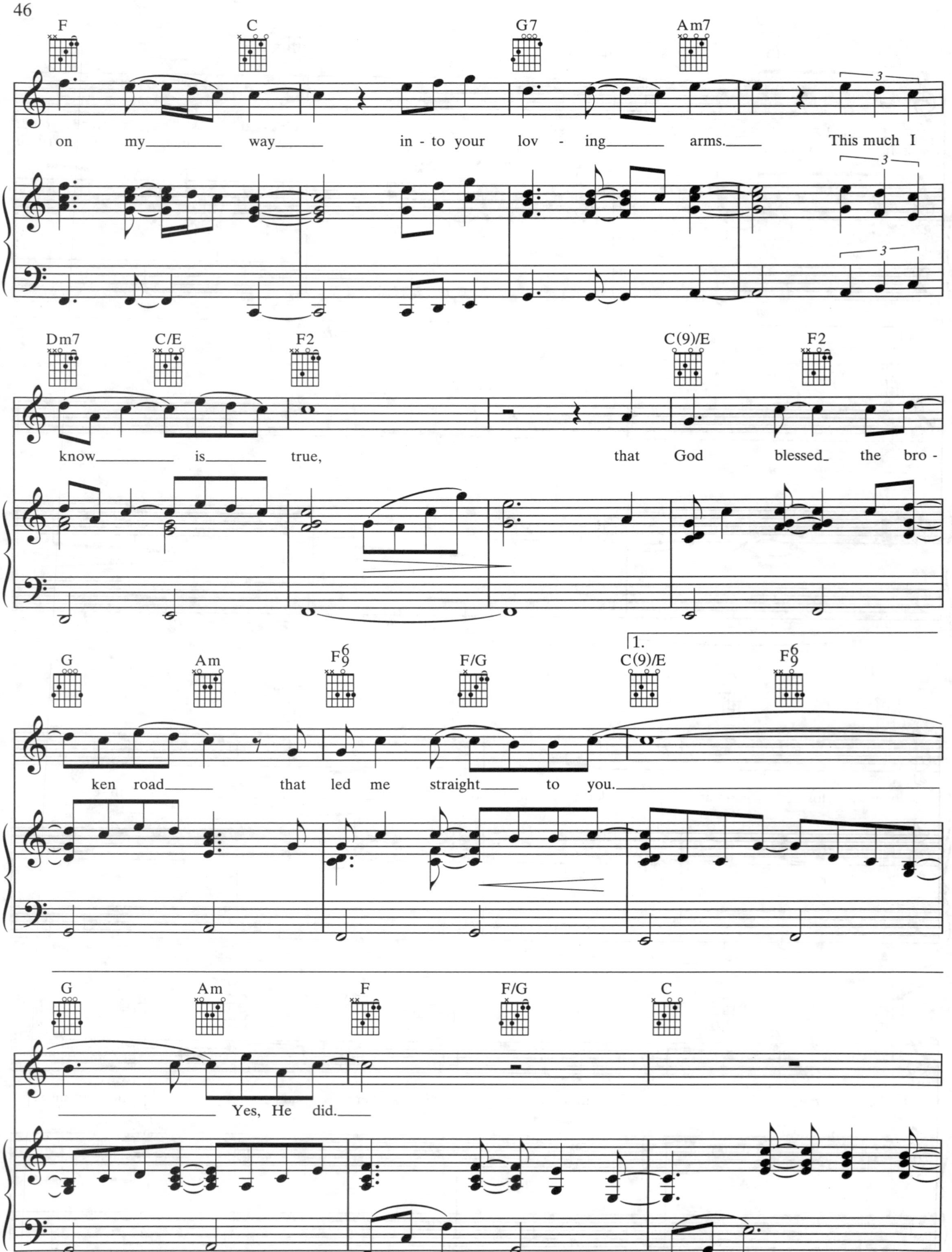
F C G7 Am7
on my way into your loving arms. This much I
3
Dm7 C/E F2 C(9)/E F2
know is true, that God blessed the bro-
G Am F6/9 F/G C(9)/E F6/9
1.
ken road that led me straight to you.
G Am F F/G C
Yes, He did.

C(9)/E
F6/9
G
Am
F
G
C
2. I
2.
F/C
C
F
C
(Inst. solo ad lib....
G
C
F
Am
Dm
C
C/B
C
Now I'm just a -
...end solo)

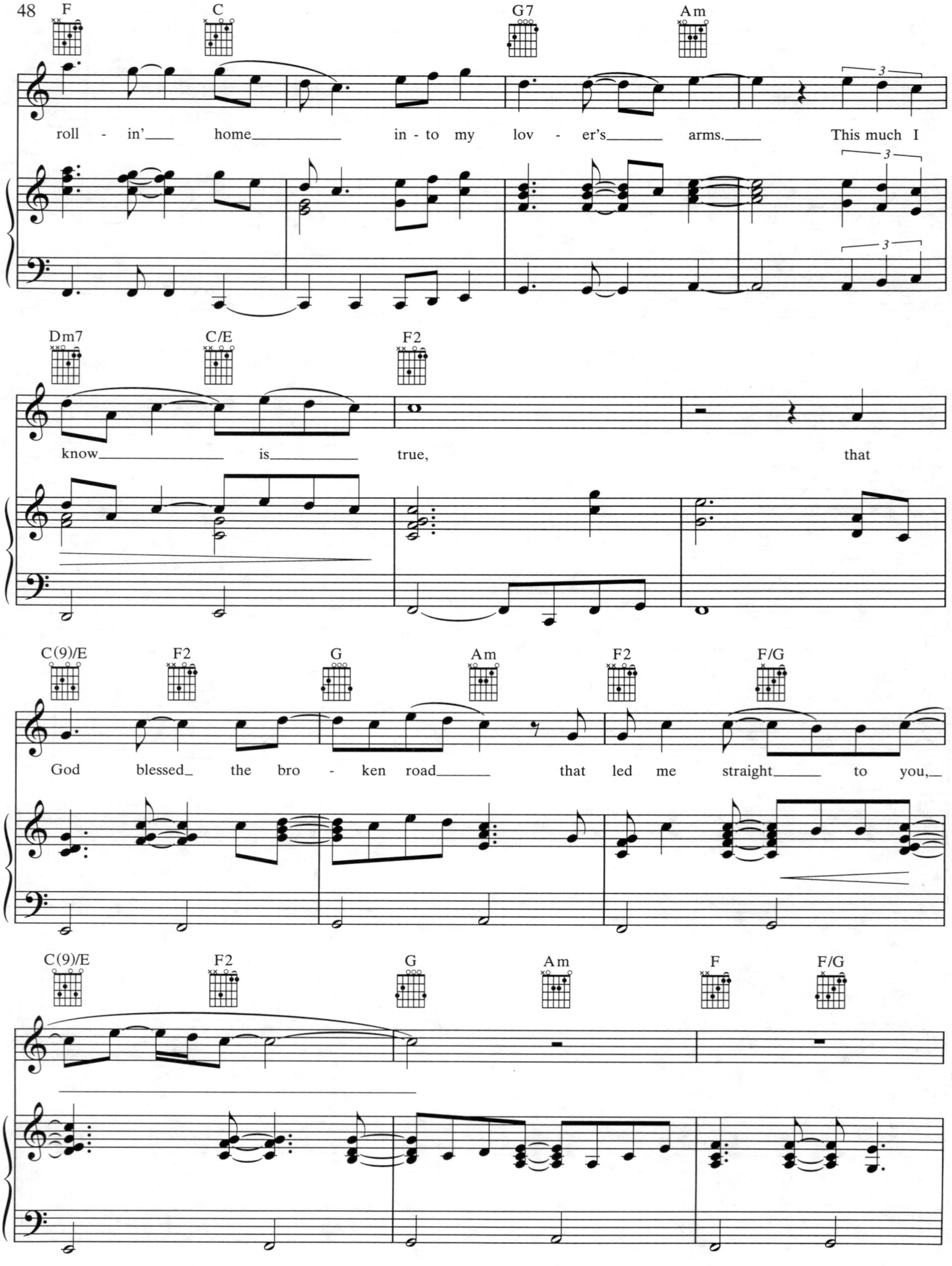
F
C
G7
Am
roll - in' home in - to my lov - er's arms. This much I
3
Dm7
C/E
F2
know is true, that
C(9)/E
F2
G
Am
F2
F/G
God blessed the bro - ken road that led me straight to you,
C(9)/E
F2
G
Am
F
F/G

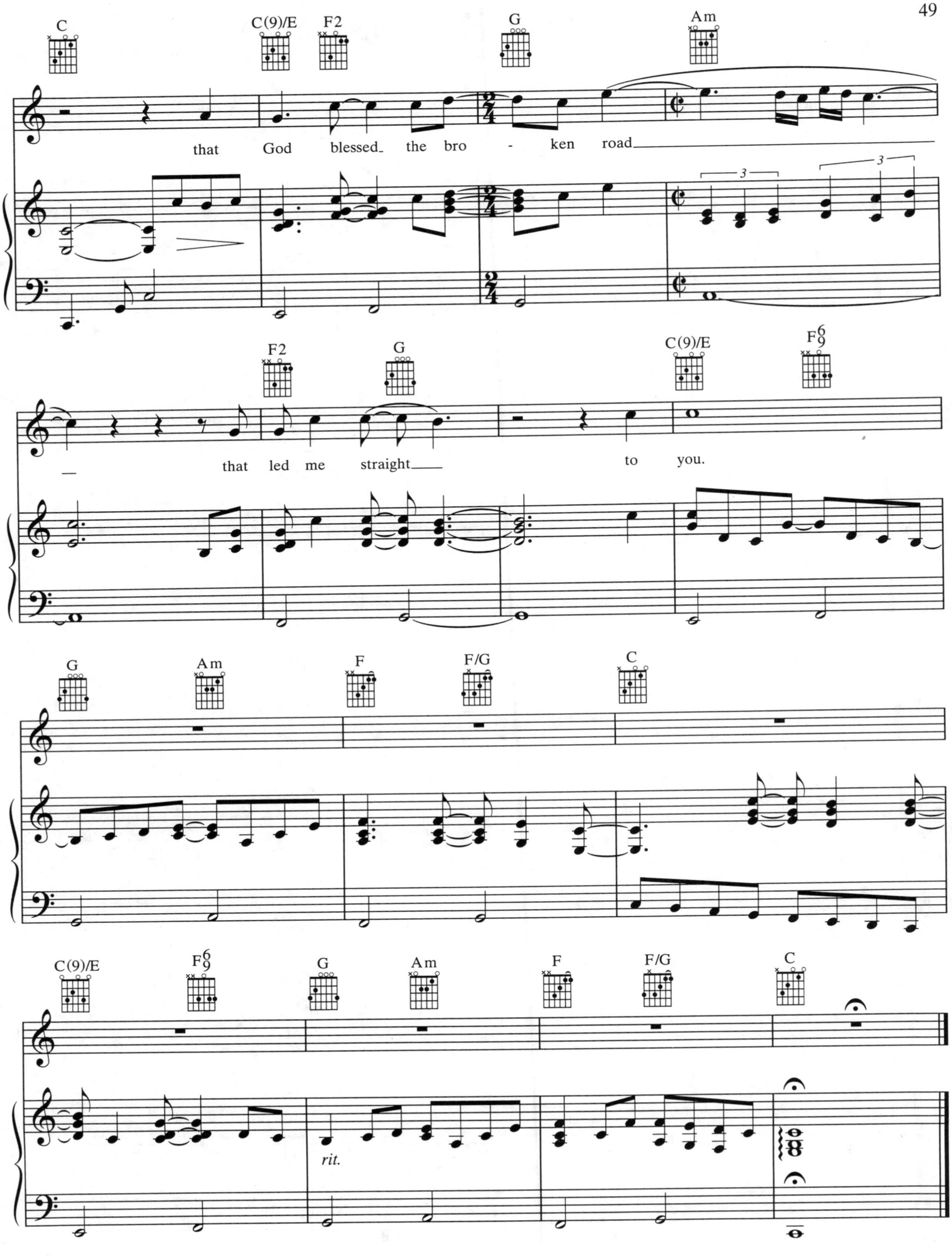
C C(9)/E F2 G Am
that God blessed the bro - ken road
F2 G C(9)/E F6/9
that led me straight to you.
G Am F F/G C
C(9)/E F6/9 G Am F F/G C
rit.

THE BUMPER OF MY SUV

Words and Music by
CHELY WRIGHT

Slowly ♩ = 76
B♭(9)
F/A
E♭(9)/G
B♭/F
mf
(with pedal)
E♭
F7sus
B♭
Verses 1 & 2:
B♭(9)
1. I've got a bright red stick-er on the
brother, Chris,
Cm11
E♭(9)
B♭(9)
back of my car. Says, "U - nit - ed States Ma - rines." And
he's been in for more than four - teen years now. Our
Cm11
E♭(9)
yes - ter - day a la - dy in a min - i van held up her mid - dle fin - ger at me.
dad was in the Na - vy dur - ing Vi - et - nam, did his du - ty then he got out.

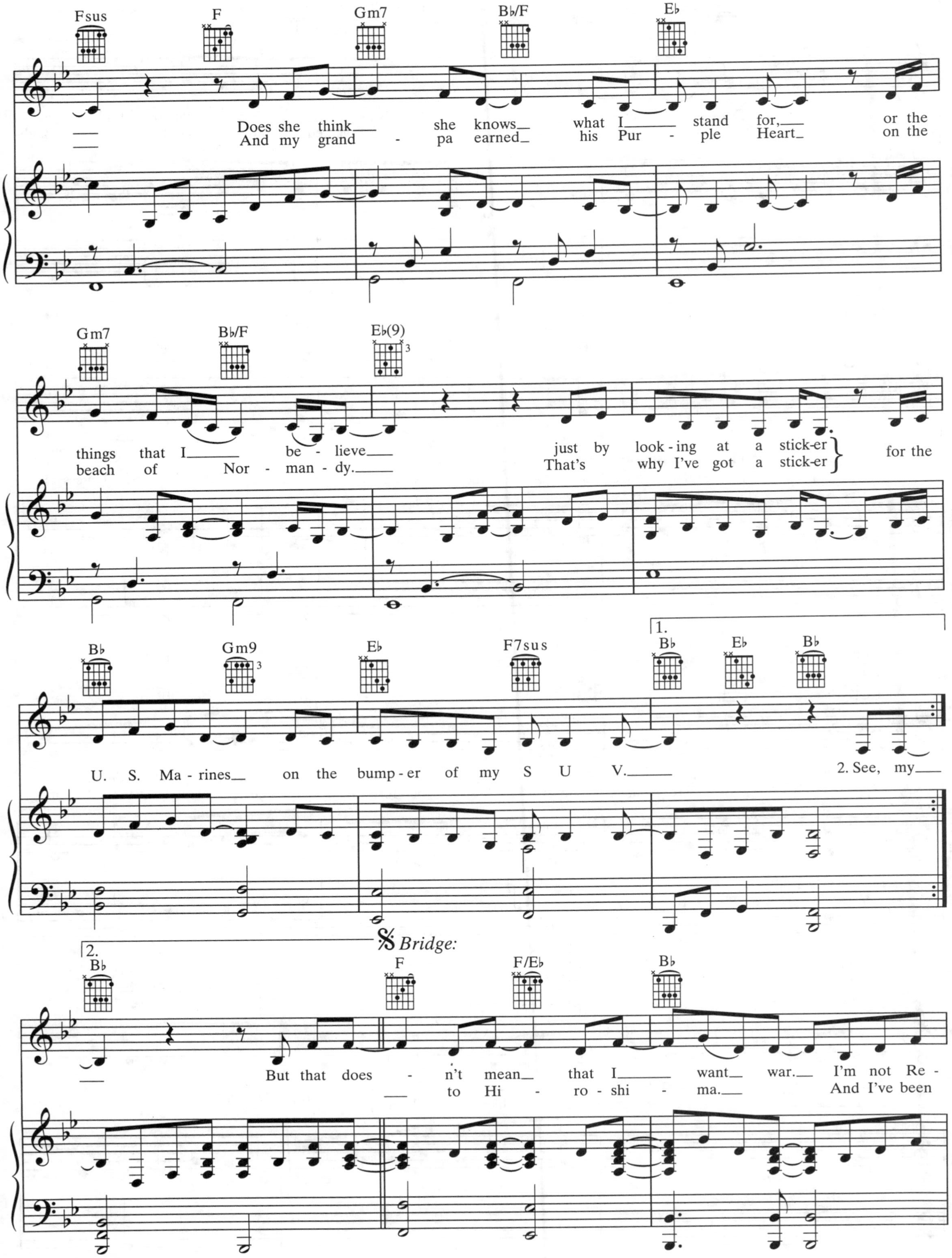
Fsus F Gm7 B♭/F E♭
Does she think she knows what I stand for, or the
And my grand - pa earned his Pur - ple Heart on the
Gm7 B♭/F E♭(9)
things that I be - lieve just by look - ing at a stick - er for the
beach of Nor - man - dy. That's why I've got a stick - er
B♭ Gm9 E♭ F7sus
1. B♭ E♭ B♭
U. S. Ma - rines on the bump - er of my S U V.
2. See, my
2. B♭
Bridge:
F F/E♭ B♭
But that does - n't mean that I want war. I'm not Re -
to Hi - ro - shi - ma. And I've been

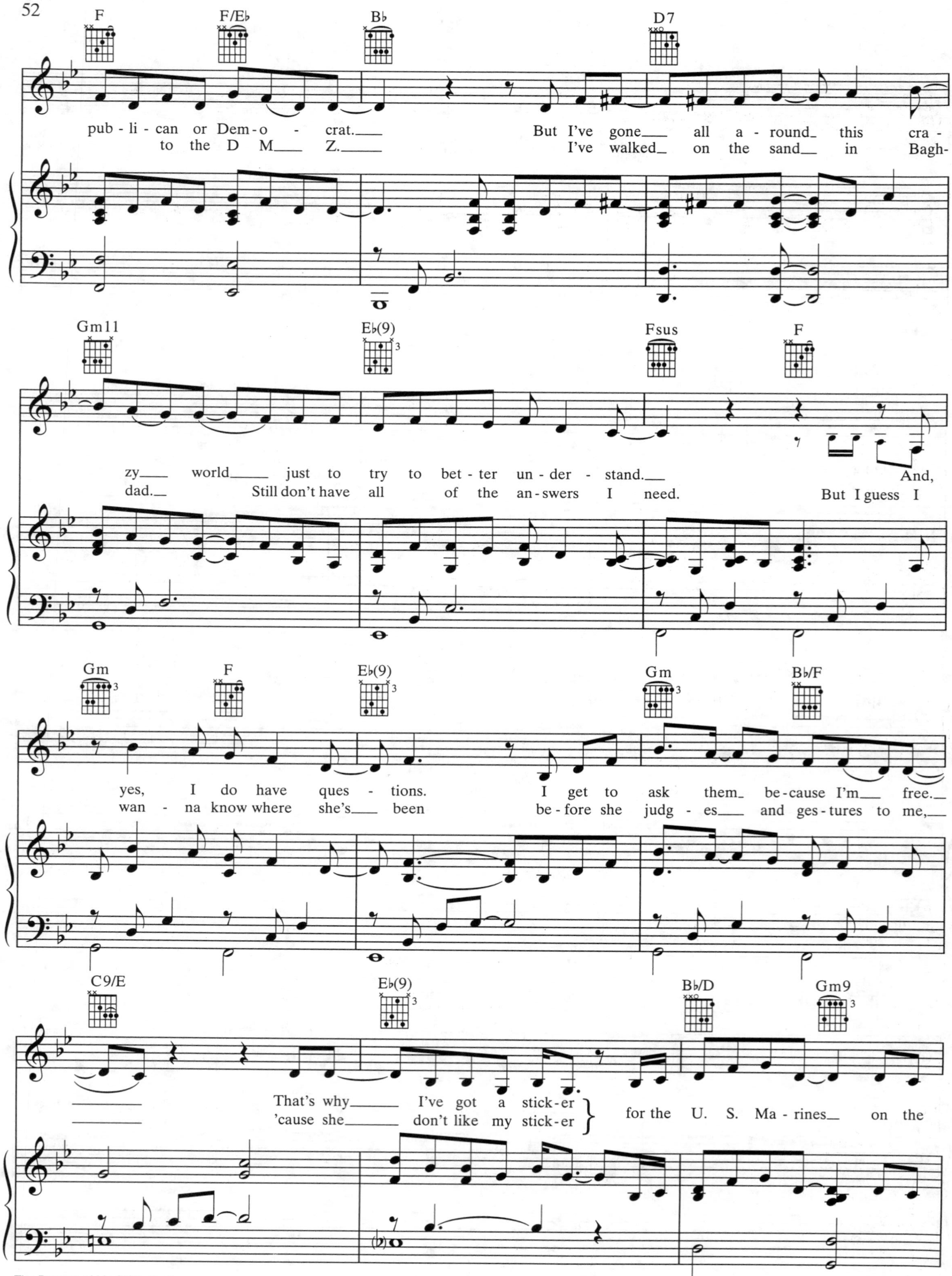
F
F/E♭
B♭
D7
pub - li - can or Dem - o - crat.
to the D M Z.
But I've gone all a - round this cra -
I've walked on the sand in Bagh-
Gm11
E♭(9)
Fsus
F
zy world just to try to bet - ter un - der - stand.
dad. Still don't have all of the an - swers I need.
And,
But I guess I
Gm
F
E♭(9)
Gm
B♭/F
yes, I do have ques - tions. I get to ask them be-cause I'm free.
wan - na know where she's been be - fore she judg - es and ges - tures to me,
C9/E
E♭(9)
B♭/D
Gm9
That's why I've got a stick - er
'cause she don't like my stick - er
for the U. S. Ma - rines on the

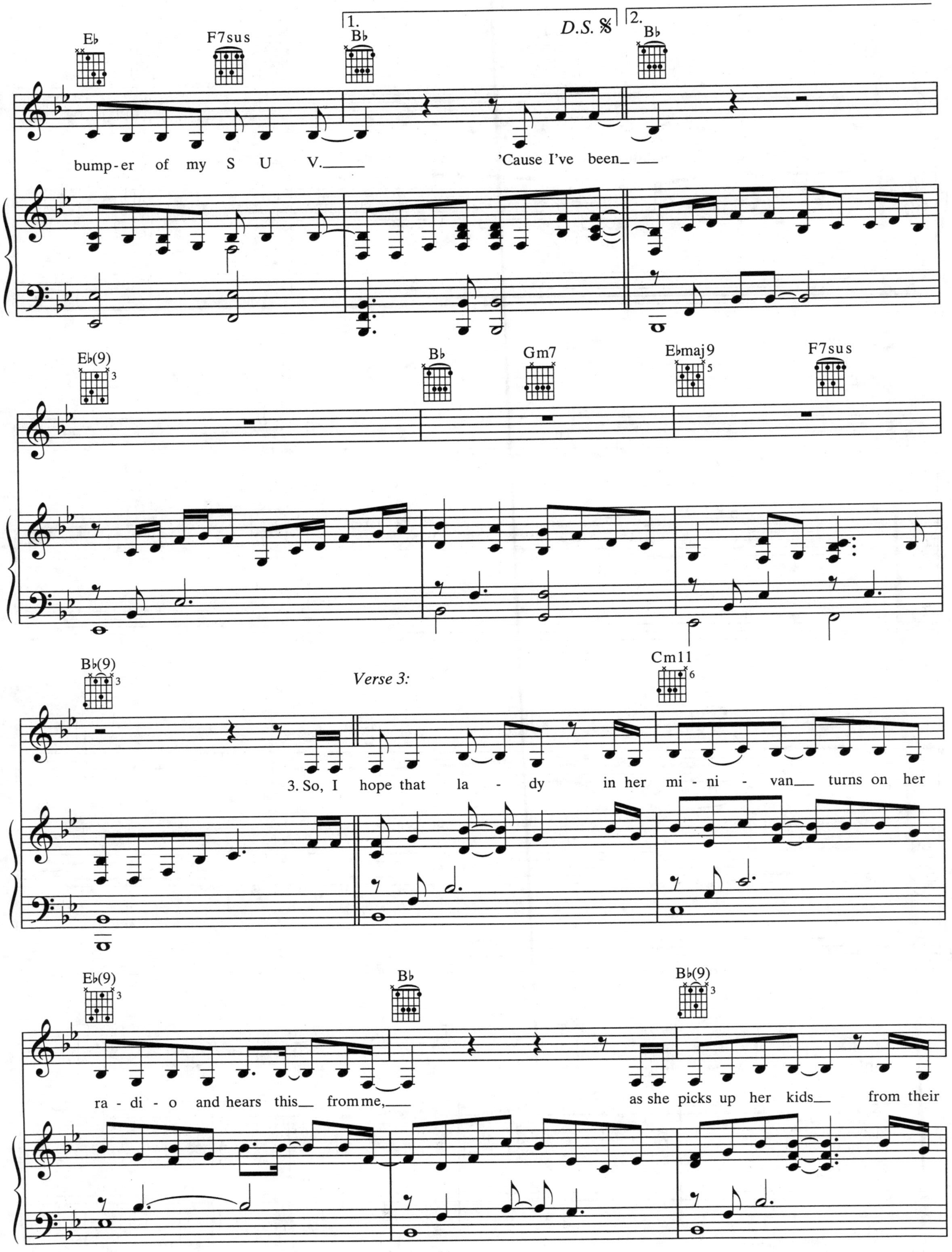
1.
D.S. 𝄋
2.
E♭
F7sus
B♭
bump-er of my S U V.
'Cause I've been
E♭(9)
B♭
Gm7
E♭maj9
F7sus
B♭(9)
Verse 3:
Cm11
3. So, I hope that la - dy in her mi - ni - van turns on her
E♭(9)
B♭
B♭(9)
ra - di - o and hears this from me,
as she picks up her kids from their

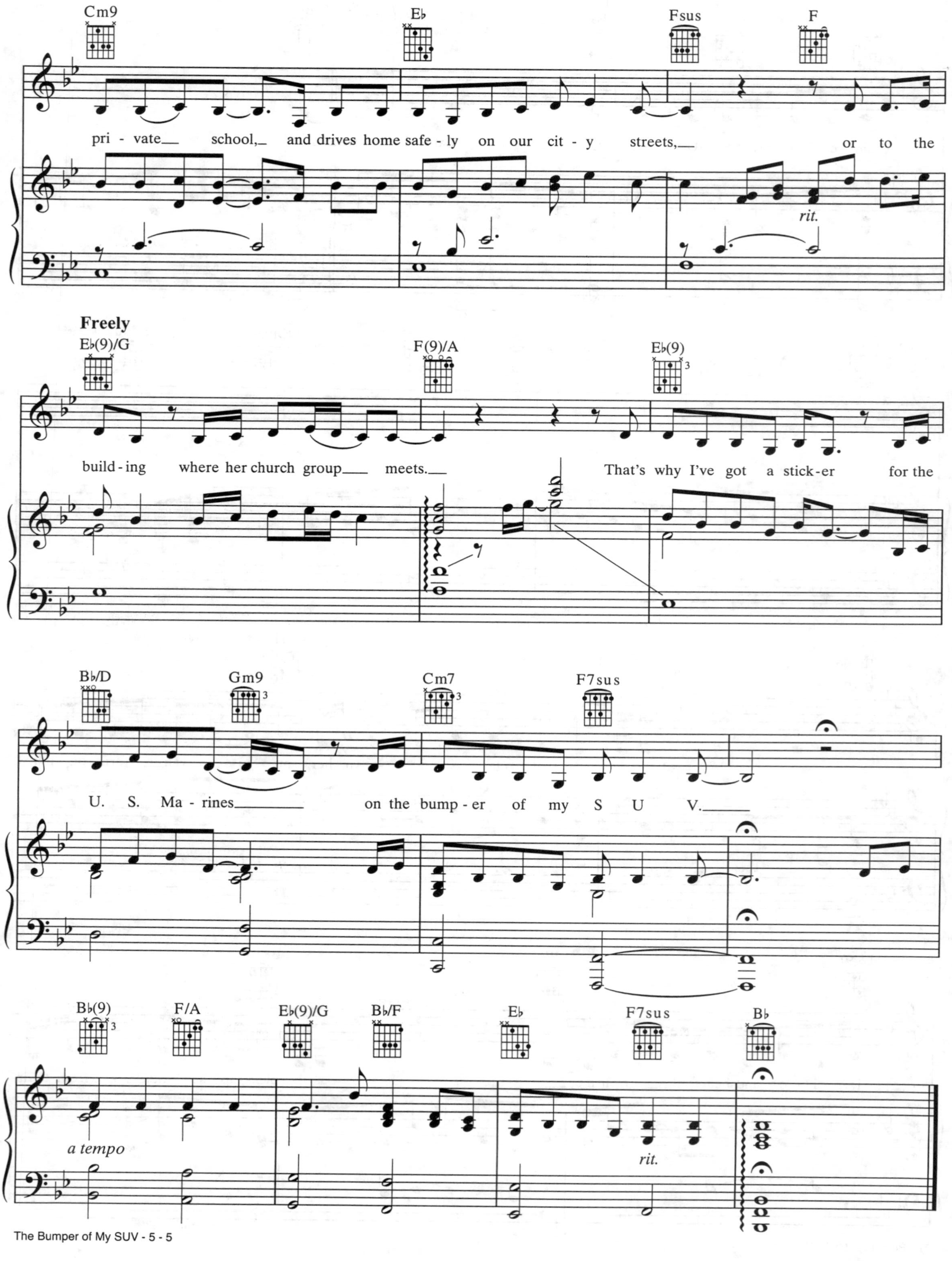
Cm9
Eb
Fsus
F
pri - vate school, and drives home safe - ly on our cit - y streets, or to the
rit.
Freely
Eb(9)/G
F(9)/A
Eb(9)
build - ing where her church group meets. That's why I've got a stick - er for the
Bb/D
Gm9
Cm7
F7sus
U. S. Ma - rines on the bump - er of my S U V.
Bb(9)
F/A
Eb(9)/G
Bb/F
Eb
F7sus
Bb
a tempo
rit.

BUT I DO LOVE YOU

Words and Music by
DIANE WARREN

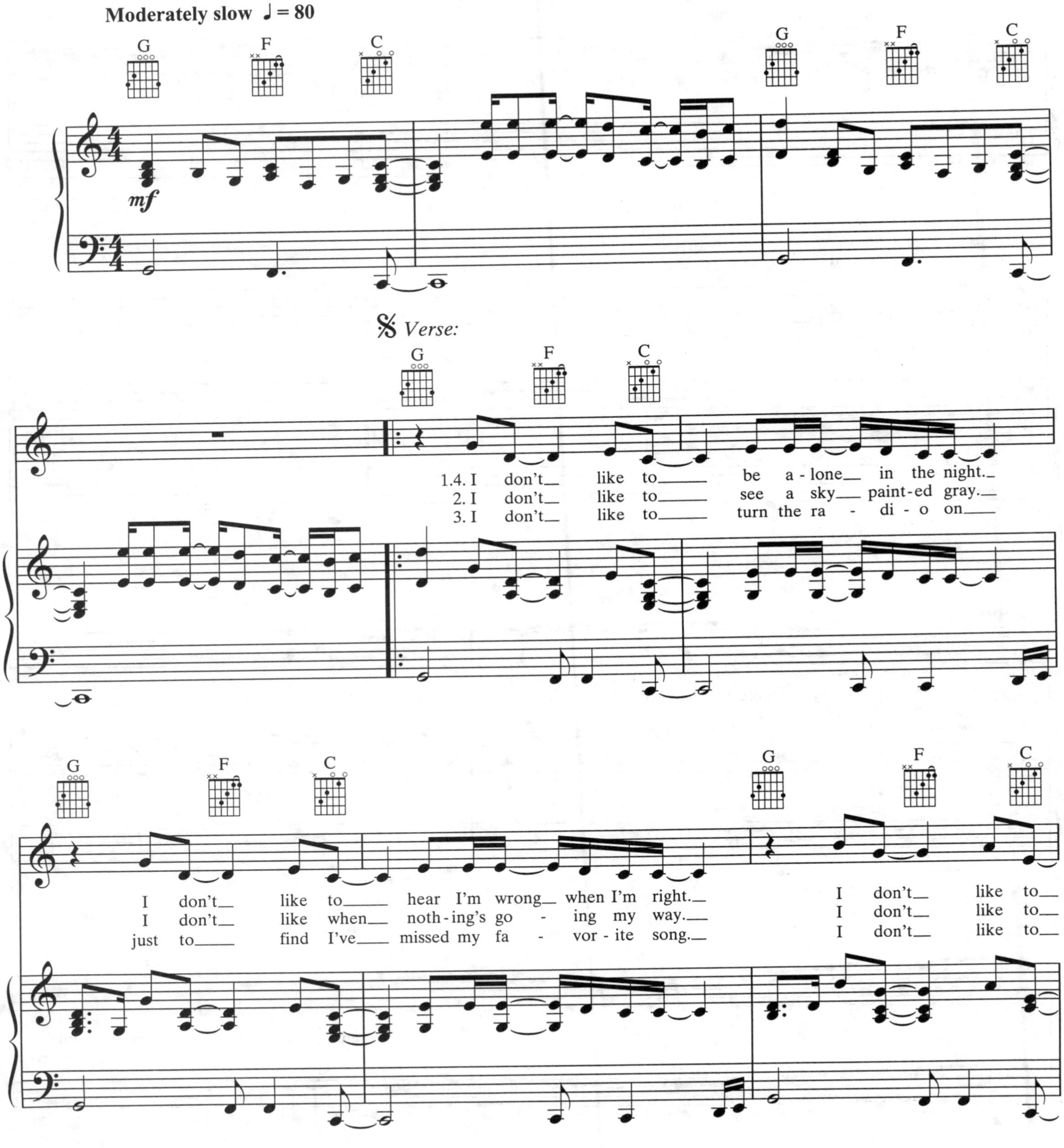

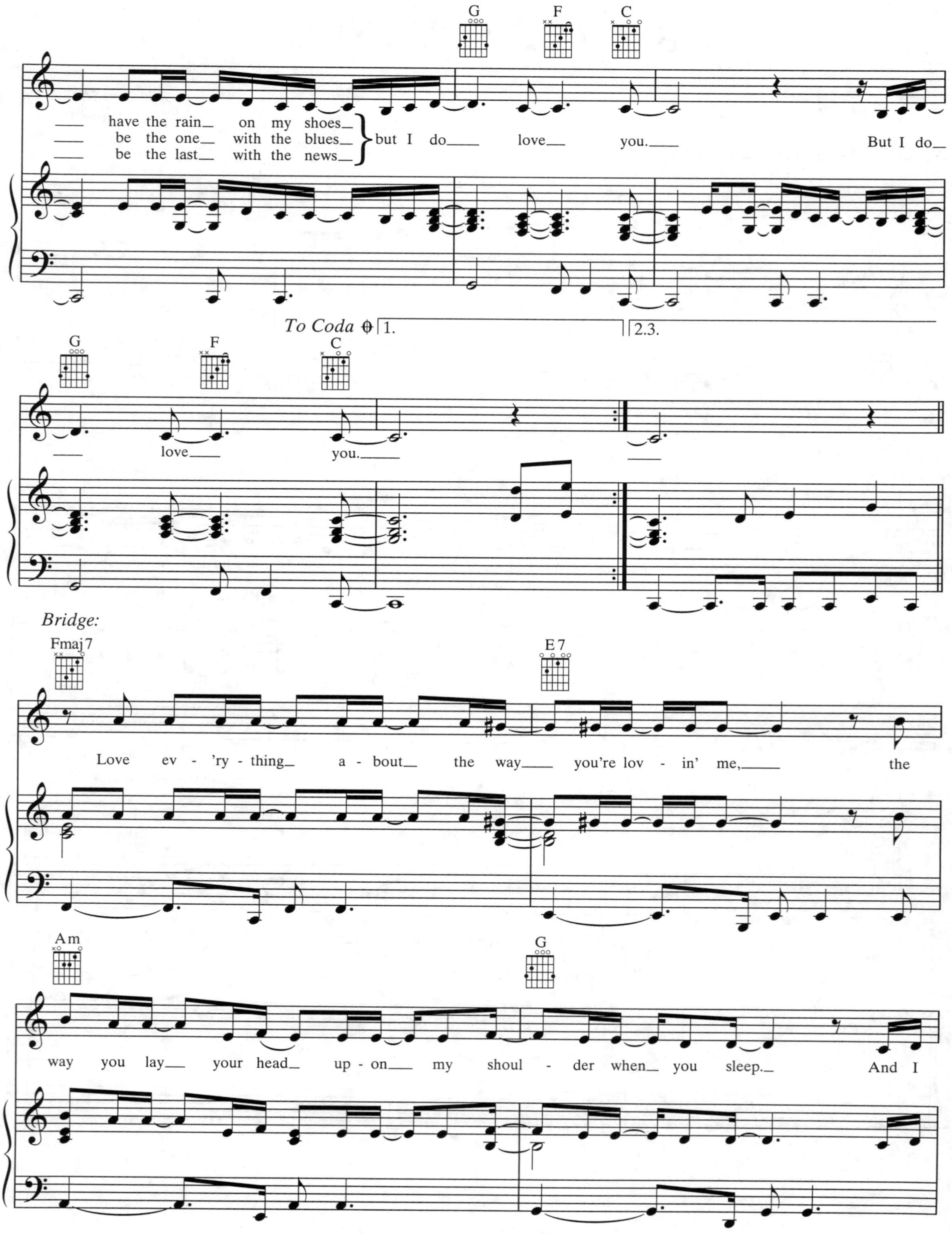
G
F
C
have the rain on my shoes
be the one with the blues
be the last with the news
but I do love you.
But I do
To Coda
1.
2.3.
G
F
C
love you.
Bridge:
Fmaj7
E7
Love ev - 'ry - thing a - bout the way you're lov - in' me, the
Am
G
way you lay your head up - on my shoul - der when you sleep. And I

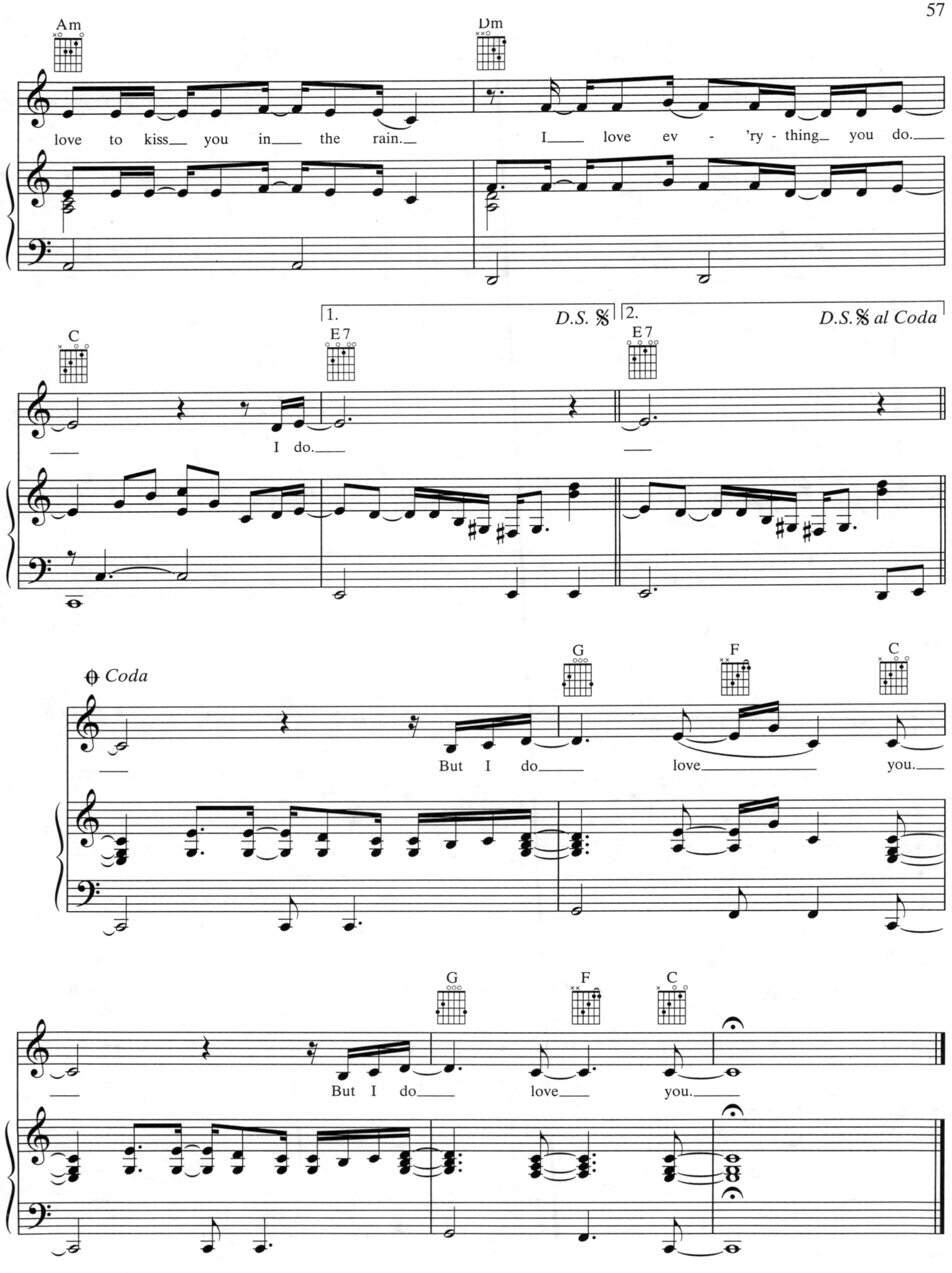
Am
Dm
love to kiss you in the rain.
I love ev - 'ry - thing you do.
C
1.
E7
D.S. 𝄋
2.
E7
D.S. 𝄋 al Coda
I do.
Coda
G
F
C
But I do love you.
G
F
C
But I do love you.

COWBOY TAKE ME AWAY

Words and Music by
MARTIE SEIDEL and
MARCUS HUMMON

Moderately slow

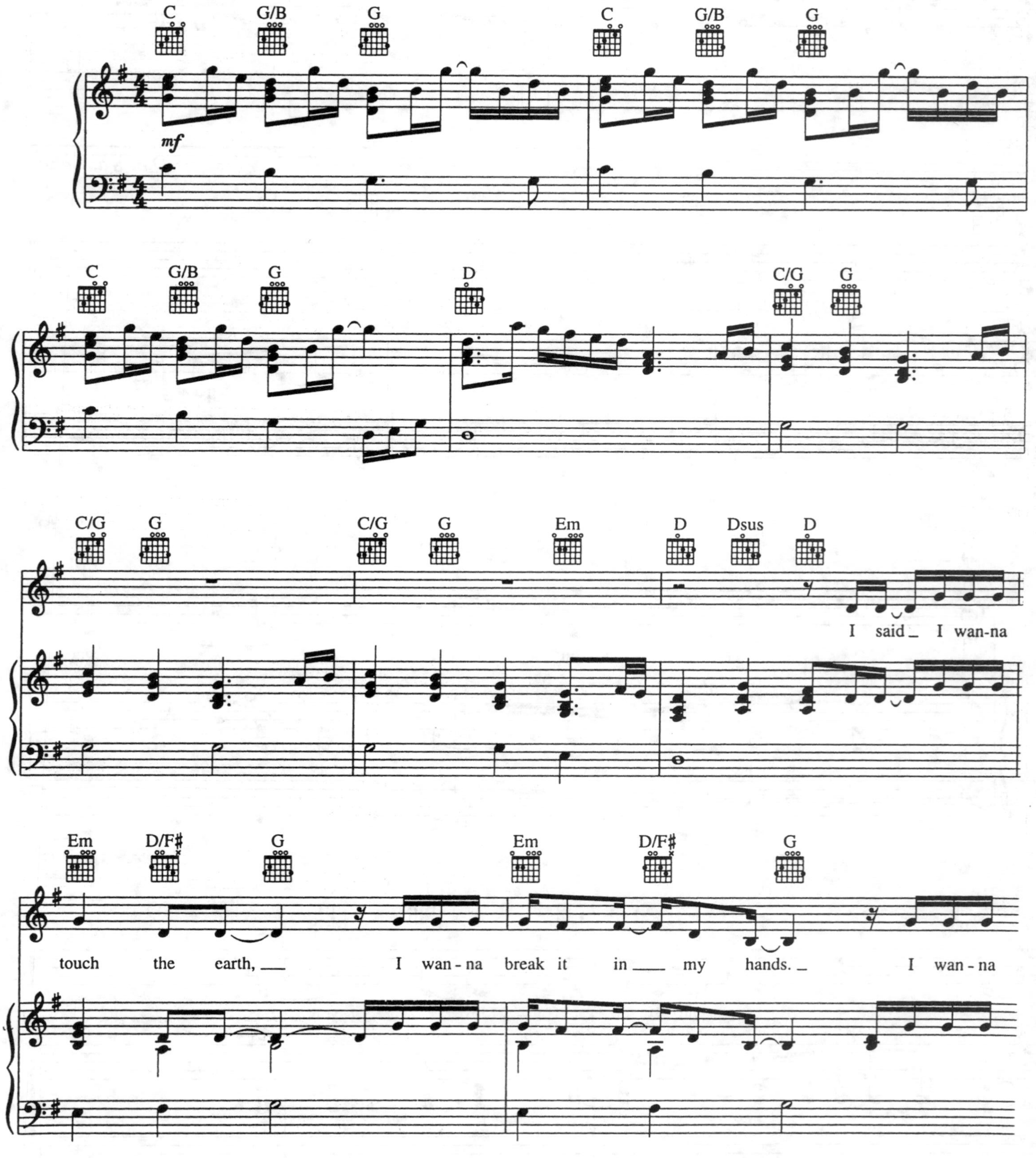

Original key: F♯ major. This edition has been transposed up one half-step to be more playable.

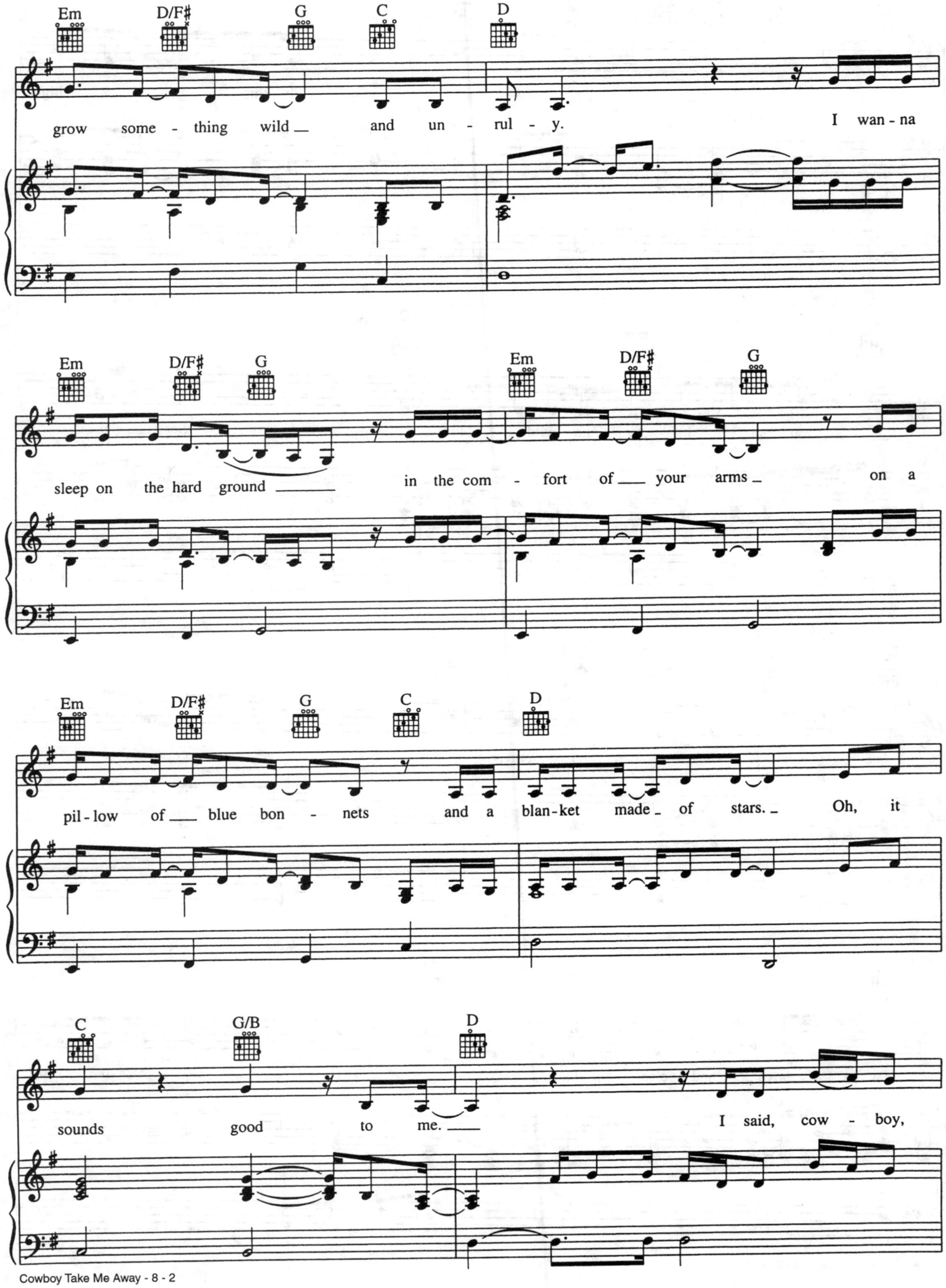
Em D/F# G C D
grow some - thing wild and un - rul - y. I wan - na
Em D/F# G Em D/F# G
sleep on the hard ground in the com - fort of your arms on a
Em D/F# G C D
pil - low of blue bon - nets and a blan - ket made of stars. Oh, it
C G/B D
sounds good to me. I said, cow - boy,

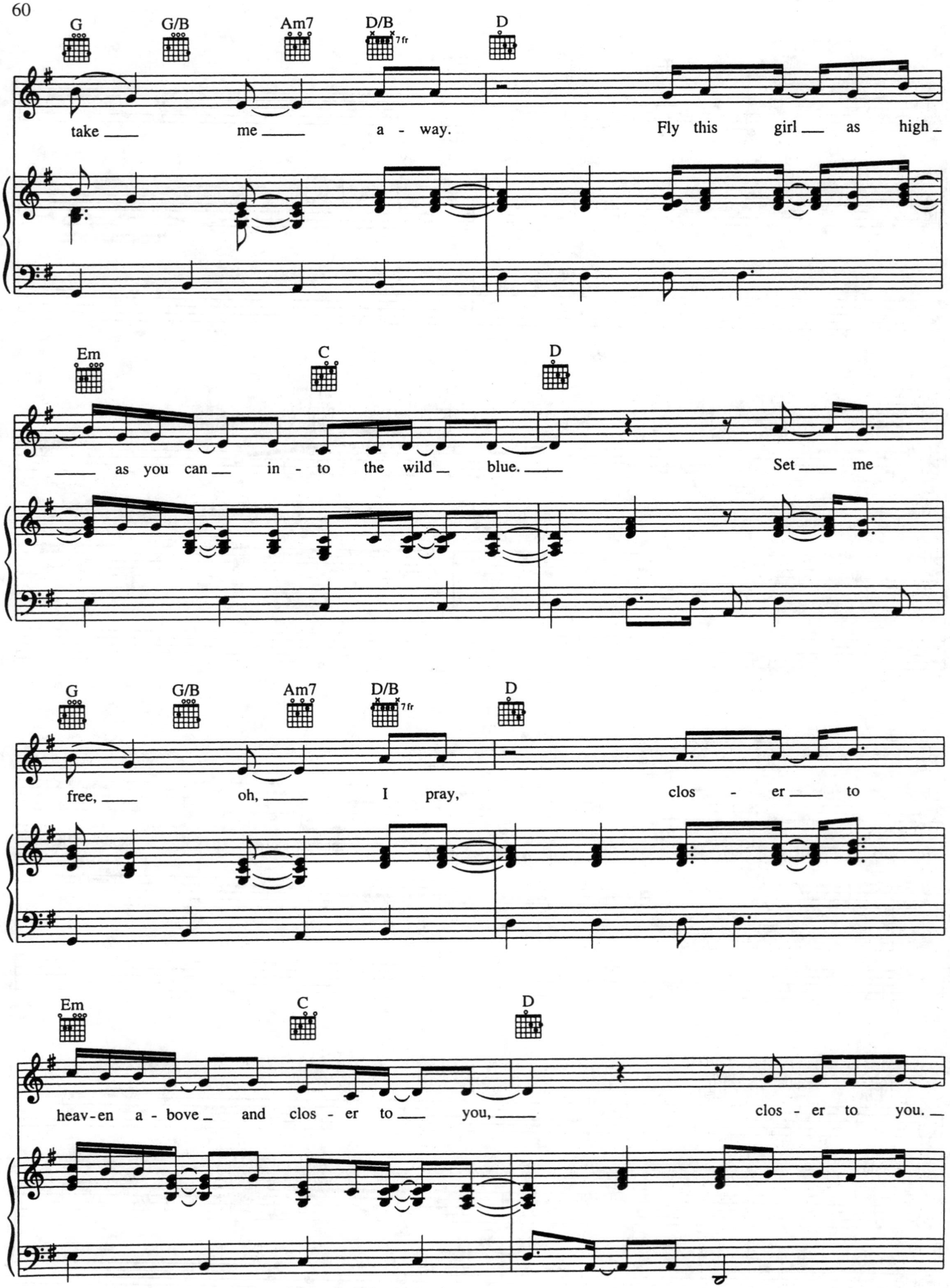
G G/B Am7 D/B 7fr D
take me a - way. Fly this girl as high
Em C D
as you can in - to the wild blue. Set me
G G/B Am7 D/B 7fr D
free, oh, I pray, clos - er to
Em C D
heav-en a - bove and clos - er to you, clos - er to you.

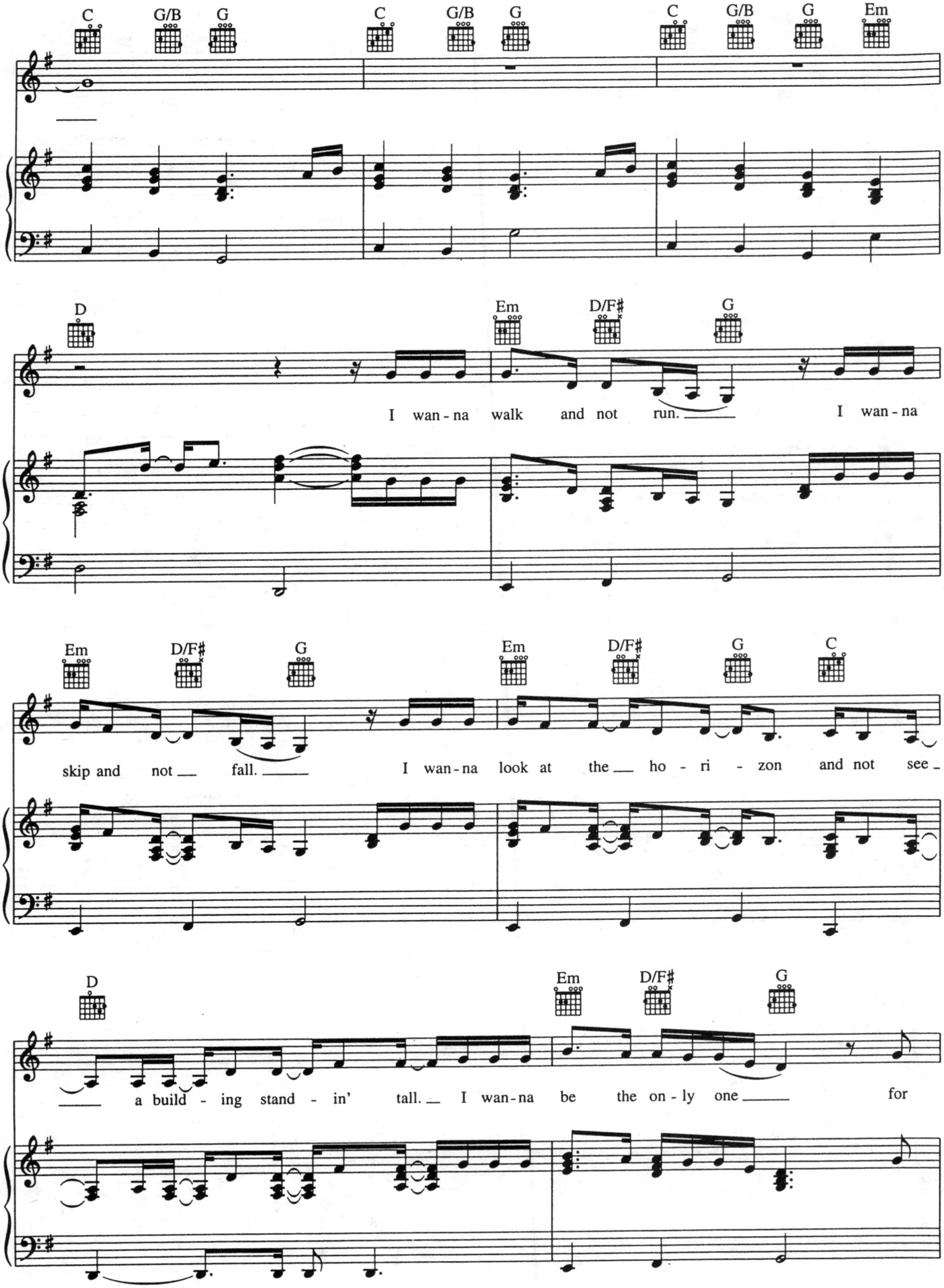
C G/B G C G/B G C G/B G Em
D Em D/F# G
I wan-na walk and not run. I wan-na
Em D/F# G Em D/F# G C
skip and not fall. I wan-na look at the ho - ri - zon and not see
D Em D/F# G
a build - ing stand - in' tall. I wan-na be the on-ly one for

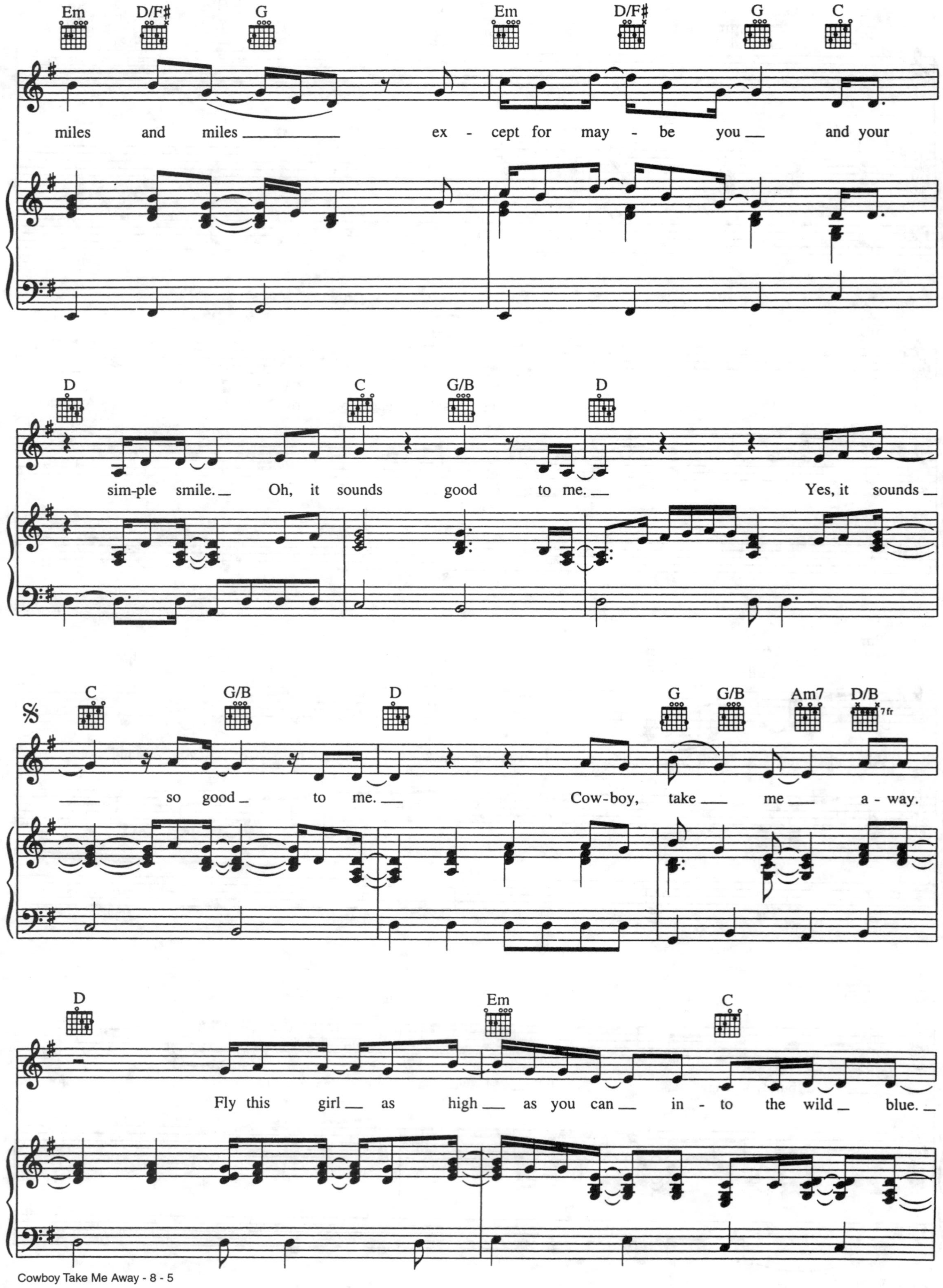
Em D/F♯ G Em D/F♯ G C
miles and miles ex - cept for may - be you and your
D C G/B D
sim-ple smile. Oh, it sounds good to me. Yes, it sounds
C G/B D G G/B Am7 D/B
7fr
so good to me. Cow-boy, take me a - way.
D Em C
Fly this girl as high as you can in - to the wild blue.

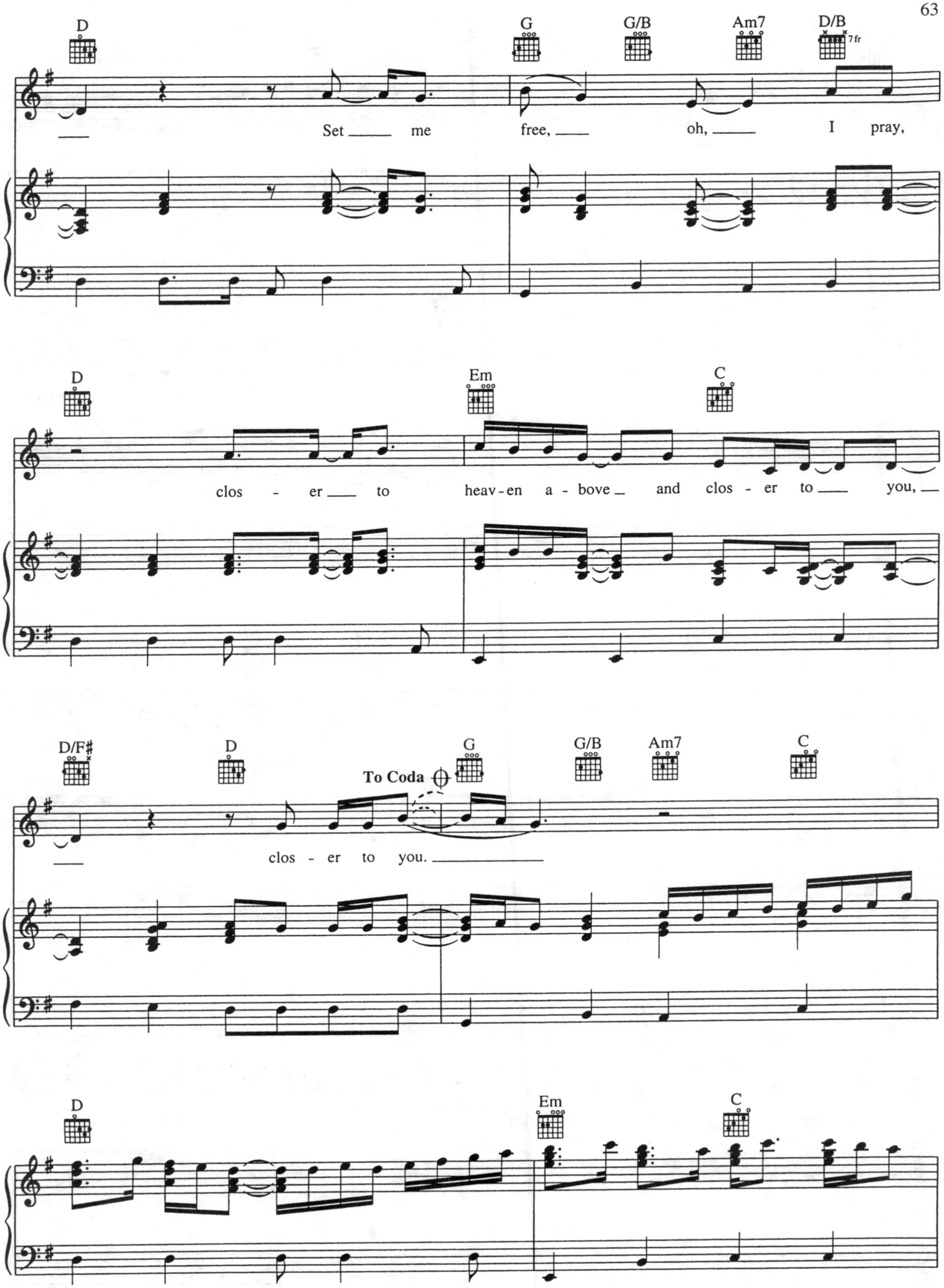
D
G
G/B
Am7
D/B
7fr
Set me free, oh, I pray,
D
Em
C
clos - er to heav-en a - bove and clos - er to you,
D/F#
D
To Coda
G
G/B
Am7
C
clos - er to you.
D
Em
C

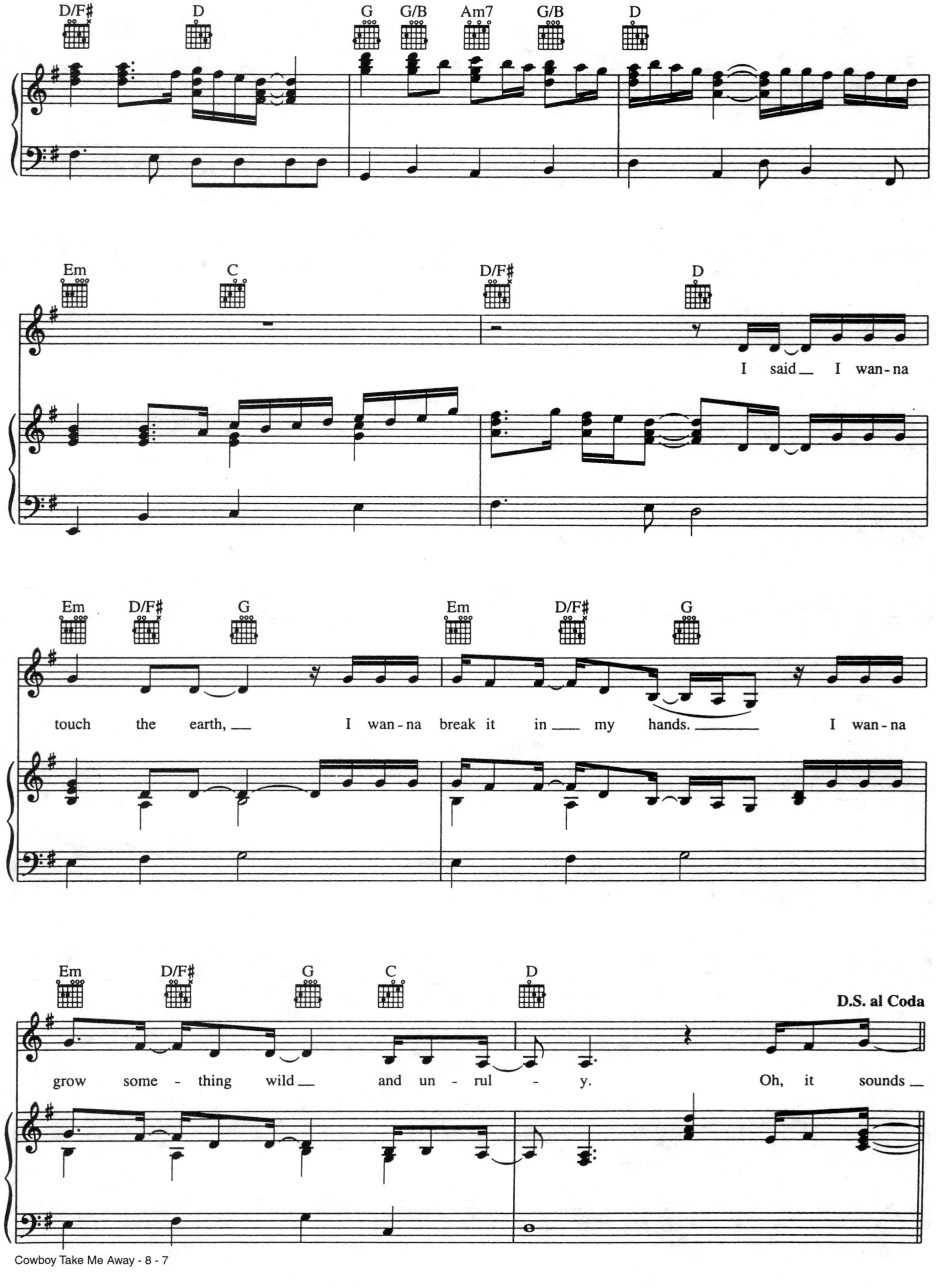
D/F#
D
G
G/B
Am7
G/B
D
Em
C
D/F#
D
I said I wan-na
Em
D/F#
G
Em
D/F#
G
touch the earth,
I wan-na break it in my hands.
I wan-na
Em
D/F#
G
C
D
D.S. al Coda
grow some - thing wild and un - rul - y.
Oh, it sounds

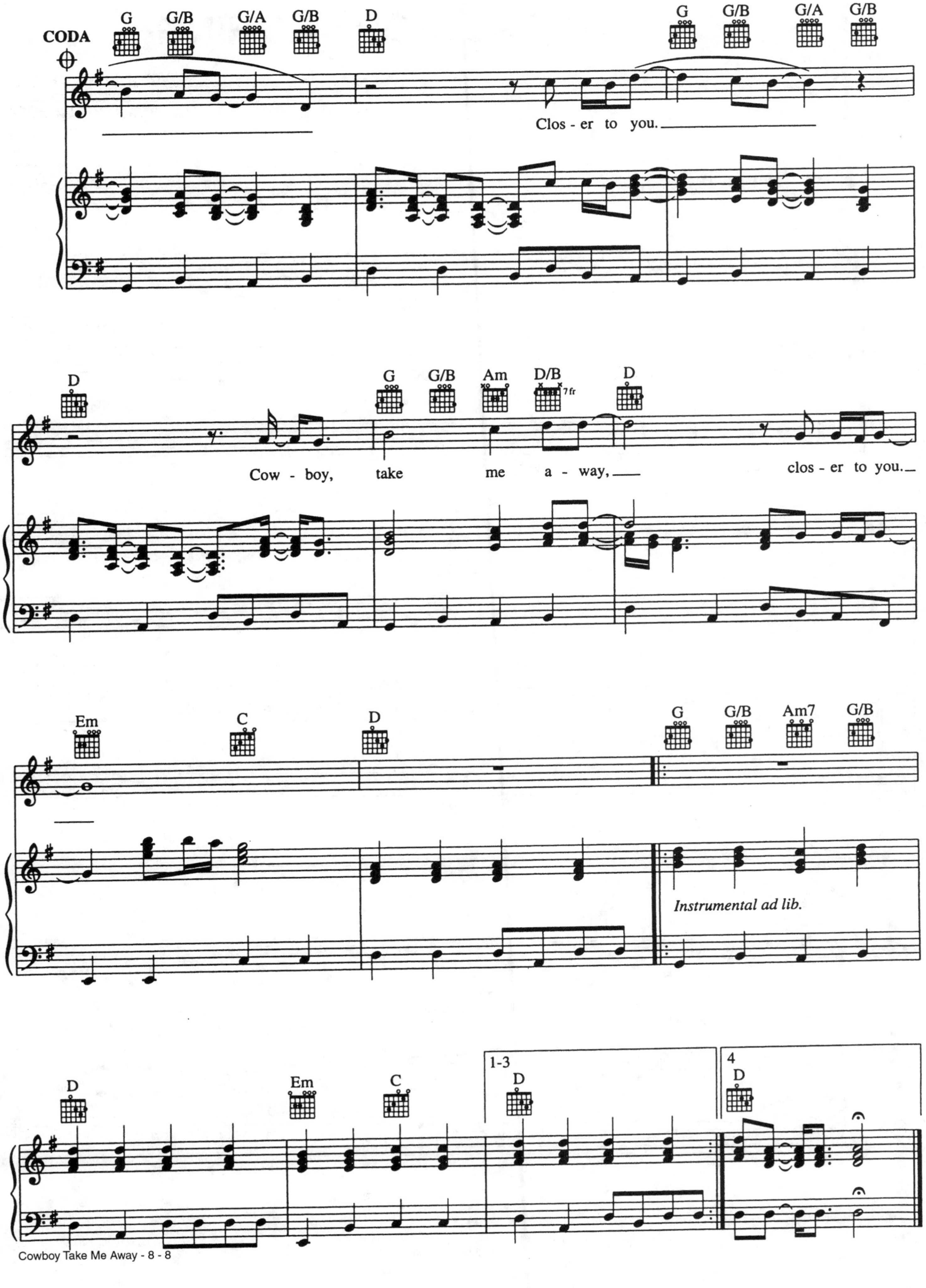
CODA
G
G/B
G/A
G/B
D
G
G/B
G/A
G/B
Clos - er to you.
D
G
G/B
Am
D/B
7 fr
D
Cow - boy, take me a - way,
clos - er to you.
Em
C
D
G
G/B
Am7
G/B
Instrumental ad lib.
D
Em
C
1-3
D
4
D

DON'T WORRY 'BOUT A THING

Words and Music by
JASON DEERE
and KRISTYN OSBORN

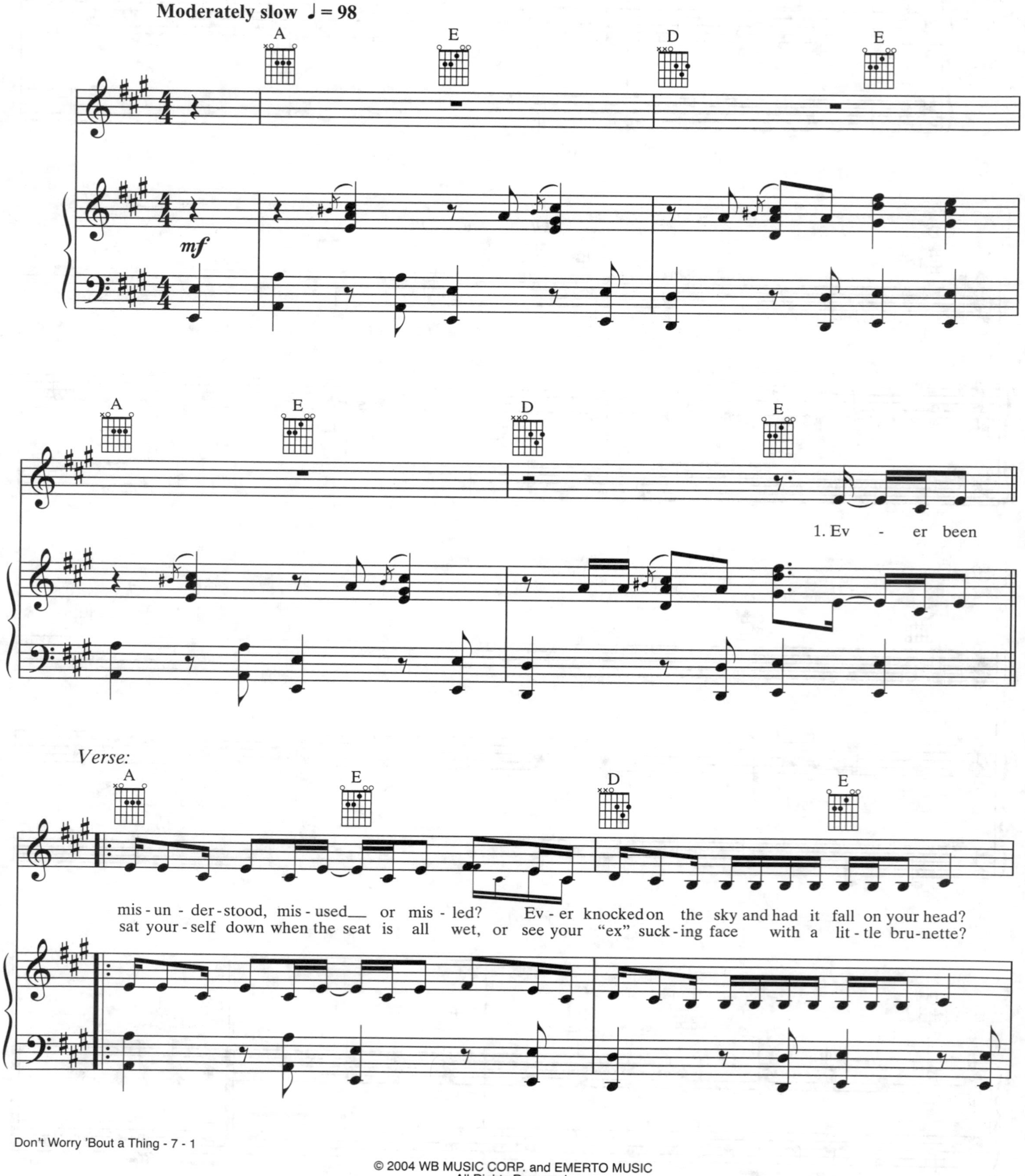

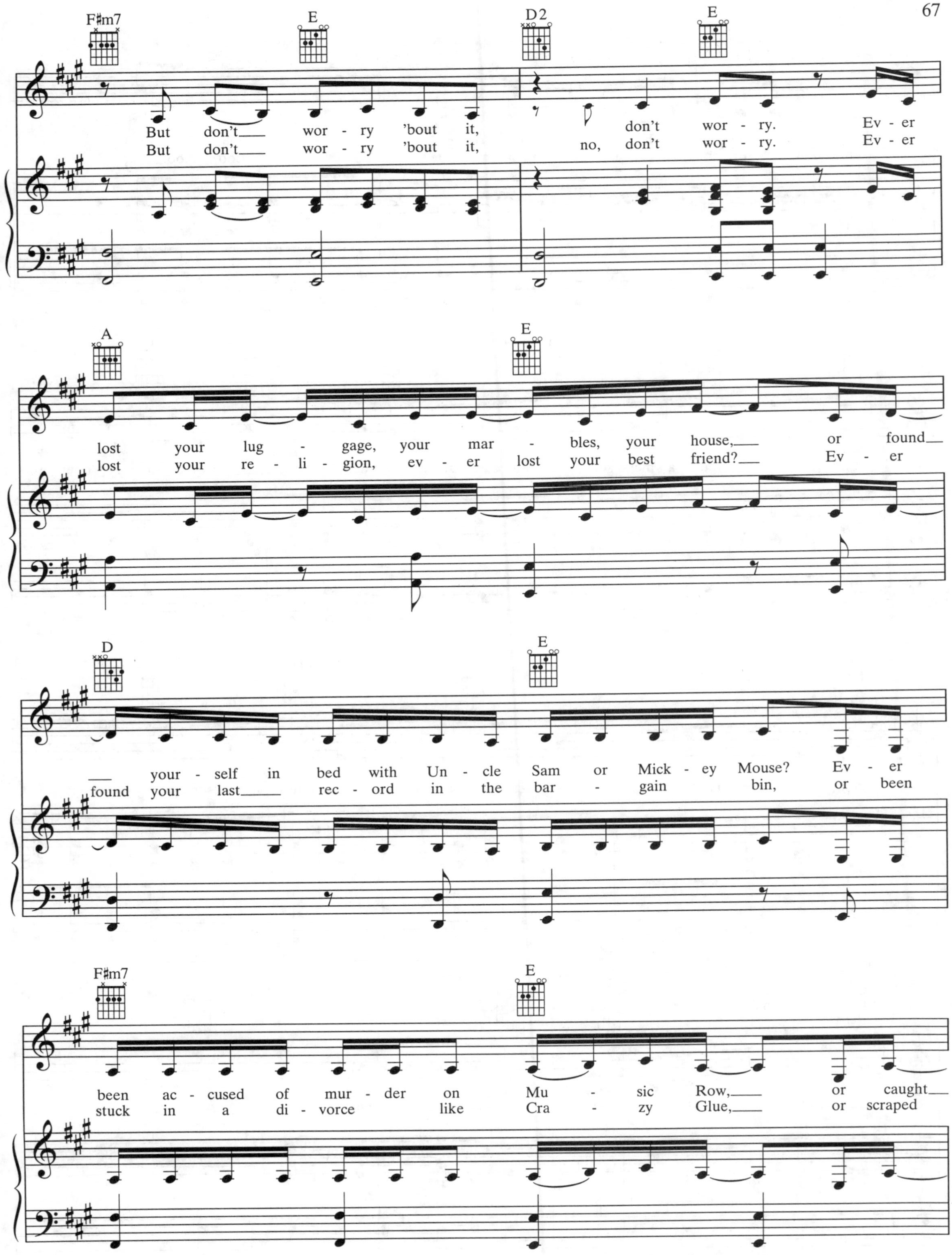
F#m7 E D2 E
But don't___ wor - ry 'bout it, don't wor - ry. Ev - er
But don't___ wor - ry 'bout it, no, don't wor - ry. Ev - er
A E
lost your lug - gage, your mar - bles, your house,___ or found___
lost your re - li - gion, ev - er lost your best friend?___ Ev - er
D E
___ your - self in bed with Un - cle Sam or Mick - ey Mouse? Ev - er
found your last___ rec - ord in the bar - gain bin, or been
F#m7 E
been ac - cused of mur - der on Mu - sic Row,___ or caught___
stuck in a di - vorce like Cra - zy Glue,___ or scraped

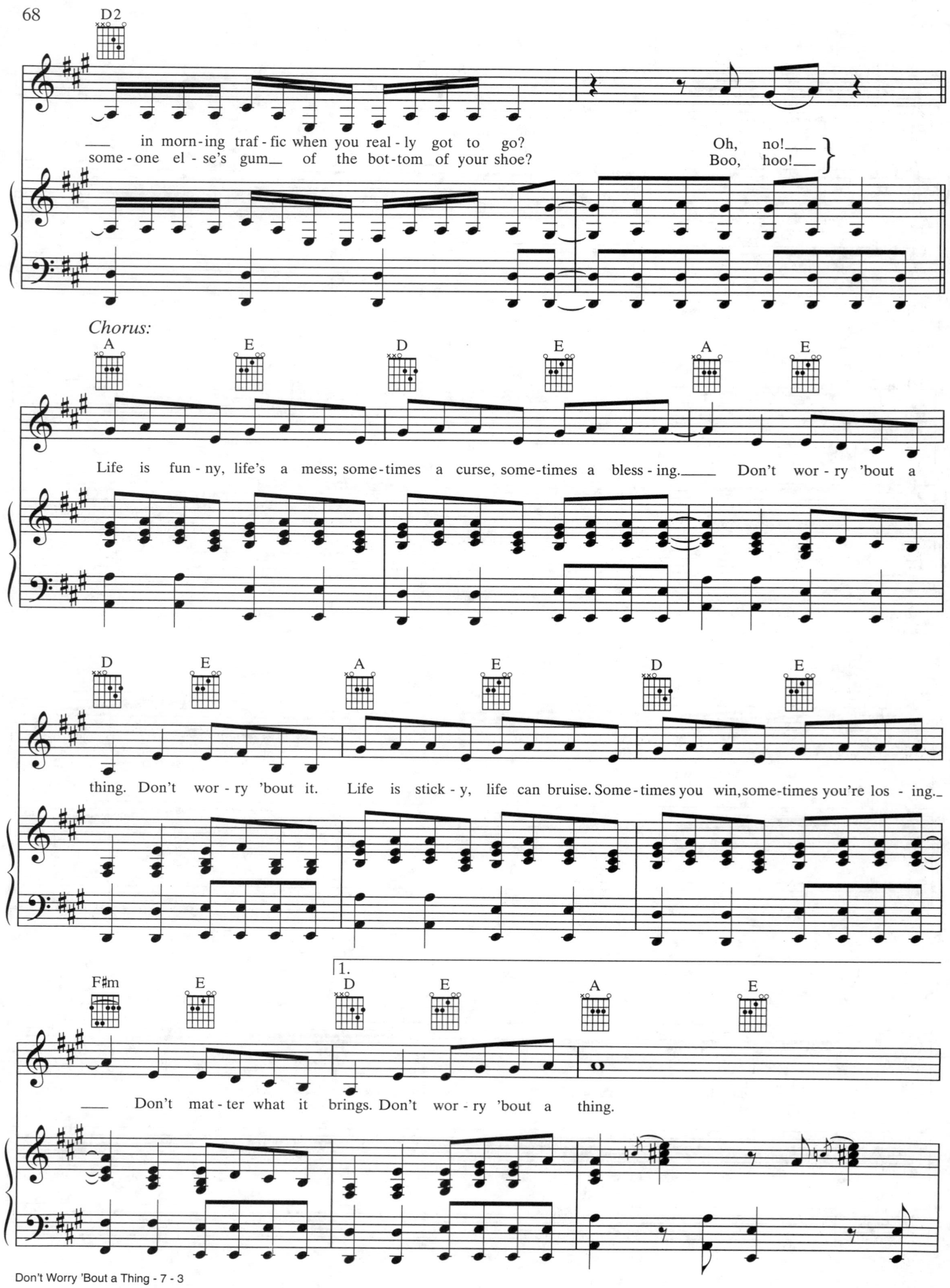
D2
in morn-ing traf - fic when you real - ly got to go?
Oh, no!
some - one el - se's gum of the bot - tom of your shoe?
Boo, hoo!
Chorus:
A E D E A E
Life is fun - ny, life's a mess; some - times a curse, some - times a bless - ing. Don't wor - ry 'bout a
D E A E D E
thing. Don't wor - ry 'bout it. Life is stick - y, life can bruise. Some - times you win, some - times you're los - ing.
1.
F♯m E D E A E
Don't mat - ter what it brings. Don't wor - ry 'bout a thing.

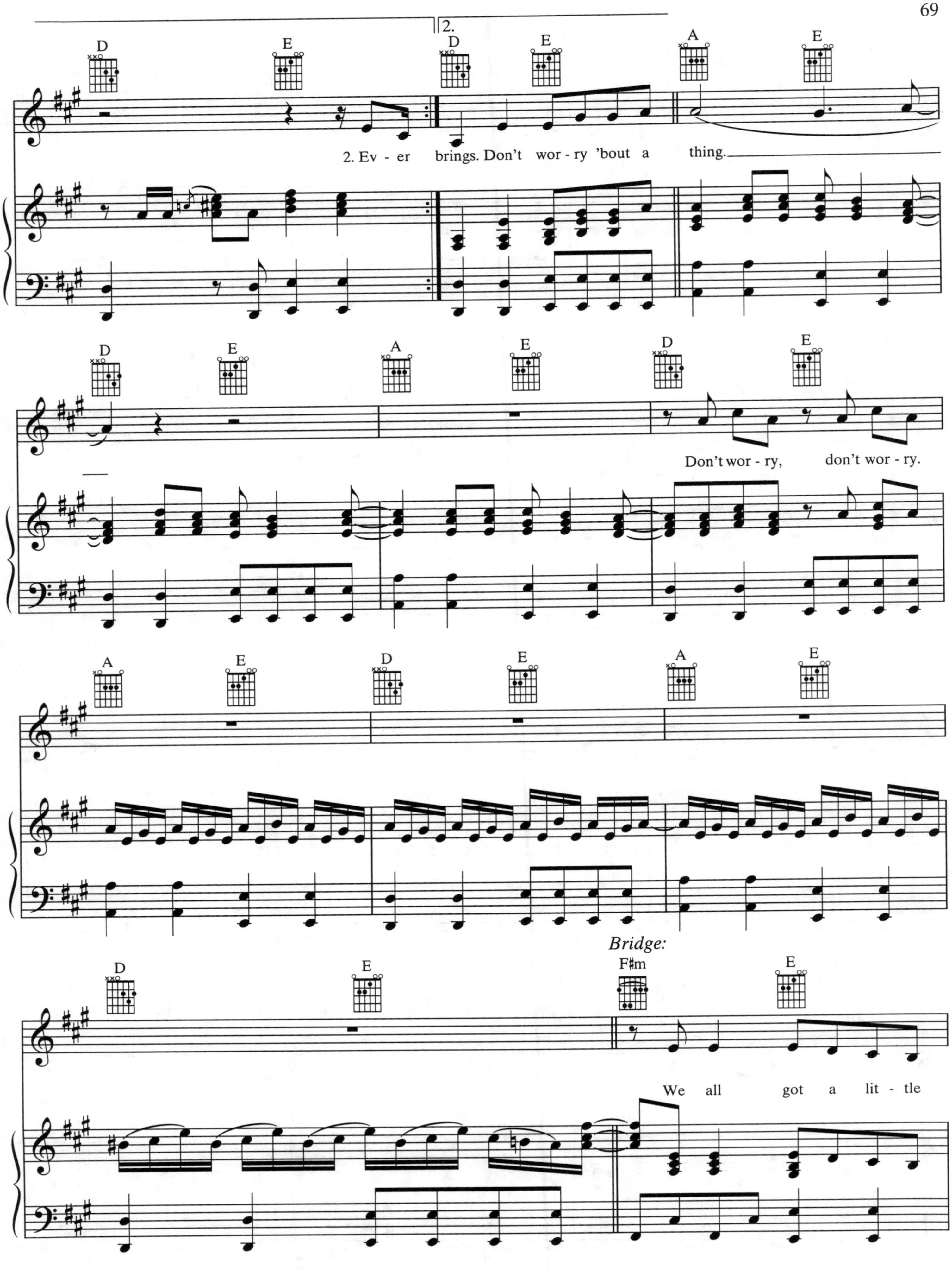
2.
D
E
D
E
A
E
2. Ev - er brings. Don't wor - ry 'bout a thing.
D
E
A
E
D
E
Don't wor - ry, don't wor - ry.
A
E
D
E
A
E
Bridge:
D
E
F♯m
E
We all got a lit - tle

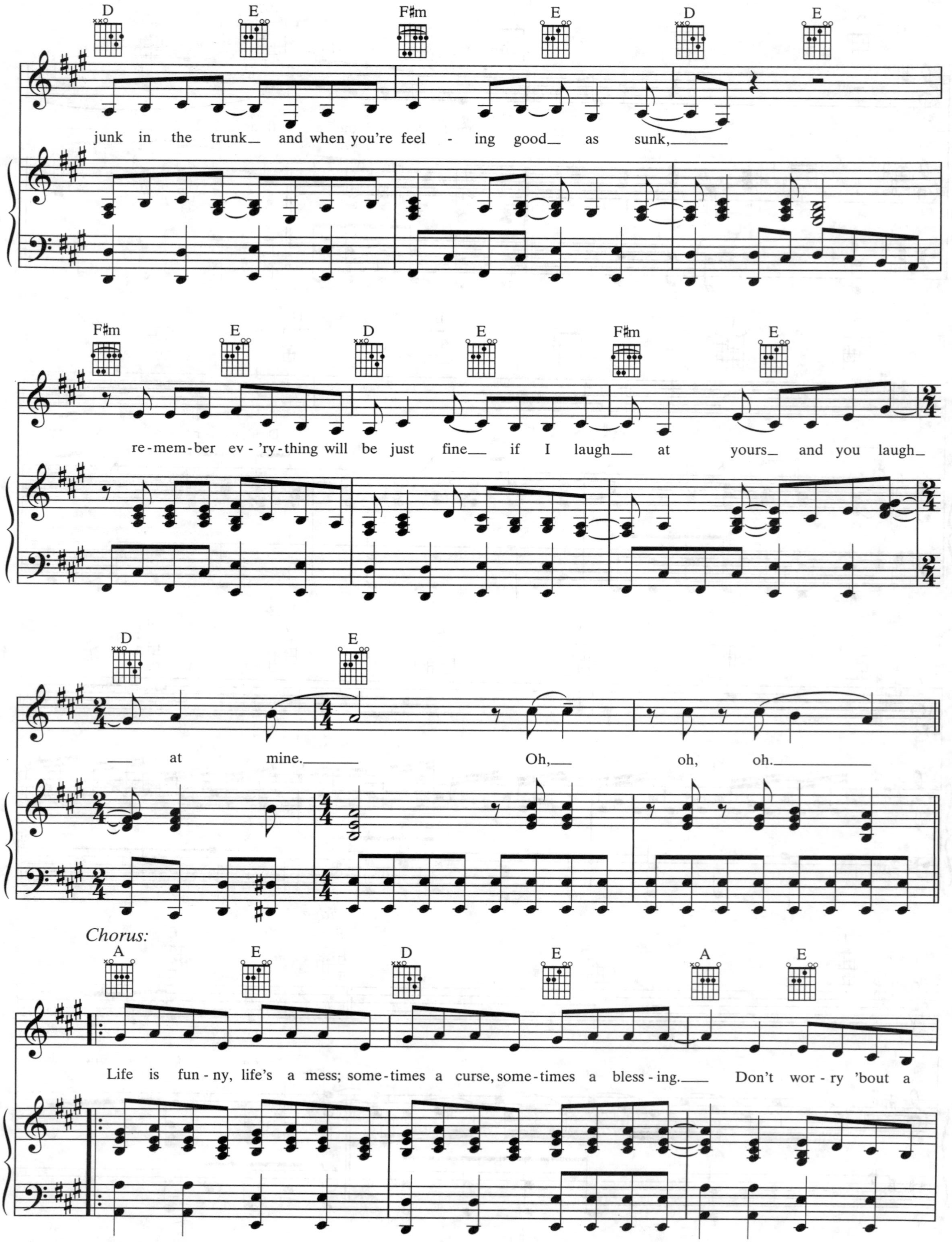
D E F♯m E D E
junk in the trunk_ and when you're feel - ing good_ as sunk,_
F♯m E D E F♯m E
re-mem-ber ev - 'ry-thing will be just fine_ if I laugh_ at yours_ and you laugh_
D E
_ at mine._ Oh,_ oh, oh._
Chorus:
A E D E A E
Life is fun-ny, life's a mess; some-times a curse, some-times a bless-ing._ Don't wor-ry 'bout a

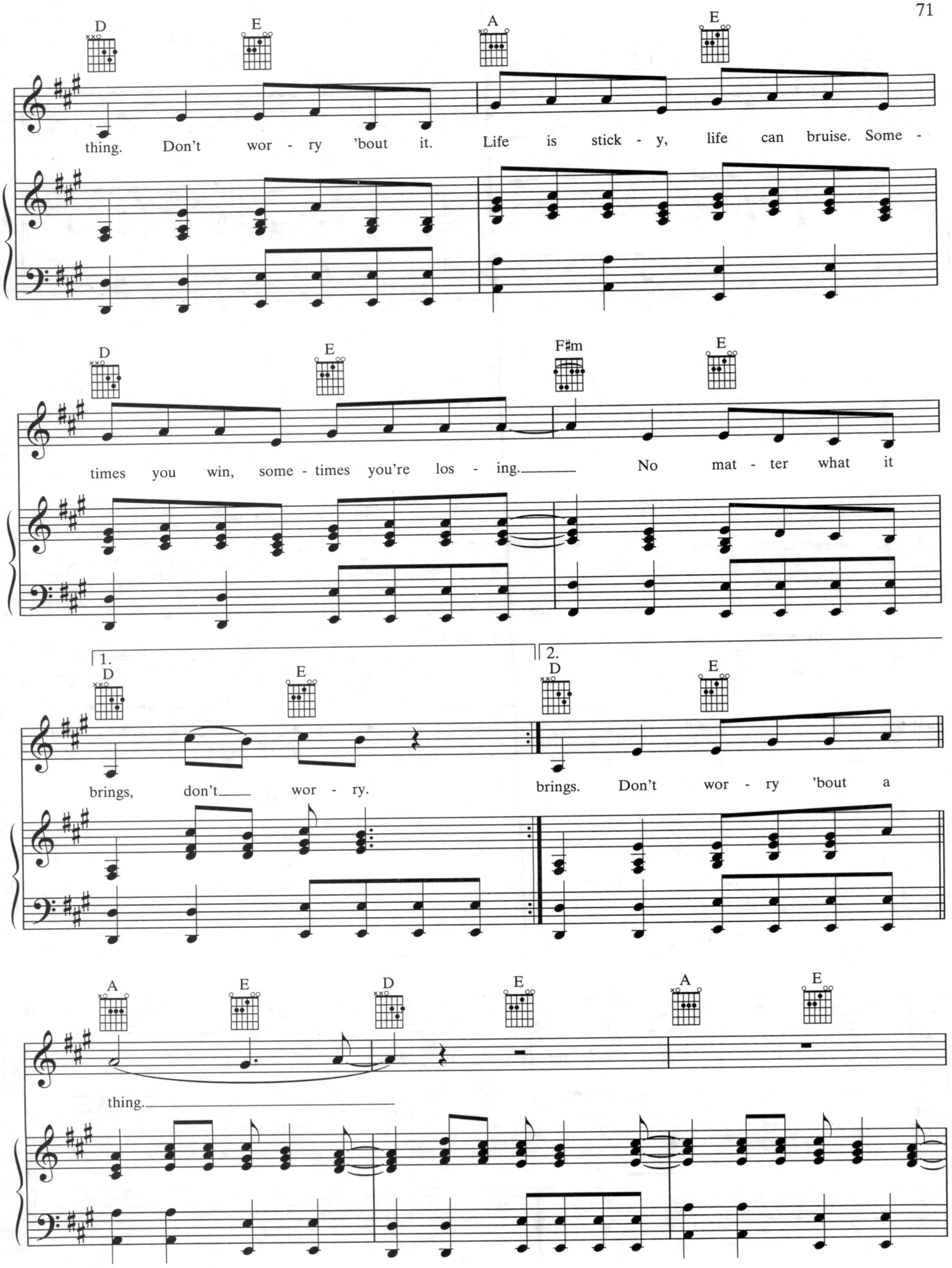
D E A E
thing. Don't wor - ry 'bout it. Life is stick - y, life can bruise. Some -
D E F♯m E
times you win, some - times you're los - ing. No mat - ter what it
1. D E
brings, don't wor - ry.
2. D E
brings. Don't wor - ry 'bout a
A E D E A E
thing.

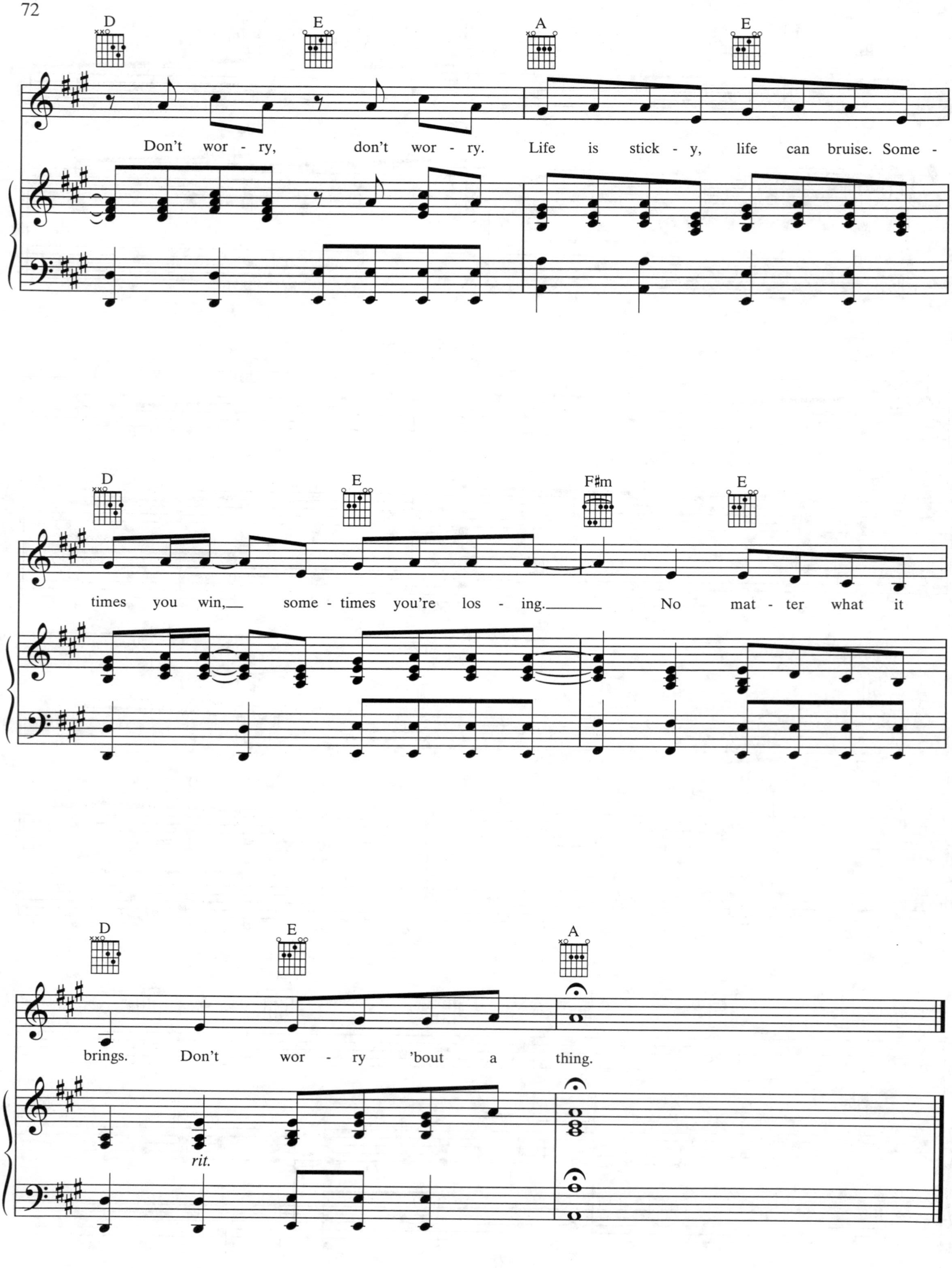
D
E
A
E
Don't wor - ry, don't wor - ry. Life is stick - y, life can bruise. Some -
D
E
F♯m
E
times you win, some - times you're los - ing. No mat - ter what it
D
E
A
brings. Don't wor - ry 'bout a thing.
rit.

GIRLS LIE TOO

Words and Music by
TIM NICHOLS,
CONNIE HARRINGTON
and KELLEY LOVELACE

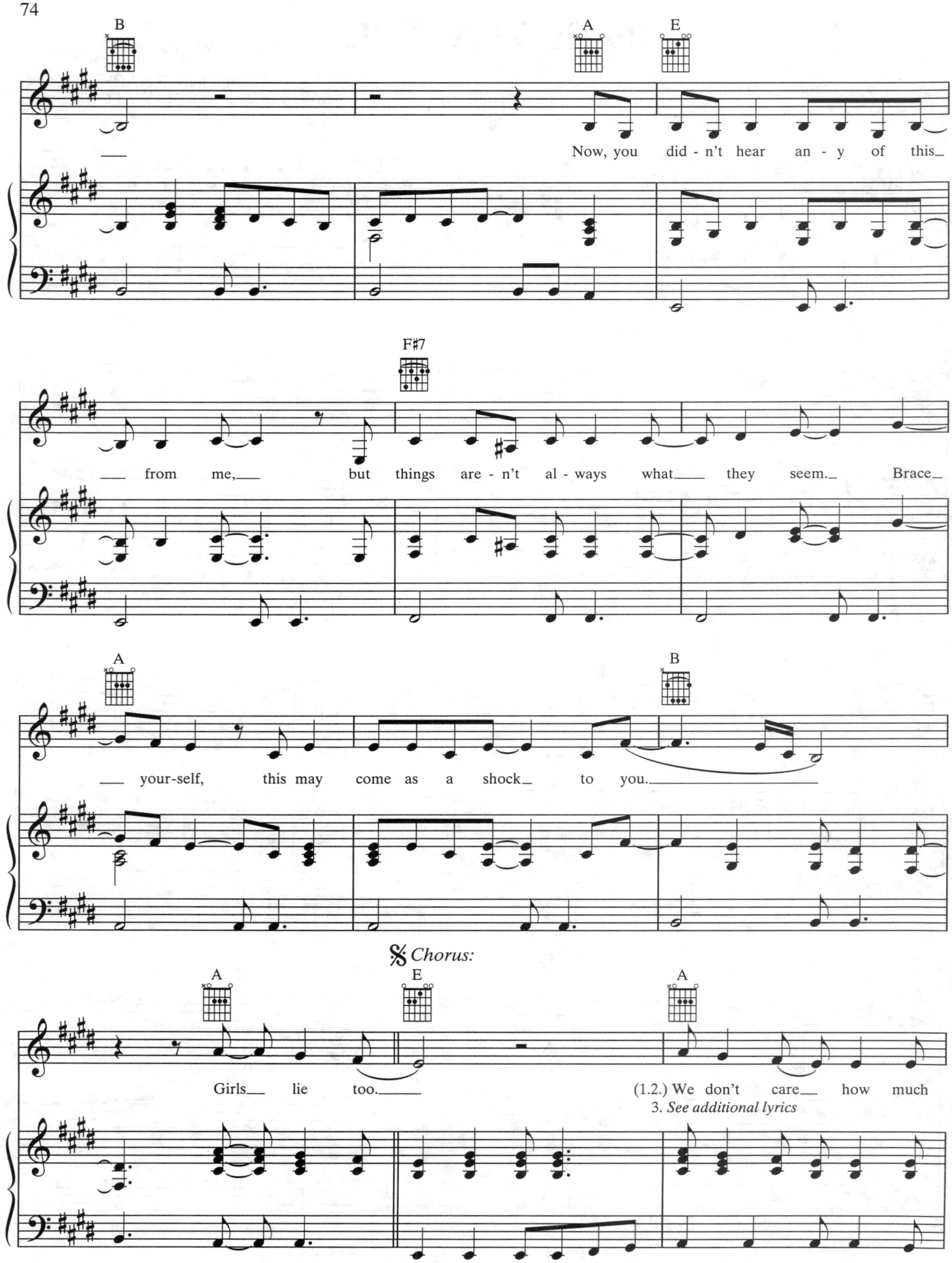
B
A
E
Now, you did - n't hear an - y of this
F♯7
from me, but things are - n't al - ways what they seem. Brace
A
B
your-self, this may come as a shock to you.
Chorus:
A
E
A
Girls lie too.
(1.2.) We don't care how much
3. See additional lyrics

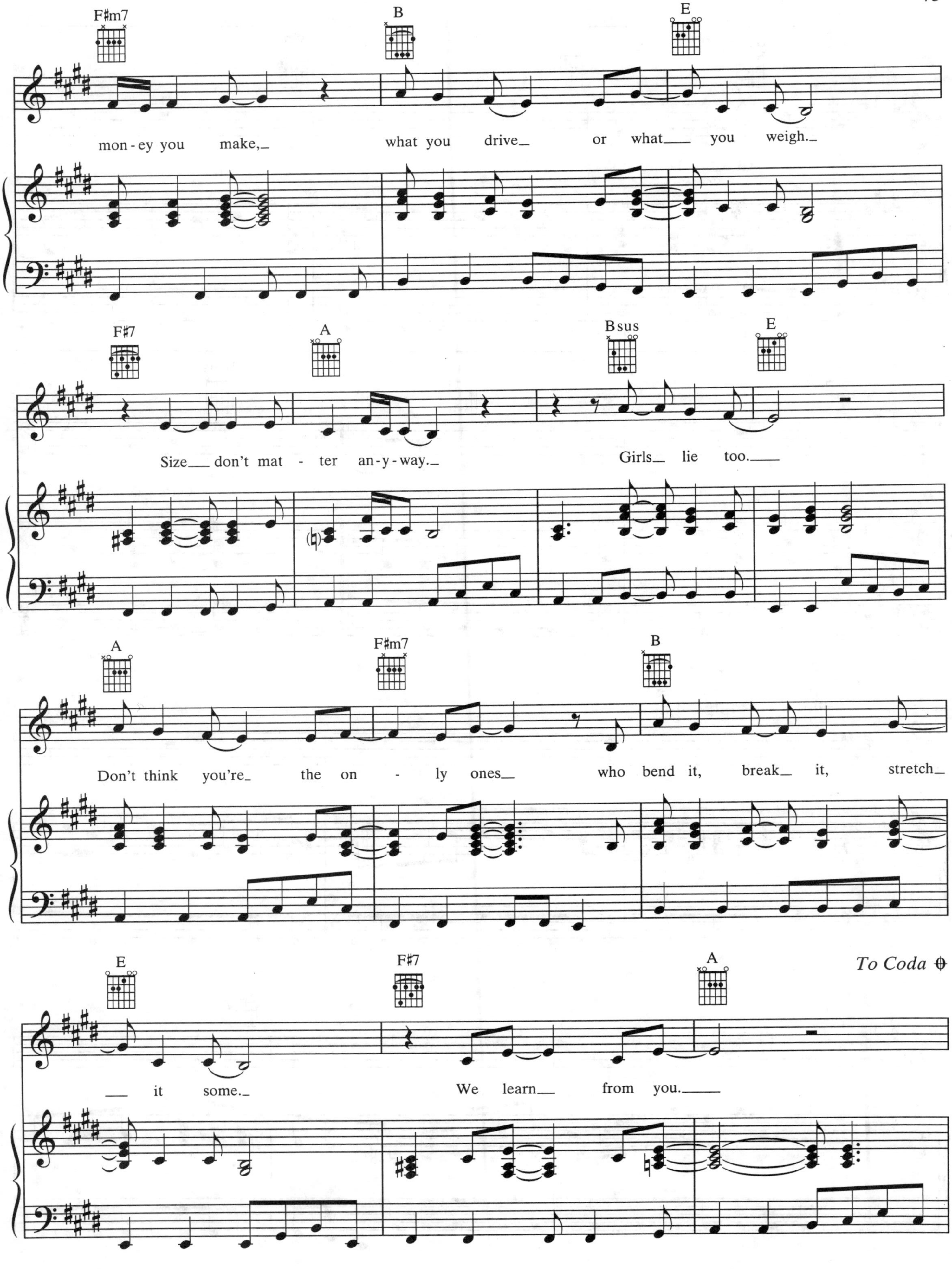
F♯m7
B
E
mon-ey you make,_ what you drive_ or what___ you weigh._
F♯7
A
Bsus
E
Size___ don't mat - ter an-y-way._ Girls_ lie too.___
A
F♯m7
B
Don't think you're_ the on - ly ones_ who bend it, break_ it, stretch_
E
F♯7
A
To Coda
___ it some._ We learn___ from you.____

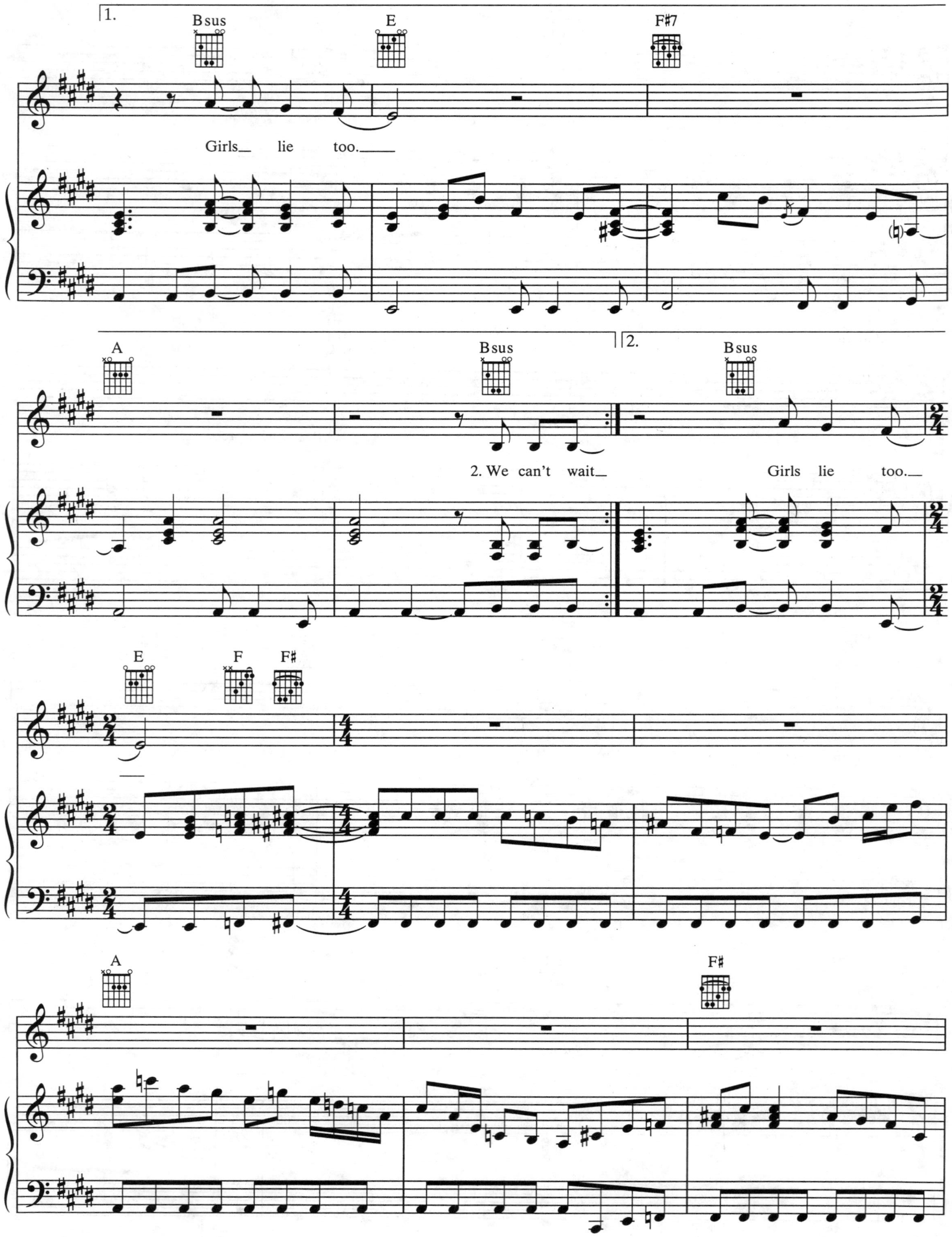
1.
Bsus
E
F♯7
Girls lie too.
A
Bsus
2.
Bsus
2. We can't wait
Girls lie too.
E
F
F♯
A
F♯

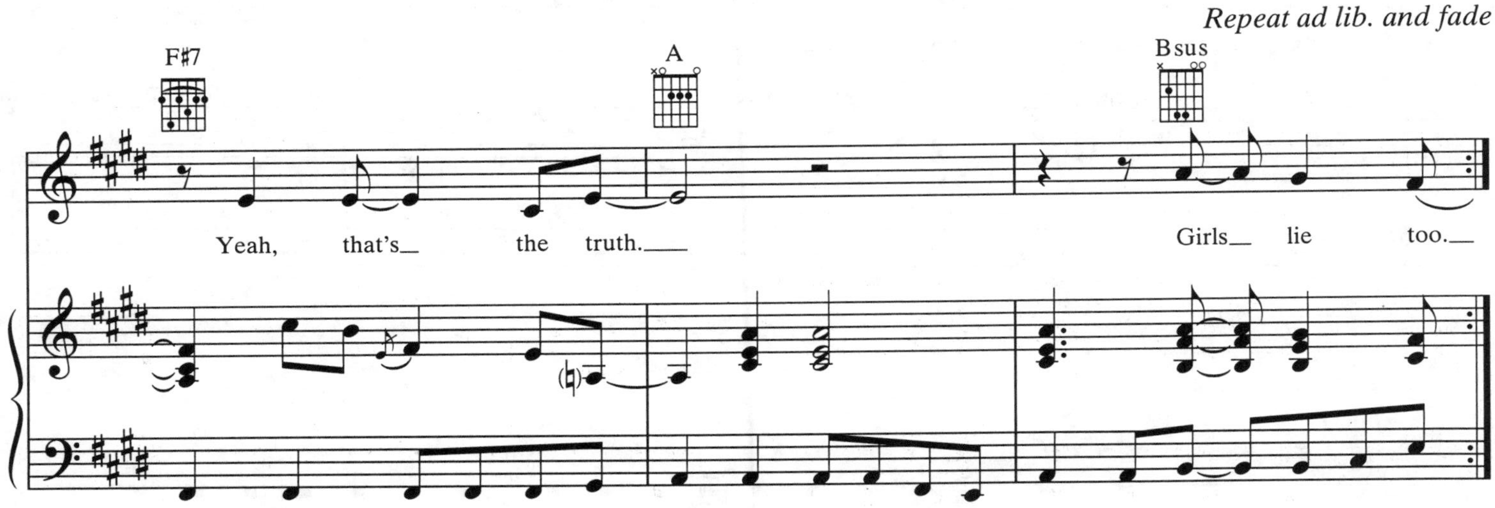

Verse 2:
We can't wait to hear about your round of golf.
We love to see deer heads hanging on the wall.
And we like Hooter's for their hotwings too.
Other guys never cross our minds.
We don't wonder what it might be like.
How could it be any better than it is with you?
(To Chorus:)

Chorus 3:
Yeah, girls lie too.
We always forgive and forget.
The cards and flowers you never sent
Will never be brought up again.
Girls lie too.
Old gray sweatpants turn us on.
We like your friends and we love your mom.
And that's the truth.
Girls lie too.
(To Coda)

GOOD MORNING BEAUTIFUL

Words and Music by
TODD CERNEY and ZACK LYLE

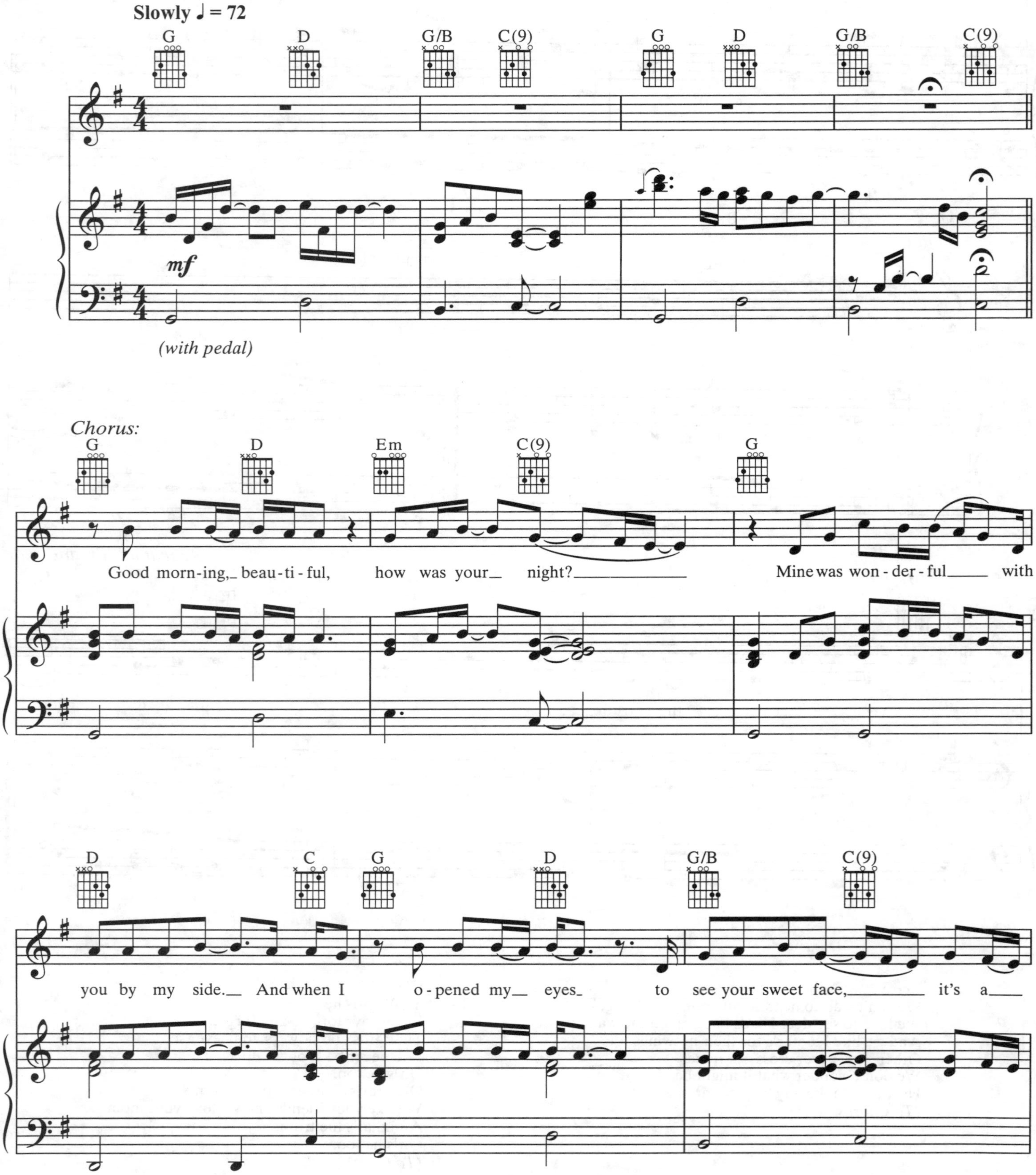

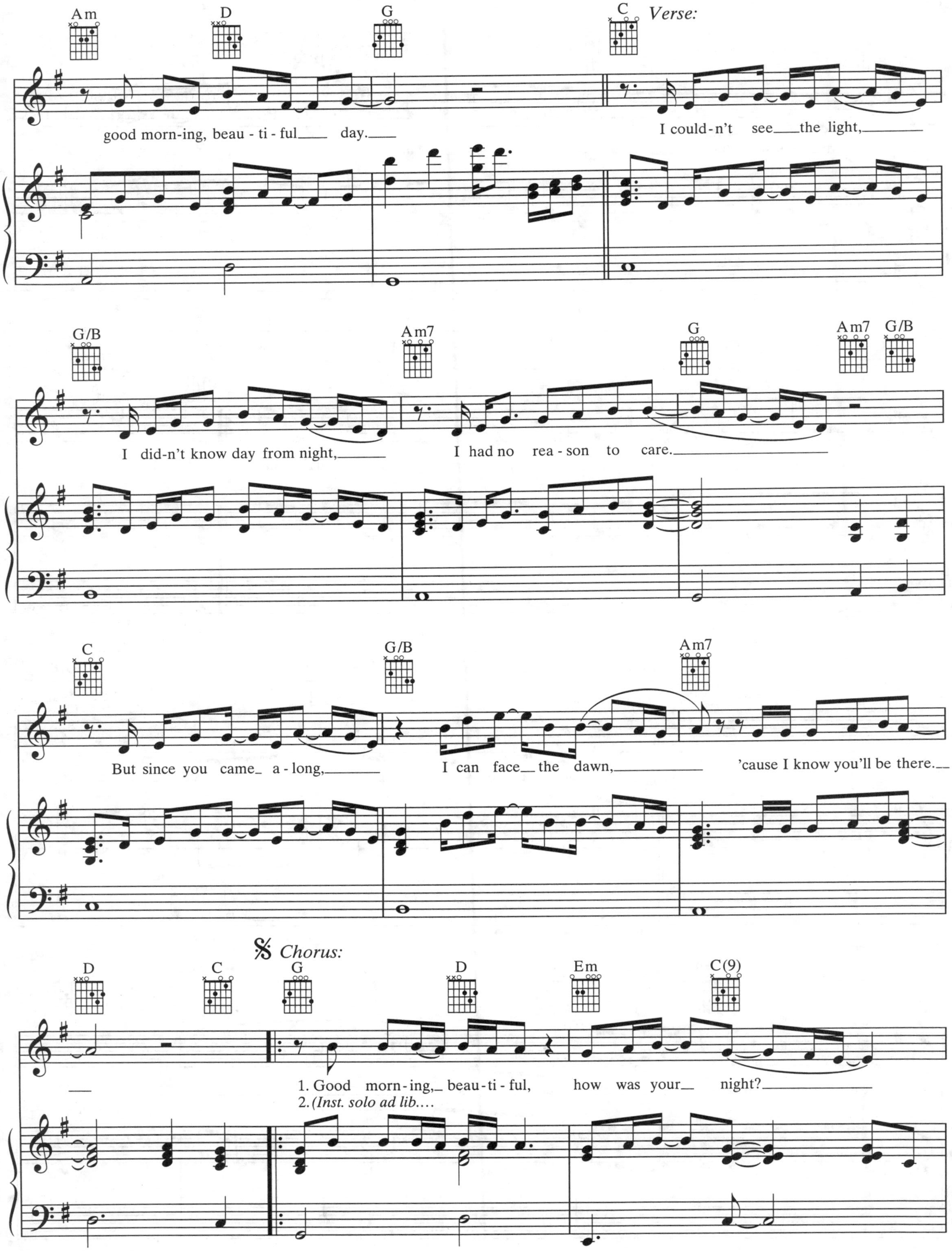
Am
D
G
C
Verse:
good morn-ing, beau - ti - ful day.
I could-n't see the light,
G/B
Am7
G
Am7
G/B
I did-n't know day from night,
I had no rea - son to care.
C
G/B
Am7
But since you came a - long,
I can face the dawn,
'cause I know you'll be there.
Chorus:
D
C
G
D
Em
C(9)
1. Good morn-ing, beau - ti - ful, how was your night?
2. (Inst. solo ad lib....

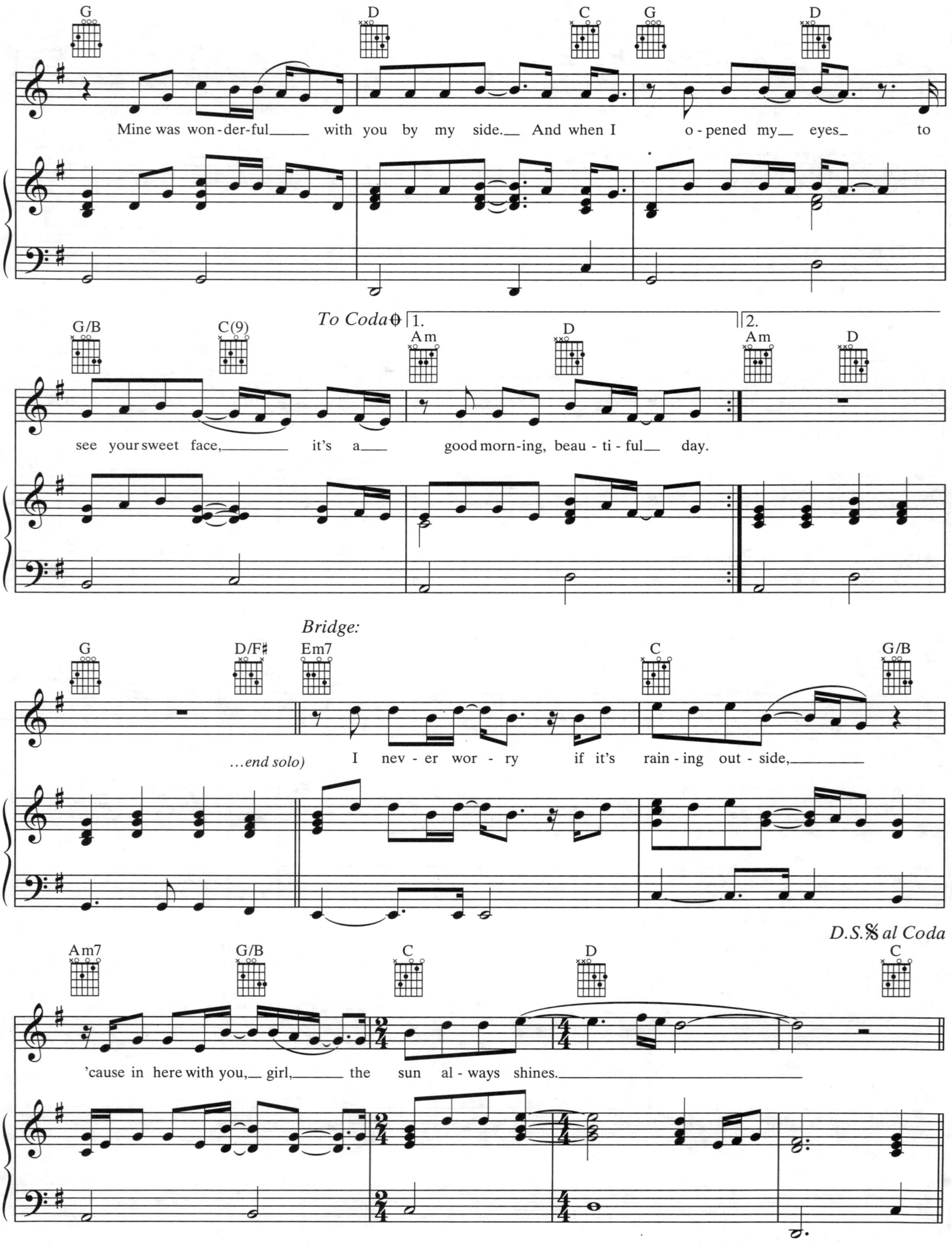
G D C G D
Mine was won-der-ful with you by my side. And when I o-pened my eyes to
G/B C(9) To Coda 1. Am D 2. Am D
see your sweet face, it's a good morn-ing, beau-ti-ful day.
Bridge:
G D/F# Em7 C G/B
...end solo) I nev-er wor-ry if it's rain-ing out-side,
D.S. al Coda
Am7 G/B C D C
'cause in here with you, girl, the sun al-ways shines.

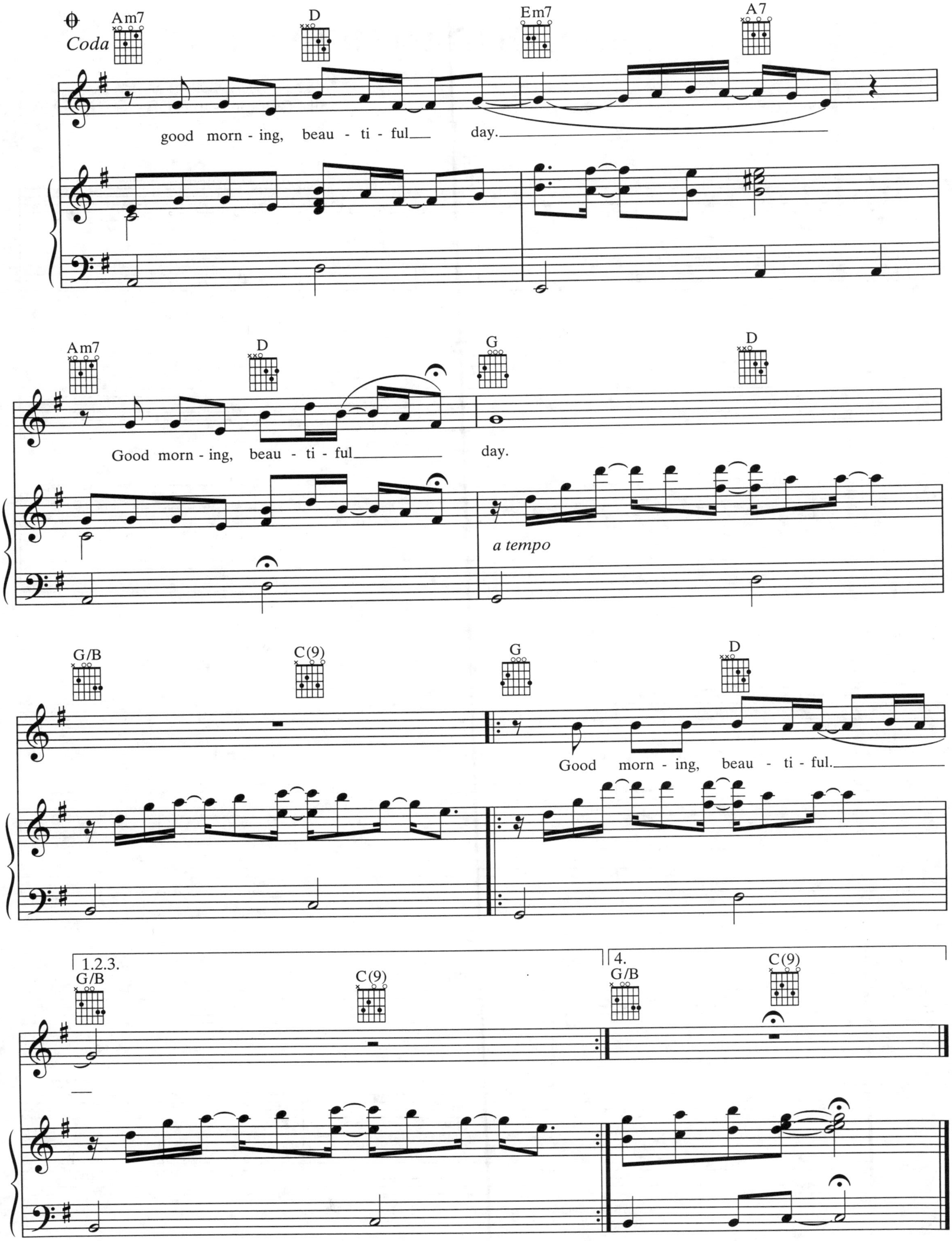
Coda
Am7
D
Em7
A7
good morn - ing, beau - ti - ful day.
G
Good morn - ing, beau - ti - ful day.
a tempo
G/B
C(9)
Good morn - ing, beau - ti - ful.
1.2.3.
4.

THE GOOD STUFF

Words and Music by
JIM COLLINS and CRAIG WISEMAN

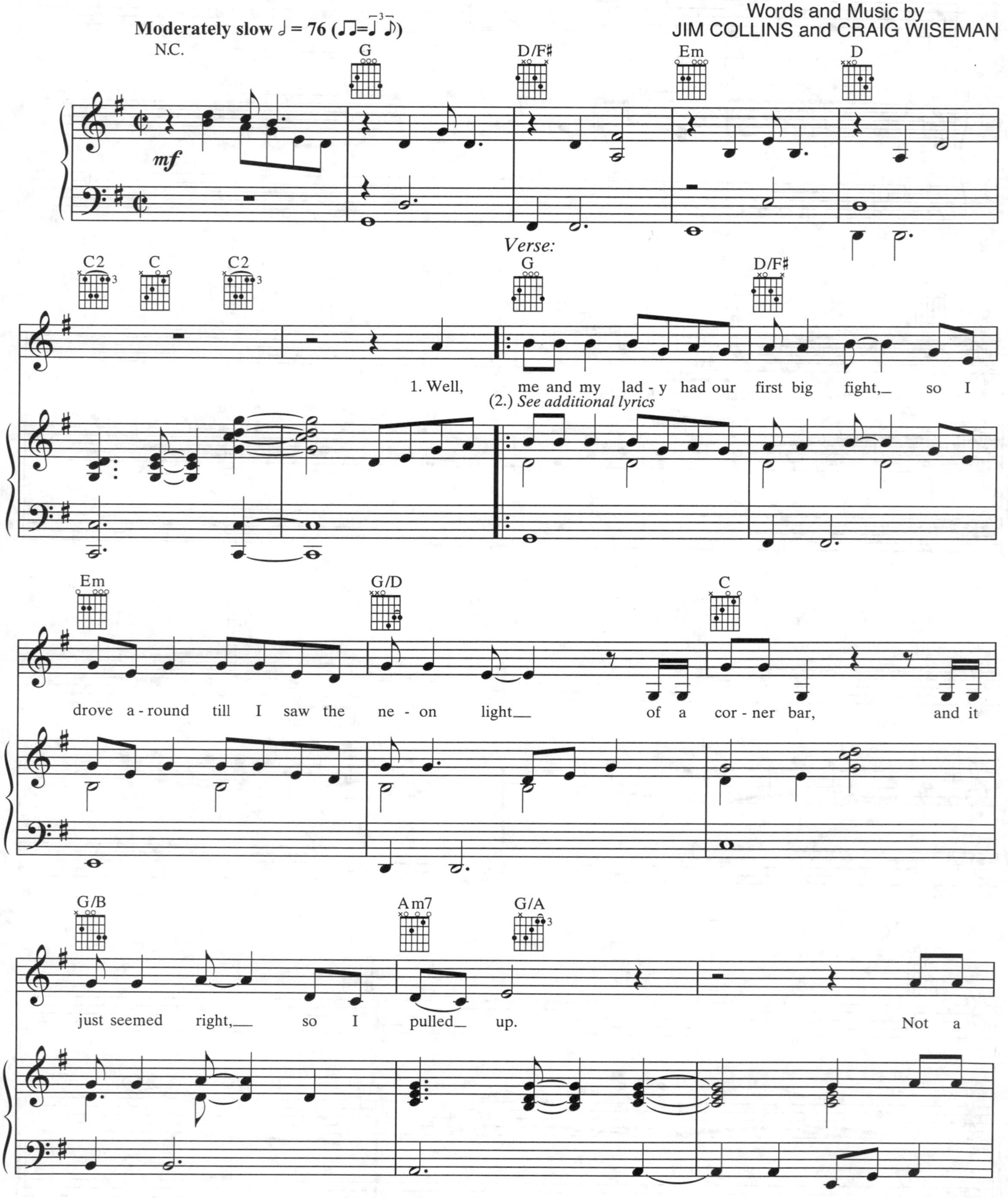

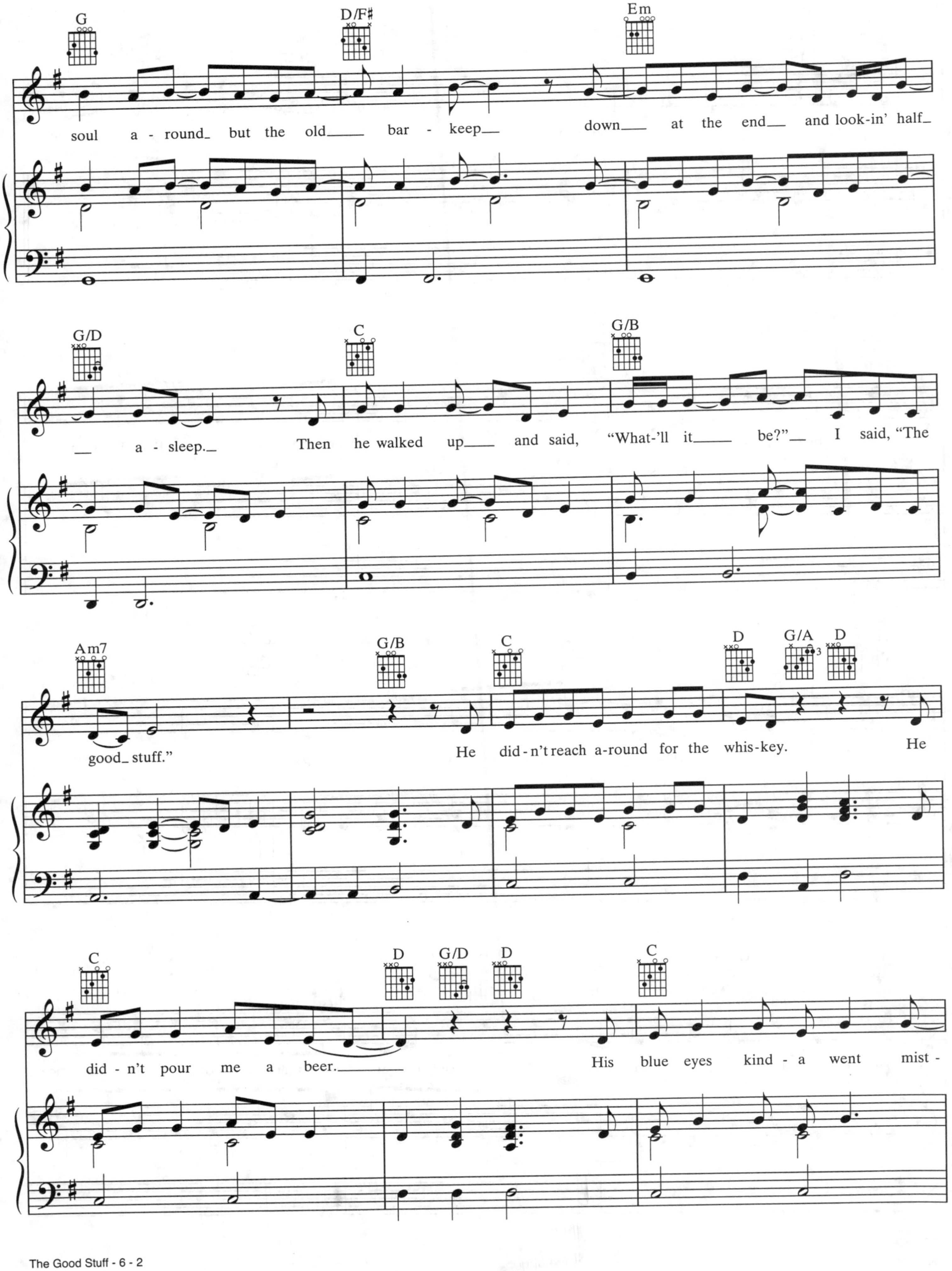
G D/F# Em
soul a - round_ but the old___ bar - keep__ down___ at the end__ and look-in' half_
G/D C G/B
__ a - sleep._ Then he walked up___ and said, "What-'ll it____ be?"__ I said, "The
Am7 G/B C D G/A D
good_ stuff." He did - n't reach a-round for the whis-key. He
C D G/D D C
did - n't pour me a beer.______ His blue eyes kind - a went mist -

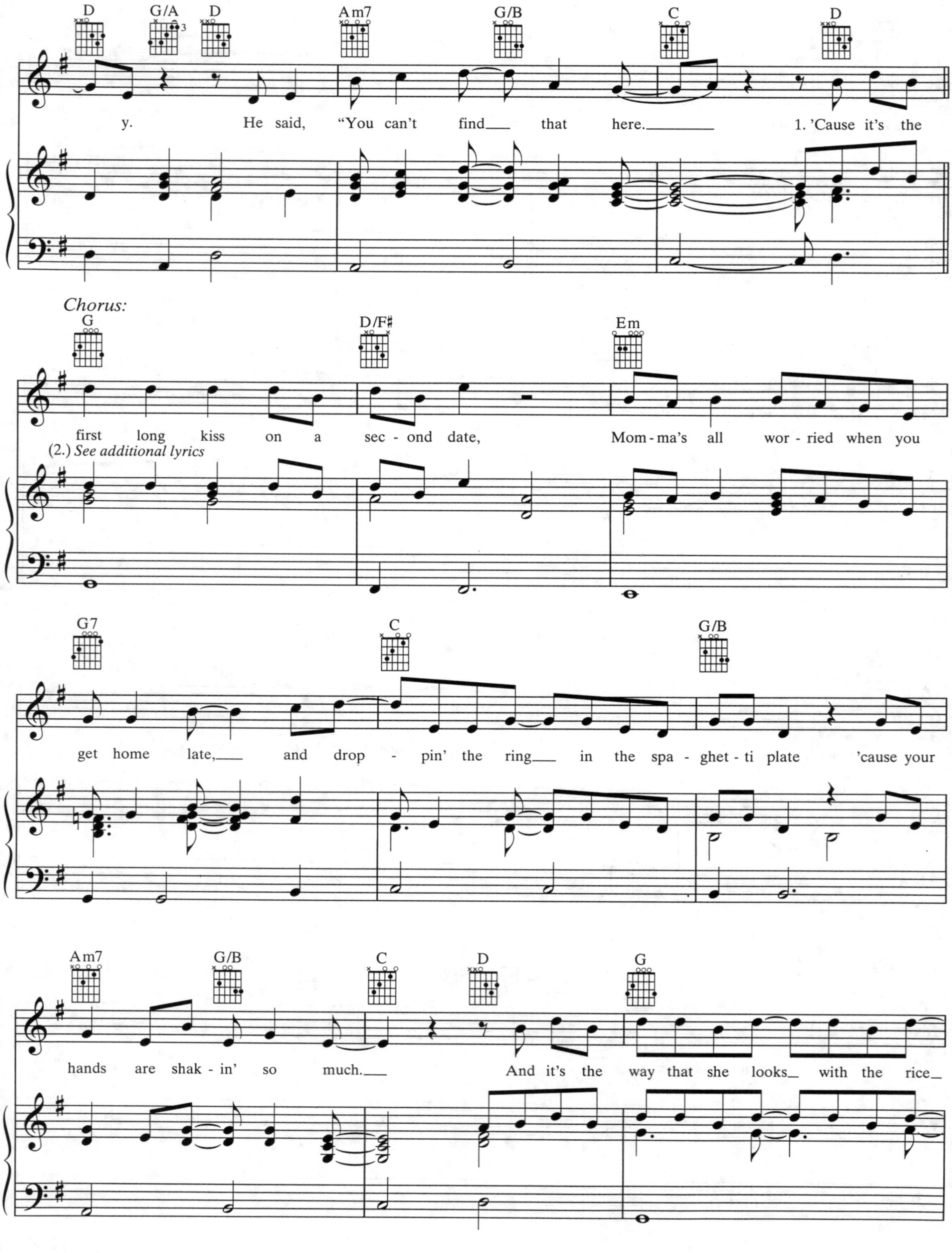
D G/A D Am7 G/B C D
y. He said, "You can't find___ that here.________ 1. 'Cause it's the
Chorus:
G D/F♯ Em
first long kiss on a sec - ond date, Mom - ma's all wor - ried when you
(2.) See additional lyrics
G7 C G/B
get home late,___ and drop - pin' the ring___ in the spa - ghet - ti plate 'cause your
Am7 G/B C D G
hands are shak - in' so much.___ And it's the way that she looks_ with the rice_

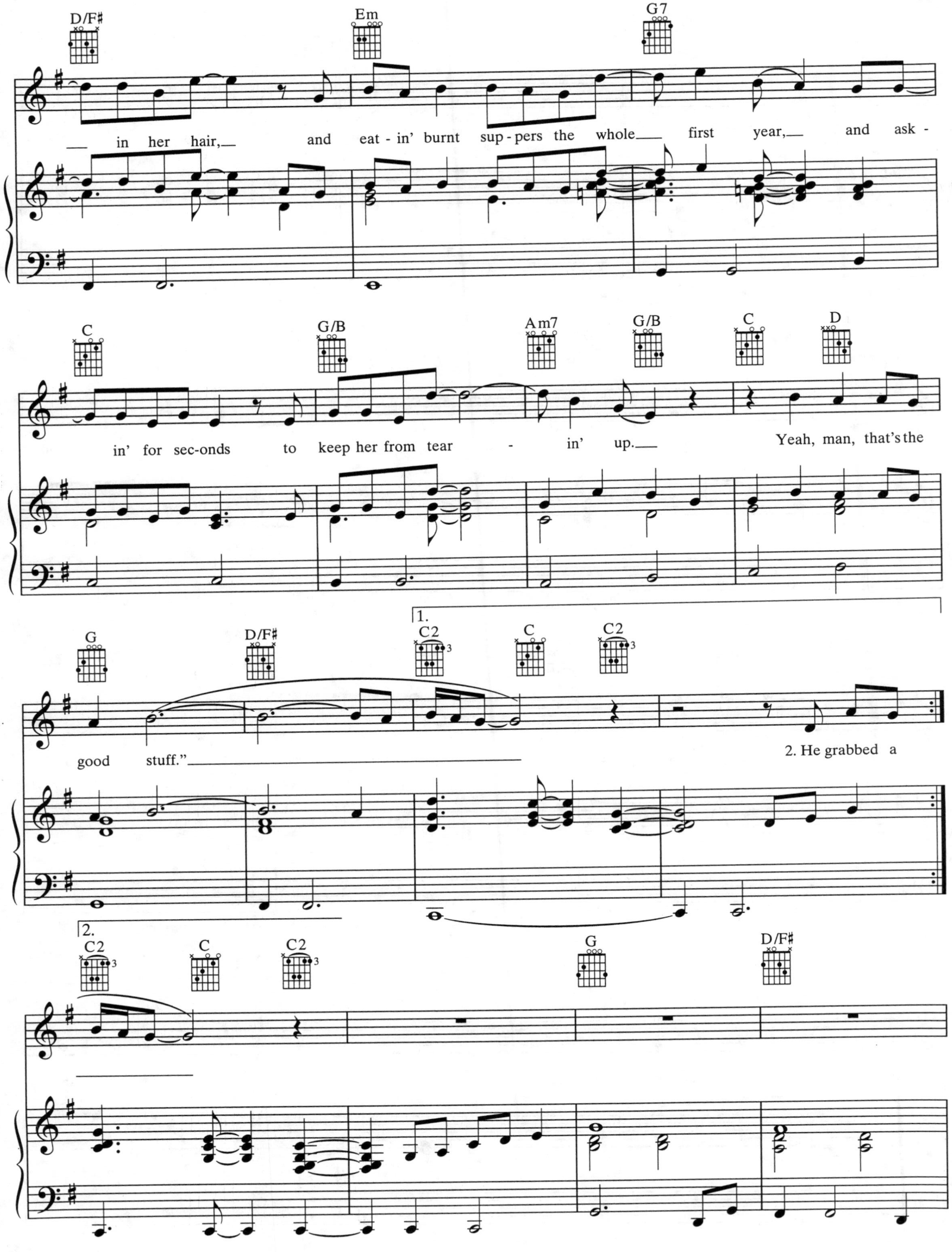
D/F♯
Em
G7
in her hair, and eat - in' burnt sup - pers the whole first year, and ask -
C
G/B
Am7
G/B
C
D
in' for sec - onds to keep her from tear - in' up. Yeah, man, that's the
1.
G
D/F♯
C2
C
C2
good stuff."
2. He grabbed a
2.
C2
C
C2
G
D/F♯

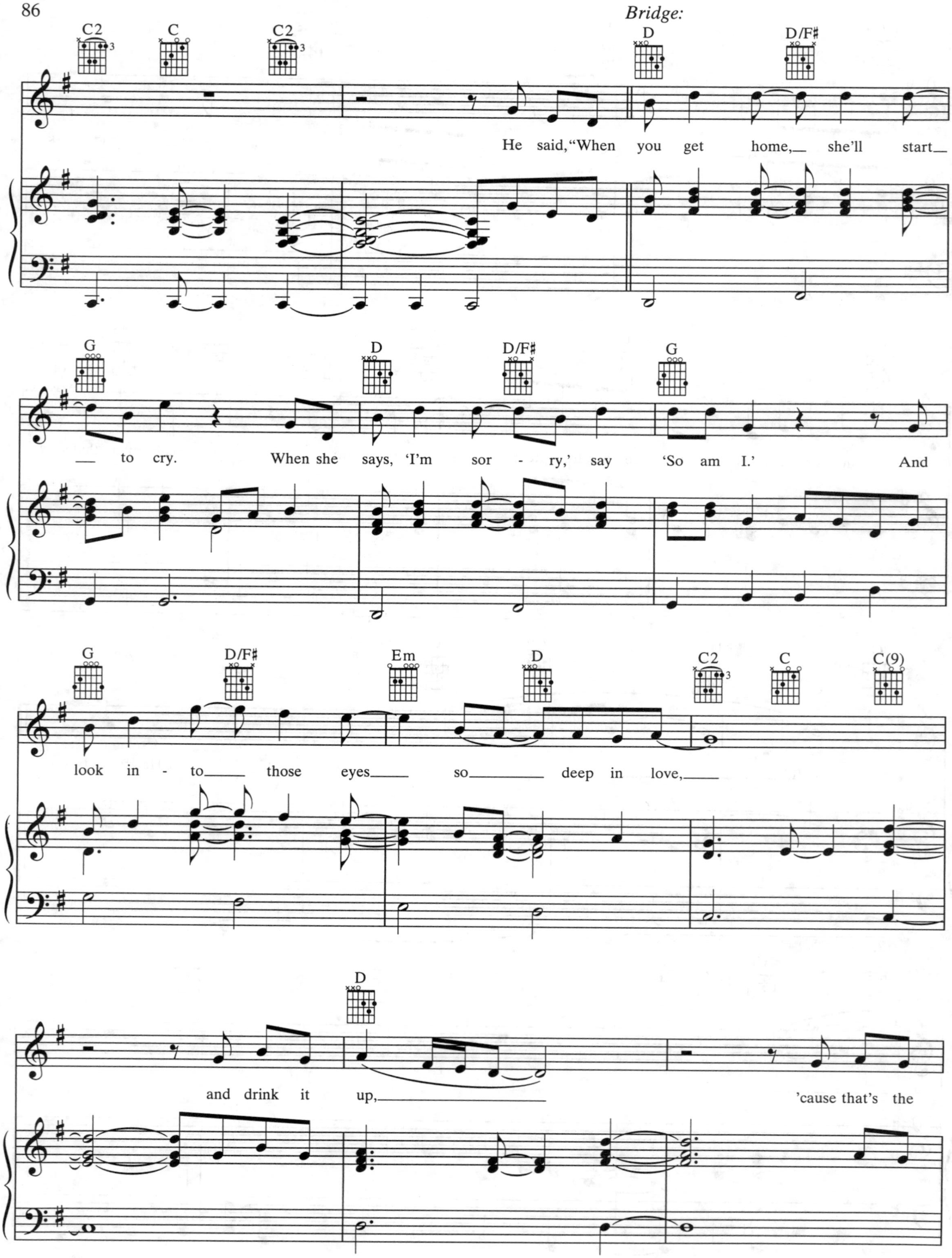
Bridge:
C2
C
C2
D
D/F#
He said, "When you get home,__ she'll start__
G
D
D/F#
G
__ to cry. When she says, 'I'm sor - ry,' say 'So am I.' And
G
D/F#
Em
D
C2
C
C(9)
look in - to___ those eyes___ so___ deep in love,___
D
and drink it up,___ 'cause that's the

Verse 2:
He grabbed a carton of milk and he poured a glass.
And I smiled, and I said, "I'll have some of that."
We sat there and talked as an hour passed, like old friends.
I saw a black and white picture, and he caught my stare.
It was a pretty girl with bouffant hair.
He said, "That's my Bonnie, taken 'bout a year after we wed."
He said, "I spent five years in the bottle
When the cancer took her from me.
But I've been sober three years now,
'Cause the one thing stronger than the whiskey...

Chorus 2:
Was the sight of her holdin' our baby girl,
The way she adored that string of pearls
I gave her the day that our youngest boy Earl
Married his high school love.
And it's a new t-shirt, sayin' 'I'm a grandpa,'
Bein' right there as the time got small,
And holdin' her hand when the good Lord called her up.
Yeah, man, that's the good stuff."
(To Bridge:)

HAVE YOU FORGOTTEN?

Words and Music by
WYNN VARBLE and DARRYL WADE WORLEY

Moderately slow ♩ = 80
G
C(9)
G
C(9)
mf
Verse:
G
1. I hear peo - ple say - ing___ we don't need this war.
2. They took all the foot - age___ off my T V,
C(9)
But I say there's some___ things___ worth fight - ing for.
said it's too dis - turb - ing___ for you and me.
G
What a - bout our free - dom___ and this piece of ground?___
It - 'll just breed an - ger,___ that's what the ex - perts say.___

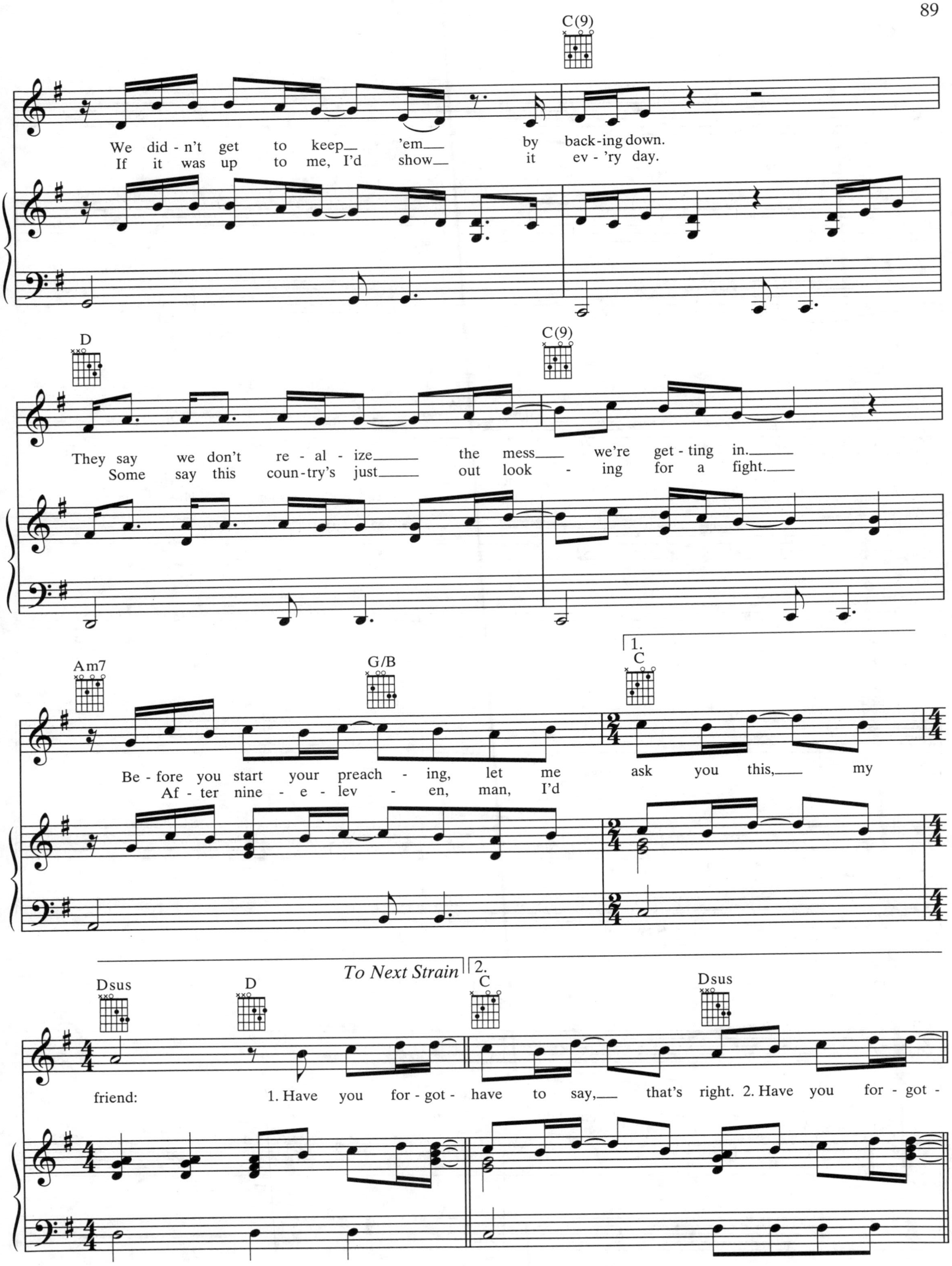
C(9)
We did - n't get to keep__ 'em__ by back-ing down.
If it was up to me, I'd show__ it ev - 'ry day.
D
C(9)
They say we don't re - al - ize____ the mess____ we're get - ting in.____
Some say this coun-try's just____ out look - ing for a fight.____
Am7
G/B
1.
C
Be - fore you start your preach - ing, let me ask you this,___ my
Af - ter nine - e - lev - en, man, I'd
To Next Strain
2.
C
Dsus
D
friend: 1. Have you for - got - have to say,___ that's right. 2. Have you for - got -

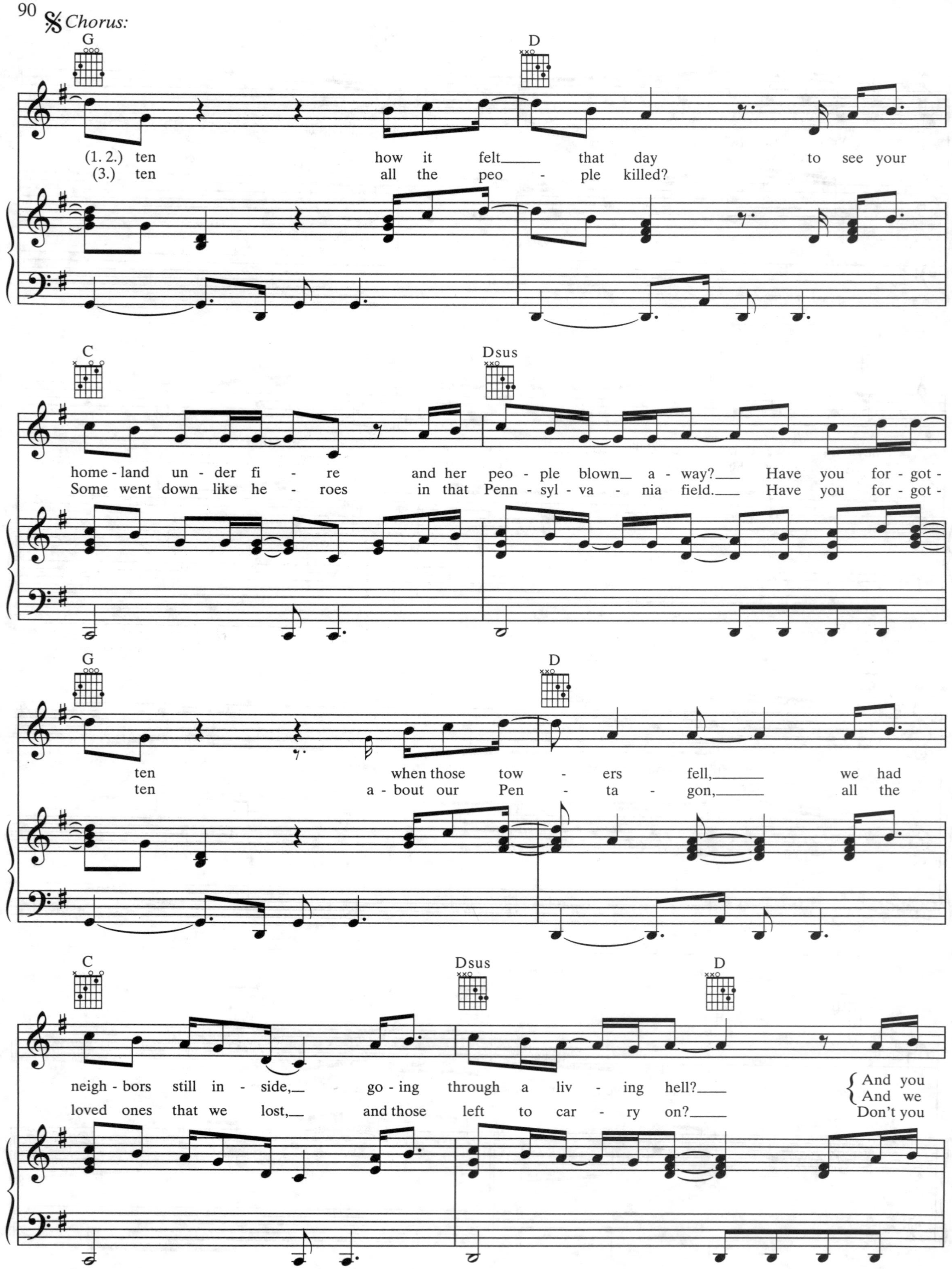
Chorus:
G
D
(1. 2.) ten how it felt___ that day to see your
(3.) ten all the peo - ple killed?
C
Dsus
home - land un - der fi - re and her peo - ple blown_ a - way?___ Have you for - got -
Some went down like he - roes in that Penn - syl - va - nia field.___ Have you for - got -
G
D
ten when those tow - ers fell,___ we had
ten a - bout our Pen - ta - gon,___ all the
C
Dsus
D
neigh - bors still in - side,_ go - ing through a liv - ing hell?___ And you
And we
loved ones that we lost,_ and those left to car - ry on?___ Don't you

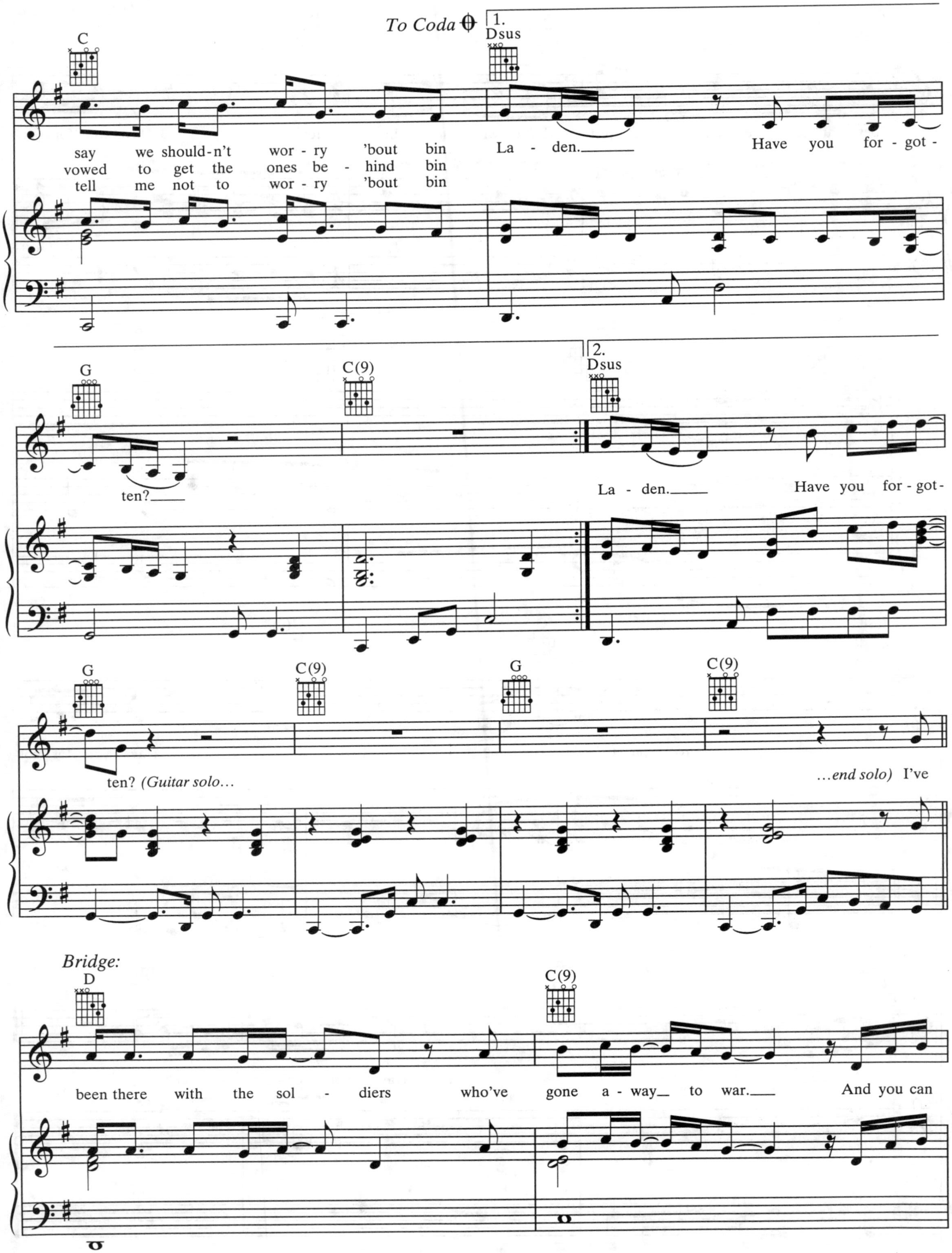
To Coda
1.
2.
C
Dsus
G
C(9)
D
Bridge:
say we should-n't wor - ry 'bout bin La - den.
vowed to get the ones be - hind bin
tell me not to wor - ry 'bout bin
Have you for - got -
ten?
La - den.
Have you for - got-
ten? (Guitar solo...
...end solo) I've
been there with the sol - diers who've gone a - way to war.
And you can

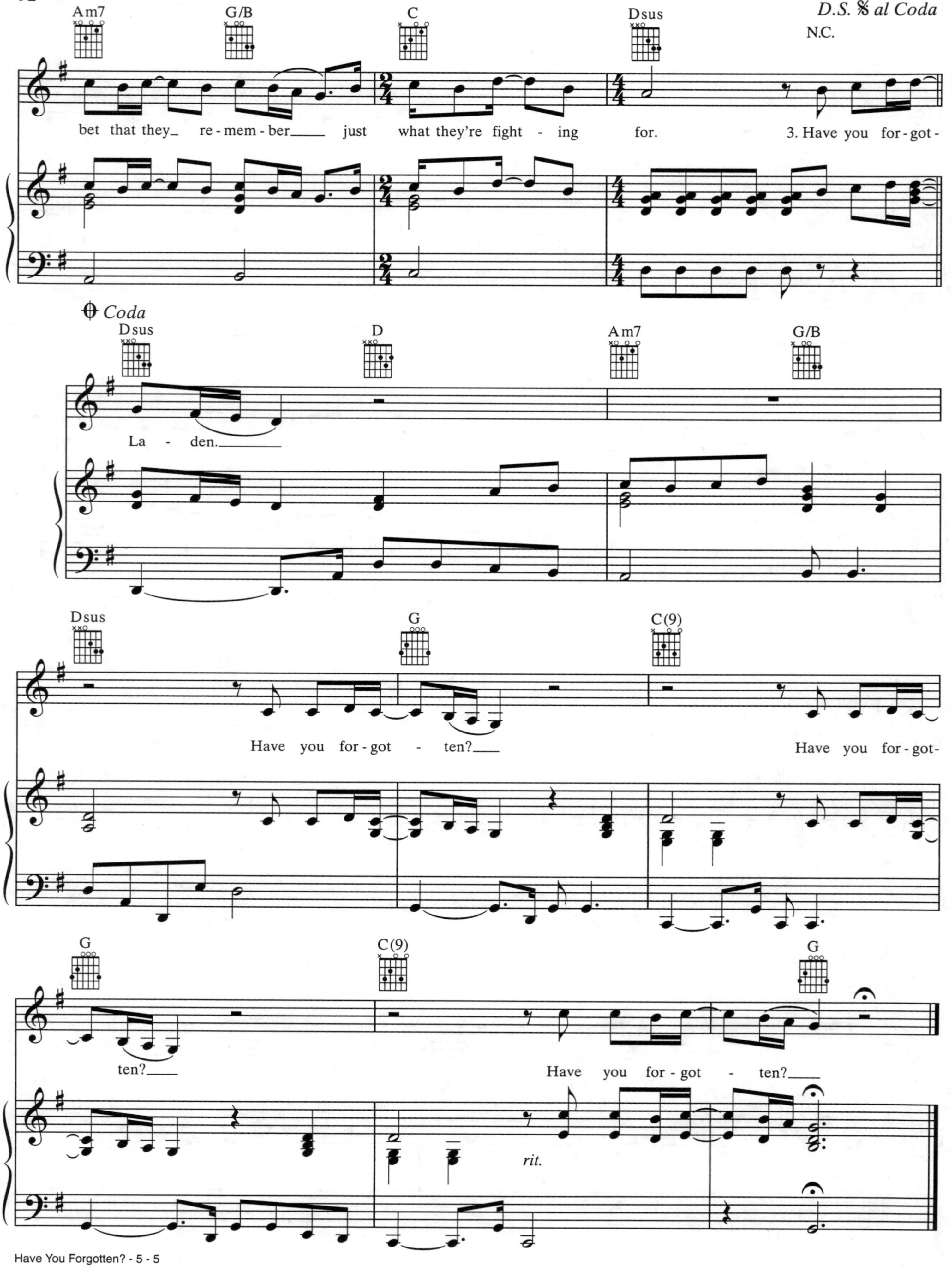
D.S. 𝄋 al Coda
N.C.
Am7
G/B
C
Dsus
bet that they_ re-mem-ber___ just what they're fight - ing for. 3. Have you for-got-
𝄌 Coda
Dsus
D
Am7
G/B
La - den.___
Dsus
G
C(9)
Have you for-got - ten?___ Have you for-got-
G
C(9)
G
ten?___ Have you for-got - ten?___
rit.

KISS THIS

Words and Music by
PHILIP DOUGLAS, AARON TIPPIN
and THEA TIPPIN

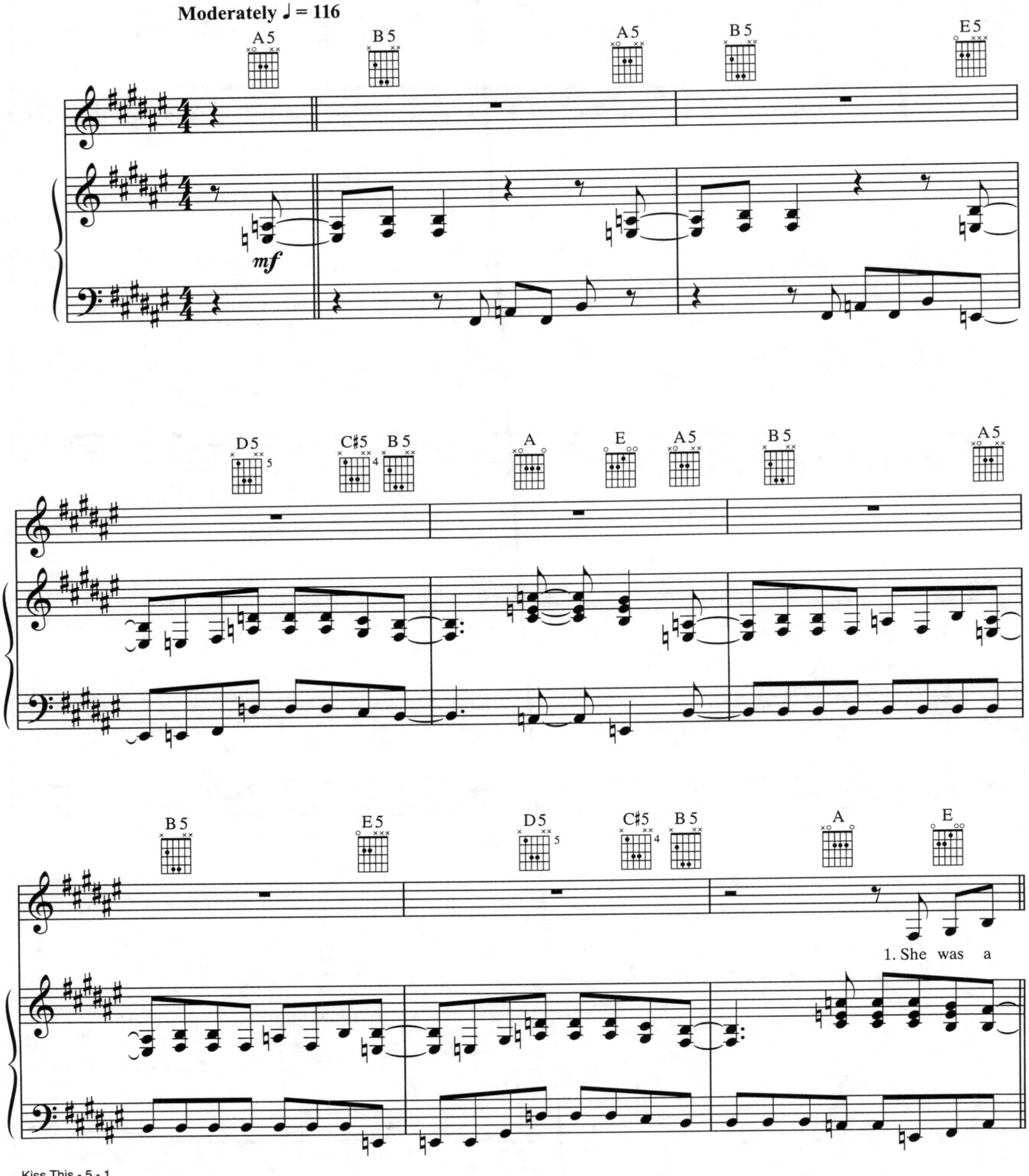

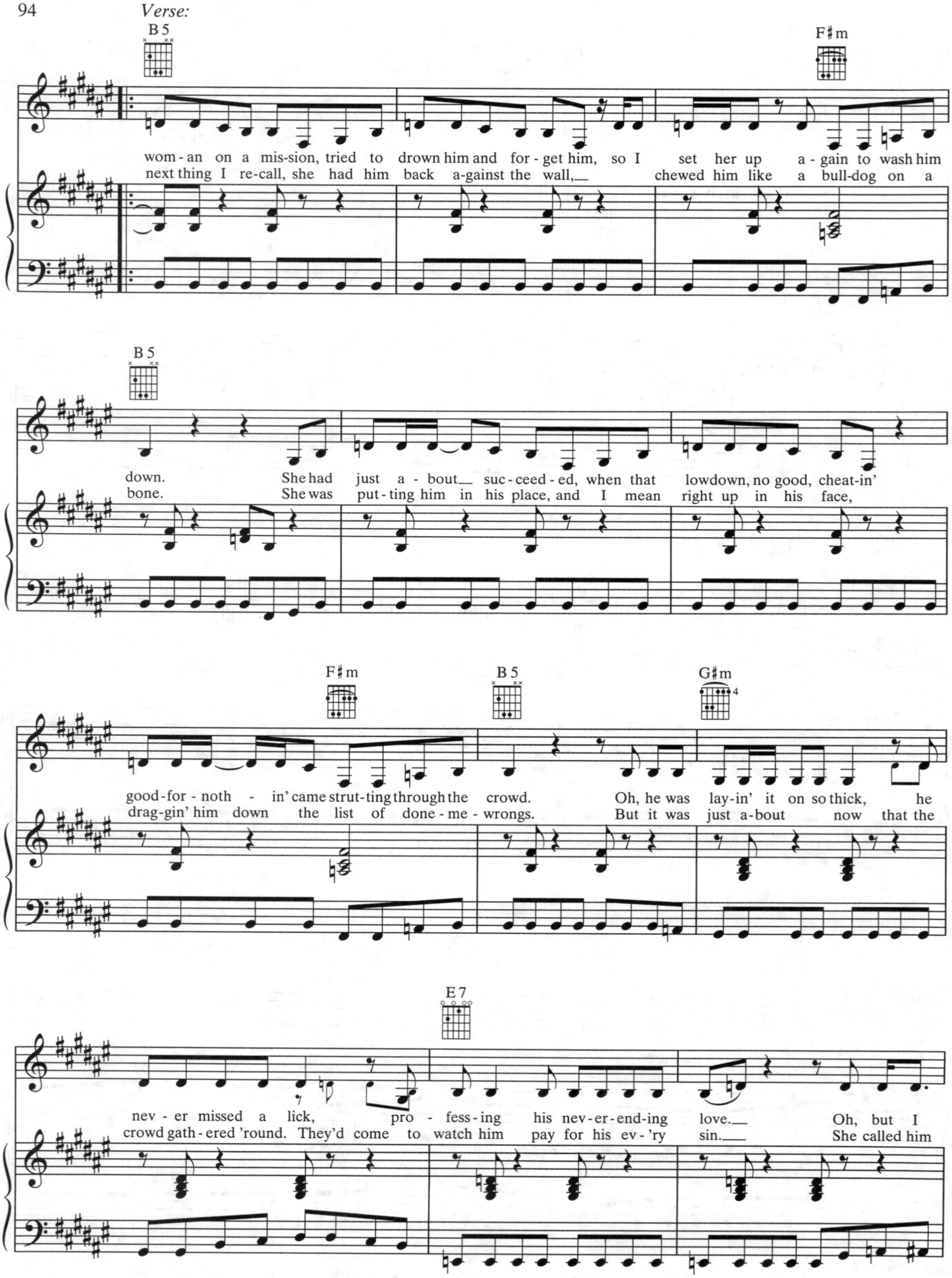
Verse:
B5
F♯m
wom-an on a mis-sion, tried to drown him and for-get him, so I set her up a-gain to wash him
next thing I re-call, she had him back a-gainst the wall,
chewed him like a bull-dog on a
B5
down. She had just a-bout suc-ceed-ed, when that lowdown, no good, cheat-in'
bone. She was put-ting him in his place, and I mean right up in his face,
F♯m
B5
G♯m
good-for-noth-in' came strut-ting through the crowd. Oh, he was lay-in' it on so thick, he
drag-gin' him down the list of done-me-wrongs. But it was just a-bout now that the
E7
nev-er missed a lick, pro-fess-ing his nev-er-end-ing love. Oh, but I
crowd gath-ered 'round. They'd come to watch him pay for his ev-'ry sin. She called him

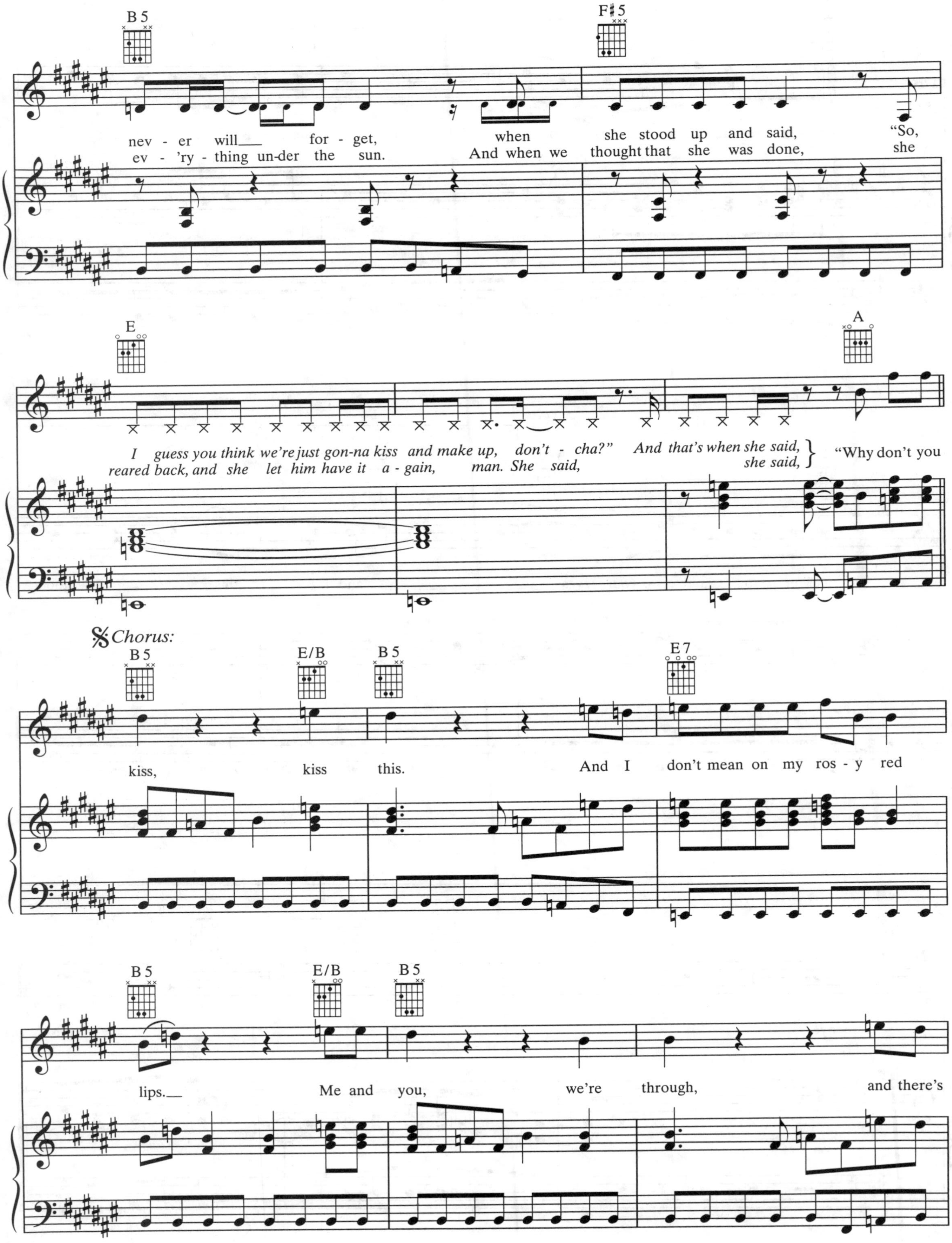
B 5
F♯5
never will___ for - get, when she stood up and said, "So,
ev - 'ry - thing un-der the sun. And when we thought that she was done, she
E
A
I guess you think we're just gon-na kiss and make up, don't - cha?" And that's when she said,
reared back, and she let him have it a - gain, man. She said, she said,
"Why don't you
Chorus:
B 5
E/B
B 5
E 7
kiss, kiss this. And I don't mean on my ros - y red
B 5
E/B
B 5
lips.__ Me and you, we're through, and there's

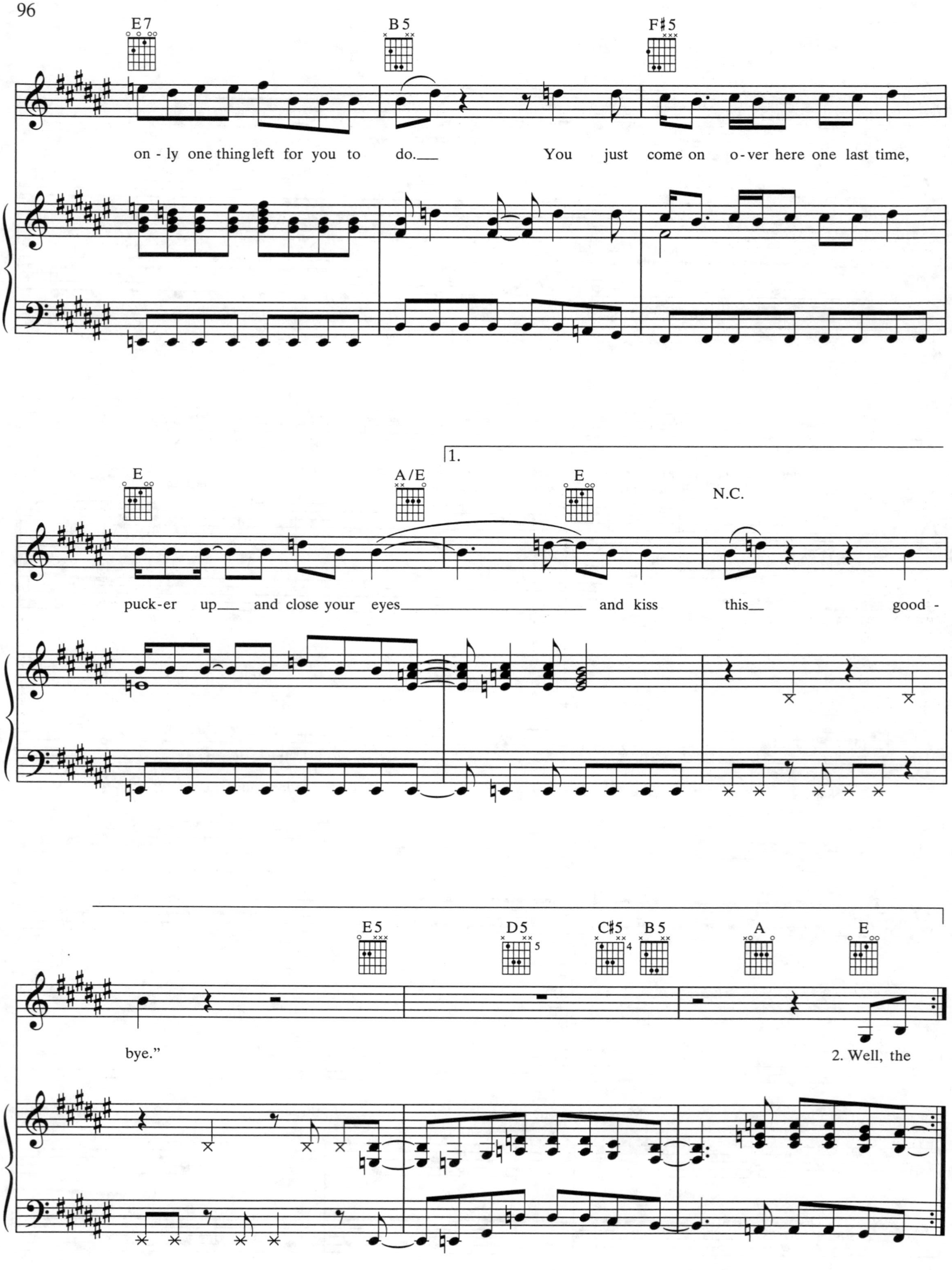
E7
B5
F♯5
on - ly one thing left for you to do.___ You just come on o - ver here one last time,
E
A/E
1.
E
N.C.
puck-er up___ and close your eyes___ and kiss this___ good -
E5
D5
C♯5
B5
A
E
bye."
2. Well, the

2.
D.S. 𝄋
3.
E
E
N.C.
B 5
and kiss,
and kiss
this
good -
bye.
Kiss
this
good - bye."

I BREATHE IN, I BREATHE OUT

Words and Music by
CHRIS CAGLE and JON ROBBIN

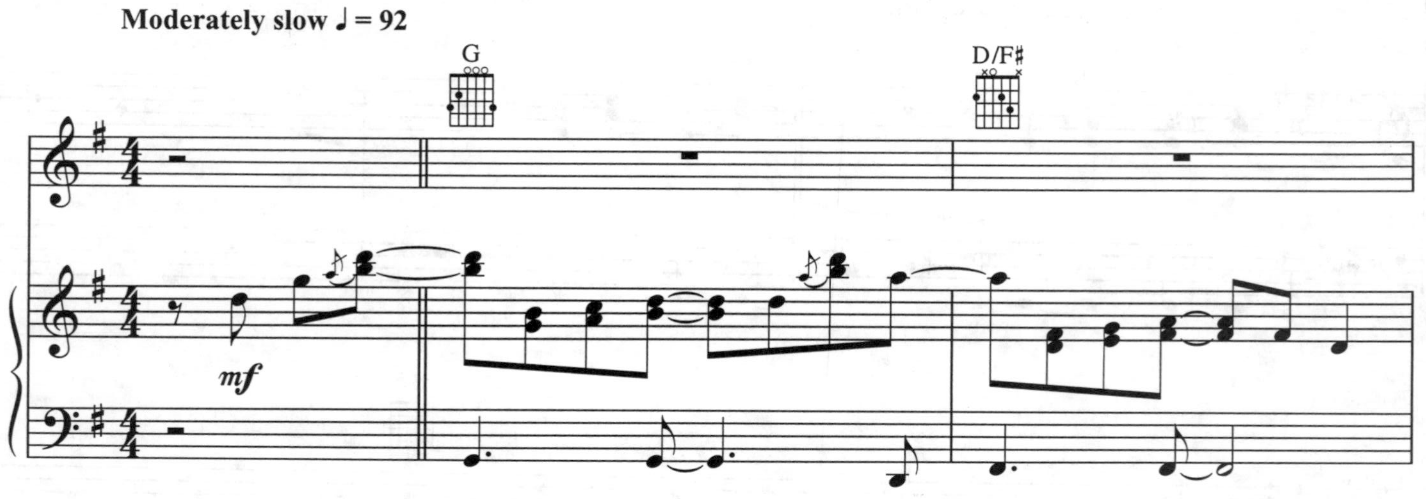
Moderately slow ♩ = 92
G
D/F♯
mf

C(9)
Verse:
G
1. Late - ly I've___ been run -
2. See additional lyrics

D/F♯
C(9)
nin' in - to our___ old friends.__ And

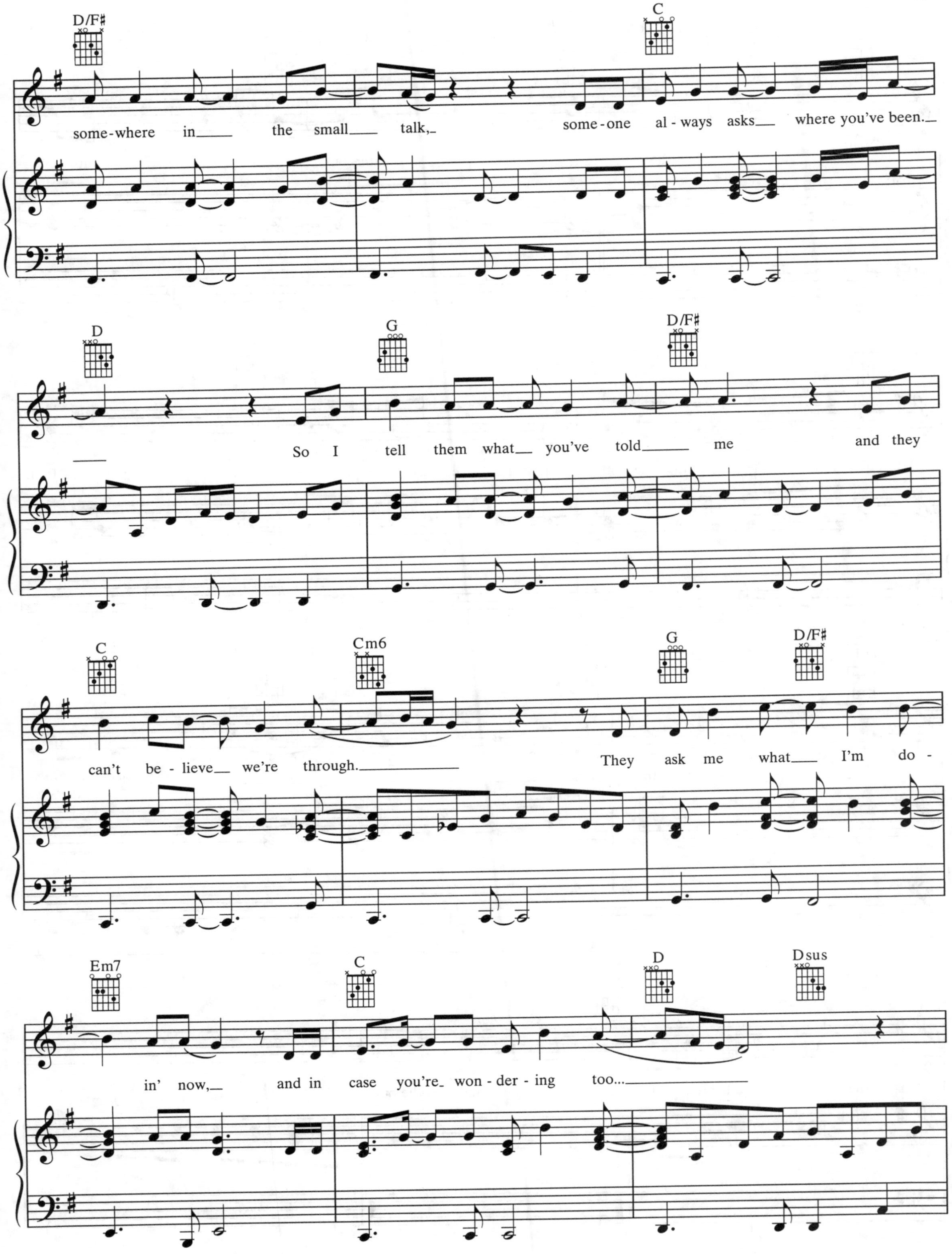
D/F♯
C
some-where in___ the small___ talk,_ some-one al-ways asks___ where you've been.__
D
G
D/F♯
So I tell them what__ you've told____ me and they
C
Cm6
G
D/F♯
can't be-lieve__ we're through.________ They ask me what___ I'm do-
Em7
C
D
Dsus
in' now,__ and in case you're_ won-der-ing too...________

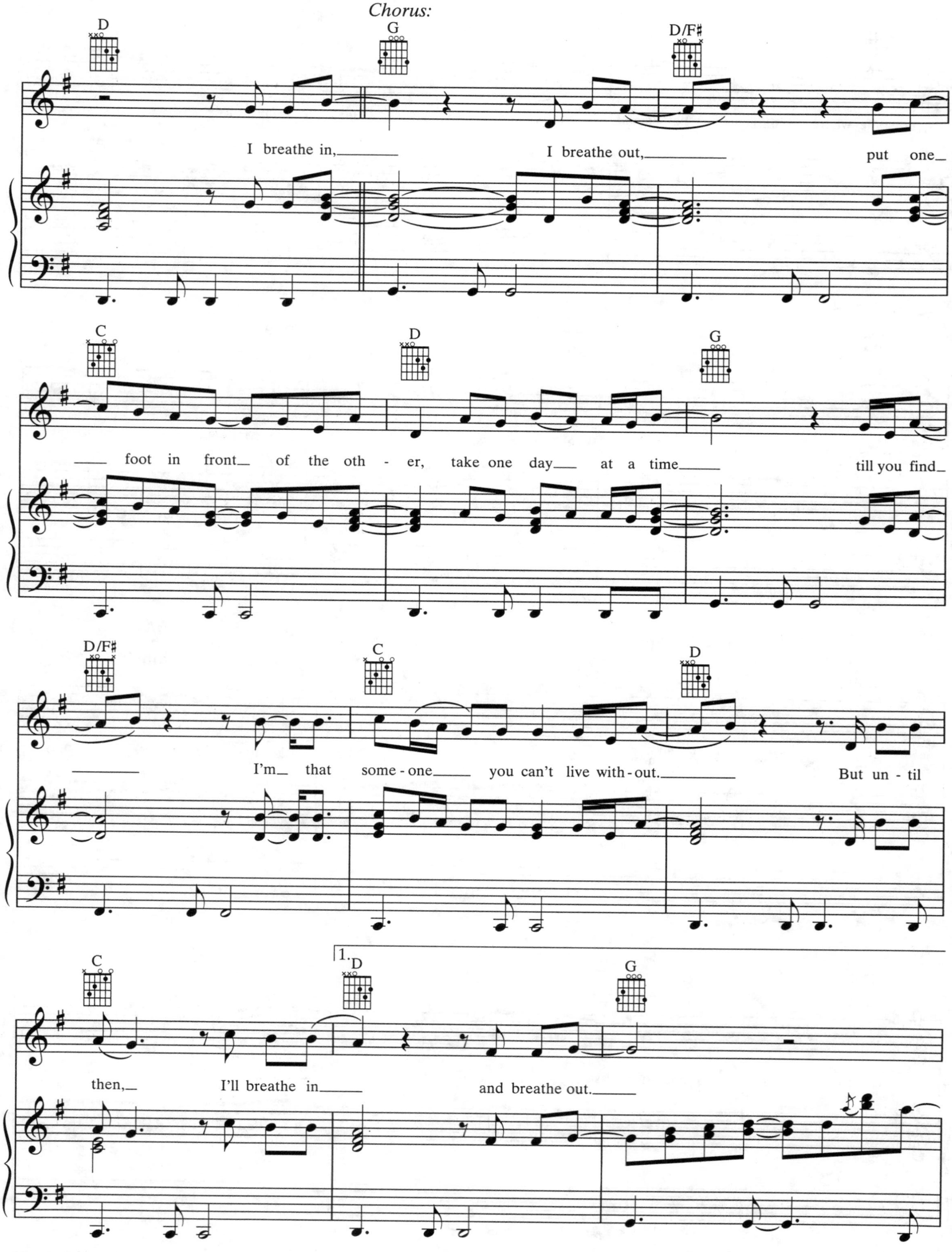
Chorus:
D
G
D/F♯
I breathe in,
I breathe out,
put one
C
D
G
foot in front of the oth - er, take one day at a time
till you find
D/F♯
C
D
I'm that some - one you can't live with - out.
But un - til
C
1.
D
G
then,
I'll breathe in
and breathe out.

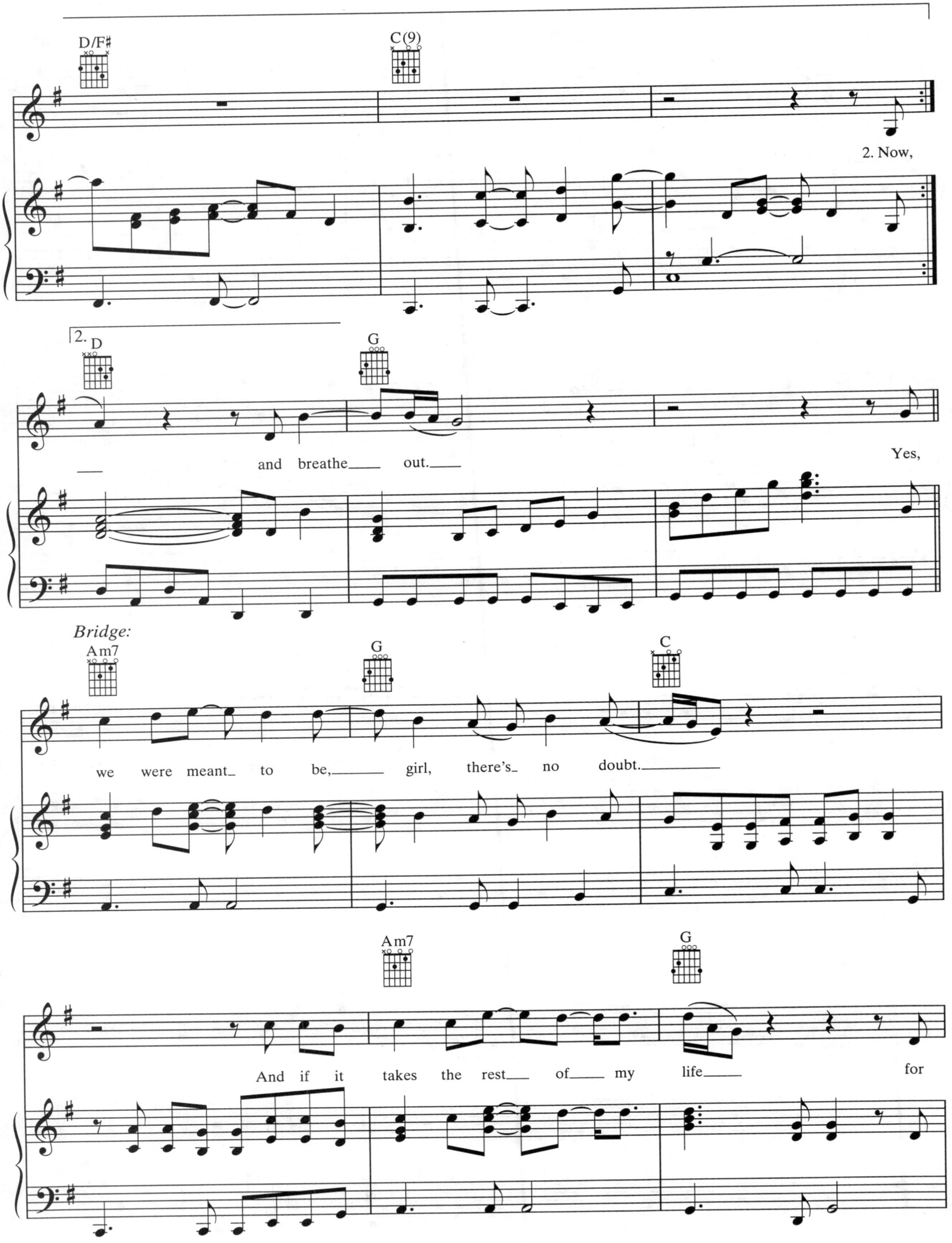
D/F♯
C(9)
2. Now,
2.
D
G
and breathe out.
Yes,
Bridge:
Am7
G
C
we were meant to be, girl, there's no doubt.
Am7
G
And if it takes the rest of my life
for

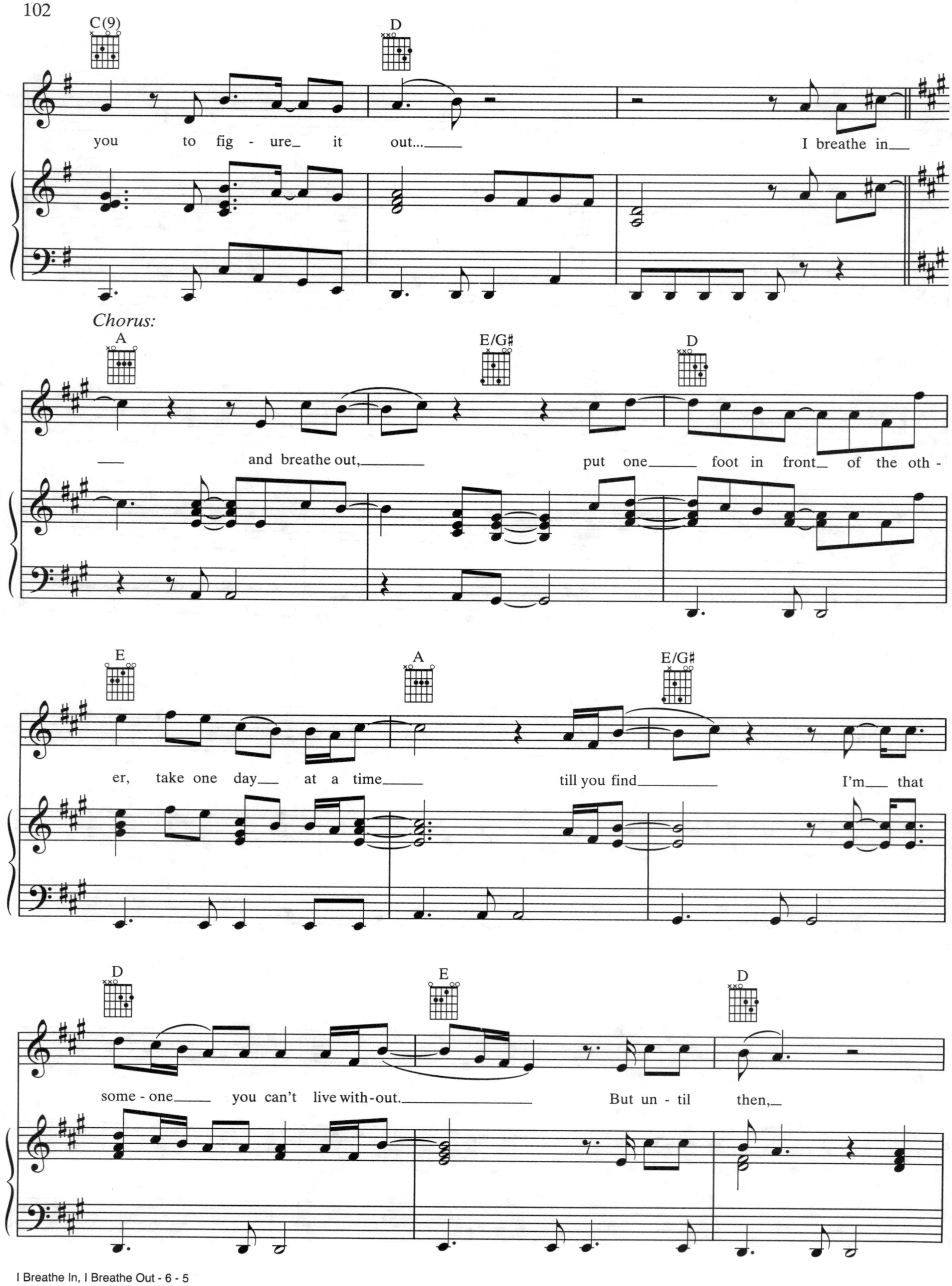
C(9)
D
you to fig - ure_ it out...___
I breathe in__
Chorus:
A
E/G♯
D
___ and breathe out,___
put one___ foot in front_ of the oth -
E
A
E/G♯
er, take one day__ at a time___
till you find___
I'm__ that
D
E
D
some - one___ you can't live with-out.___
But un - til then,_

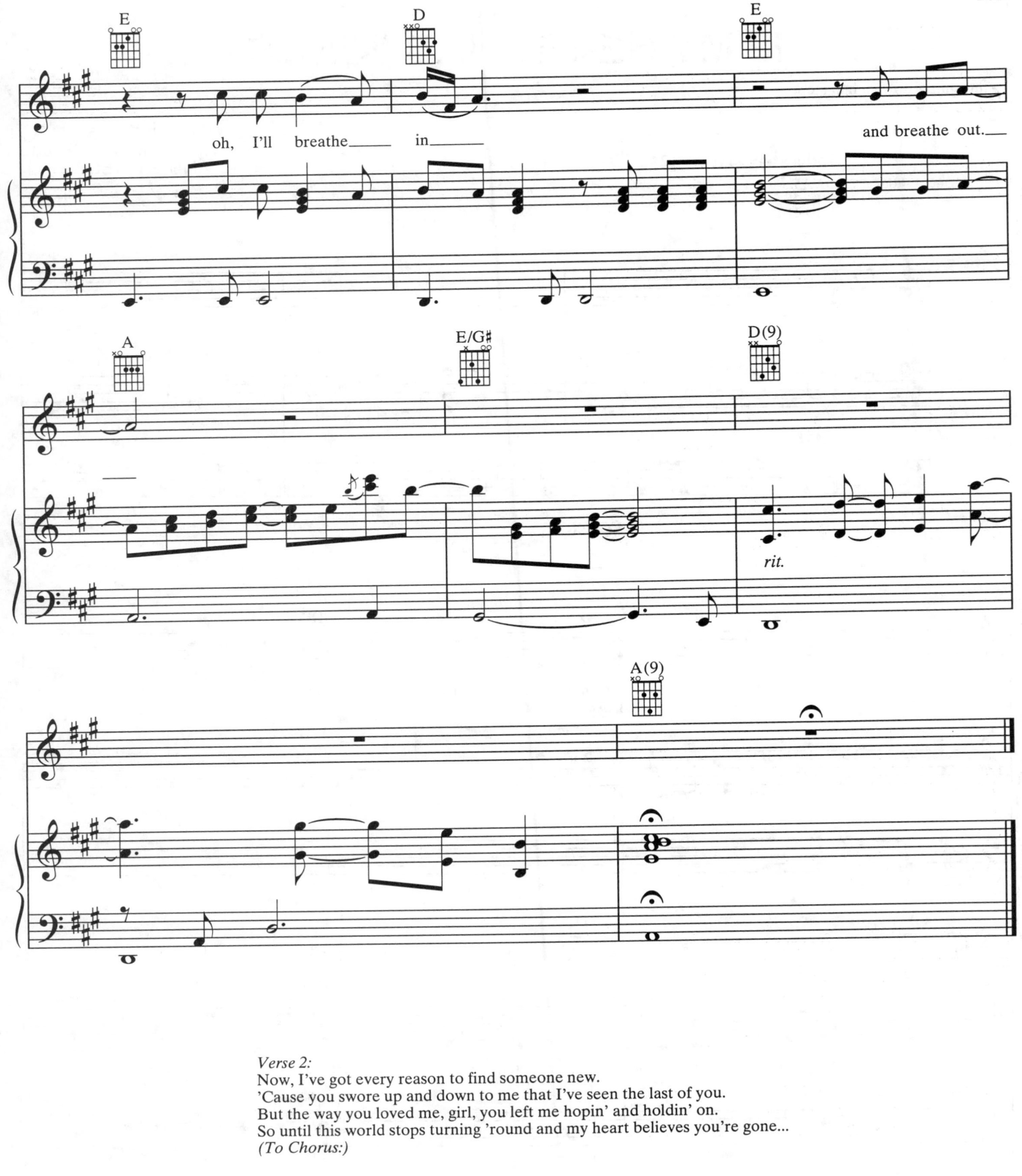

Verse 2:
Now, I've got every reason to find someone new.
'Cause you swore up and down to me that I've seen the last of you.
But the way you loved me, girl, you left me hopin' and holdin' on.
So until this world stops turning 'round and my heart believes you're gone...
(To Chorus:)

IF MY HEART HAD WINGS

Tune guitar down a half step:
⑥ = E♭ ③ = G♭
⑤ = A♭ ② = B♭
④ = D♭ ① = E♭

Words and Music by
J. FRED KNOBLOCH and
ANNIE ROBOFF

Moderately fast ♩ = 124

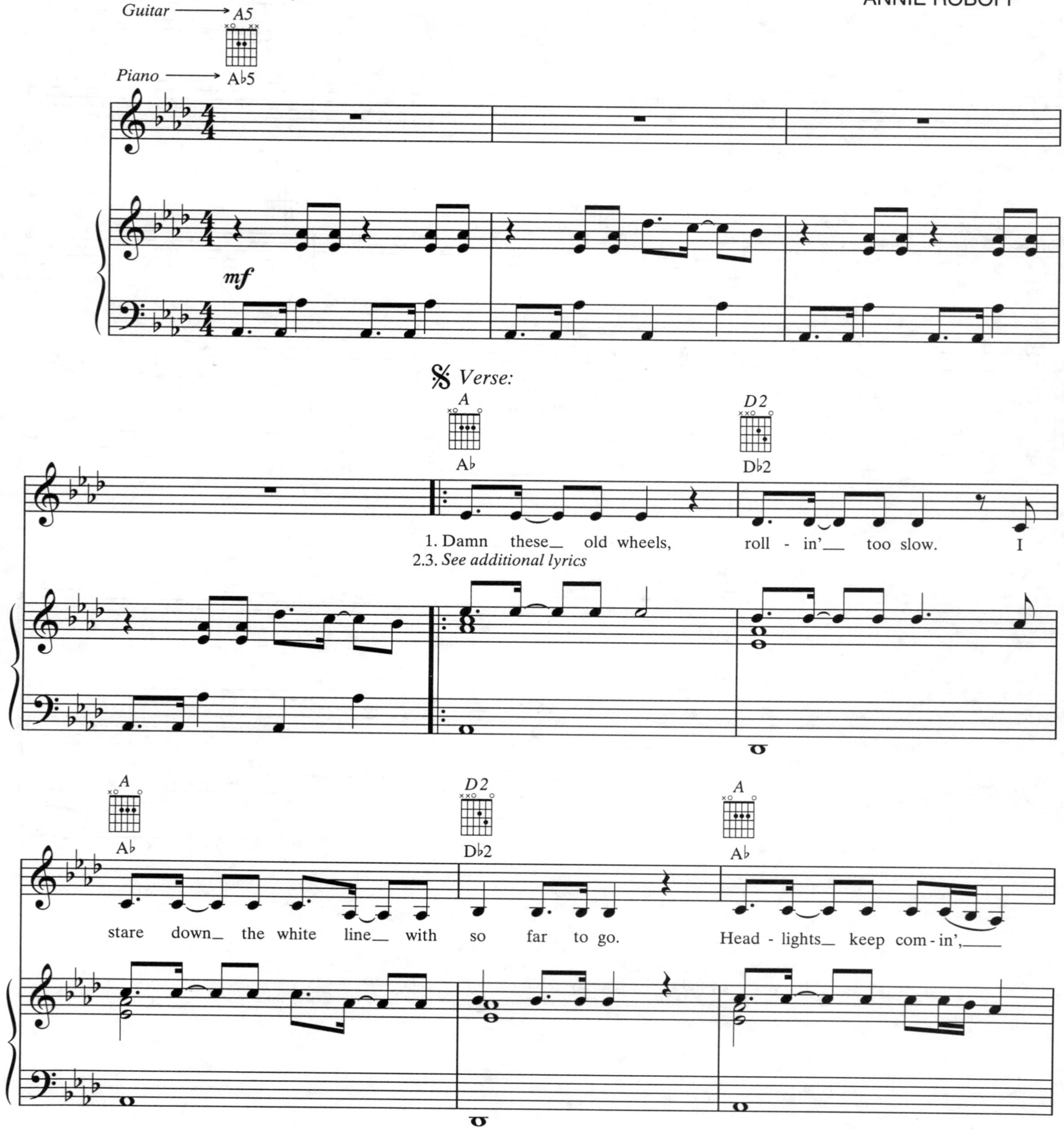
Guitar → A5
Piano → A♭5
mf
Verse:
A
A♭
D2
D♭2
1. Damn these_ old wheels, roll - in'_ too slow. I
2.3. See additional lyrics
stare down_ the white line_ with so far to go. Head - lights_ keep com - in',___

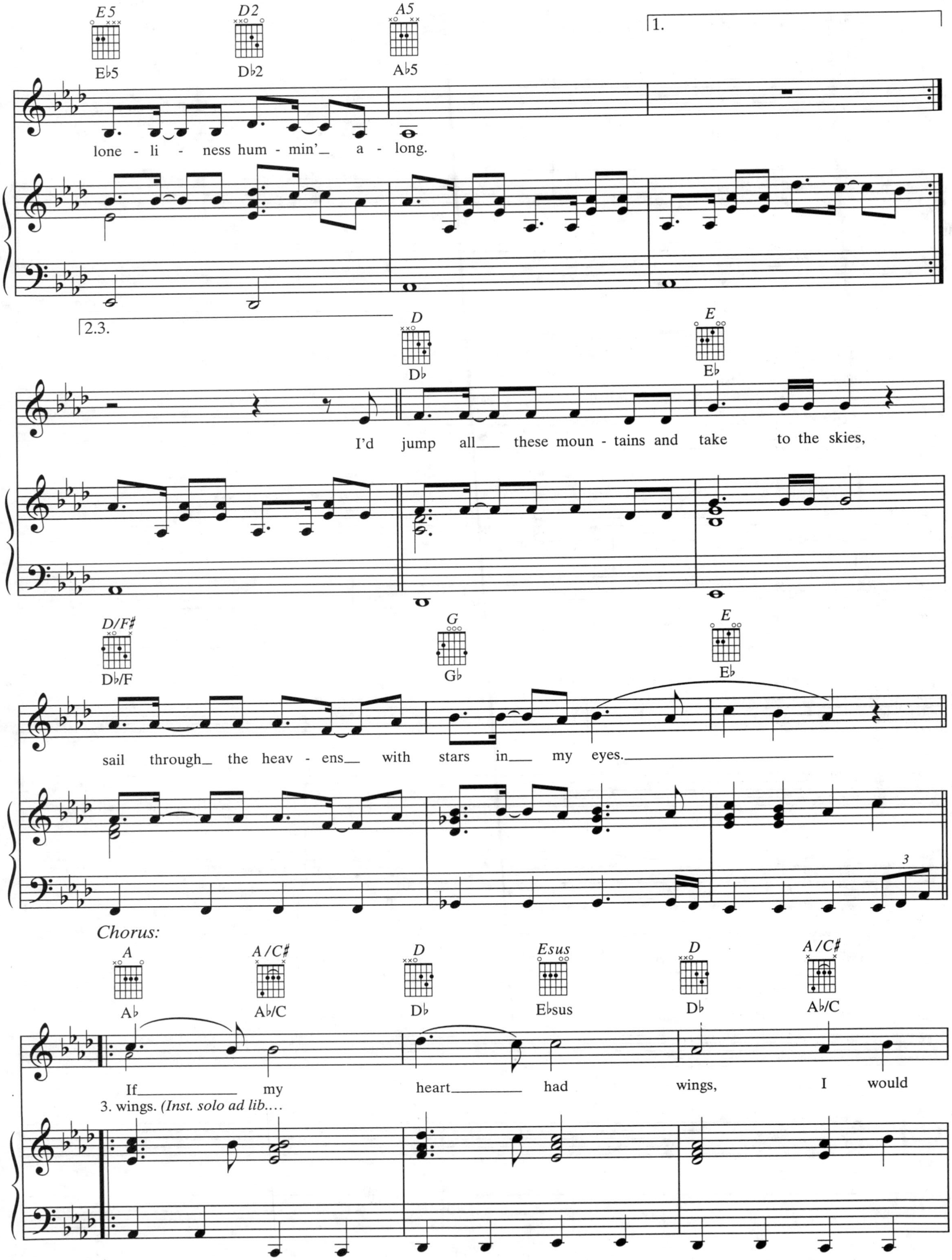
E5
D2
A5
E♭5
D♭2
A♭5
1.
lone - li - ness hum - min' a - long.
2.3.
D
E
D♭
E♭
I'd jump all these moun - tains and take to the skies,
D/F♯
G
E
D♭/F
G♭
E♭
sail through the heav - ens with stars in my eyes.
3
Chorus:
A
A/C♯
D
Esus
D
A/C♯
A♭
A♭/C
D♭
E♭sus
D♭
A♭/C
If my heart had wings, I would
3. wings. (Inst. solo ad lib....

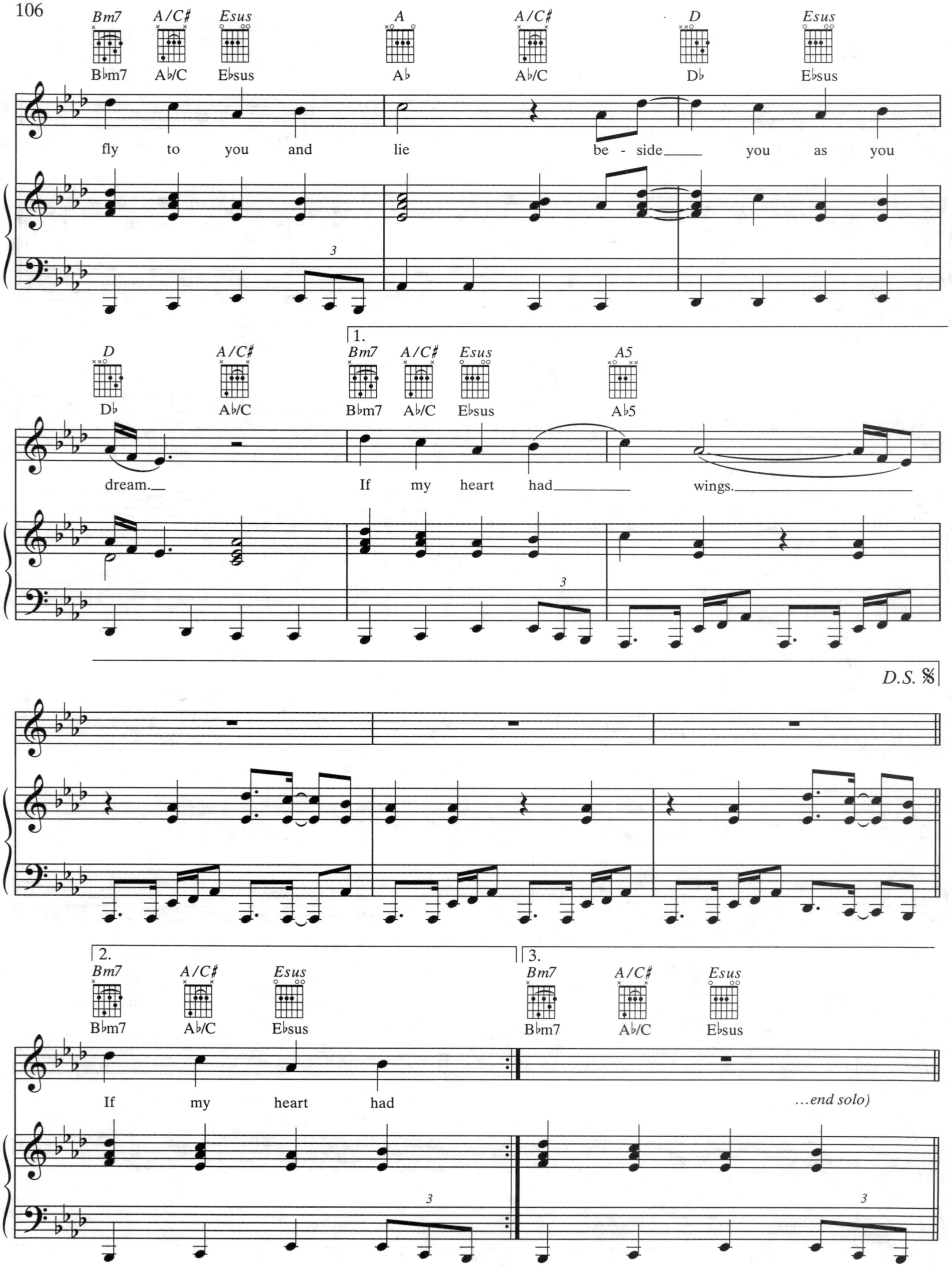
Bm7 A/C♯ Esus A A/C♯ D Esus
B♭m7 A♭/C E♭sus A♭ A♭/C D♭ E♭sus
fly to you and lie be - side you as you
D A/C♯
D♭ A♭/C
dream.
1.
Bm7 A/C♯ Esus A5
B♭m7 A♭/C E♭sus A♭5
If my heart had wings.
D.S. 𝄋
2.
Bm7 A/C♯ Esus
B♭m7 A♭/C E♭sus
If my heart had
3.
Bm7 A/C♯ Esus
B♭m7 A♭/C E♭sus
…end solo)

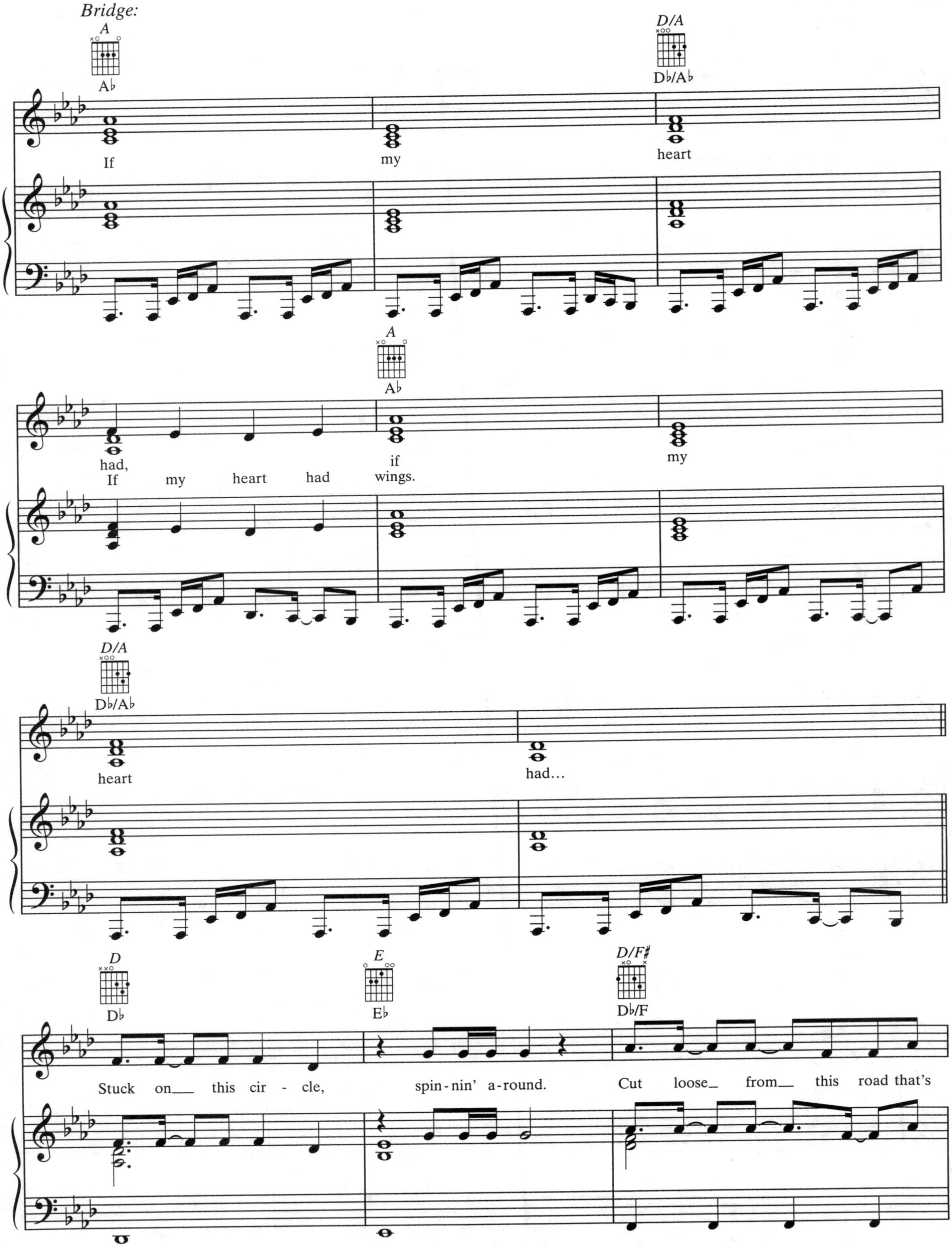
Bridge:
A
Ab
If
my
D/A
Db/Ab
heart
had,
If my heart had
A
Ab
if
wings.
my
D/A
Db/Ab
heart
had…
D
Db
Stuck on___ this cir - cle,
E
Eb
spin - nin' a - round.
D/F#
Db/F
Cut loose_ from___ this road that's

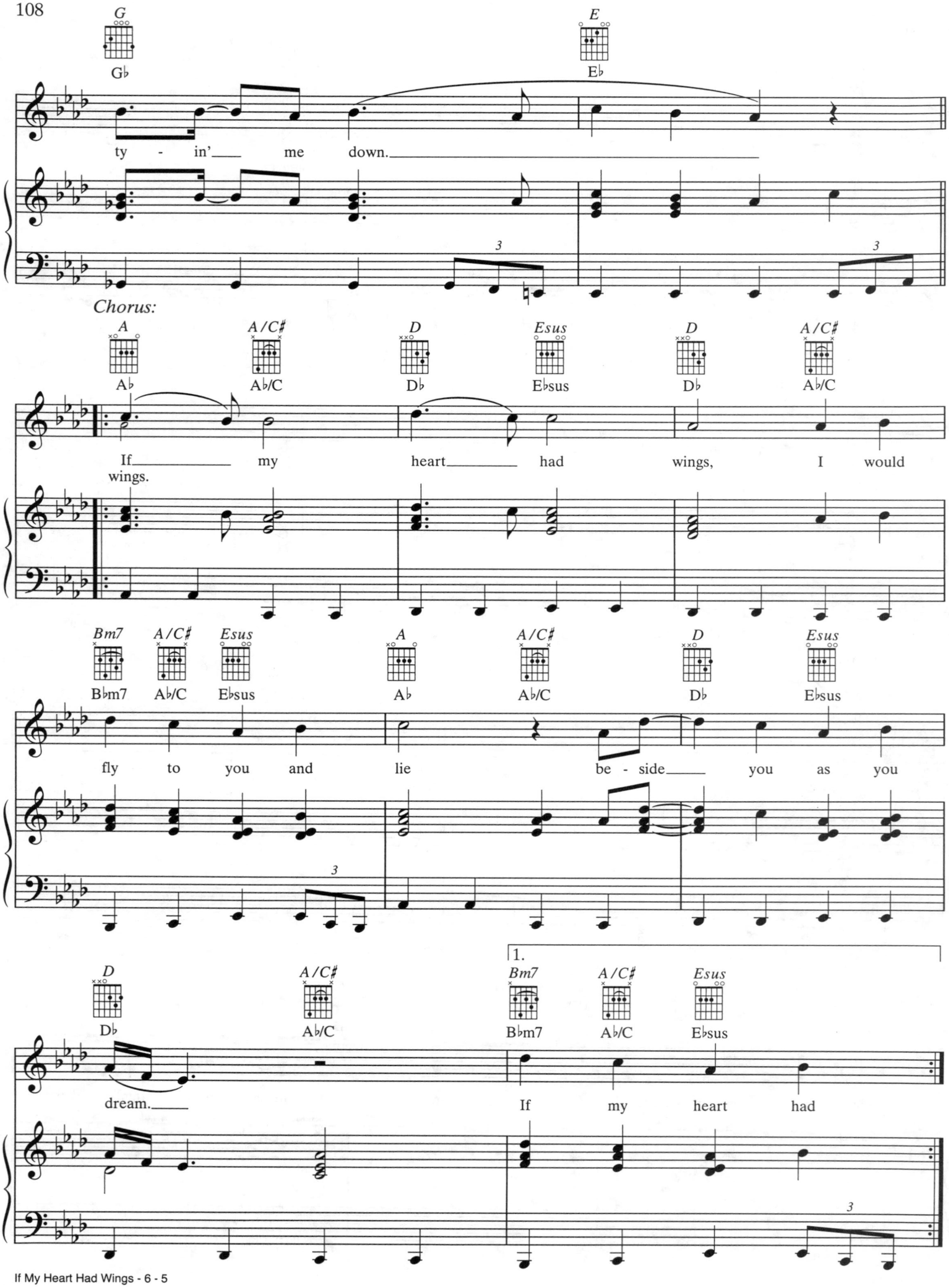
G
E
G♭
E♭
ty - in' me down.
3
3
Chorus:
A
A/C♯
D
Esus
D
A/C♯
A♭
A♭/C
D♭
E♭sus
D♭
A♭/C
If my heart had wings, I would
wings.
Bm7
A/C♯
Esus
A
A/C♯
D
Esus
B♭m7
A♭/C
E♭sus
A♭
A♭/C
D♭
E♭sus
fly to you and lie be - side you as you
3
1.
D
A/C♯
Bm7
A/C♯
Esus
D♭
A♭/C
B♭m7
A♭/C
E♭sus
dream.
If my heart had
3

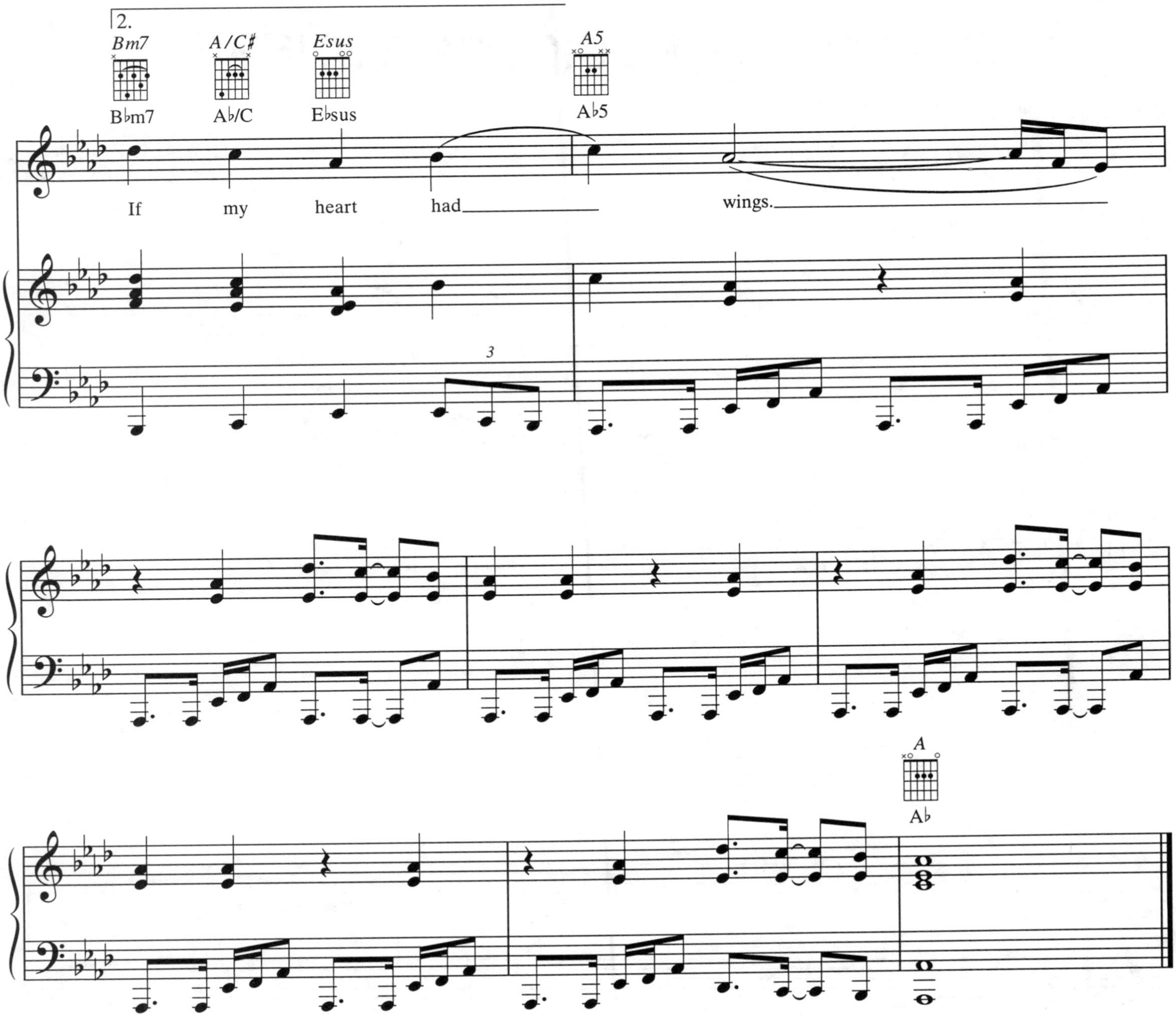

Verse 2:
Who poured this pain?
Who made these clouds?
I stare through this windshield
Thinkin' out loud.
Time keeps on crawling,
Love keeps on calling me home.

Verse 3:
We both committed.
We both agreed.
You do what you have to
To get what you need.
Feeling you near me
With so many miles in between,
Oh, Lord, it ain't easy
Out here in the dark
To keep us together so far apart.
(To Chorus:)

IT'S FIVE O'CLOCK SOMEWHERE

Words and Music by
DONALD ROLLINS
and JIM BROWN

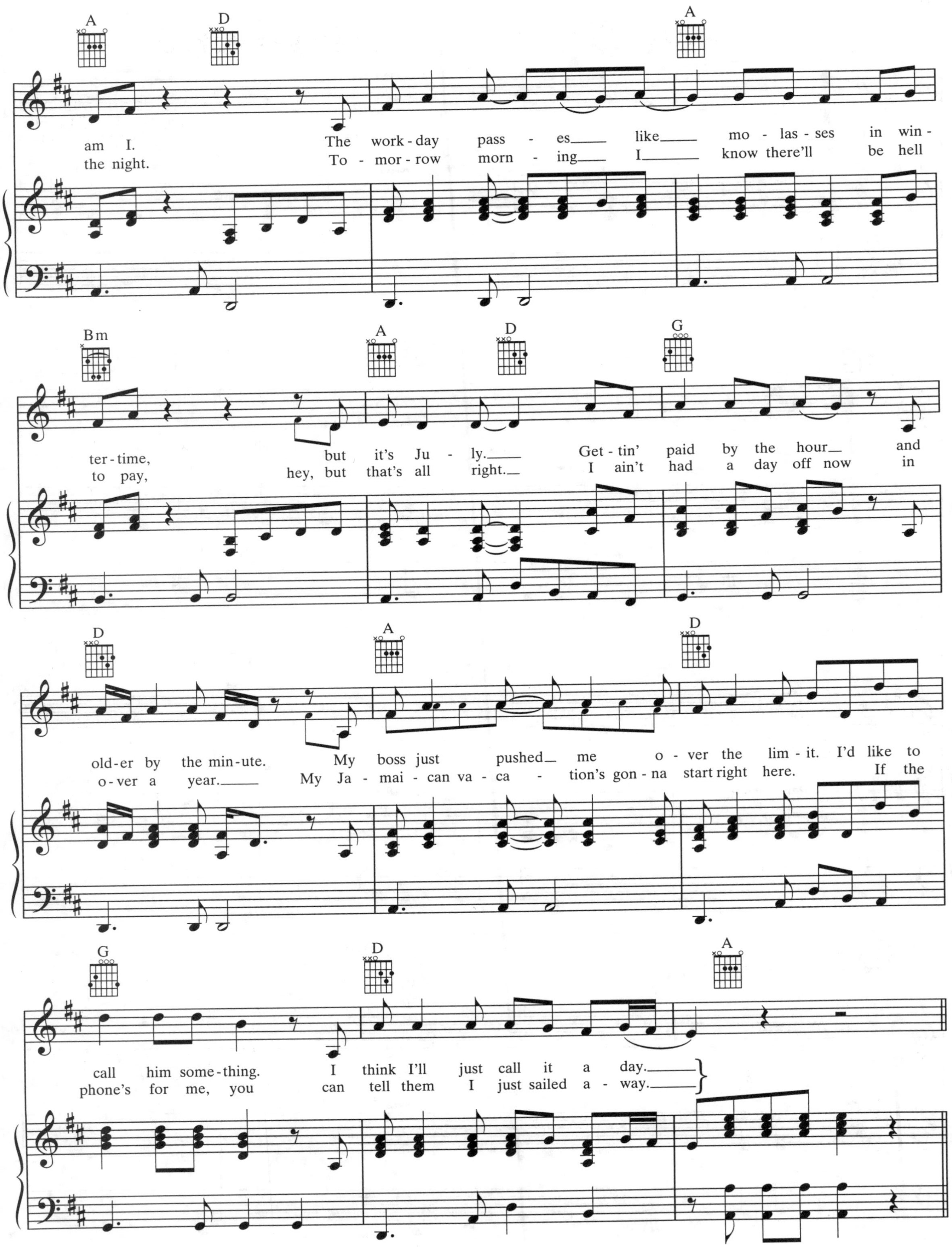
A
D
A
am I.
The work-day pass - es like mo - las - ses in win -
the night.
To - mor - row morn - ing I know there'll be hell
Bm
A
D
G
ter - time, but it's Ju - ly. Get - tin' paid by the hour and
to pay, hey, but that's all right. I ain't had a day off now in
D
A
D
old - er by the min - ute. My boss just pushed me o - ver the lim - it. I'd like to
o - ver a year. My Ja - mai - can va - ca - tion's gon - na start right here. If the
G
D
A
call him some - thing. I think I'll just call it a day.
phone's for me, you can tell them I just sailed a - way.

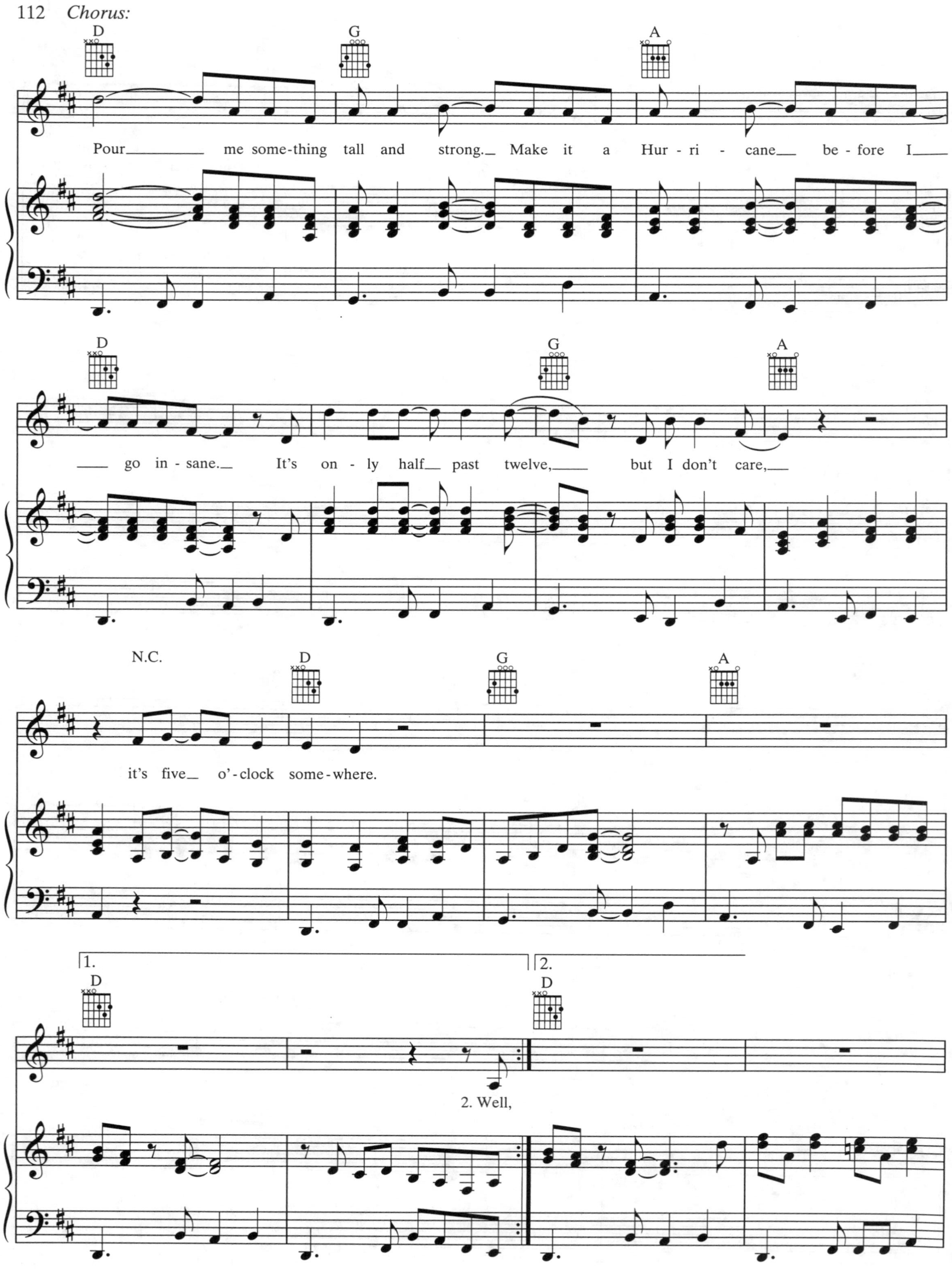
Chorus:
D
G
A
Pour me some-thing tall and strong. Make it a Hur - ri - cane be - fore I
D
G
A
go in - sane. It's on - ly half past twelve, but I don't care,
N.C.
D
G
A
it's five o'-clock some-where.
1.
D
2.
D
2. Well,

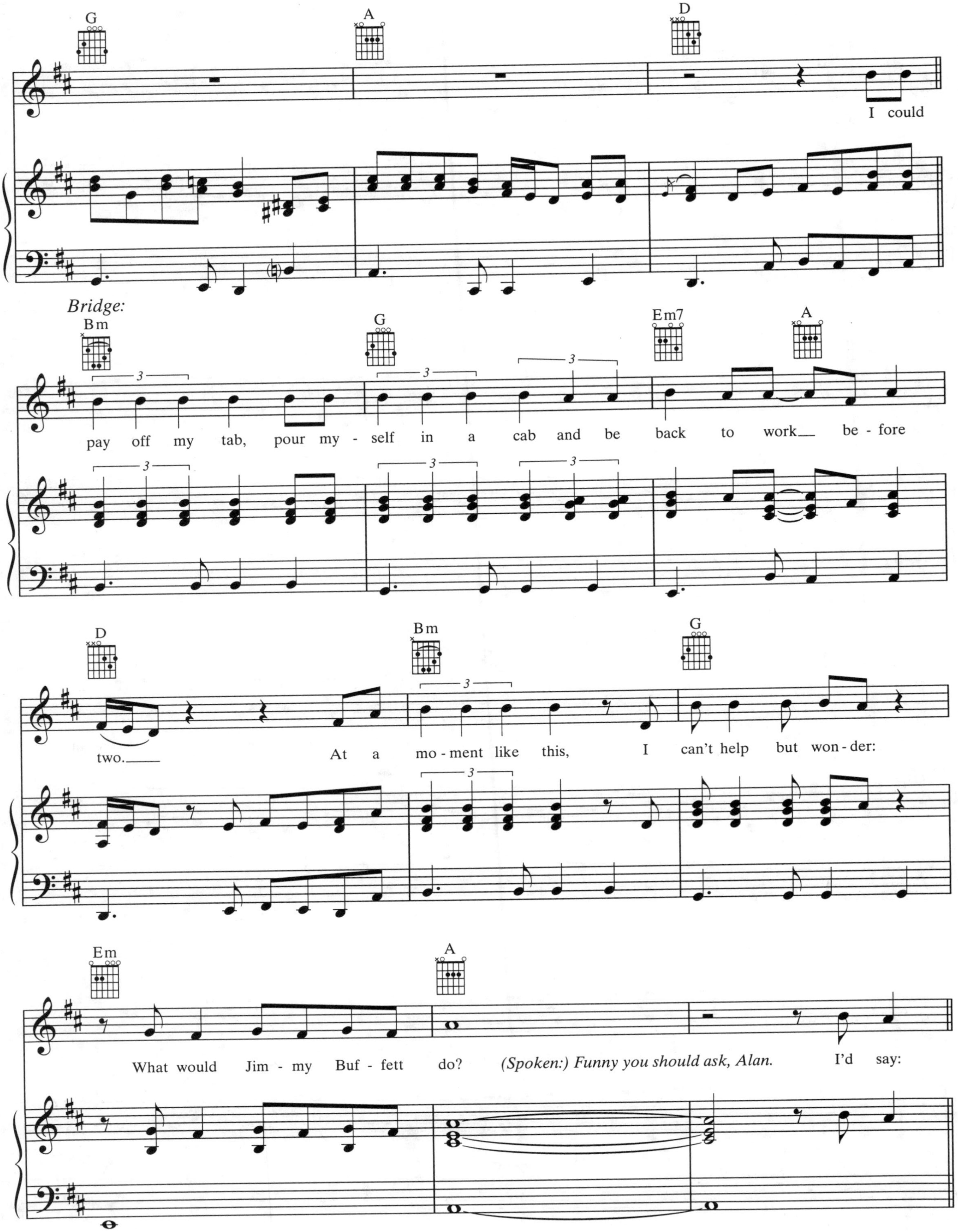
G
A
D
I could
Bridge:
Bm
G
Em7
A
pay off my tab, pour my - self in a cab and be back to work__ be - fore
D
Bm
G
two.____ At a mo - ment like this, I can't help but won - der:
Em
A
What would Jim - my Buf - fett do? (Spoken:) Funny you should ask, Alan. I'd say:

Chorus:

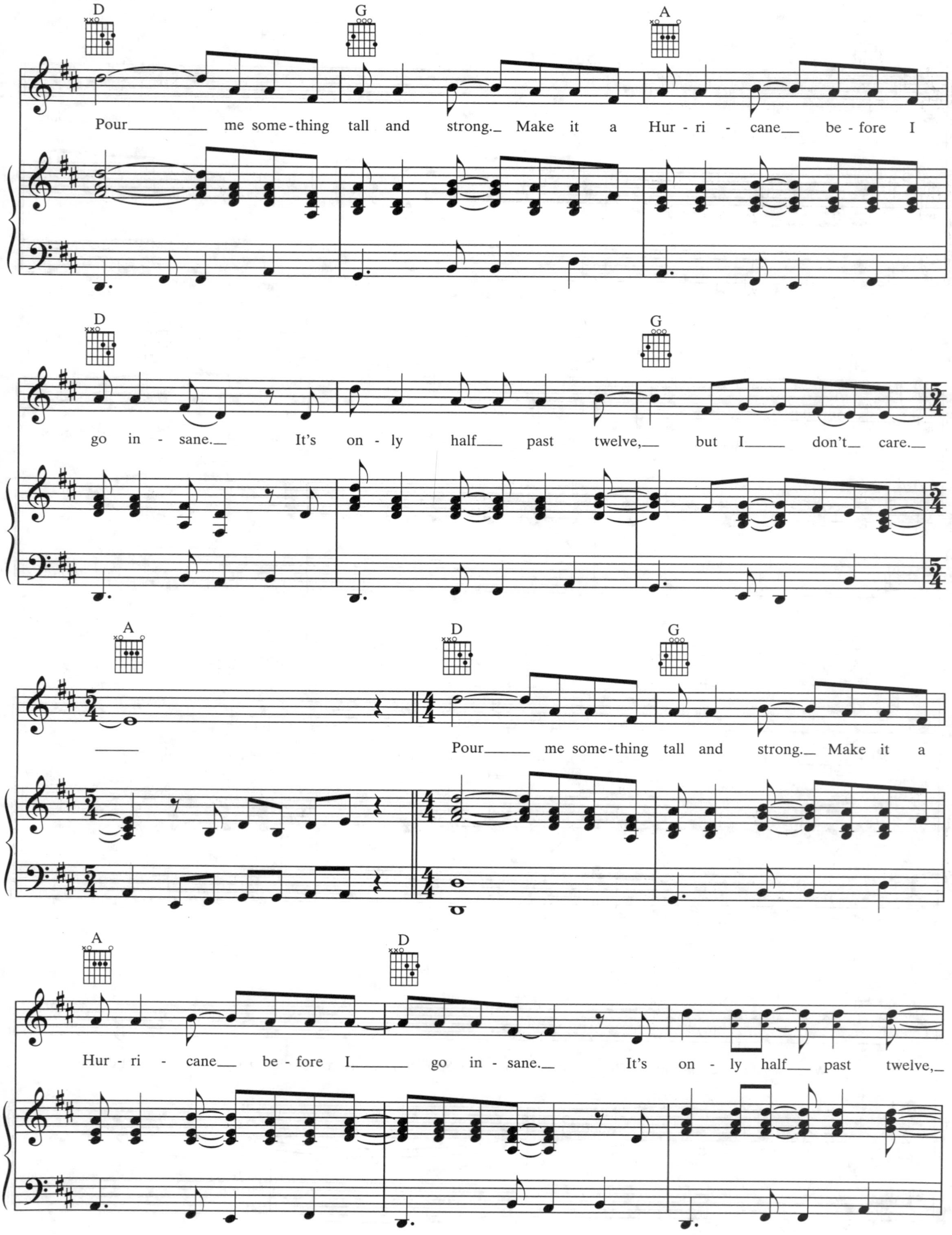
D
G
A
Pour___ me some-thing tall and strong._ Make it a Hur-ri-cane__ be-fore I
D
G
go in-sane._ It's on-ly half__ past twelve,__ but I___ don't__ care.__
A
D
G
Pour___ me some-thing tall and strong._ Make it a
A
D
Hur-ri-cane__ be-fore I___ go in-sane.__ It's on-ly half__ past twelve,_

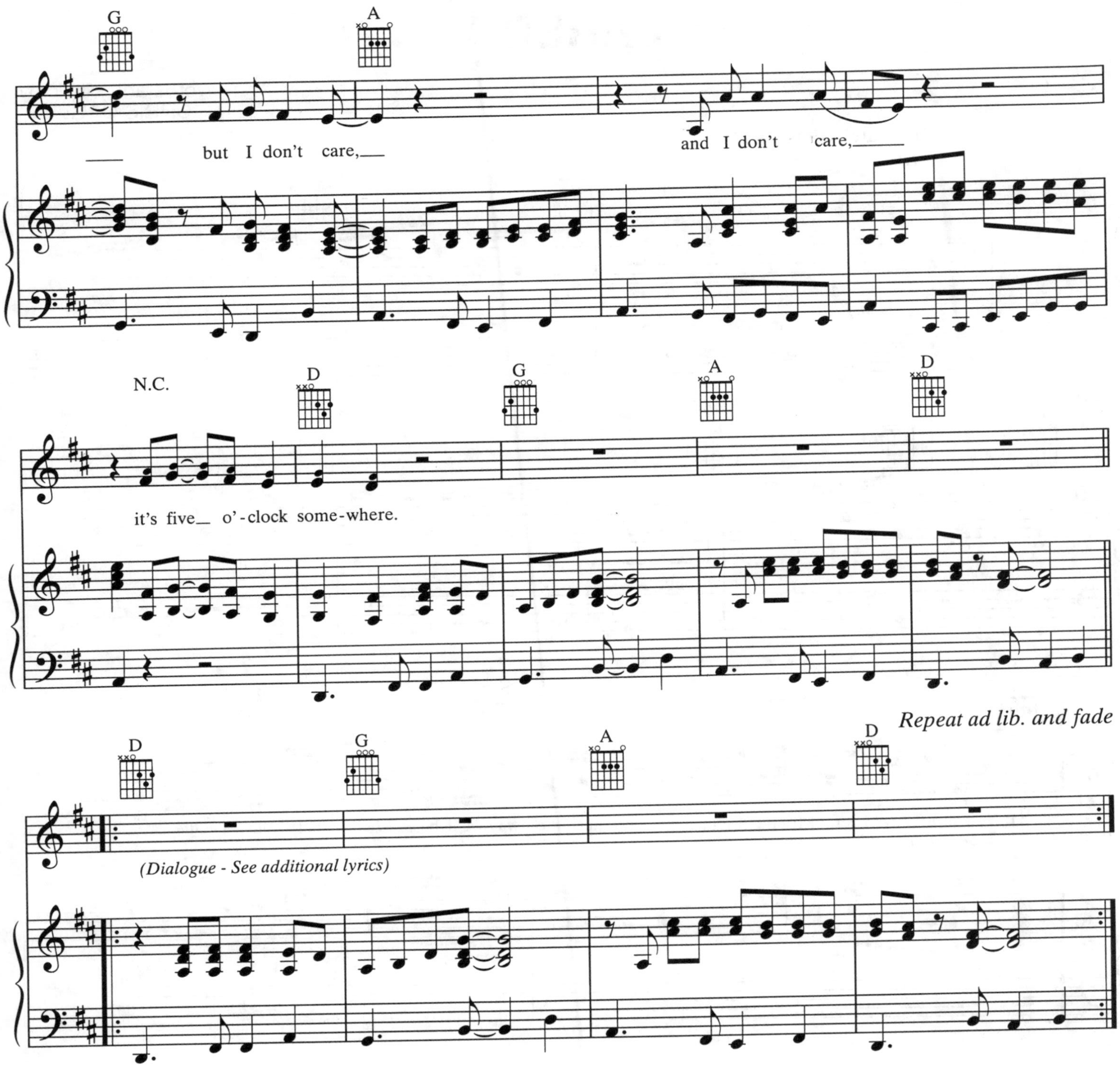

Dialogue:
Jimmy: What time zone am I on? What country am I in?
Alan: It doesn't matter. It's five o'clock somewhere.
Jimmy: It's always on five in Margaritaville, come to think of it.
Alan: I heard that.
Jimmy: You've been there, haven't you?
Alan: Yes, sir.
Jimmy: I've seen your boat there.
Alan: I've been to Margaritaville a few times.
Jimmy: All right. That's good.
Alan: Stumbled my way back.
Jimmy: OK. Just want to make sure you can keep it between the navigational beacons.
Alan: Between the bouys. I got it.
Jimmy: All right. It's five o'clock. Let's go somewhere.
Alan: I'm ready. Crank it up.
Jimmy: Let's get out of here.
Alan: I'm gone.

LAREDO

Words and Music by
CHRIS CAGLE

Moderately slow ♩ = 80
N.C.
C*
B♭
mf
F
B♭
C
B♭
F
B♭
Verse:
C
B♭
F
B♭
1. You've al-ways been a friend of mine, and that's the way we'll be___ 'til the day I die.___
2. See additional lyrics
C
B♭
F
B♭
Yeah, it's good to know_ you're on___ my___ side.

* *Original recording in D♭ major.*

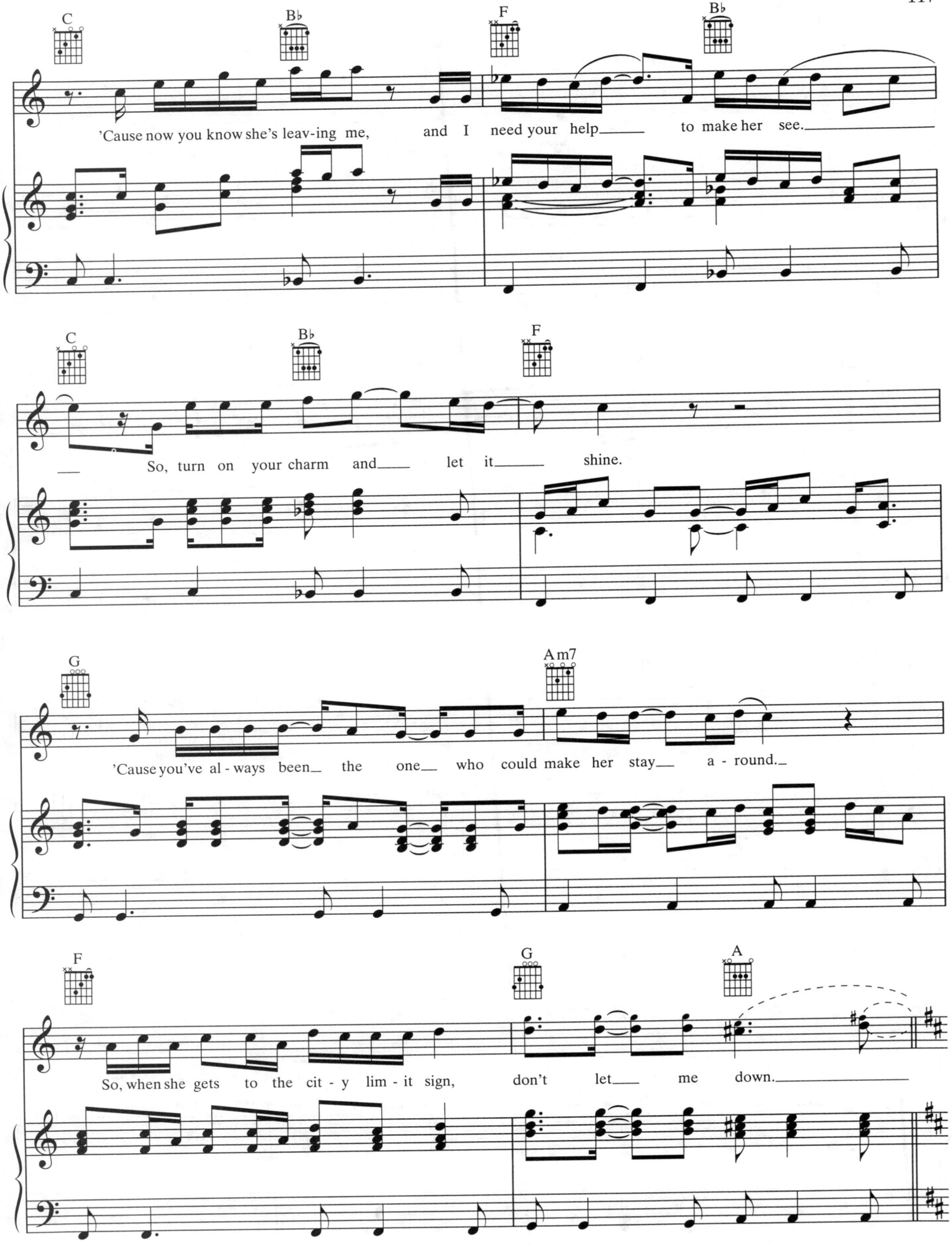
C
B♭
F
B♭
'Cause now you know she's leav-ing me, and I need your help to make her see.
C
B♭
F
So, turn on your charm and let it shine.
G
Am7
'Cause you've al-ways been the one who could make her stay a-round.
F
G
A
So, when she gets to the cit-y lim-it sign, don't let me down.

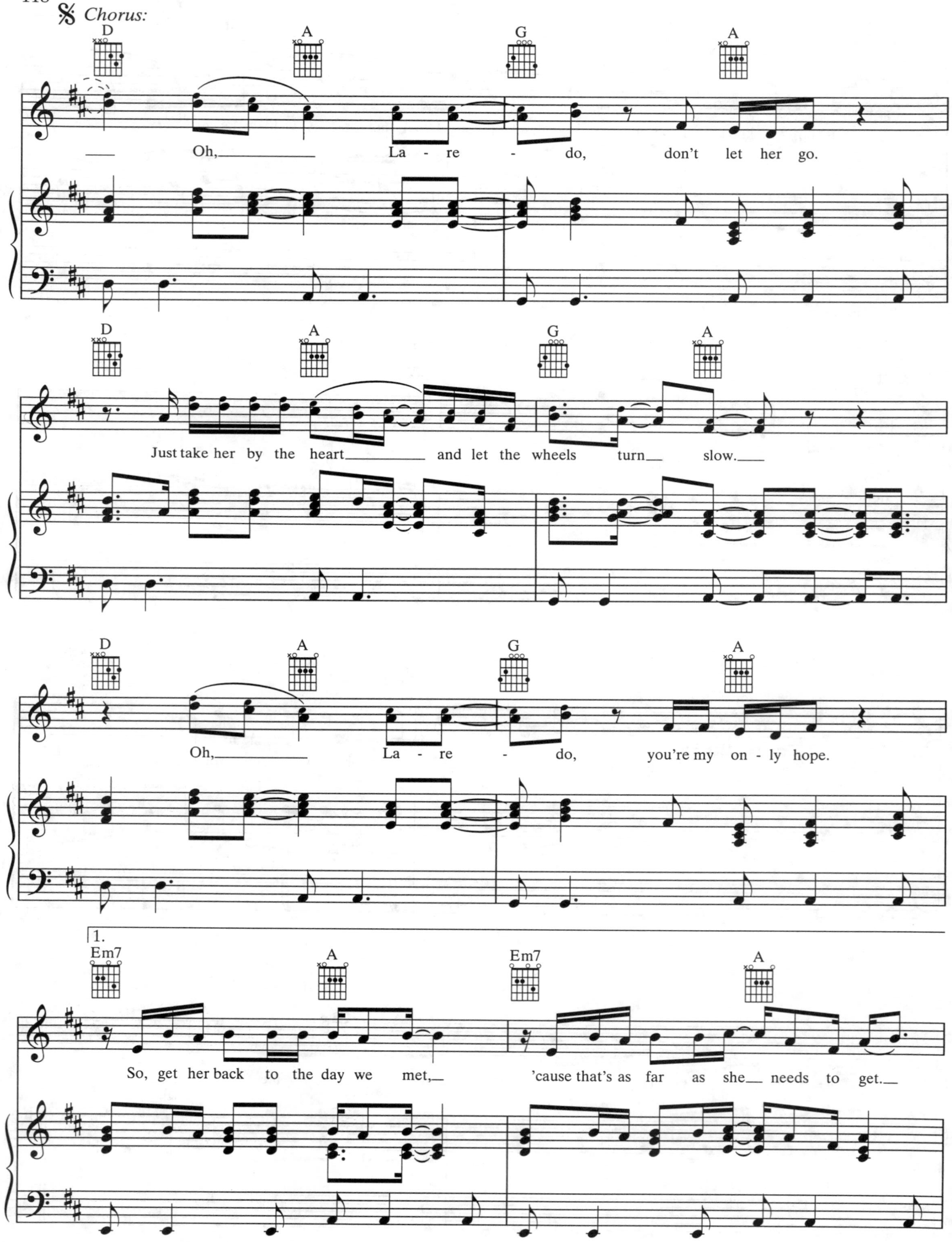
Chorus:
D
A
G
A
Oh, La - re - do, don't let her go.
D
A
G
A
Just take her by the heart and let the wheels turn slow.
D
A
G
A
Oh, La - re - do, you're my on - ly hope.
1.
Em7
A
Em7
A
So, get her back to the day we met,
'cause that's as far as she needs to get.

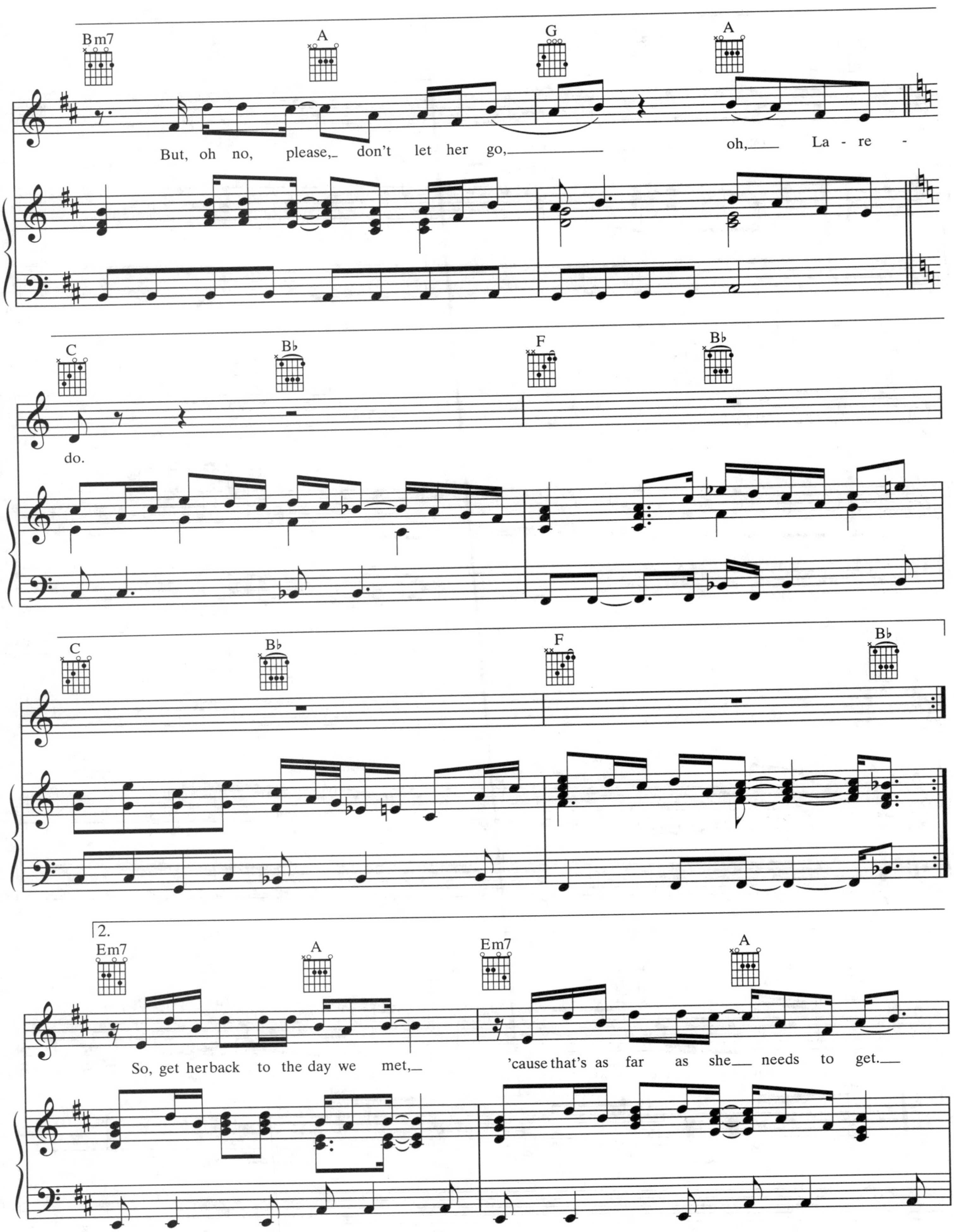
Bm7
A
G
A
But, oh no, please, don't let her go, oh, La - re -
C
B♭
F
B♭
do.
C
B♭
F
B♭
2.
Em7
A
Em7
A
So, get her back to the day we met, 'cause that's as far as she needs to get.

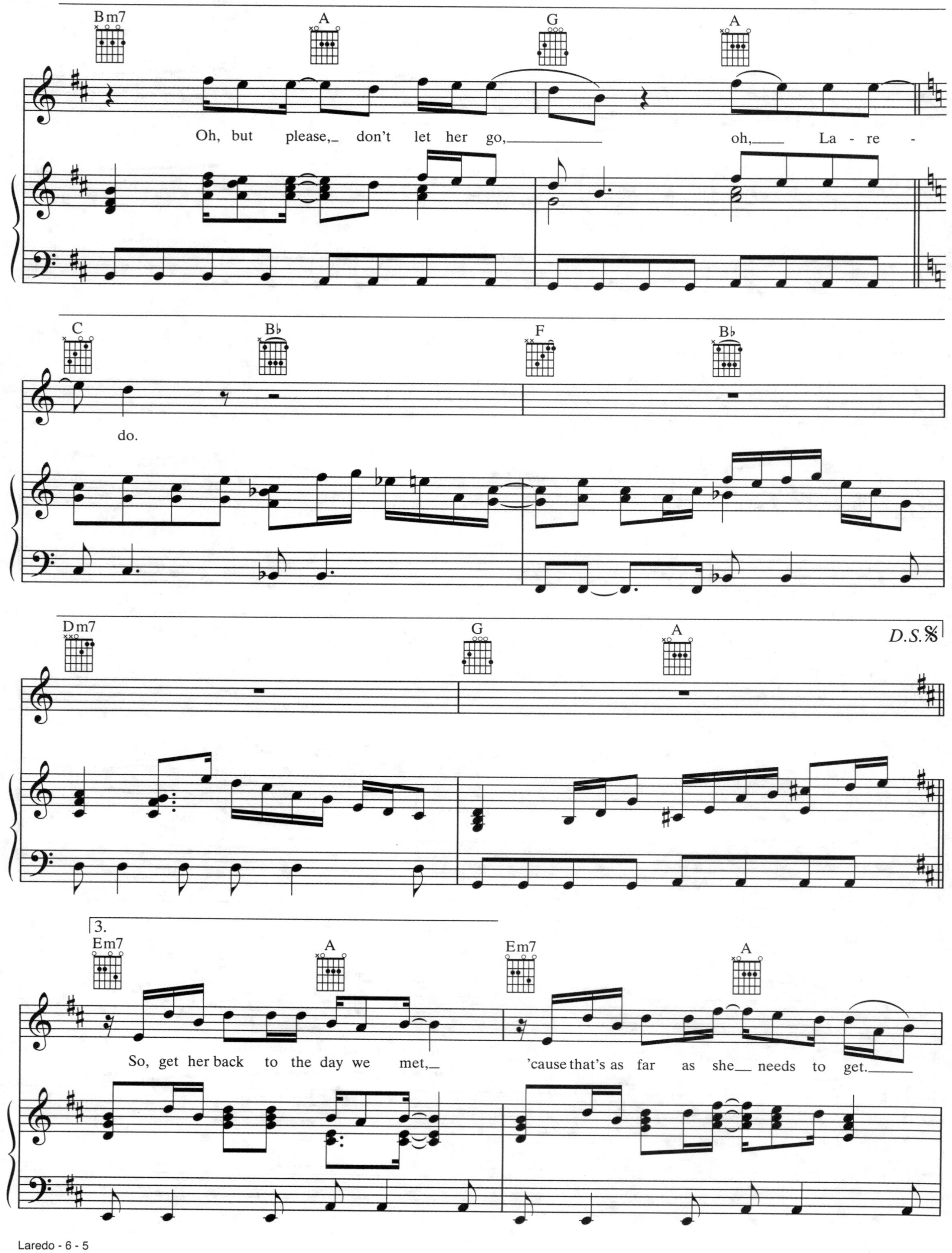
Bm7
A
G
A
Oh, but please,_ don't let her go,___ oh,___ La - re -
C
B♭
F
B♭
do.
Dm7
G
A
D.S.𝄋
3.
Em7
A
Em7
A
So, get her back to the day we met,_ 'cause that's as far as she_ needs to get.___

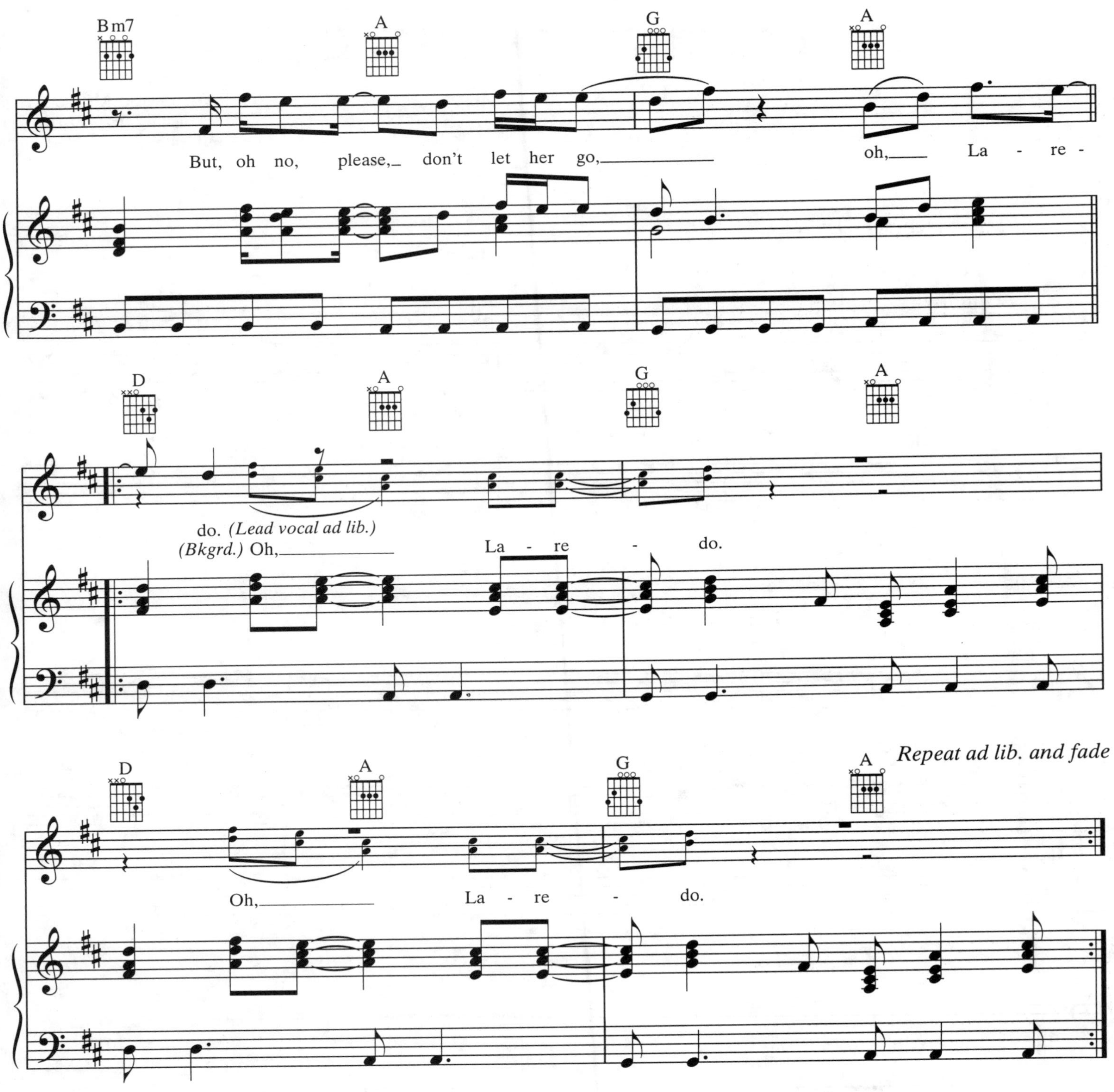

Verse 2:
Make her think about the moonlit walks
And the long, long talks by the water's edge,
With her feet hangin' off the Cane Creek Bridge.
And bring to mind the first kiss we shared
At the old town square when she drives down there,
'Cause that's a day she said she could never forget.
Keep the nights by the candlelight as an ace in the hole,
'Cause those are nights of passion that I know will bring her home.
(To Chorus:)

LET THEM BE LITTLE

Words and Music by
BILLY DEAN and
RICHIE McDONALD

Moderately slow ♩ = 72

*
C
C/E
F2
Dm
Am7
G/B
mp
(with pedal)
Verse:
C
C/E
F2
C/E
1. I can re - mem - ber when_ you fit in the palm_ of my hand._
2. I nev - er felt_ so much_ in one lit - tle ten - der_ touch.
Dm7
C/E
F2
Gsus
G
You felt so good_ in it, no big - ger than a min - ute.
I live for those_ kiss - es, your prayers_ and your wish - es.

*Original recording in D♭ major, Guitar Capo 1.

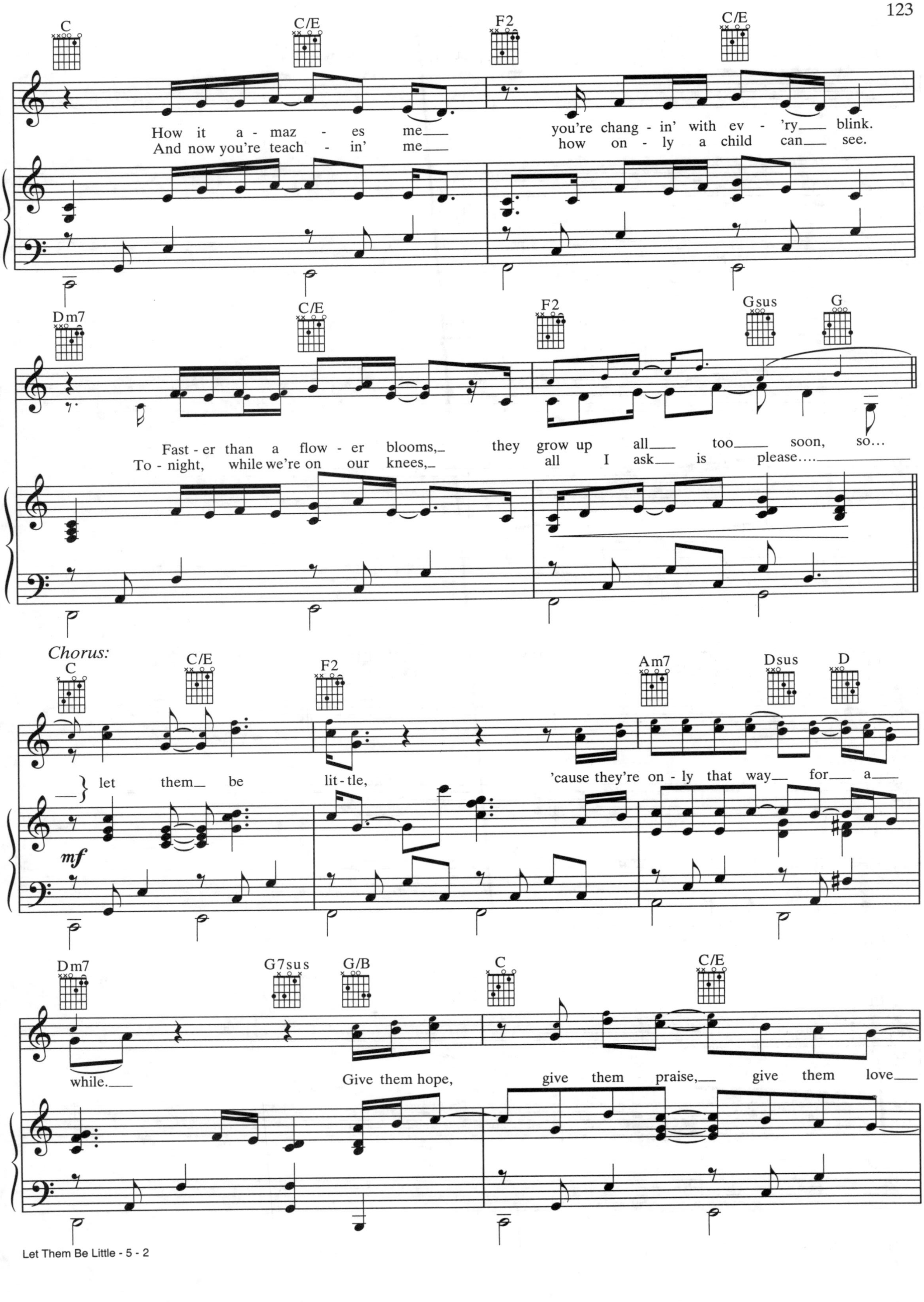
C
C/E
F2
C/E
How it a - maz - es me
you're chang - in' with ev - 'ry blink.
And now you're teach - in' me
how on - ly a child can see.
Dm7
C/E
F2
Gsus
G
Fast - er than a flow - er blooms,
they grow up all too soon, so…
To - night, while we're on our knees,
all I ask is please….
Chorus:
C
C/E
F2
Am7
Dsus
D
let them be lit - tle,
'cause they're on - ly that way for a
mf
Dm7
G7sus
G/B
C
C/E
while.
Give them hope,
give them praise,
give them love

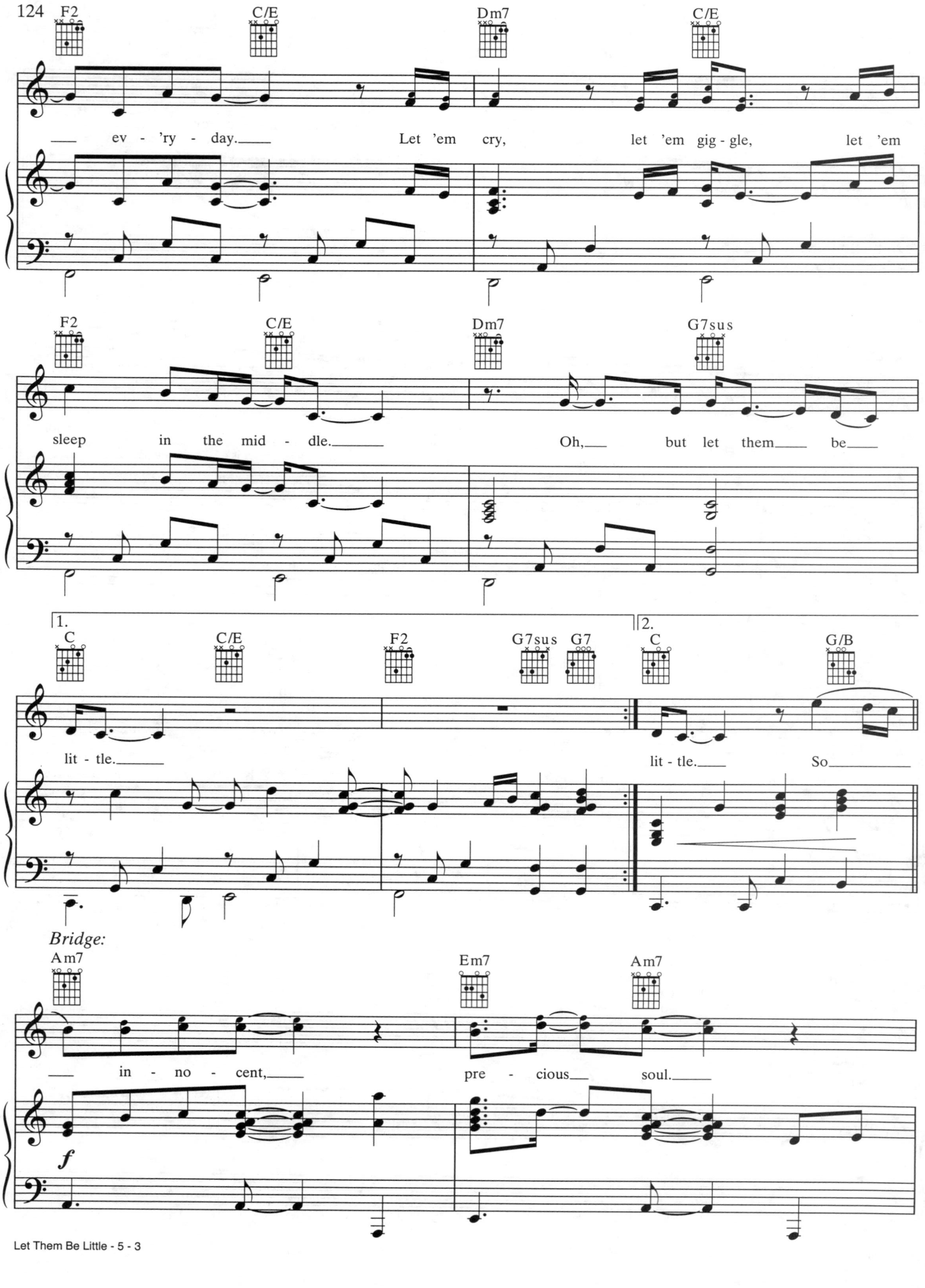
F2
C/E
Dm7
C/E
ev - 'ry - day.
Let 'em cry,
let 'em gig - gle,
let 'em
F2
C/E
Dm7
G7sus
sleep in the mid - dle.
Oh, but let them be
1.
C
C/E
F2
G7sus
G7
2.
C
G/B
lit - tle.
lit - tle.
So
Bridge:
Am7
Em7
Am7
in - no - cent,
pre - cious soul.
f

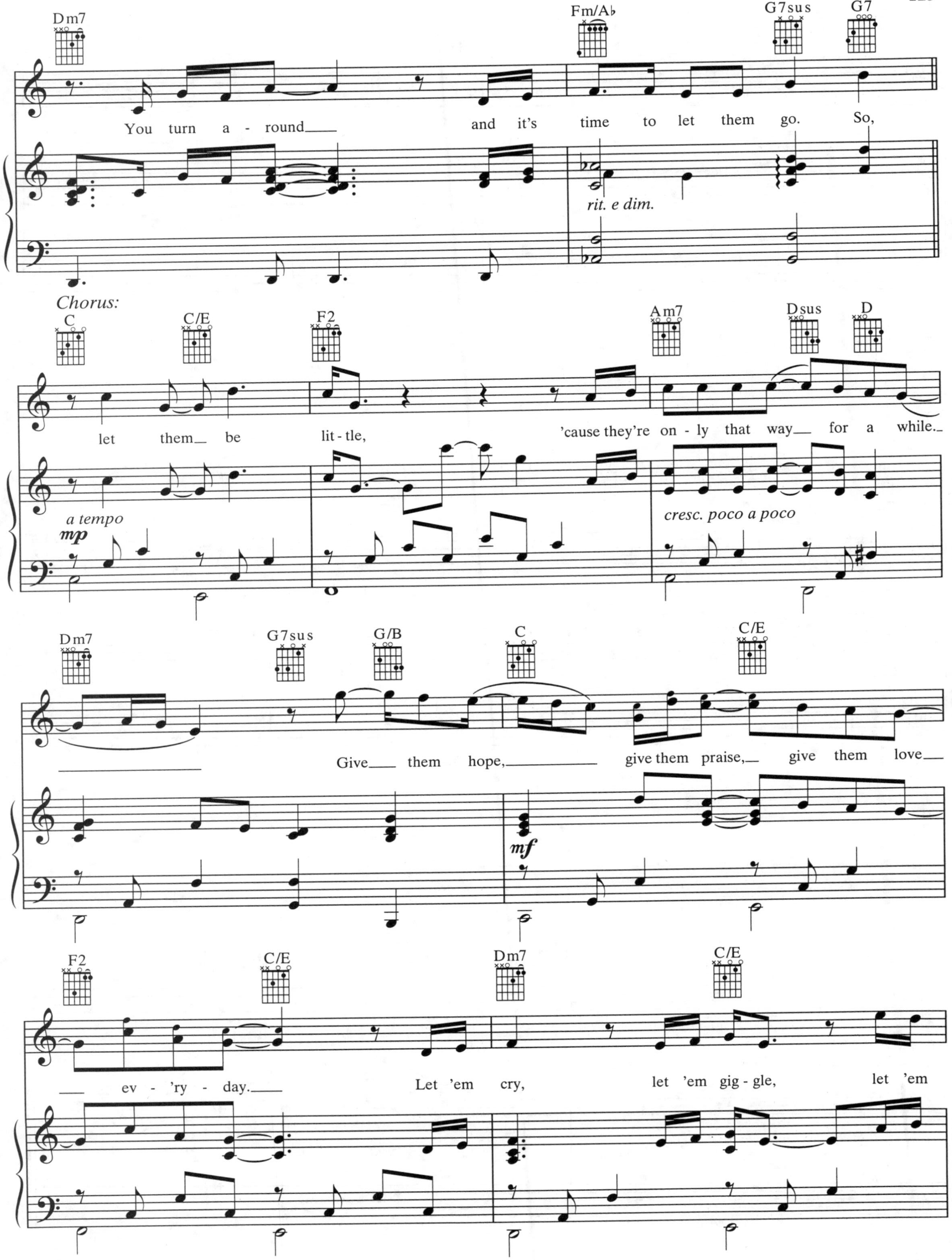
Dm7
Fm/A♭
G7sus
G7
You turn a - round___ and it's time to let them go. So,
rit. e dim.
Chorus:
C
C/E
F2
Am7
Dsus
D
let them__ be lit - tle, 'cause they're on - ly that way__ for a while._
a tempo
mp
cresc. poco a poco
Dm7
G7sus
G/B
C
C/E
Give__ them hope,______ give them praise,__ give them love__
mf
F2
C/E
Dm7
C/E
__ ev - 'ry - day.___ Let 'em cry, let 'em gig - gle, let 'em

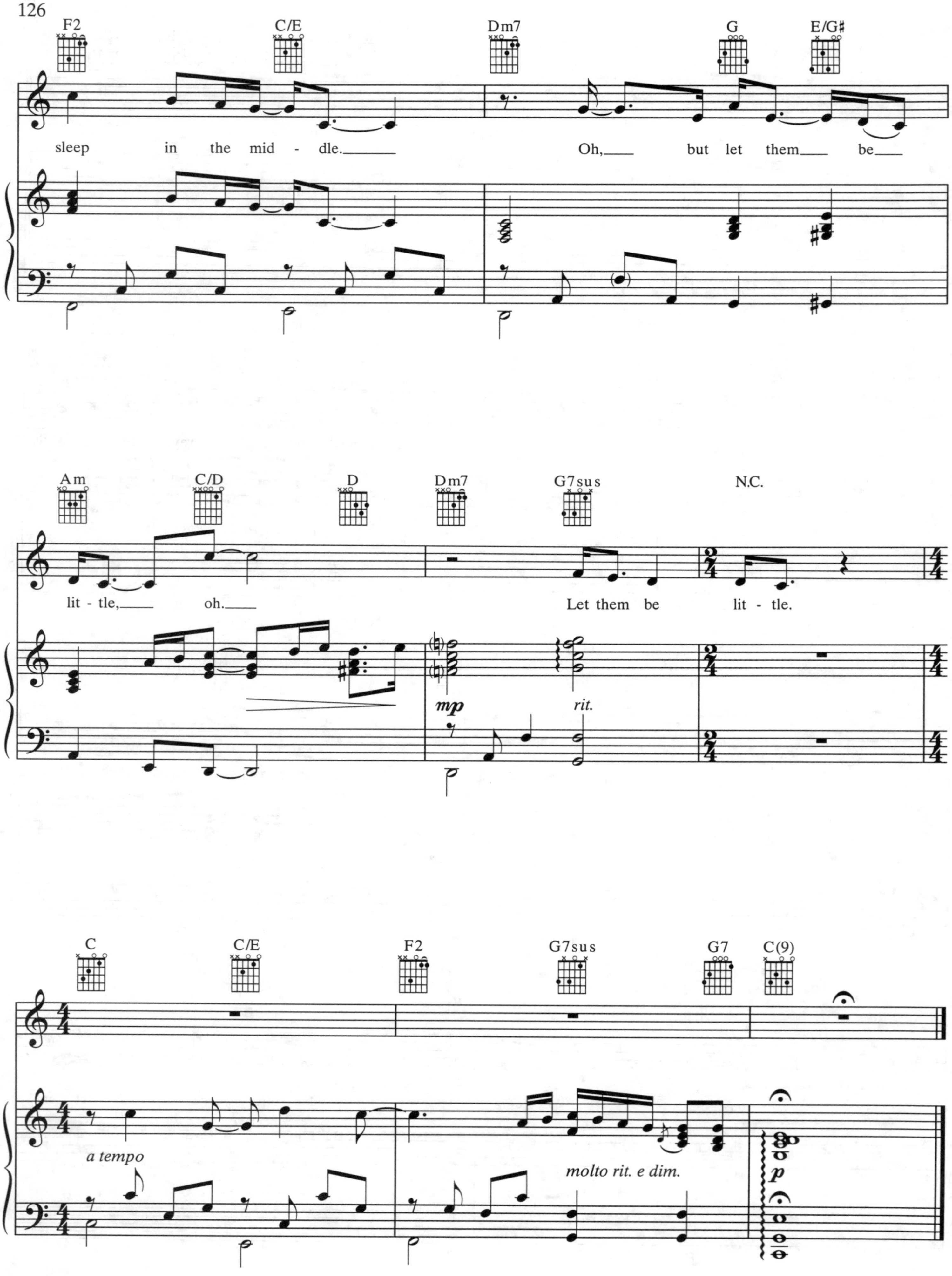
F2
C/E
Dm7
G
E/G♯
sleep in the mid - dle.
Oh, but let them be
Am
C/D
D
Dm7
G7sus
N.C.
lit - tle, oh.
Let them be lit - tle.
mp
rit.
C
C/E
F2
G7sus
G7
C(9)
a tempo
molto rit. e dim.
p

LET'S MAKE SURE WE KISS GOODBYE

Words and Music by
VINCE GILL

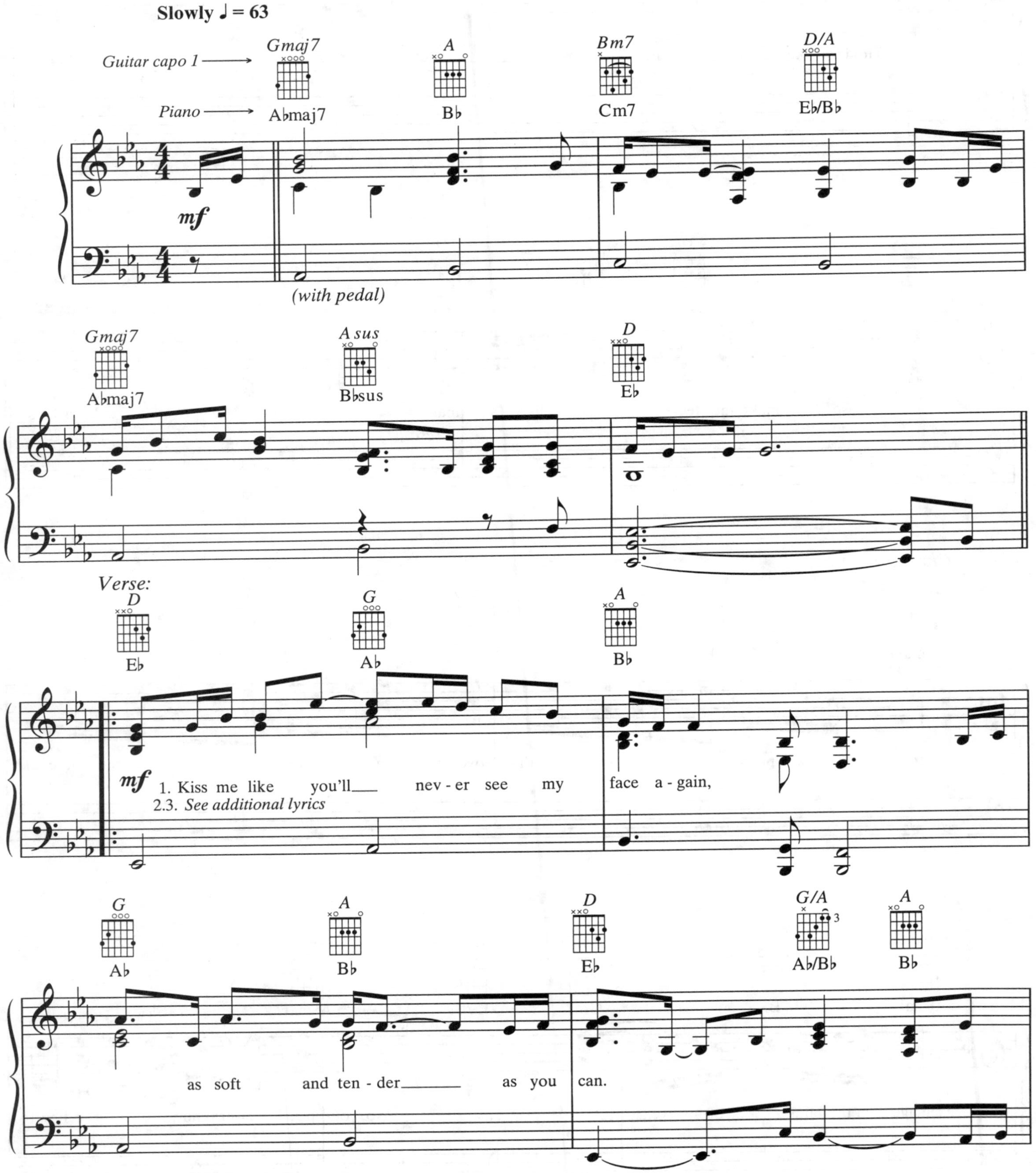

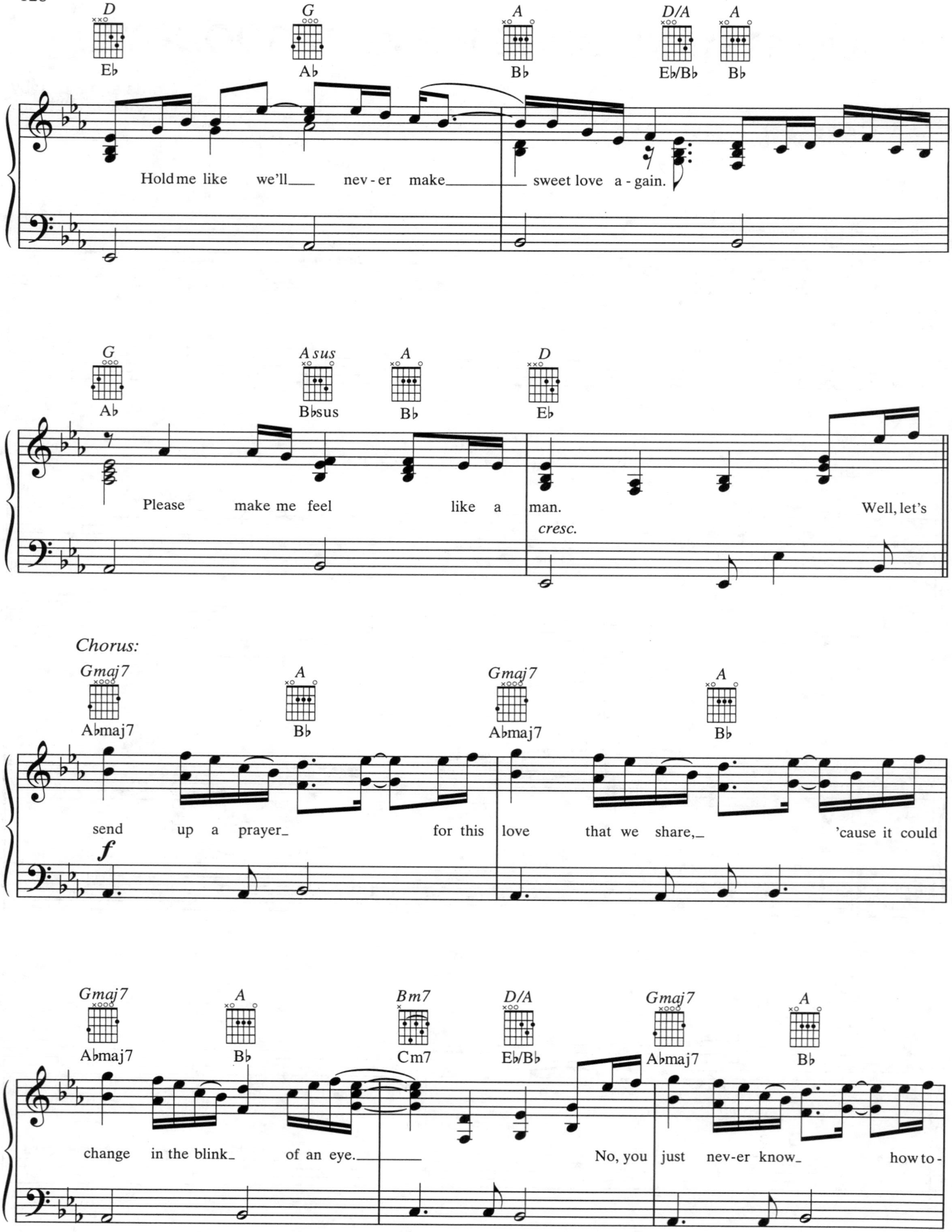
D
G
A
D/A
A
Eb
Ab
Bb
Eb/Bb
Bb
Hold me like we'll never make sweet love again.
G
Asus
A
D
Ab
Bbsus
Bb
Eb
Please make me feel like a man.
cresc.
Well, let's
Chorus:
Gmaj7
A
Gmaj7
A
Abmaj7
Bb
Abmaj7
Bb
send up a prayer for this love that we share, 'cause it could
f
Gmaj7
A
Bm7
D/A
Gmaj7
A
Abmaj7
Bb
Cm7
Eb/Bb
Abmaj7
Bb
change in the blink of an eye. No, you just never know how to-

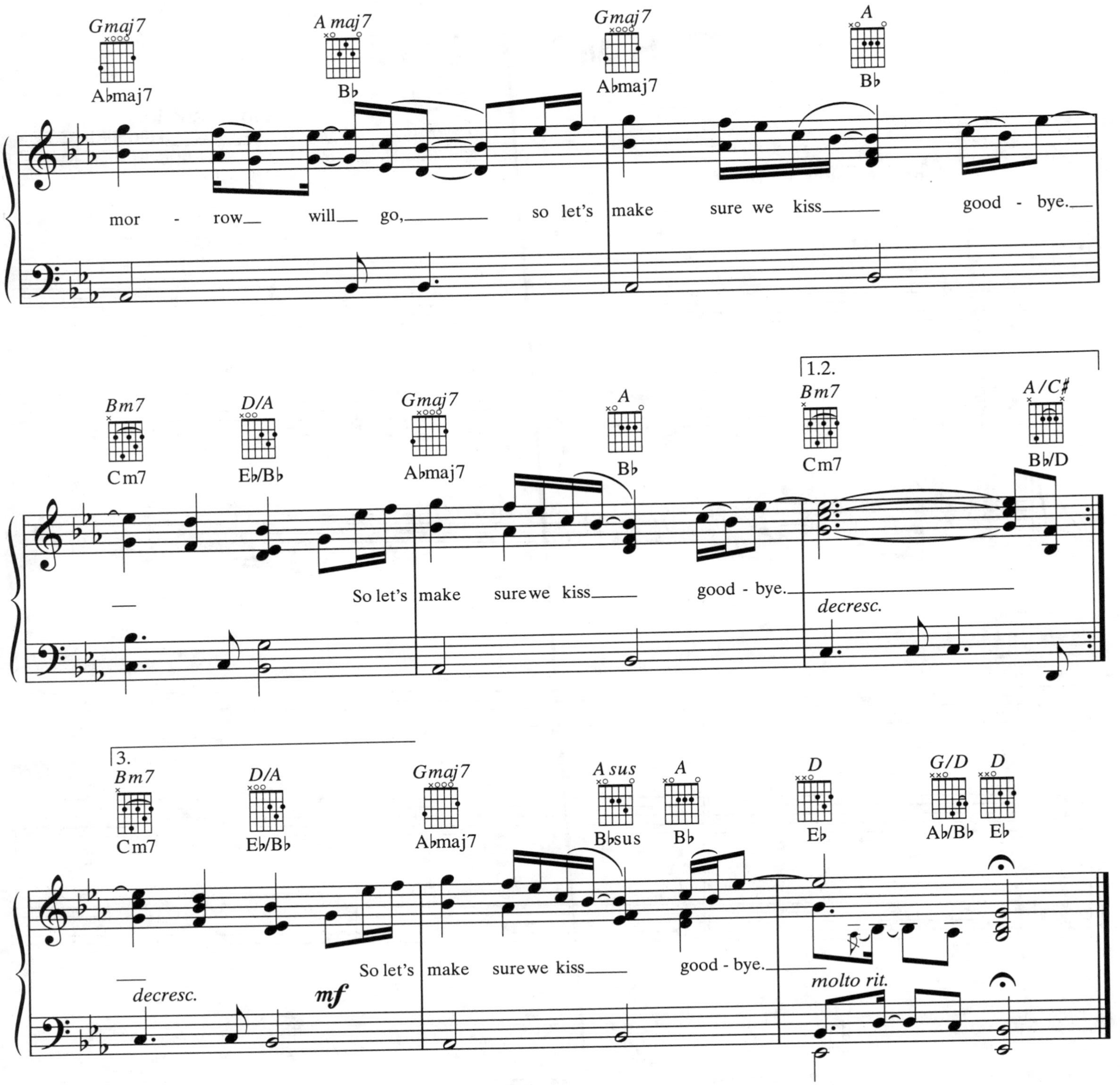

Verse 2:
Look at me just like the day we fell in love
And found the missing pieces to our soul.
You and me have always been just like the birds:
Wherever you are feels like home.
(To Chorus:)

Verse 3:
(Instrumental solo ad lib.)
(To Chorus:)

LET'S MAKE LOVE

Words and Music by
MARV GREEN, CHRIS LINDSEY,
BILL LUTHER and AIMEE MAYO

F/A
Gm
B♭/F
E♭
touch-ing you.
The on - ly thing I want to do is
B♭/F
F
E♭
E♭6
be with you,
as close to you
as I can
Chorus:
E♭maj7
B♭
F
be.
Let's make love
all night long,
un - til
mf
Gm
E♭
B♭
all our strength is gone.
Hold on tight,
just let

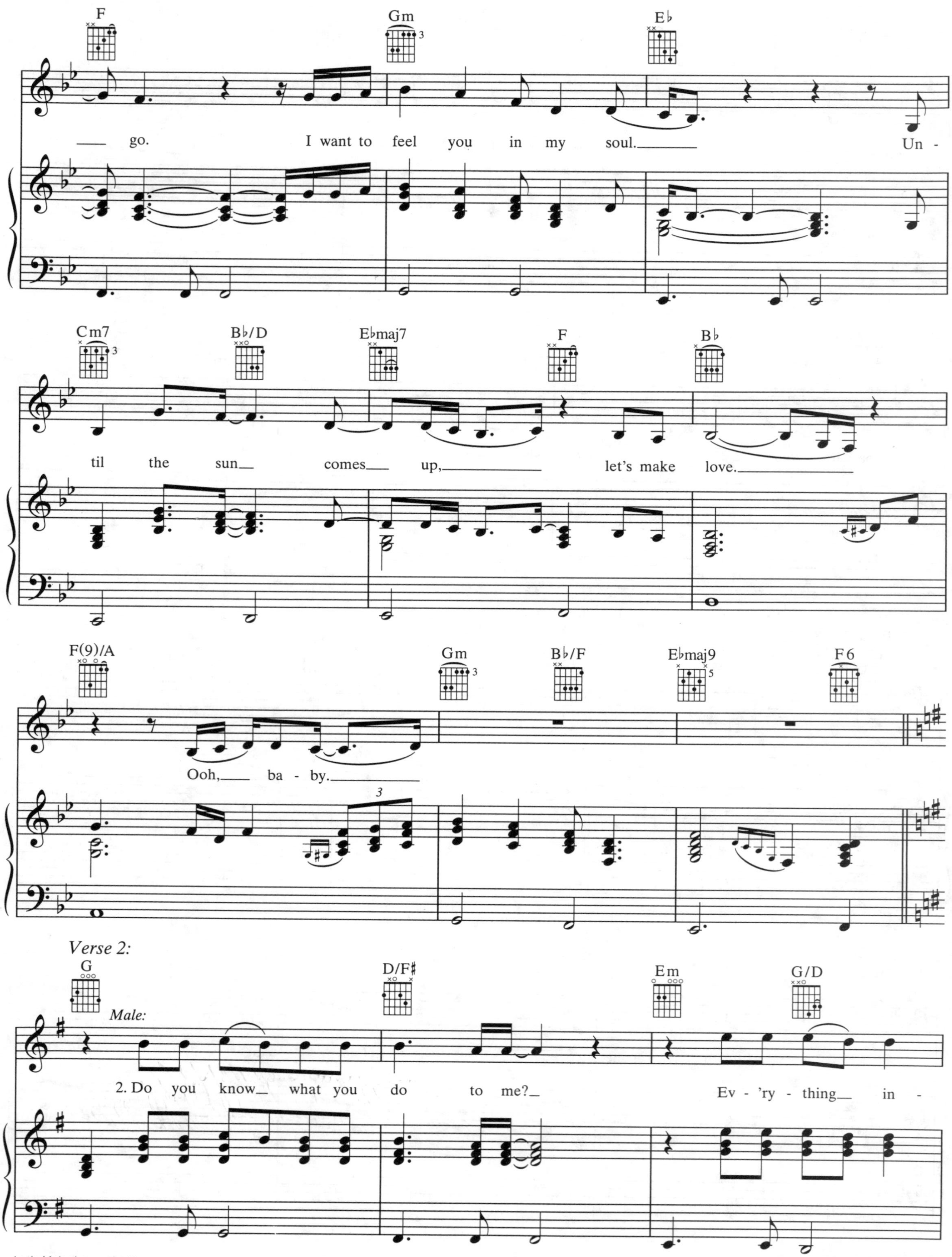
F
Gm
E♭
go. I want to feel you in my soul. Un -
Cm7
B♭/D
E♭maj7
F
B♭
til the sun comes up, let's make love.
F(9)/A
Gm
B♭/F
E♭maj9
F6
Ooh, ba - by.
3
Verse 2:
G
D/F♯
Em
G/D
Male:
2. Do you know what you do to me? Ev - 'ry - thing in -

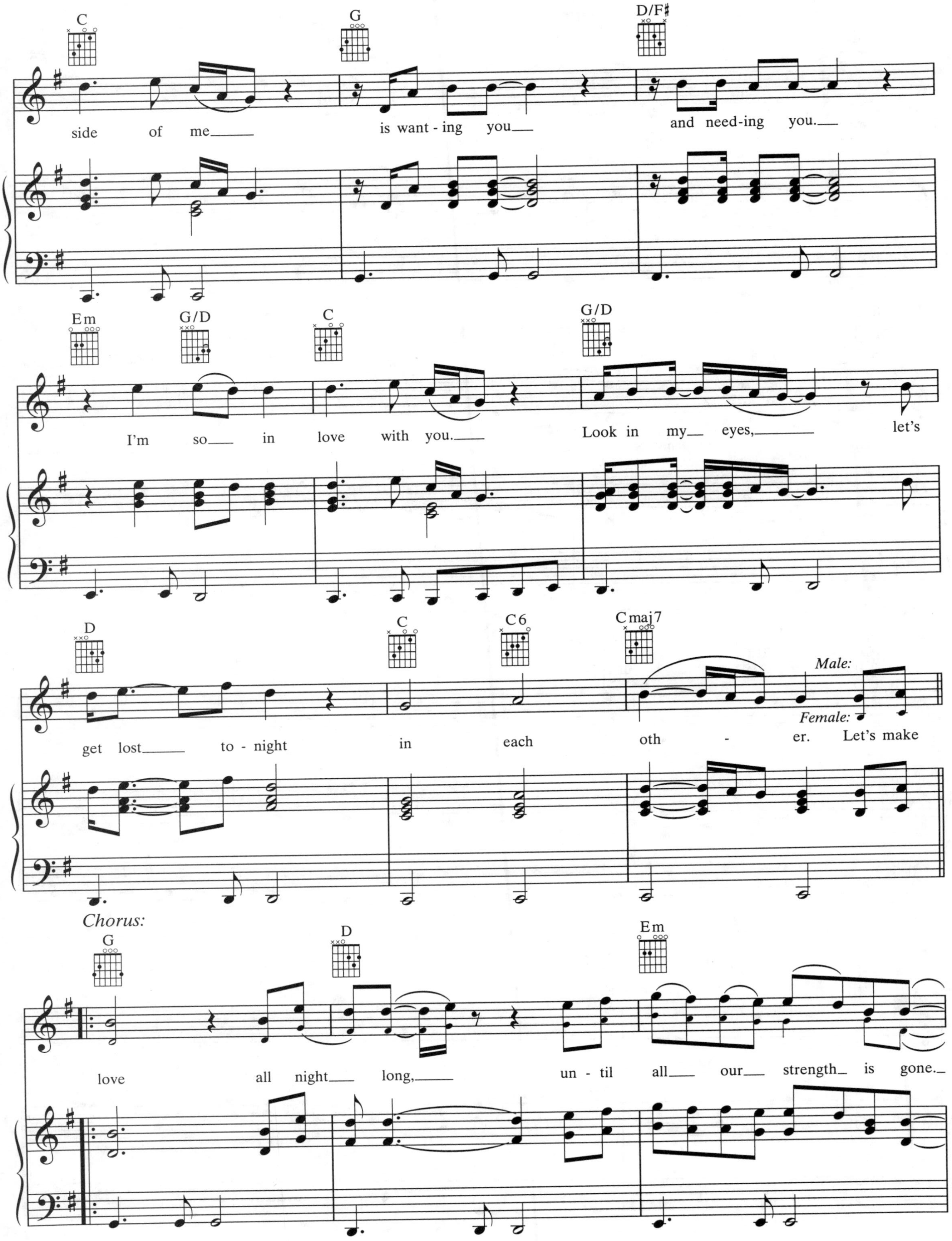
C
G
D/F♯
side of me___ is want - ing you___ and need-ing you.___
Em
G/D
C
G/D
I'm so___ in love with you.___ Look in my___ eyes,___ let's
D
C
C6
Cmaj7
Male:
Female:
get lost___ to - night in each oth - er. Let's make
Chorus:
G
D
Em
love all night___ long,___ un - til all___ our___ strength_ is gone._

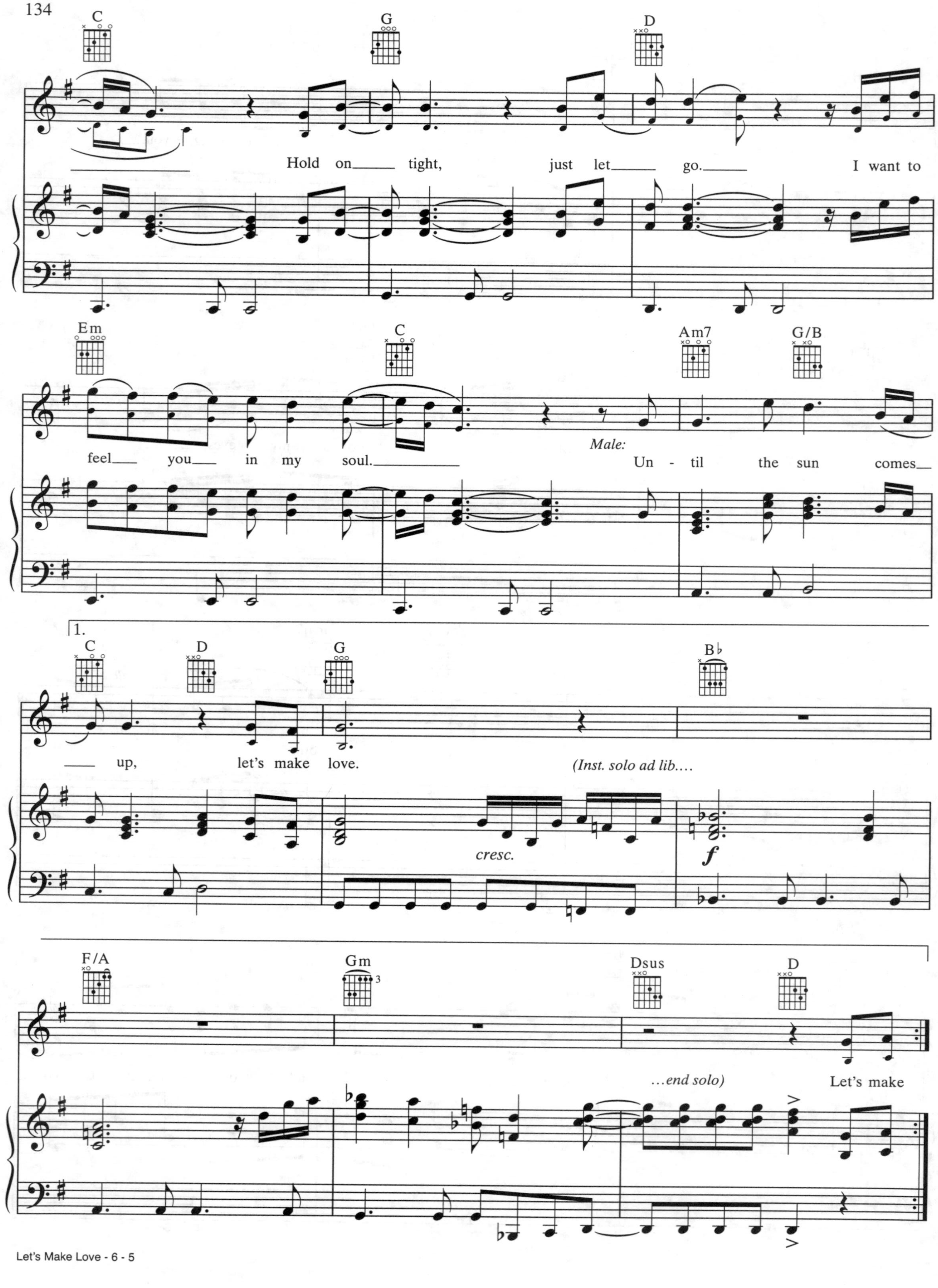
C
G
D
Hold on___ tight,
just let___ go.___
I want to
Em
C
Am7
G/B
feel___ you___ in my soul.___
Male:
Un - til the sun comes___
1.
C
D
G
B♭
___ up,
let's make love.
(Inst. solo ad lib....
cresc.
f
F/A
Gm
Dsus
D
...end solo)
Let's make

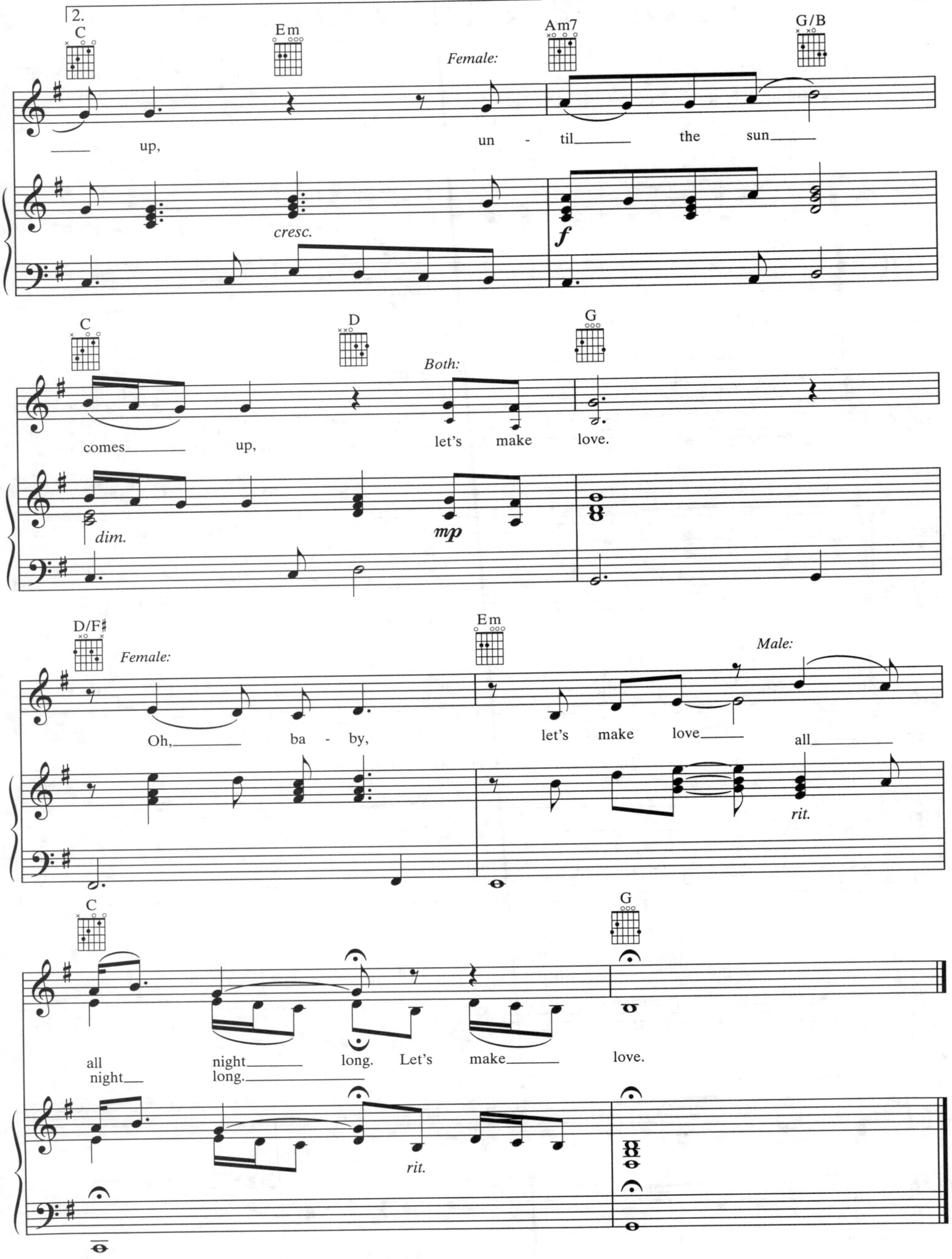
2.
C
Em
Am7
G/B
Female:
up,
un - til the sun
cresc.
f
C
D
G
Both:
comes up, let's make love.
dim.
mp
D/F♯
Em
Female:
Male:
Oh, ba - by, let's make love all
rit.
C
G
all night long. Let's make love.
night long.
rit.

LIKE WE NEVER LOVED AT ALL

Words and Music by
JOHN RICH, VICKY McGEHEE
and SCOTT SACKS

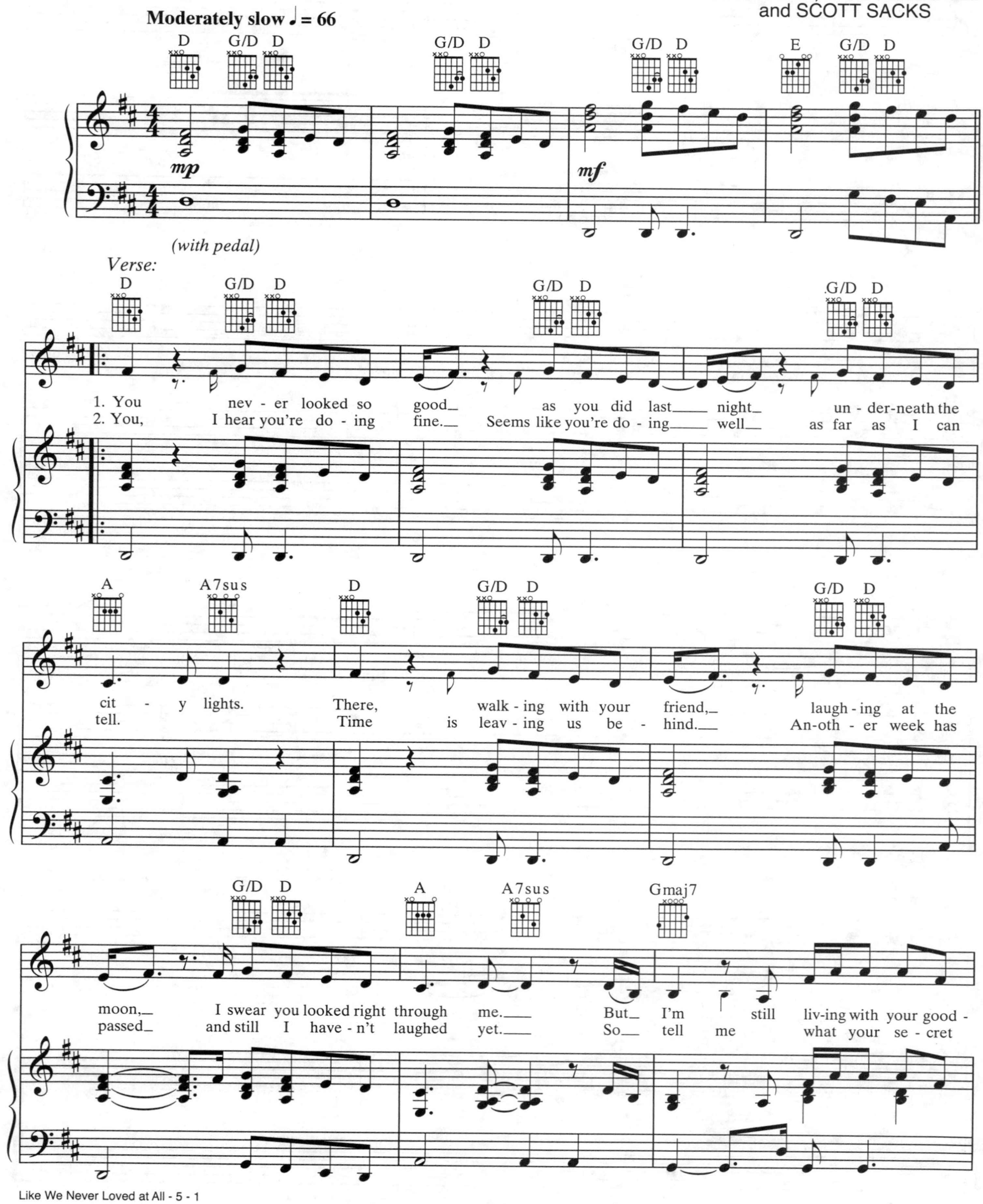

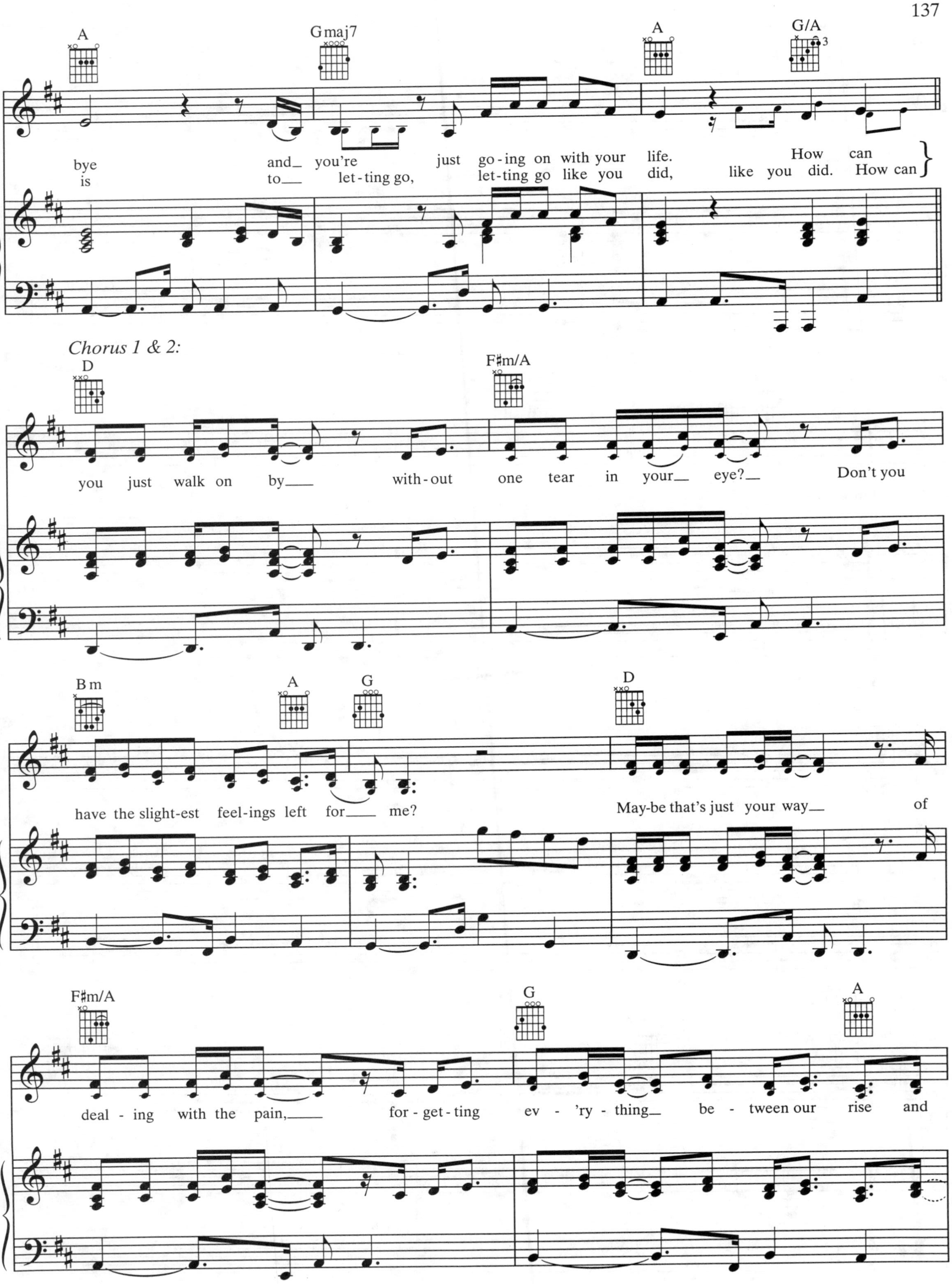
A
Gmaj7
A
G/A
bye and_ you're just go-ing on with your life. How can
is to_ let-ting go, let-ting go like you did, like you did. How can
Chorus 1 & 2:
D
F♯m/A
you just walk on by_ with-out one tear in your_ eye?_ Don't you
Bm
A
G
D
have the slight-est feel-ings left for_ me? May-be that's just your way_ of
F♯m/A
G
A
deal - ing with the pain,_ for - get - ting ev - 'ry - thing_ be - tween our rise and

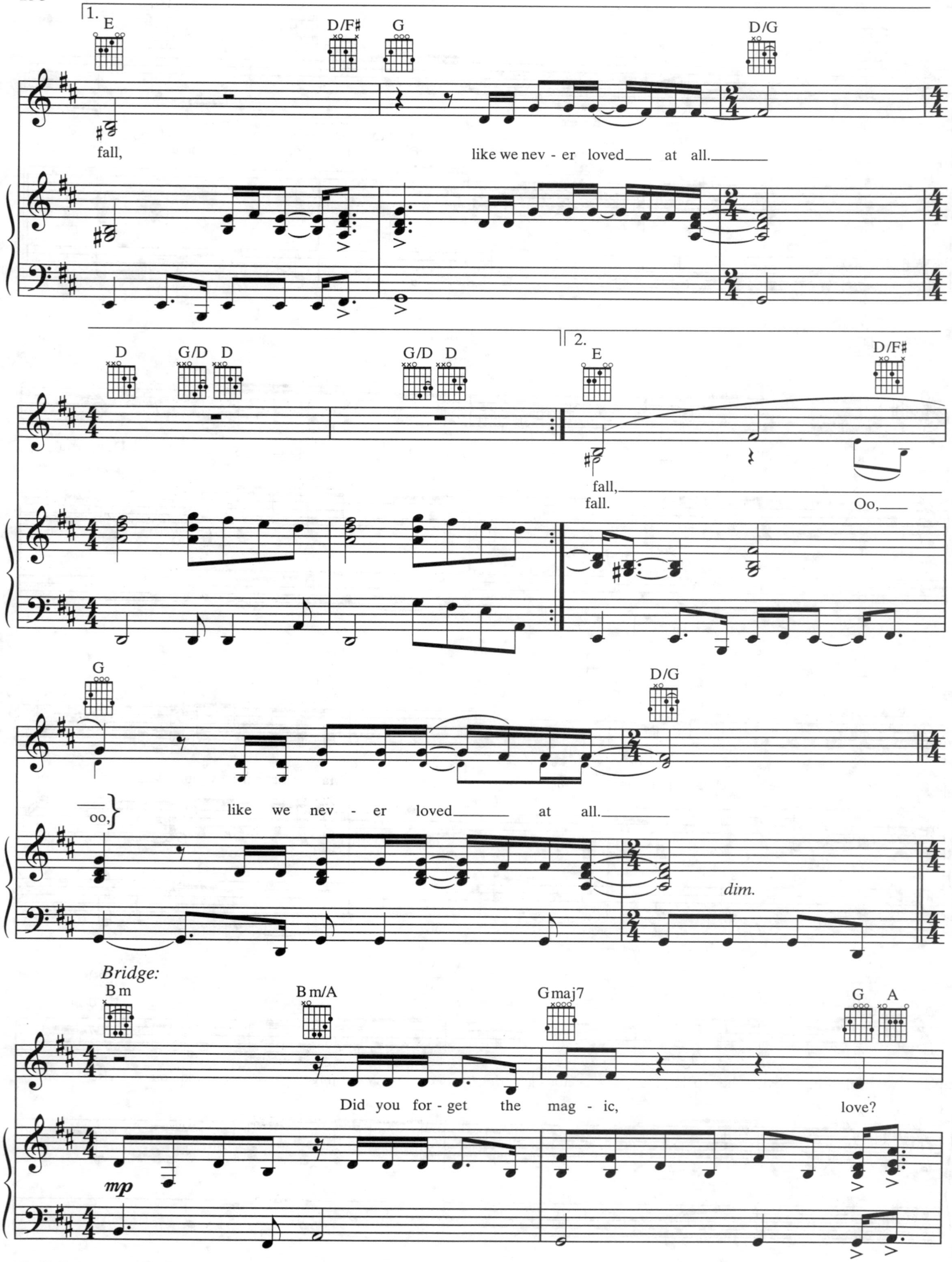
1.
E
D/F♯
G
D/G
fall,
like we nev - er loved at all.
D
G/D
D
G/D
D
2.
E
D/F♯
fall,
fall.
Oo,
G
D/G
oo,
like we nev - er loved at all.
dim.
Bridge:
Bm
Bm/A
Gmaj7
G
A
mp
Did you for - get the mag - ic, love?

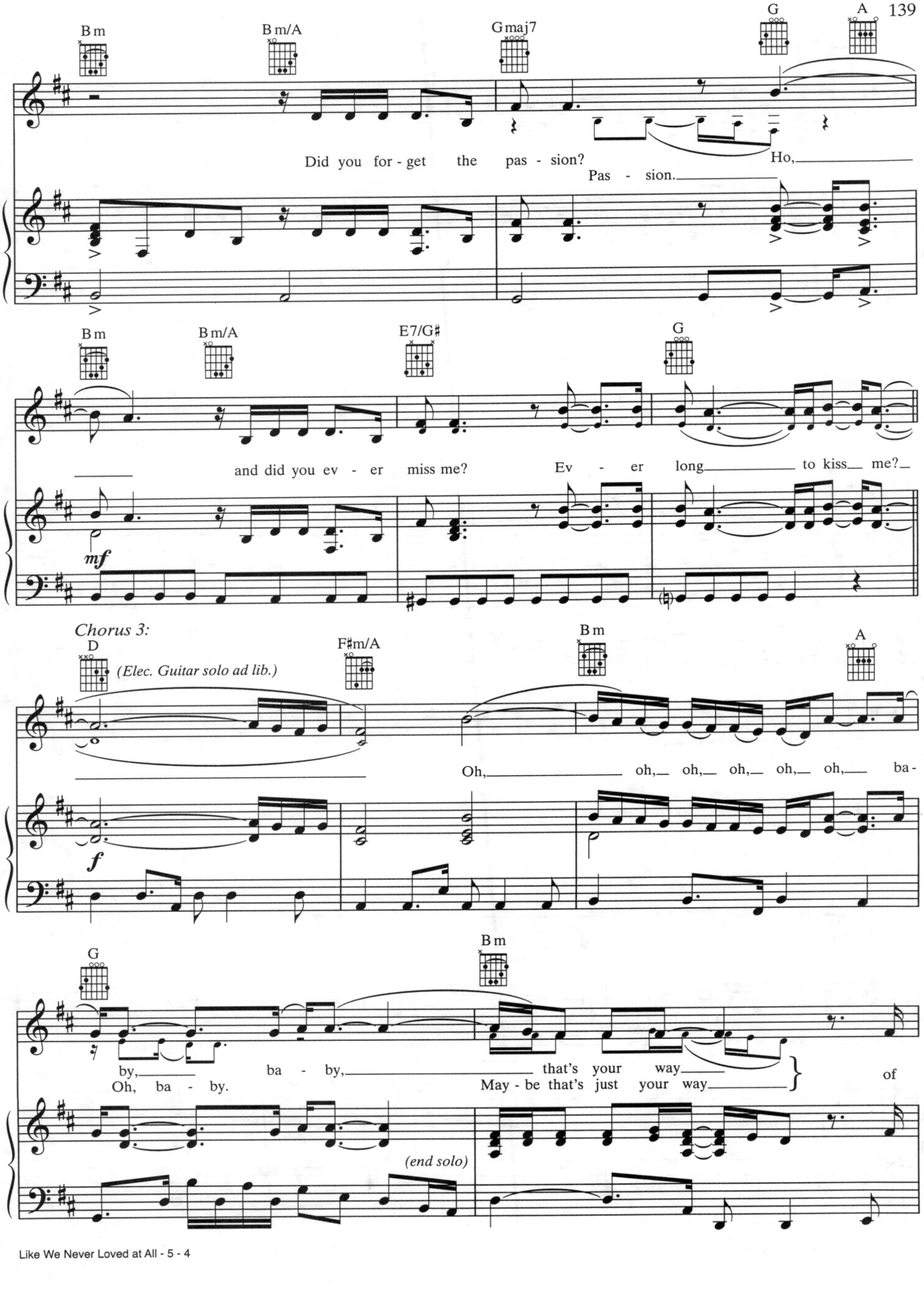
Bm
Bm/A
Gmaj7
G
A
Did you for - get the pas - sion? Ho,
Pas - sion.
Bm
Bm/A
E7/G♯
G
and did you ev - er miss me? Ev - er long to kiss me?
mf
Chorus 3:
D
(Elec. Guitar solo ad lib.)
F♯m/A
Bm
A
Oh, oh, oh, oh, oh, oh, ba -
f
G
Bm
by, ba - by, that's your way
Oh, ba - by. May - be that's just your way
of
(end solo)

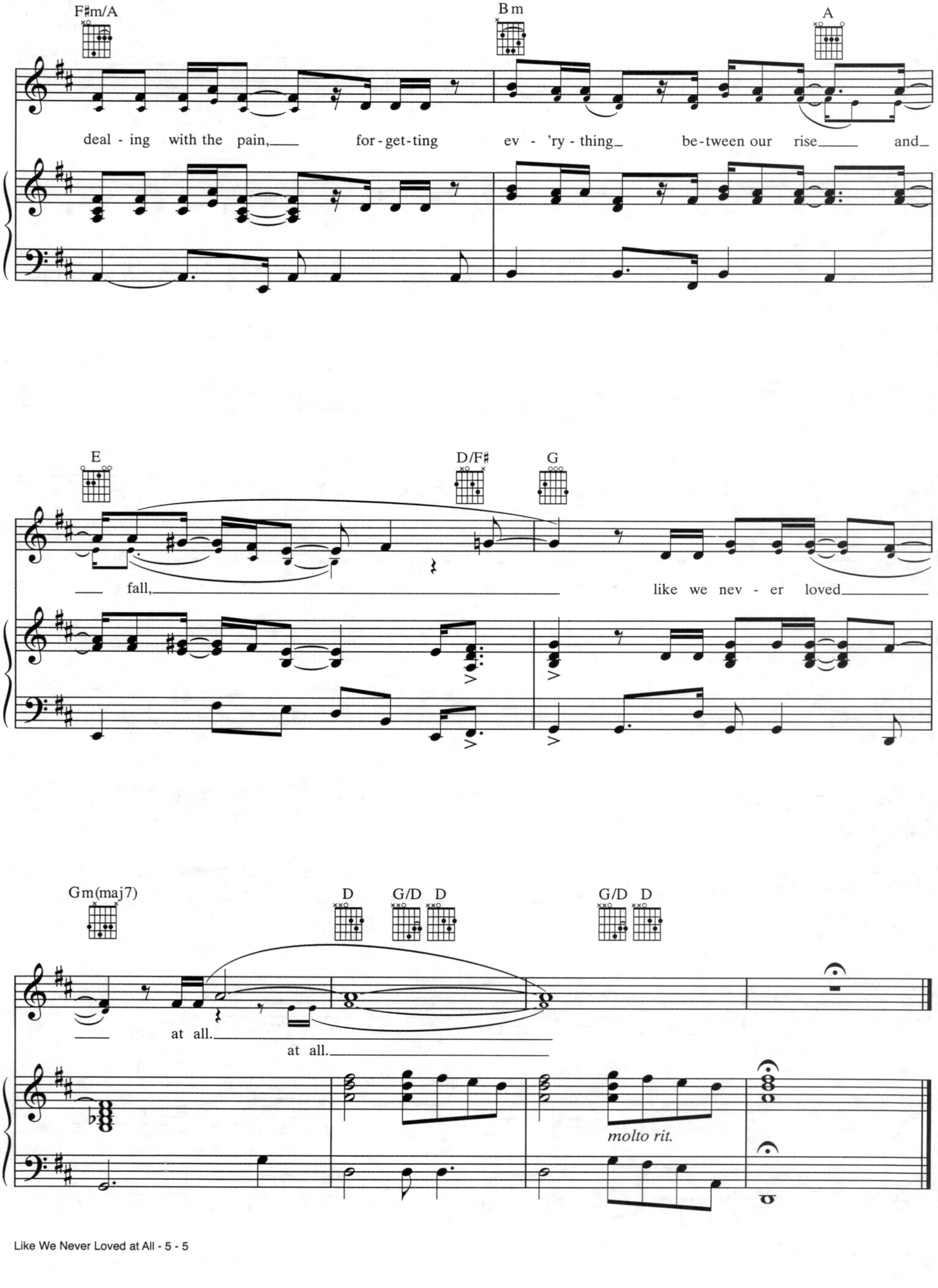
F♯m/A
Bm
A
deal - ing with the pain,
for - get - ting
ev - 'ry - thing
be - tween our rise
and
E
D/F♯
G
fall,
like we nev - er loved
Gm(maj7)
D
G/D
D
G/D
D
at all.
at all.
molto rit.

LIVE LIKE YOU WERE DYING

Words and Music by
TIM NICHOLS and
CRAIG WISEMAN

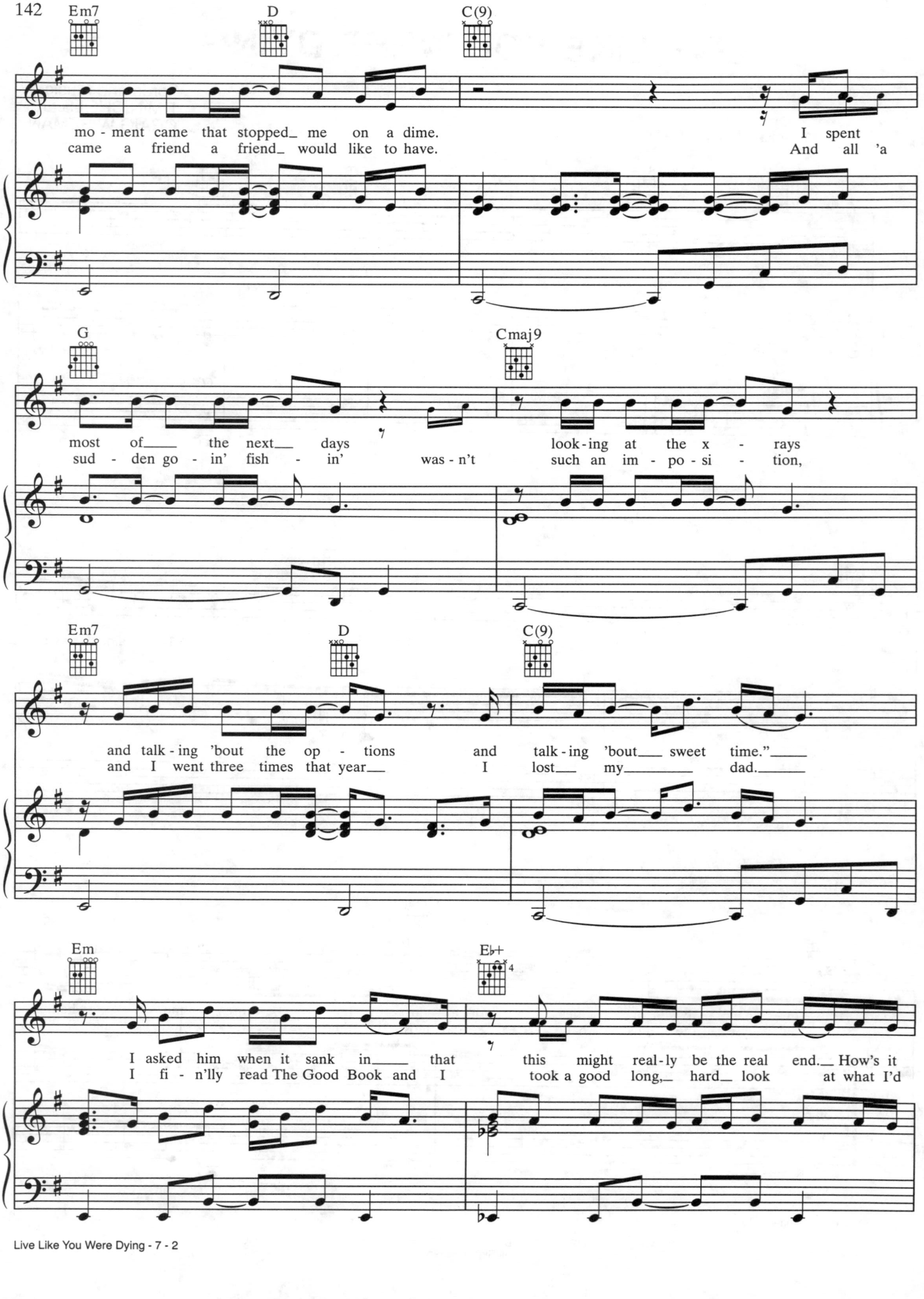
Em7
D
C(9)
mo - ment came that stopped_ me on a dime. I spent
came a friend a friend_ would like to have. And all 'a
G
Cmaj9
most of___ the next__ days looking at the x - rays
sud - den go - in' fish - in' was - n't such an im - po - si - tion,
Em7
D
C(9)
and talk - ing 'bout the op - tions and talk - ing 'bout__ sweet time." ____
and I went three times that year__ I lost__ my______ dad.____
Em
E♭+
4
I asked him when it sank in____ that this might real - ly be the real end.__ How's it
I fi - n'lly read The Good Book and I took a good long,_ hard_ look at what I'd

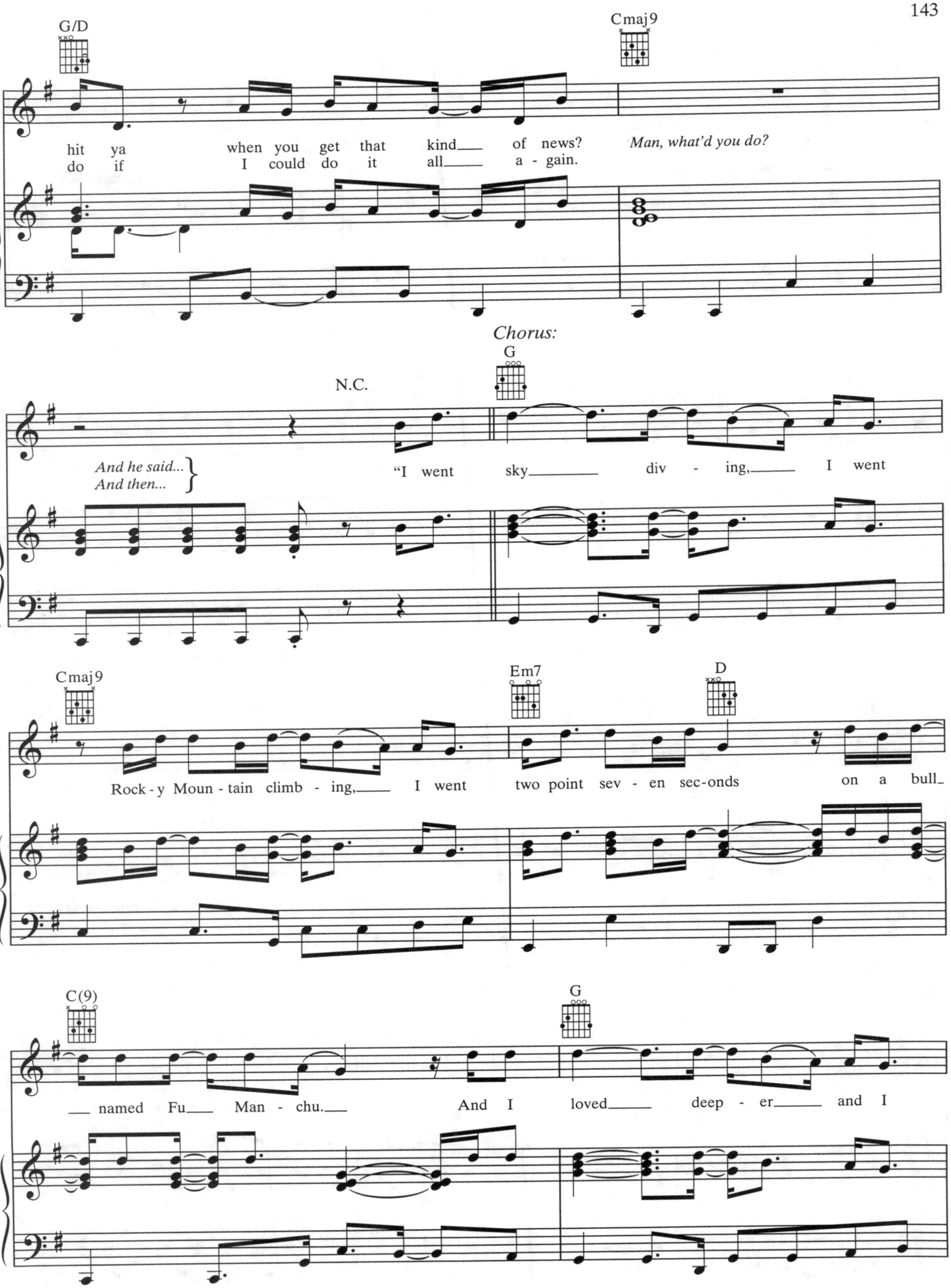
G/D
Cmaj9
hit ya when you get that kind of news?
do if I could do it all a - gain.
Man, what'd you do?
Chorus:
N.C.
G
And he said...
And then...
"I went sky div - ing, I went
Cmaj9
Em7
D
Rock - y Moun - tain climb - ing, I went two point sev - en sec - onds on a bull
C(9)
G
named Fu Man - chu. And I loved deep - er and I

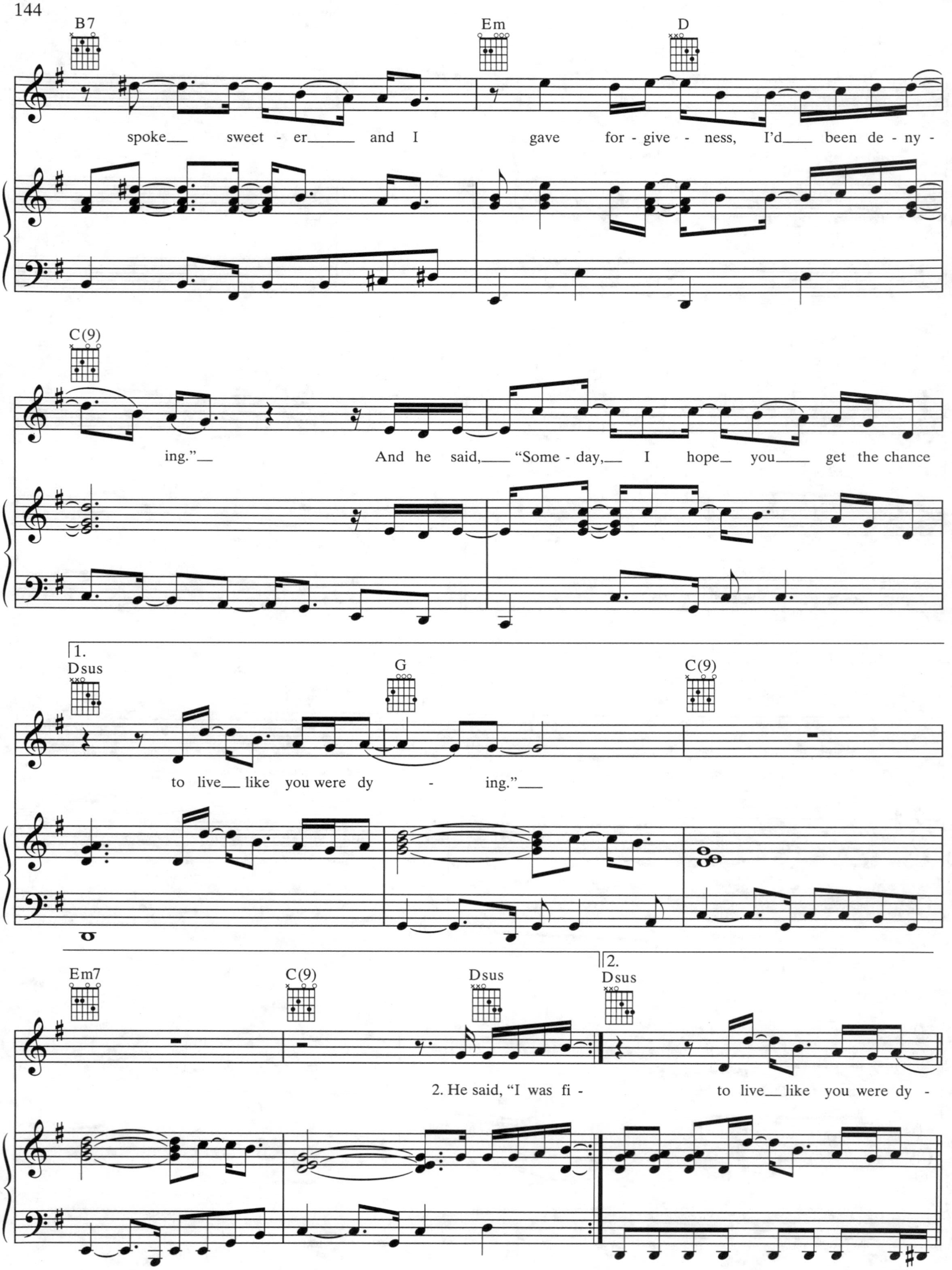
B7
Em
D
spoke__ sweet - er___ and I gave for - give - ness, I'd__ been de - ny -
C(9)
ing."__ And he said,___ "Some - day,__ I hope_ you___ get the chance
1.
Dsus
G
C(9)
to live__ like you were dy - ing."___
Em7
C(9)
Dsus
2.
Dsus
2. He said, "I was fi -
to live__ like you were dy -

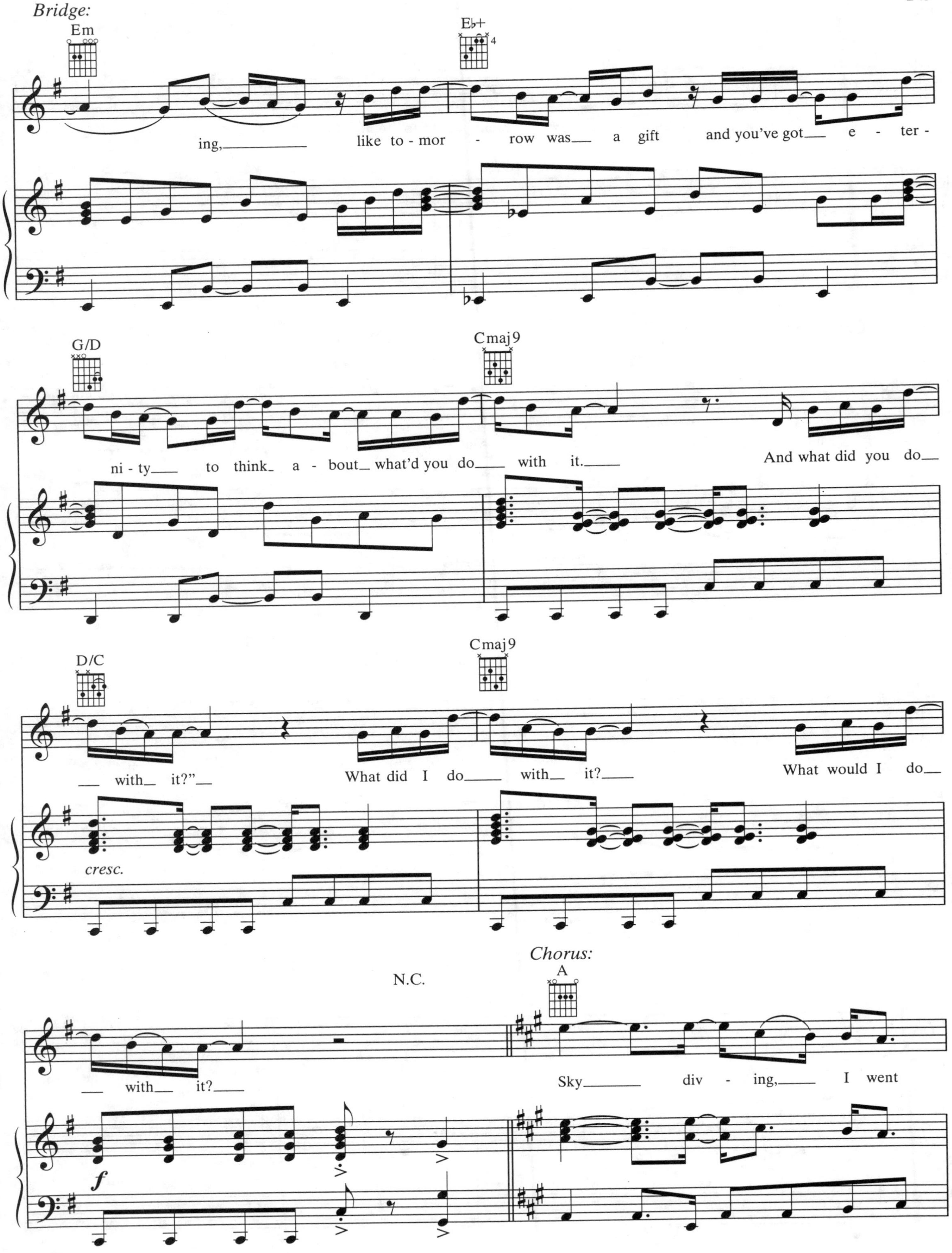
Bridge:
Em
E♭+
ing, like to - mor - row was a gift and you've got e - ter -
G/D
Cmaj9
ni - ty to think a - bout what'd you do with it.
And what did you do
D/C
Cmaj9
with it?"
What did I do with it?
What would I do
cresc.
N.C.
Chorus:
A
with it?
Sky div - ing, I went
f

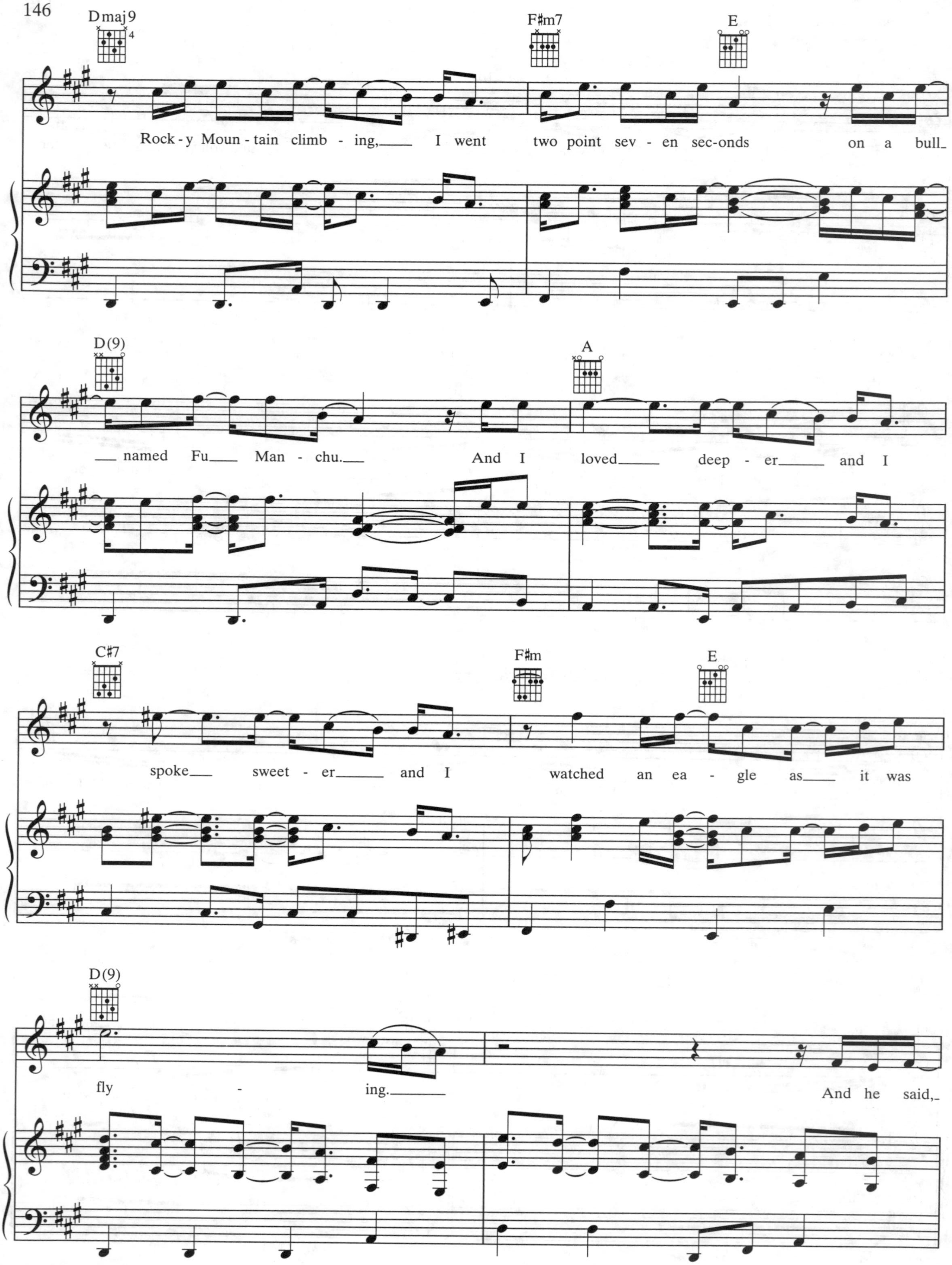
Dmaj9
F♯m7
E
Rock-y Moun-tain climb - ing, I went two point sev - en sec-onds on a bull
D(9)
A
named Fu Man - chu. And I loved deep - er and I
C♯7
F♯m
E
spoke sweet - er and I watched an ea - gle as it was
D(9)
fly - ing. And he said,

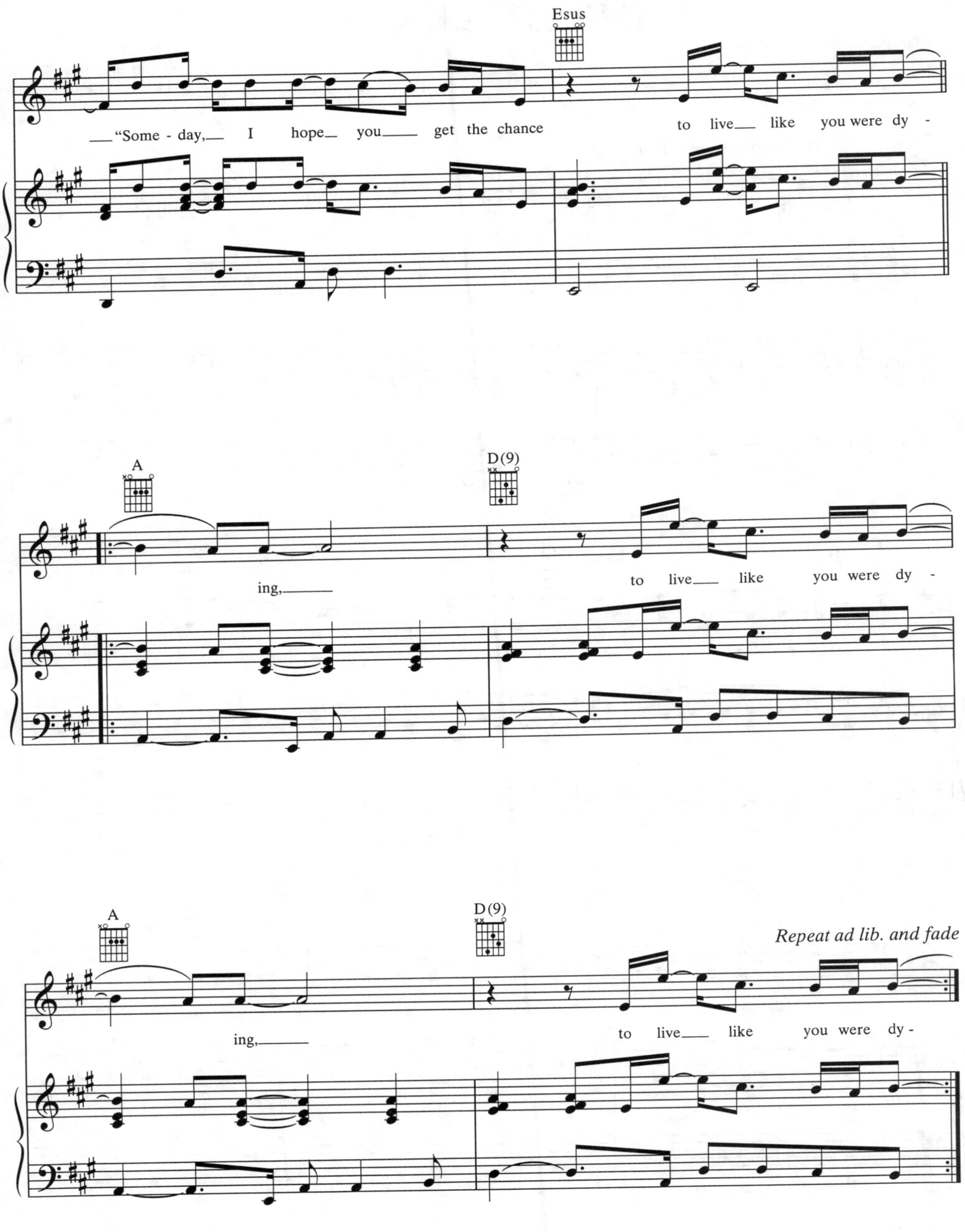
Esus
"Some - day, I hope you get the chance to live like you were dy -
A
D(9)
ing, to live like you were dy -
A
D(9)
Repeat ad lib. and fade
ing, to live like you were dy -

THE LITTLE GIRL

Tune guitar down 1/2 step, "drop D"
⑥ = D♭ ③ = G♭
⑤ = A♭ ② = B♭
④ = D♭ ① = E♭

Words and Music by
HARLEY ALLEN

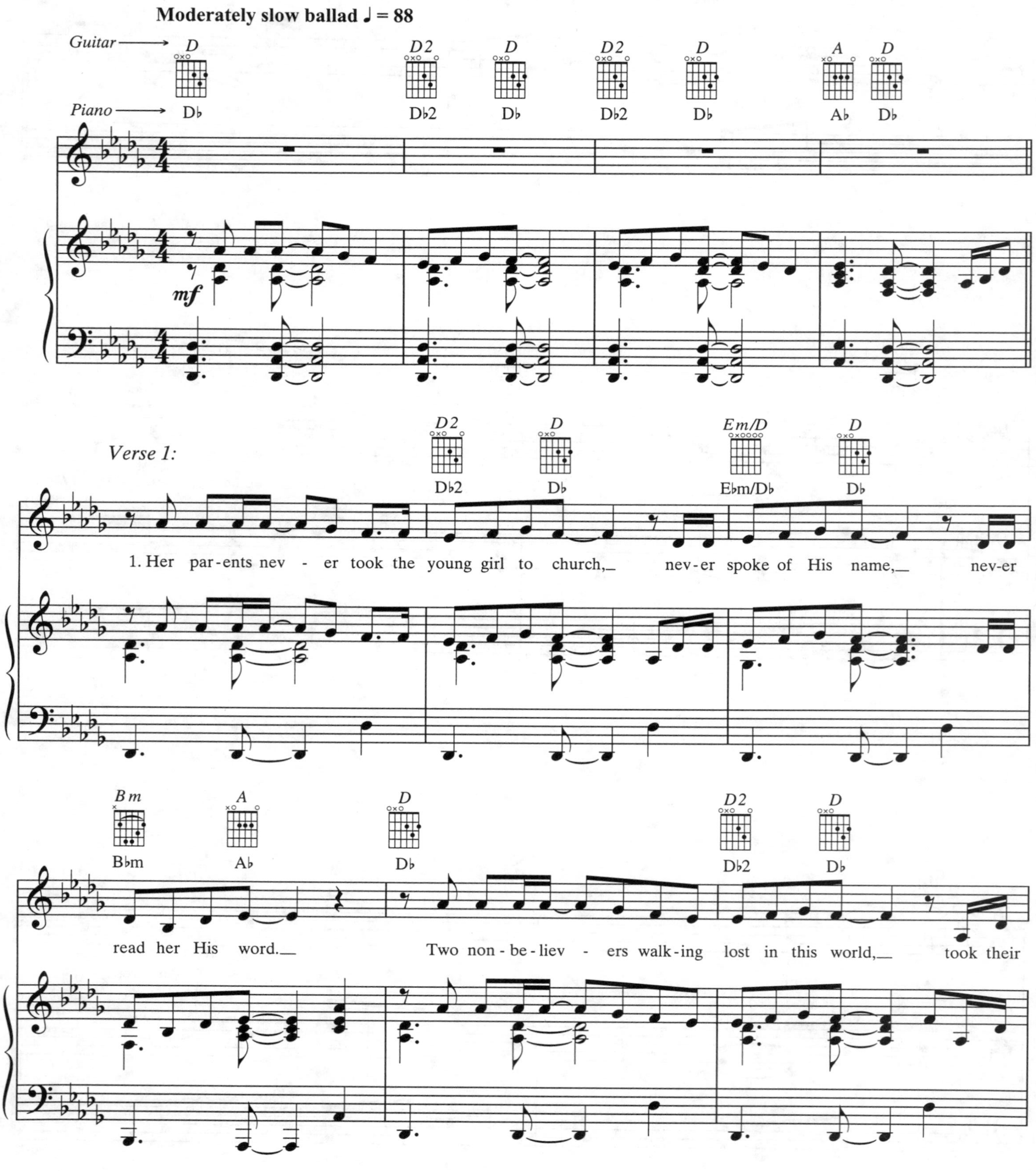
Moderately slow ballad ♩ = 88
Guitar
Piano
D D2 D D2 D A D
D♭ D♭2 D♭ D♭2 D♭ A♭ D♭
mf
Verse 1:
D2 D Em/D D
D♭2 D♭ E♭m/D♭ D♭
1. Her par-ents nev - er took the young girl to church,__ nev-er spoke of His name,__ nev-er
Bm A D D2 D
B♭m A♭ D♭ D♭2 D♭
read her His word.__ Two non-be-liev - ers walk-ing lost in this world,__ took their

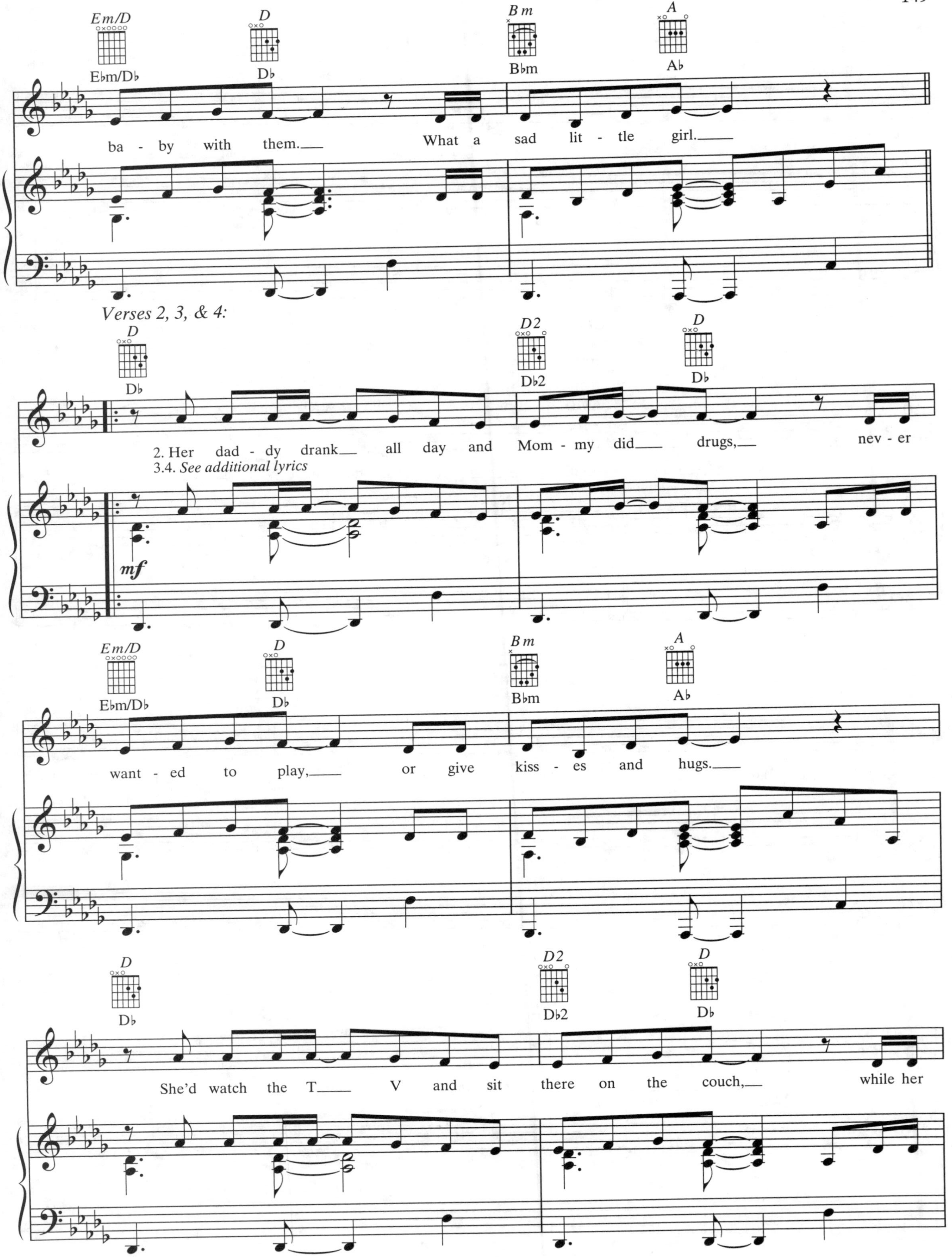
Em/D
D
Bm
A
E♭m/D♭
D♭
B♭m
A♭
ba - by with them.
What a sad lit - tle girl.
Verses 2, 3, & 4:
D
D2
D
D♭
D♭2
D♭
2. Her dad - dy drank all day and Mom - my did drugs, nev - er
3.4. See additional lyrics
mf
Em/D
D
Bm
A
E♭m/D♭
D♭
B♭m
A♭
want - ed to play, or give kiss - es and hugs.
D
D2
D
D♭
D♭2
D♭
She'd watch the T V and sit there on the couch, while her

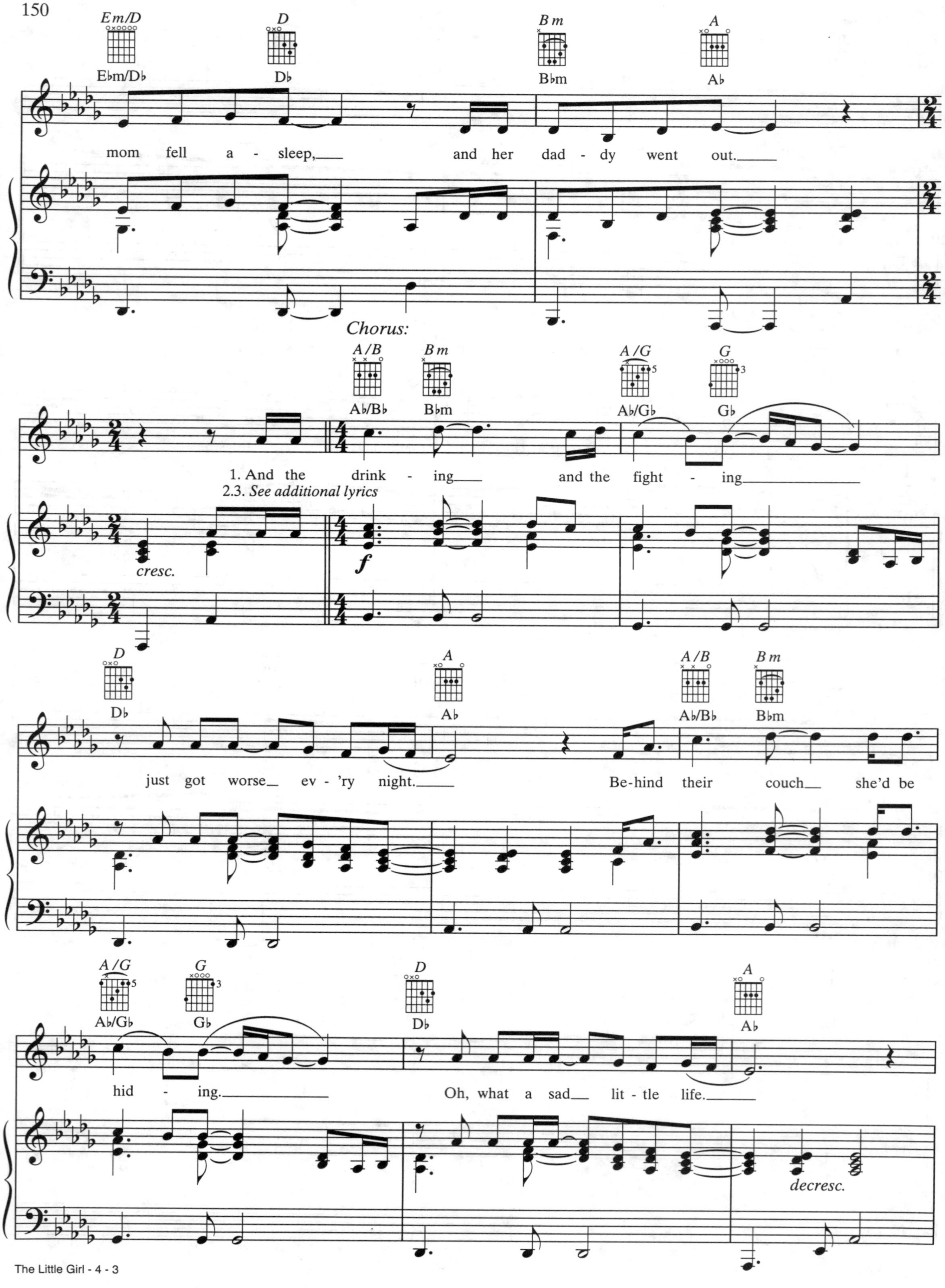
Em/D
D
Bm
A
Ebm/Db
Db
Bbm
Ab
mom fell a - sleep,
and her dad - dy went out.
Chorus:
A/B
Bm
A/G
G
Ab/Bb
Bbm
Ab/Gb
Gb
1. And the drink - ing
and the fight - ing
2.3. See additional lyrics
cresc.
f
D
A
A/B
Bm
Db
Ab
Ab/Bb
Bbm
just got worse ev - 'ry night.
Be-hind their couch she'd be
A/G
G
D
A
Ab/Gb
Gb
Db
Ab
hid - ing.
Oh, what a sad lit - tle life.
decresc.

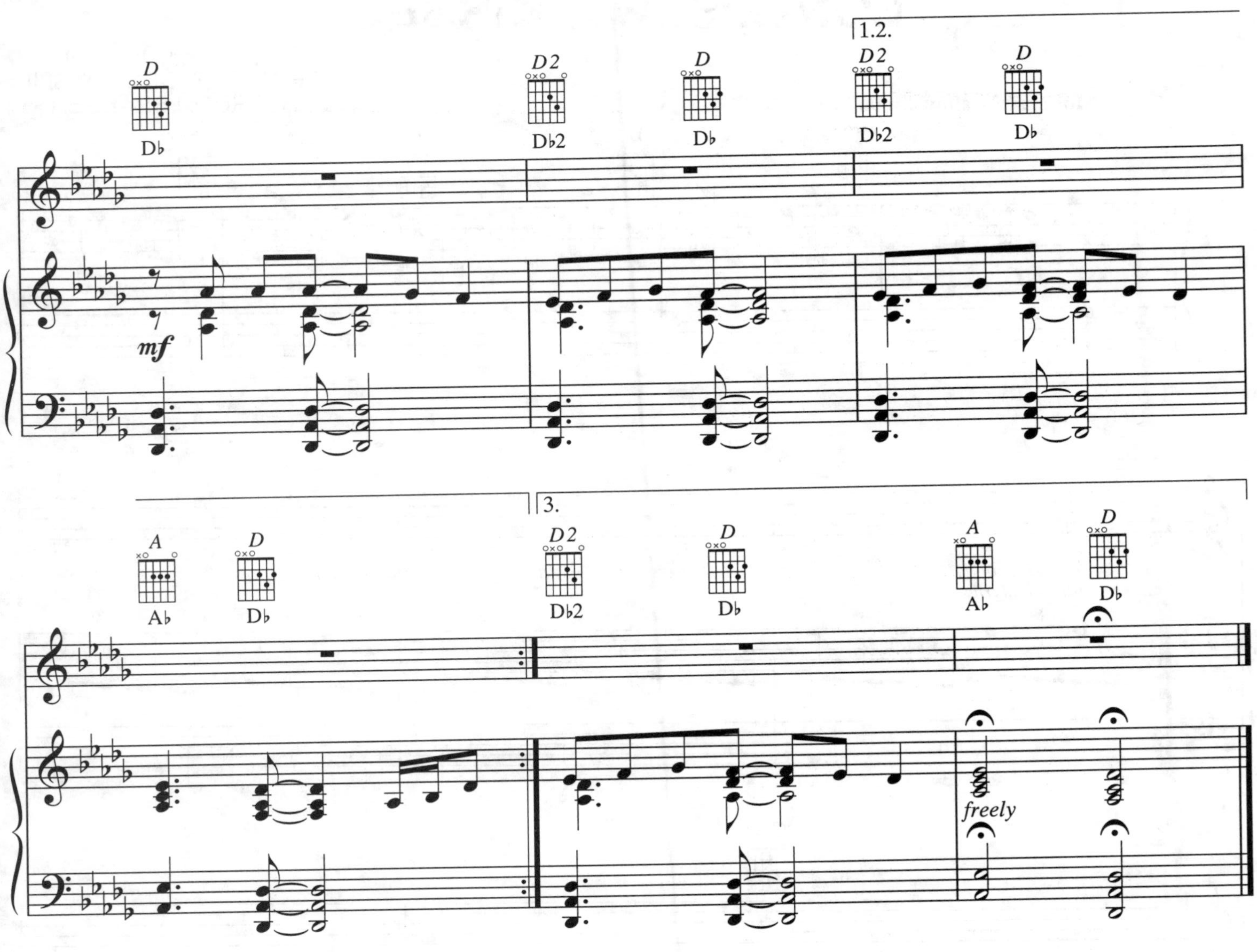

Verse 3:
And like it always does, the bad just got worse,
With every slap and every curse,
Until her daddy, in a drunk rage one night,
Used a gun on her mom and then took his life.

Chorus 2:
And some people from the city
Took the girl far away
To a new mom and a new dad,
Kisses and hugs every day.

Verse 4:
Her first day of Sunday school, the teacher walked in,
And a small little girl stared at a picture of Him.
She said, "I know that man up there on that cross.
I don't know his name, but I know he got off."

Chorus 3:
"'Cause He was there in my old house
And held me close to His side
As I hid there behind our couch
The night that my parents died."

LONG, SLOW KISSES

Words and Music by
JEFF BATES, BEN HAYSLIP
and GORDON BRADBERRY

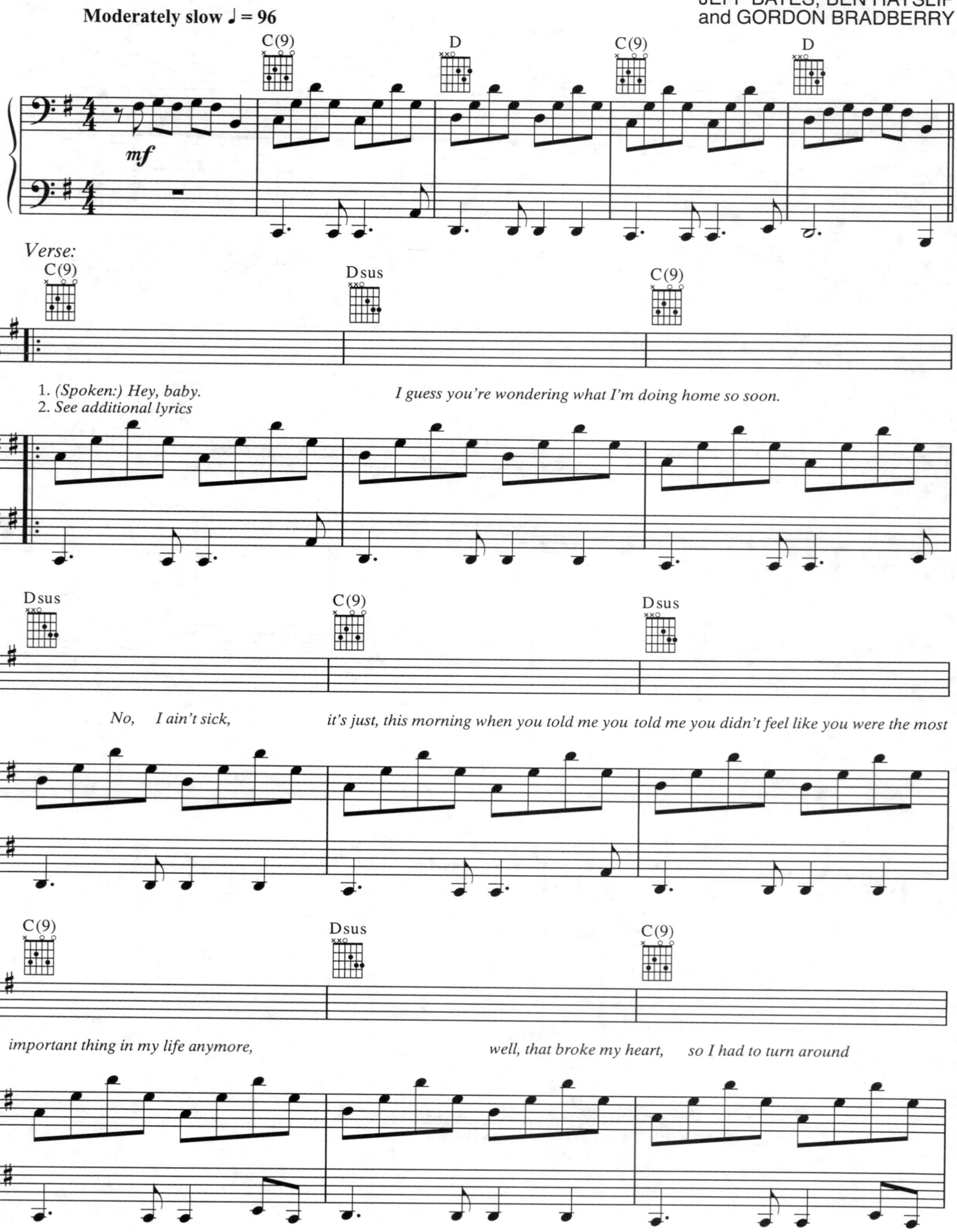
Moderately slow ♩ = 96
C(9)
D
C(9)
D
mf
Verse:
C(9)
Dsus
C(9)
1. (Spoken:) Hey, baby.
2. See additional lyrics
I guess you're wondering what I'm doing home so soon.
Dsus
C(9)
Dsus
No, I ain't sick,
it's just, this morning when you told me you told me you didn't feel like you were the most
C(9)
Dsus
C(9)
important thing in my life anymore,
well, that broke my heart, so I had to turn around

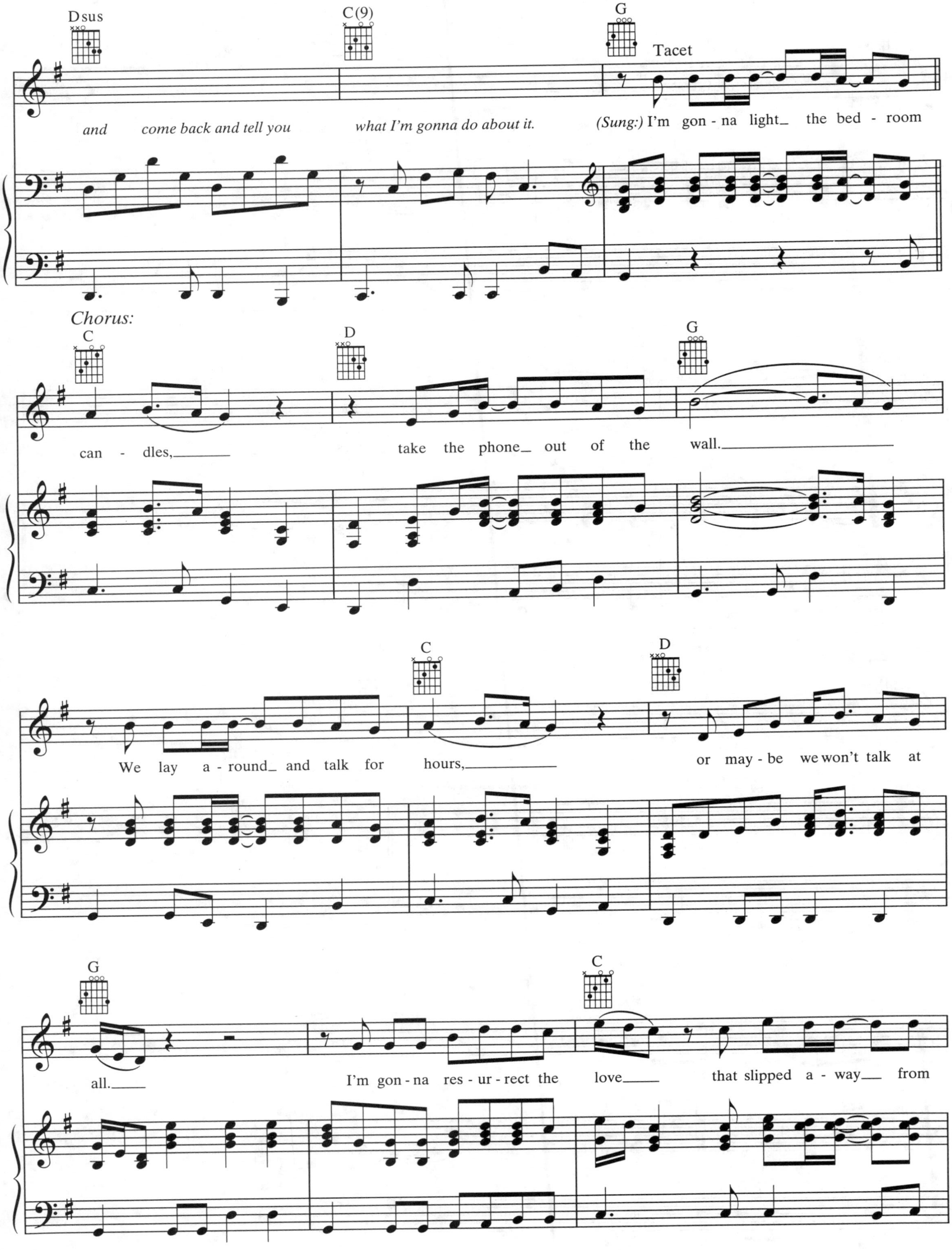
Dsus
C(9)
G
Tacet
and come back and tell you what I'm gonna do about it. (Sung:) I'm gon - na light_ the bed - room
Chorus:
C
D
G
can - dles,___ take the phone_ out of the wall.___
C
D
We lay a - round_ and talk for hours,___ or may - be we won't talk at
G
C
all.___ I'm gon - na res - ur - rect the love___ that slipped a - way___ from

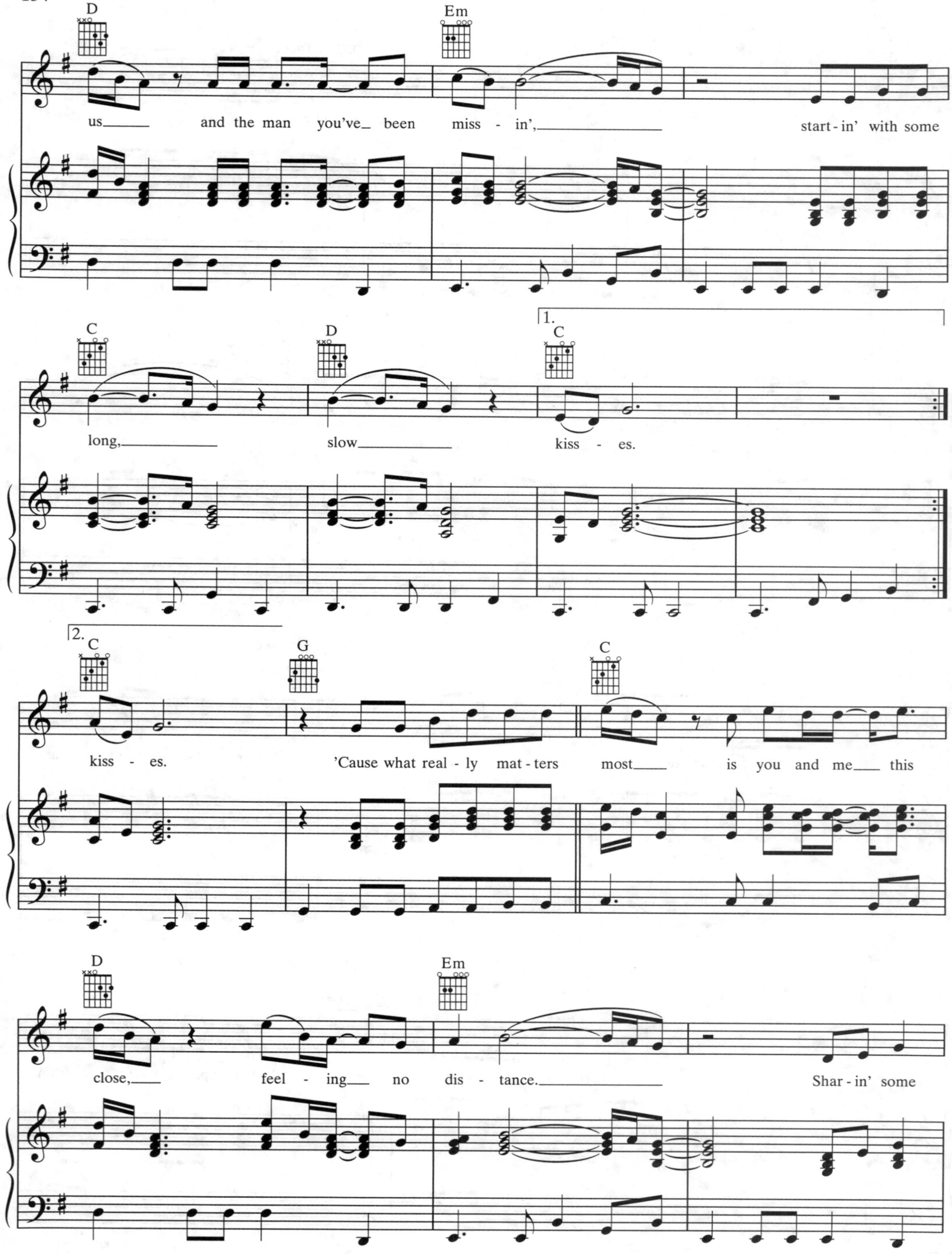
D
Em
us___ and the man you've_ been miss - in',___ start-in' with some
C
D
1.
C
long,___ slow___ kiss - es.
2.
C
G
C
kiss - es. 'Cause what real - ly mat-ters most___ is you and me___ this
D
Em
close,___ feel - ing___ no dis - tance.___ Shar - in' some

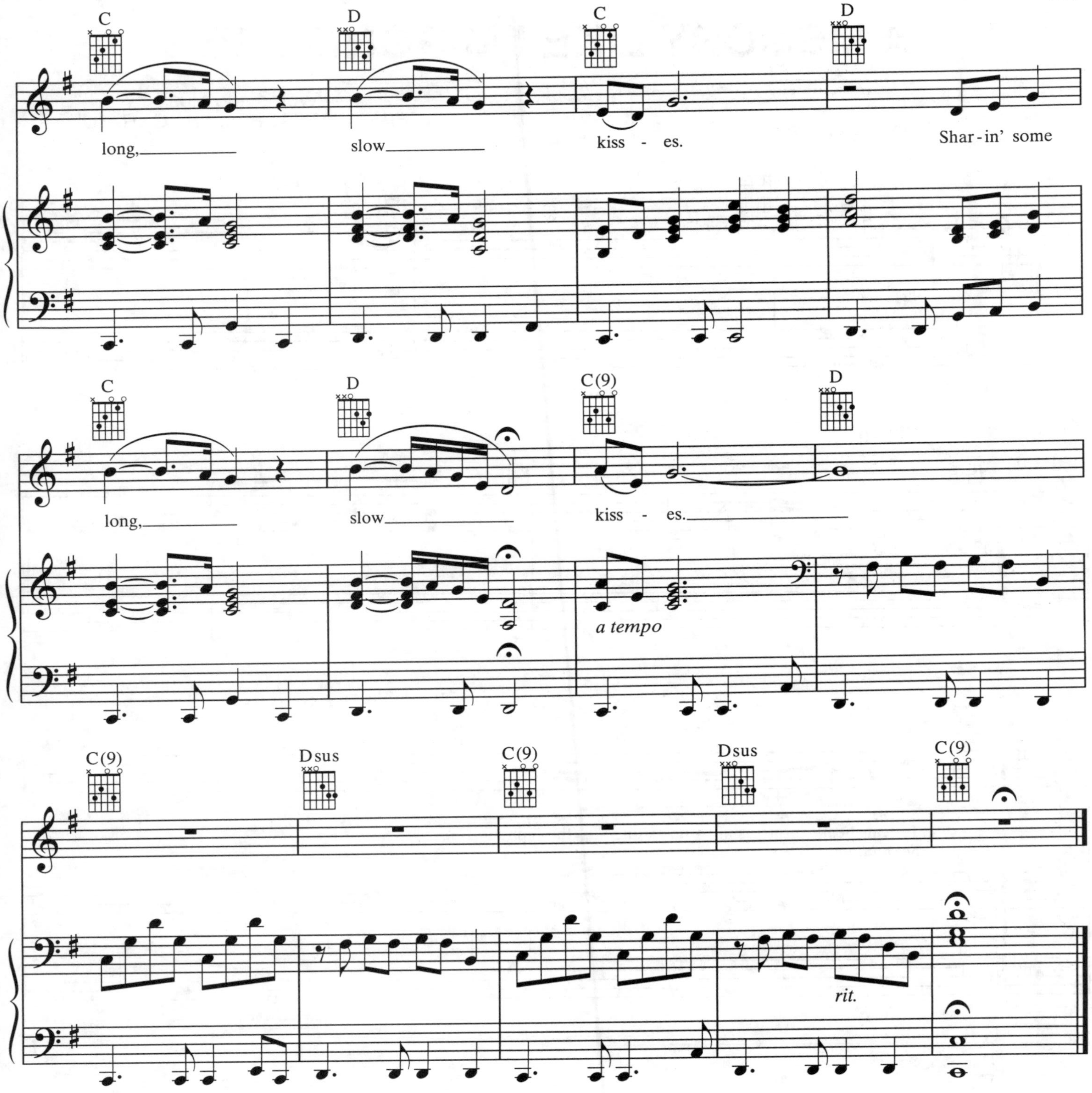

Verse 2:
(Spoken:) I just wanna let you know how ashamed I am
For making you feel that way.
Darlin', I'm so sorry.
I guess I've just been spendin'
Too much time on making a living
And way too little on making love.
But if you can just find it in your heart to forgive me
Girl, I swear from this moment on
You'll always know where you stand with me.
(To Chorus:)

A MEMORY LIKE I'M GONNA BE

Words and Music by
JERRY LASETER and ROGER MURRAH

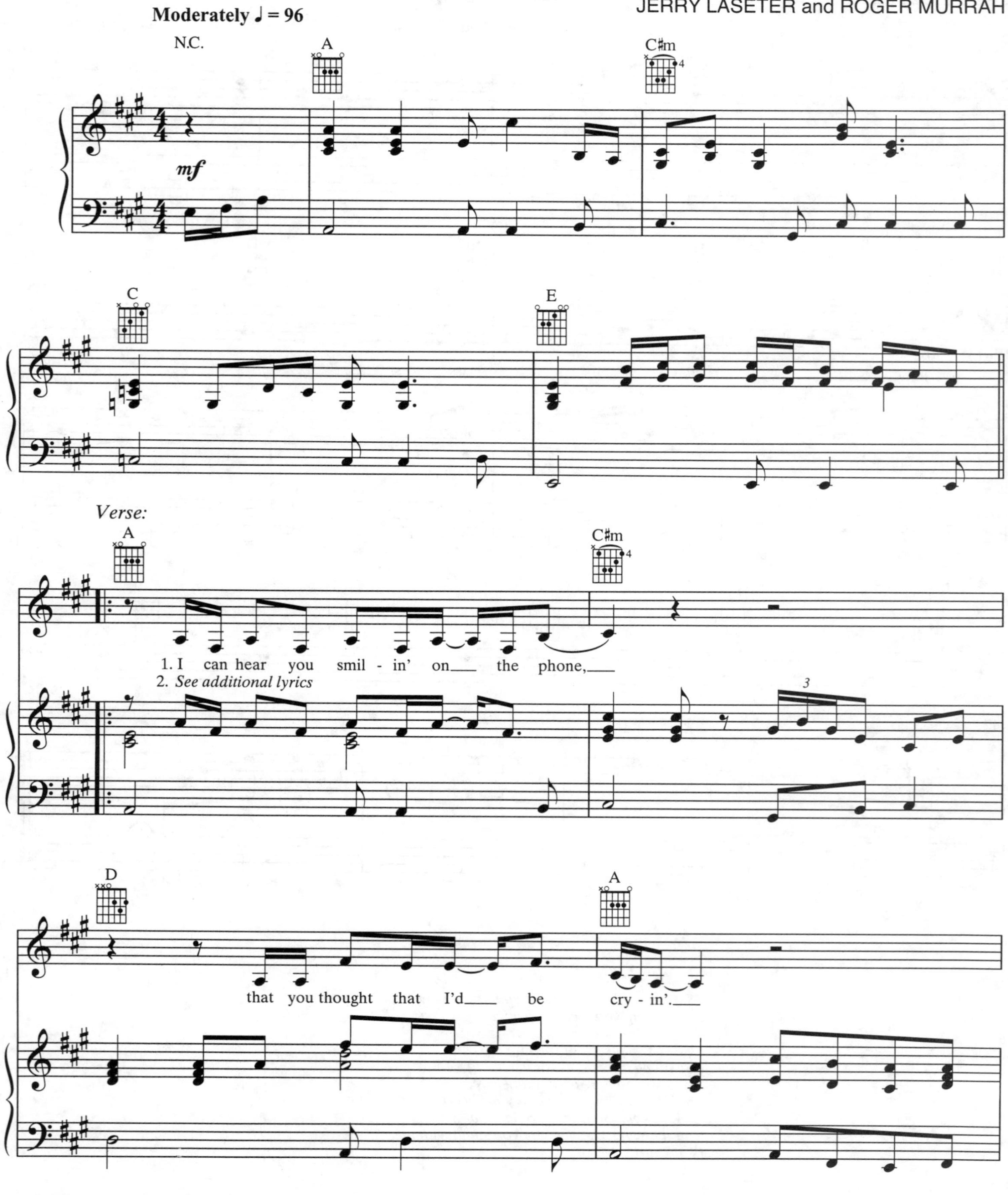

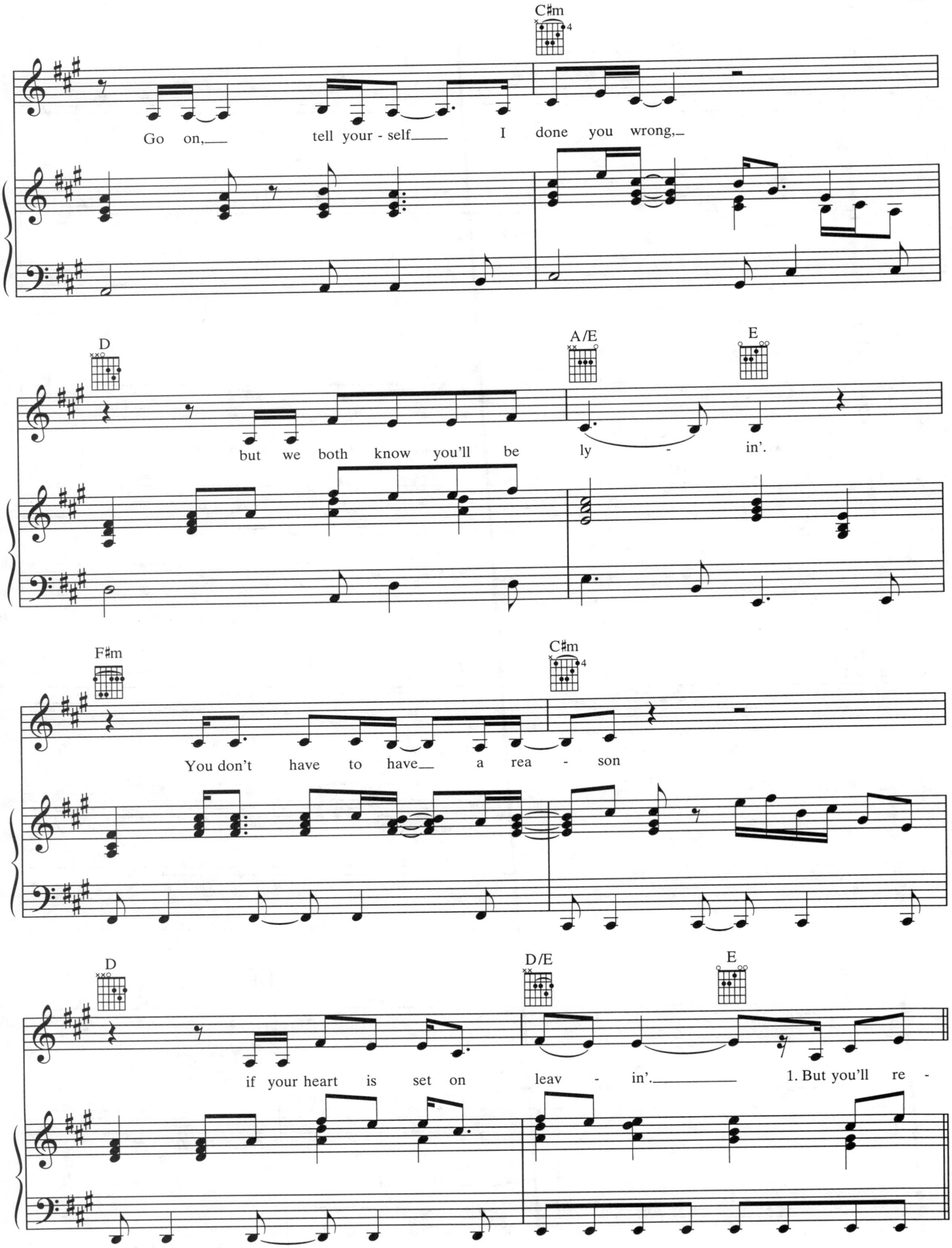
C♯m
Go on, tell your - self I done you wrong,
D
A/E
E
but we both know you'll be ly - in'.
F♯m
C♯m
You don't have to have a rea - son
D
D/E
E
if your heart is set on leav - in'. 1. But you'll re -

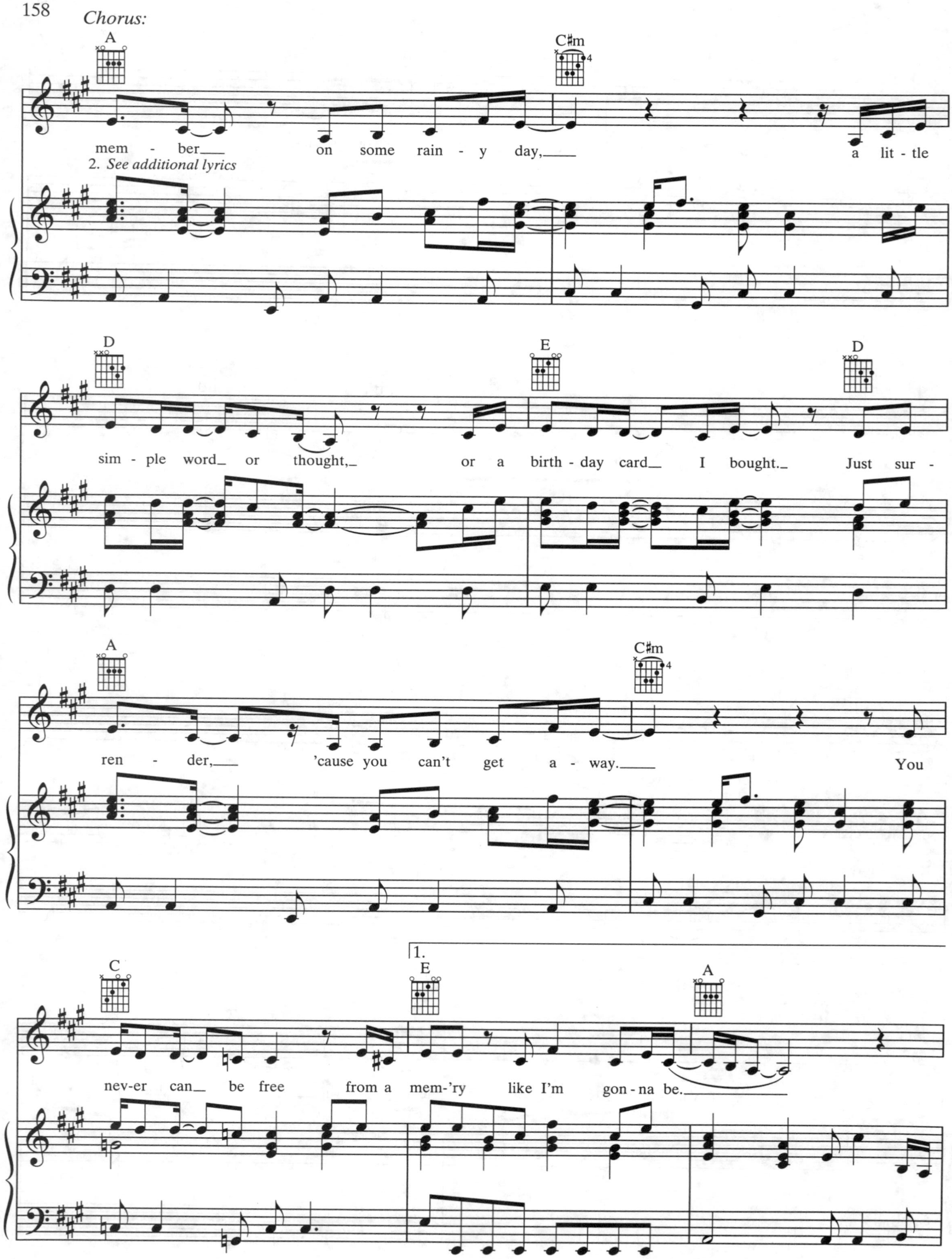
Chorus:
A
C♯m
mem - ber___ on some rain - y day,___ a lit - tle
2. See additional lyrics
D
E
D
sim - ple word_ or thought,_ or a birth - day card_ I bought._ Just sur -
A
C♯m
ren - der,___ 'cause you can't get a - way.___ You
1.
C
E
A
nev-er can_ be free from a mem-'ry like I'm gon - na be.___

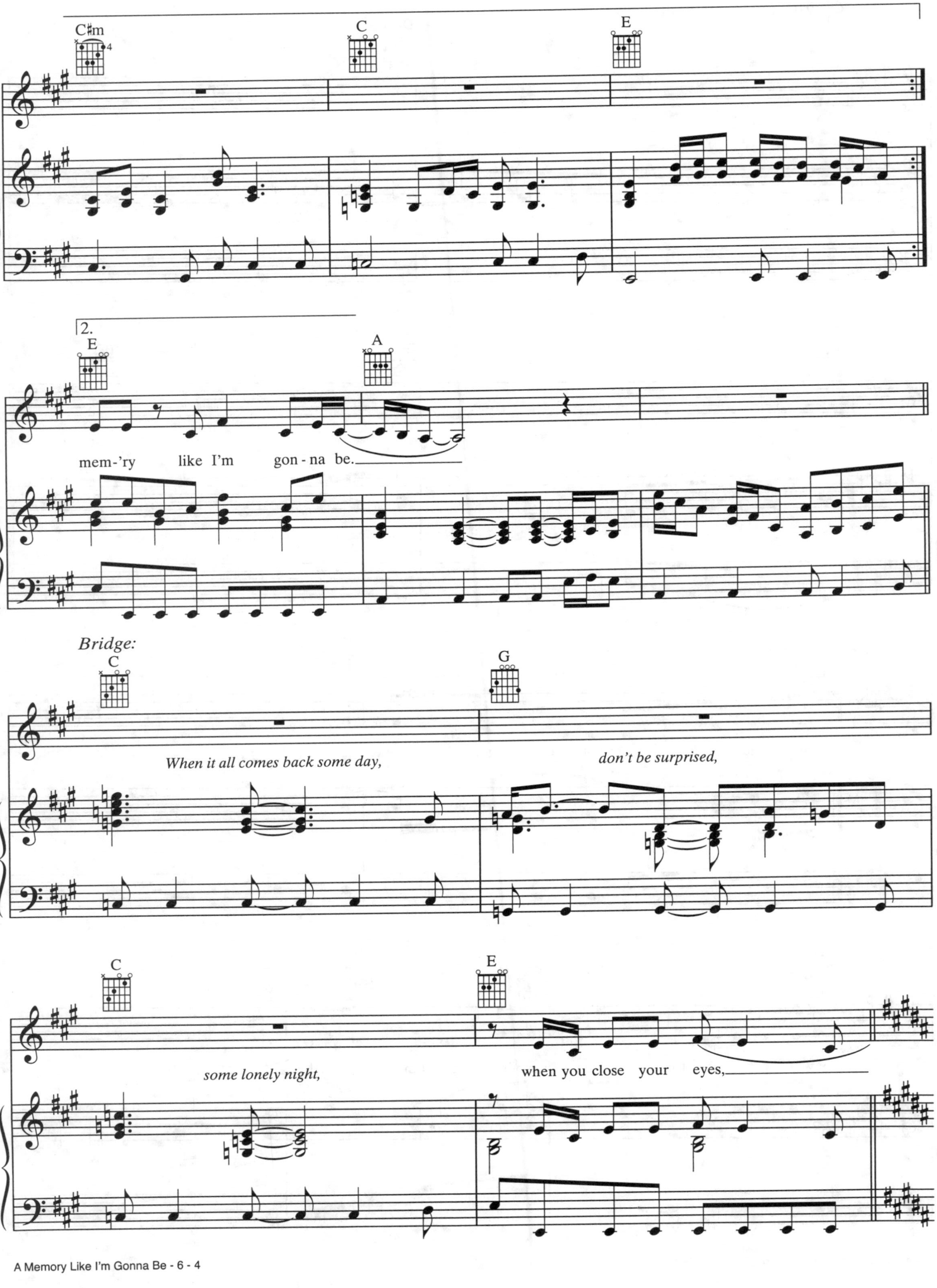
C♯m
C
E
2.
E
A
mem-'ry like I'm gon-na be.
Bridge:
C
G
When it all comes back some day,
don't be surprised,
C
E
some lonely night,
when you close your eyes,

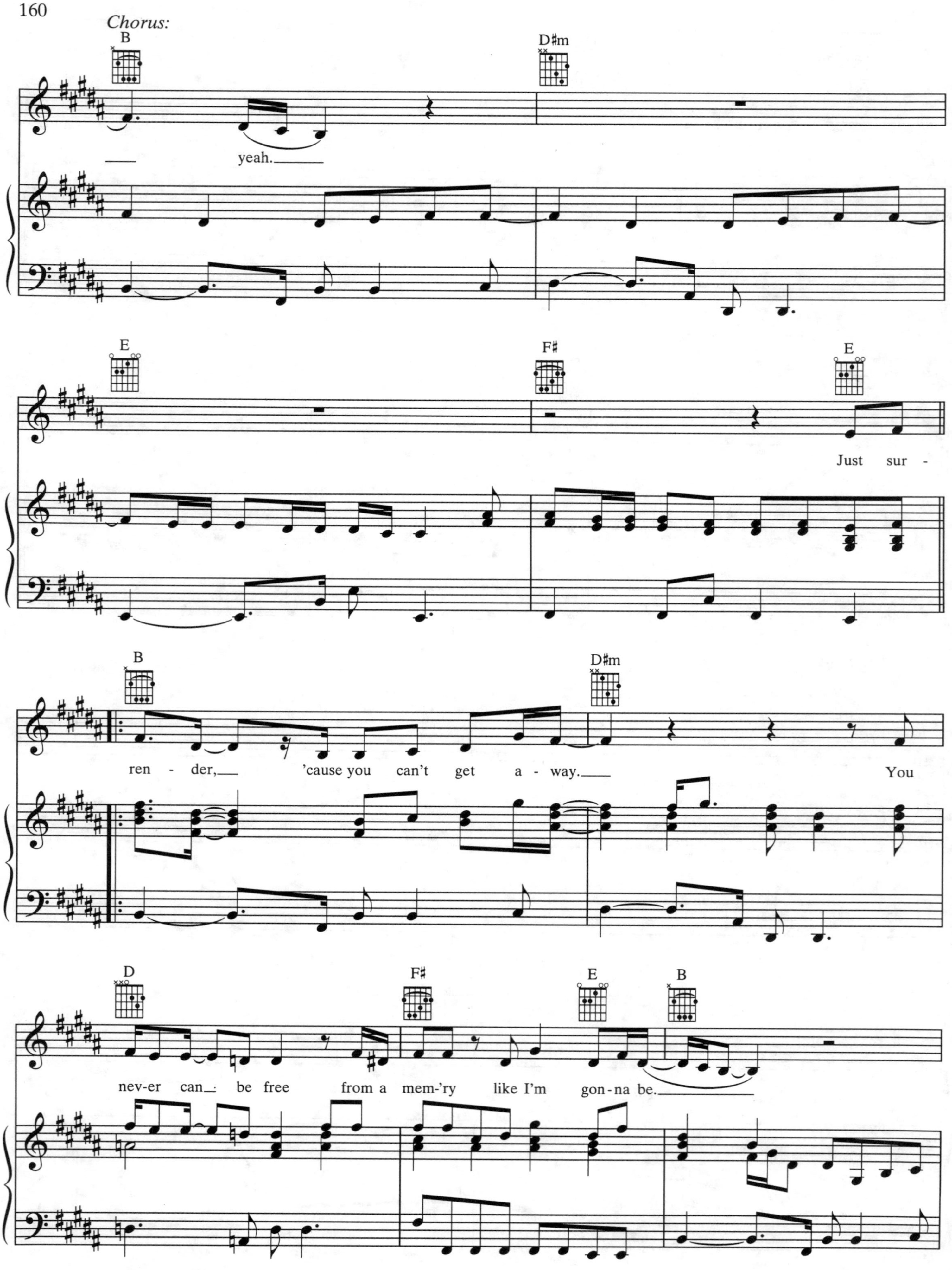
Chorus:
B
yeah.
D♯m
E
F♯
E
Just sur -
B
ren - der,
'cause you can't get a - way.
D♯m
You
D
nev-er can be free from a mem-'ry like I'm gon-na be.
F♯
E
B

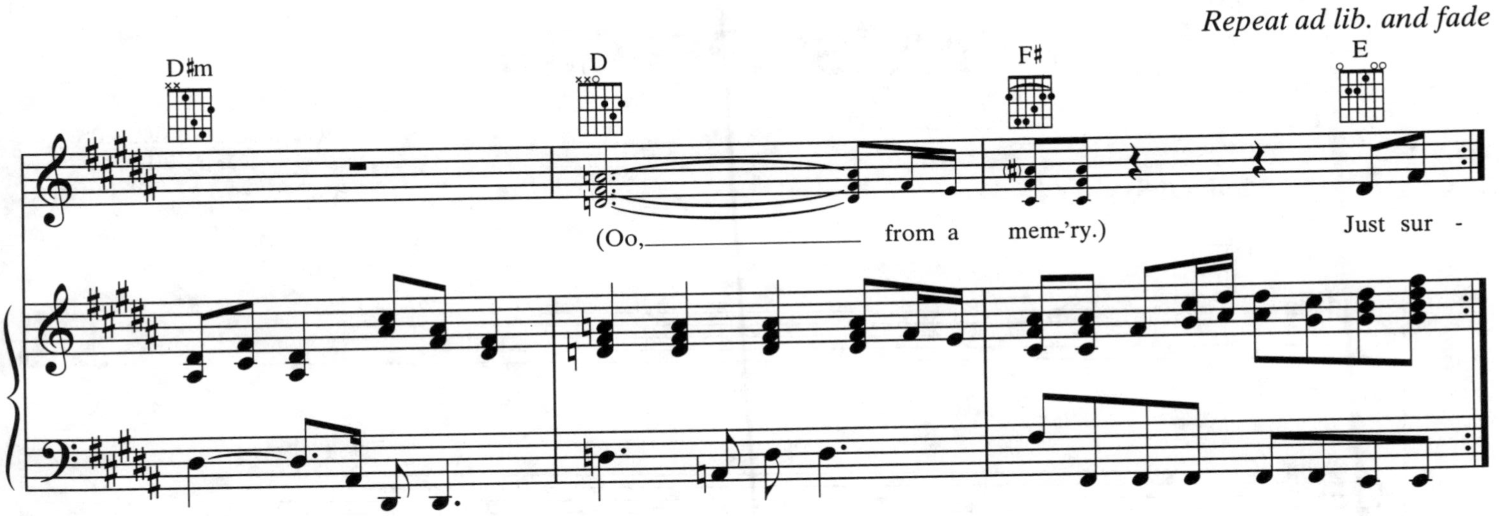

Verse 2:
Like the greener grass you beg to see,
It's just a high-heeled illusion.
Better count the cost of bein' free.
Is it worth all that you're losin'?
It may be over, but it's not ending,
'Cause there's one thing you're forgetting.

Chorus 2:
You'll remember on some rainy day
The little things we used to do,
Like that night in Baton Rouge.
Just surrender, 'cause you can't get away.
You never can be free
From a mem'ry like I'm gonna be.
(To Bridge:)

MISSISSIPPI GIRL

Words and Music by
JOHN RICH
and ADAM SHOENFELD

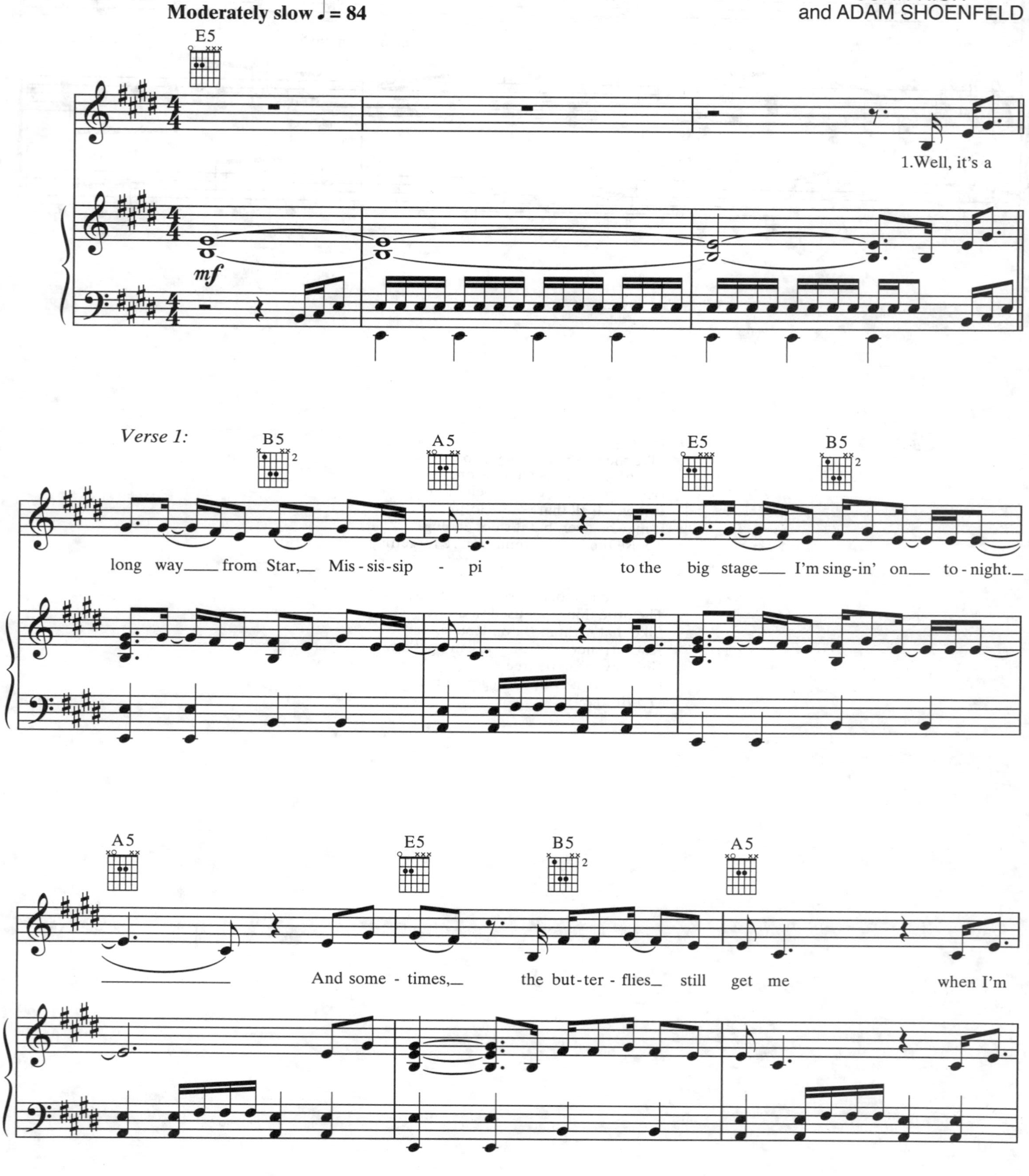

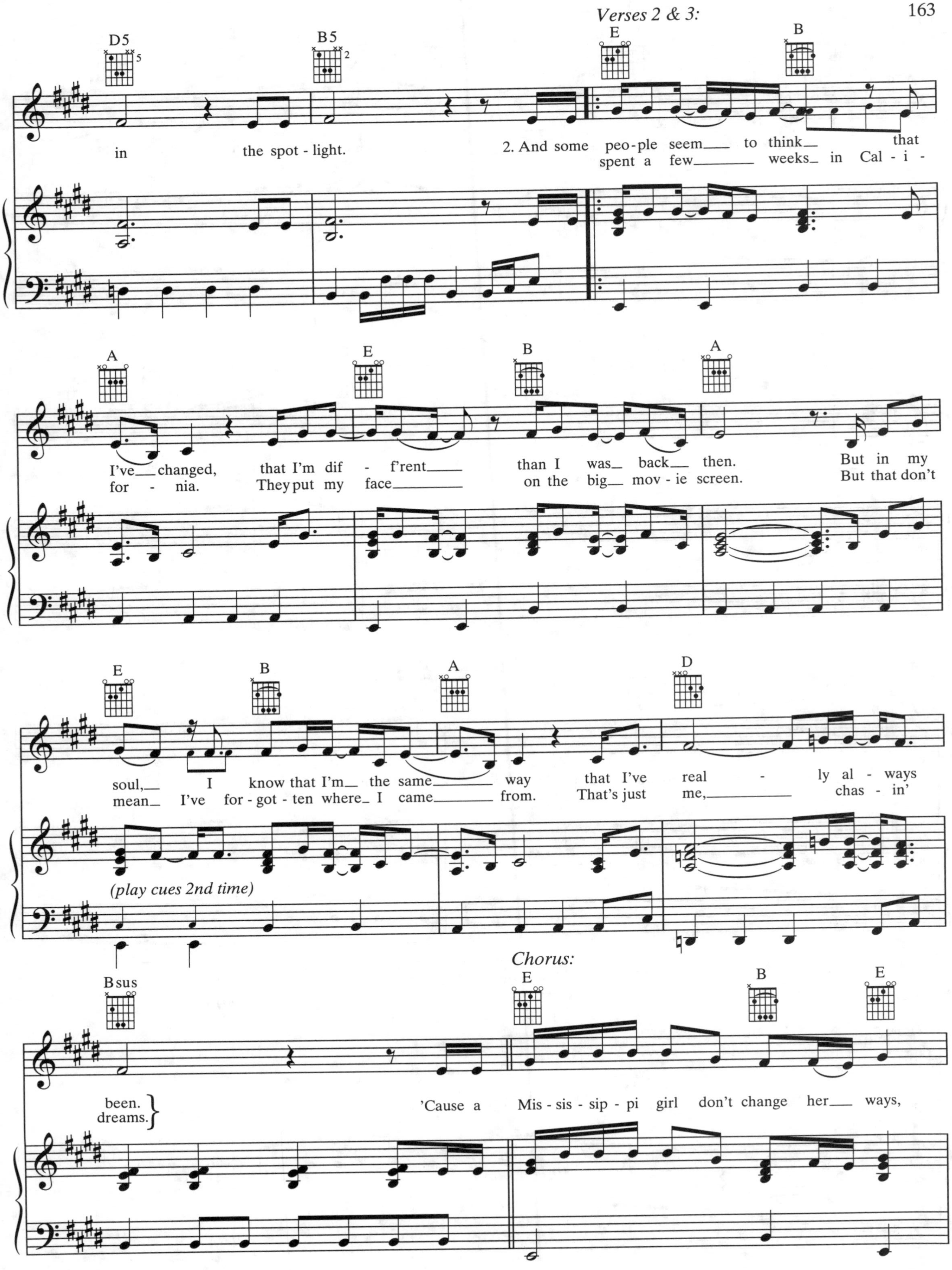
Verses 2 & 3:
D5
B5
E
B
in the spot - light.
2. And some peo - ple seem___ to think___ that
spent a few_______ weeks_ in Cal - i -
A
E
B
A
I've___ changed, that I'm dif - f'rent___ than I was_ back___ then. But in my
for - nia. They put my face_______ on the big___ mov - ie screen. But that don't
E
B
A
D
soul,___ I know that I'm___ the same_______ way that I've real - ly al - ways
mean___ I've for - got - ten where_ I came_______ from. That's just me,_______ chas - in'
(play cues 2nd time)
Chorus:
Bsus
E
B
E
been.
dreams.
'Cause a Mis - sis - sip - pi girl don't change her___ ways,

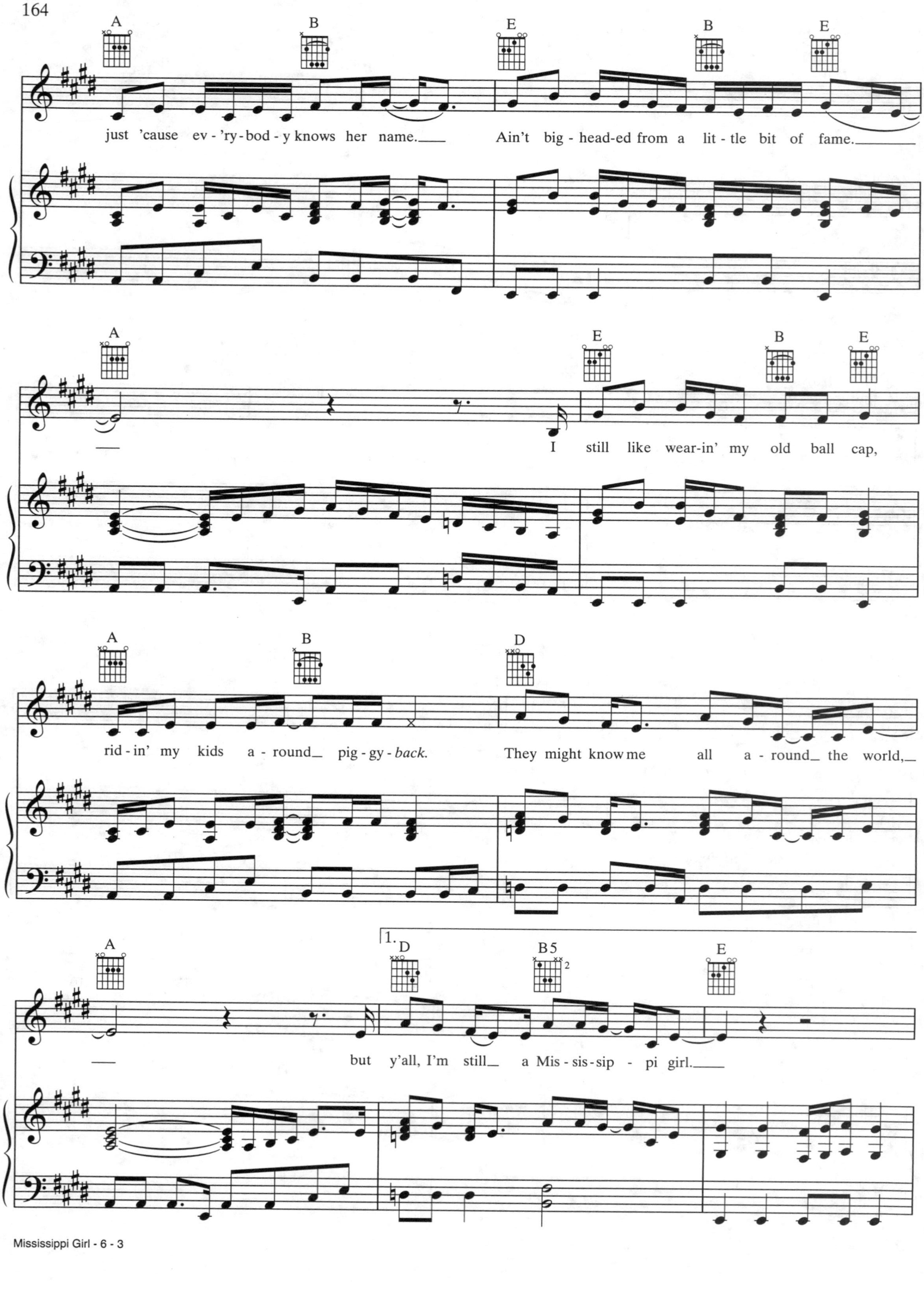
A B E B E
just 'cause ev - 'ry-bod - y knows her name.___ Ain't big - head-ed from a lit - tle bit of fame.___
A E B E
I still like wear-in' my old ball cap,
A B D
rid - in' my kids a - round_ pig - gy - back. They might know me all a - round_ the world,_
A D B5 E
1.
but y'all, I'm still_ a Mis - sis - sip - pi girl.___

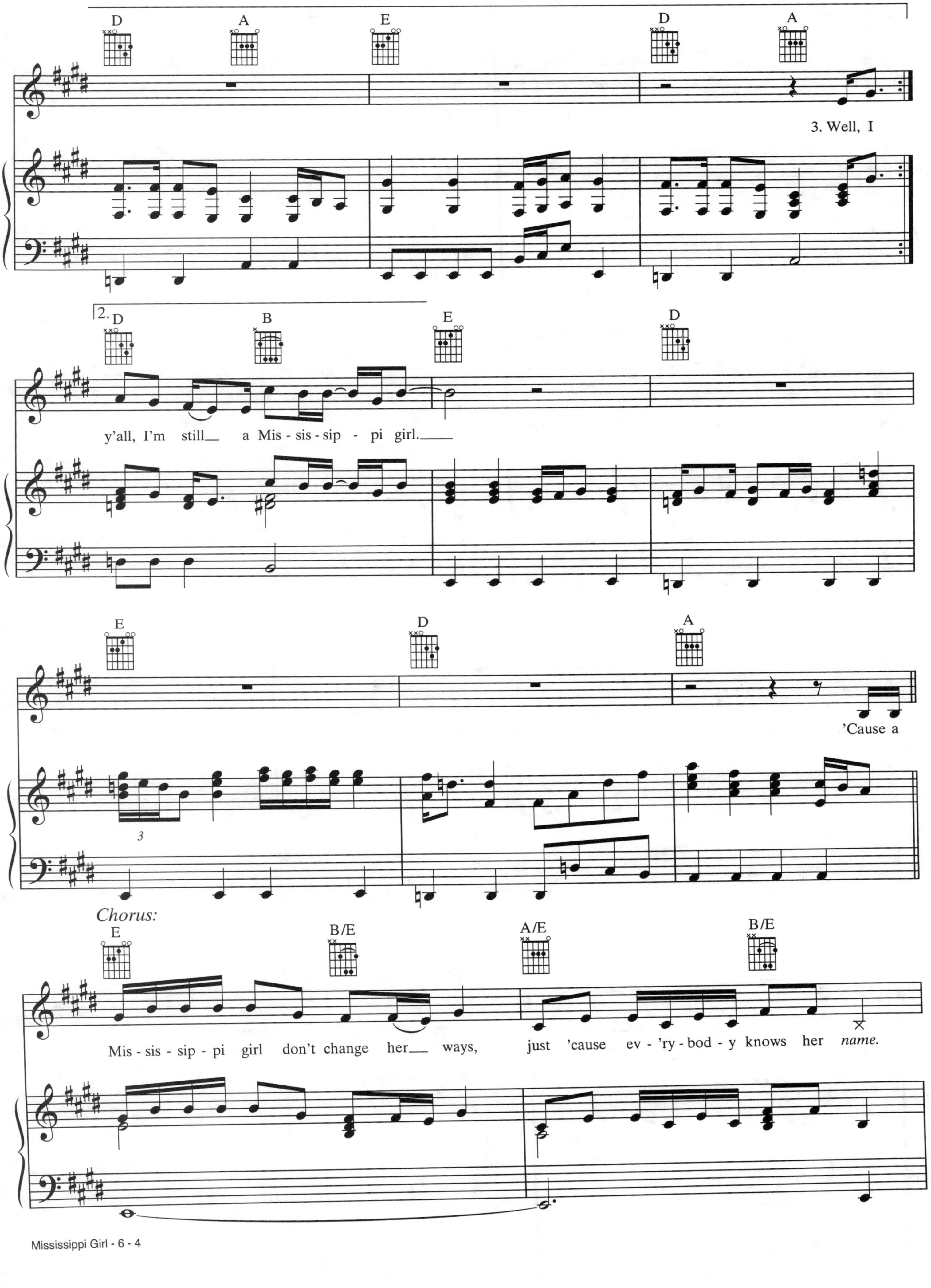
D
A
E
D
A
3. Well, I
2.
D
B
E
D
y'all, I'm still__ a Mis - sis - sip - pi girl.____
E
D
A
3
'Cause a
Chorus:
E
B/E
A/E
B/E
Mis - sis - sip - pi girl don't change her__ ways, just 'cause ev - 'ry - bod - y knows her name.

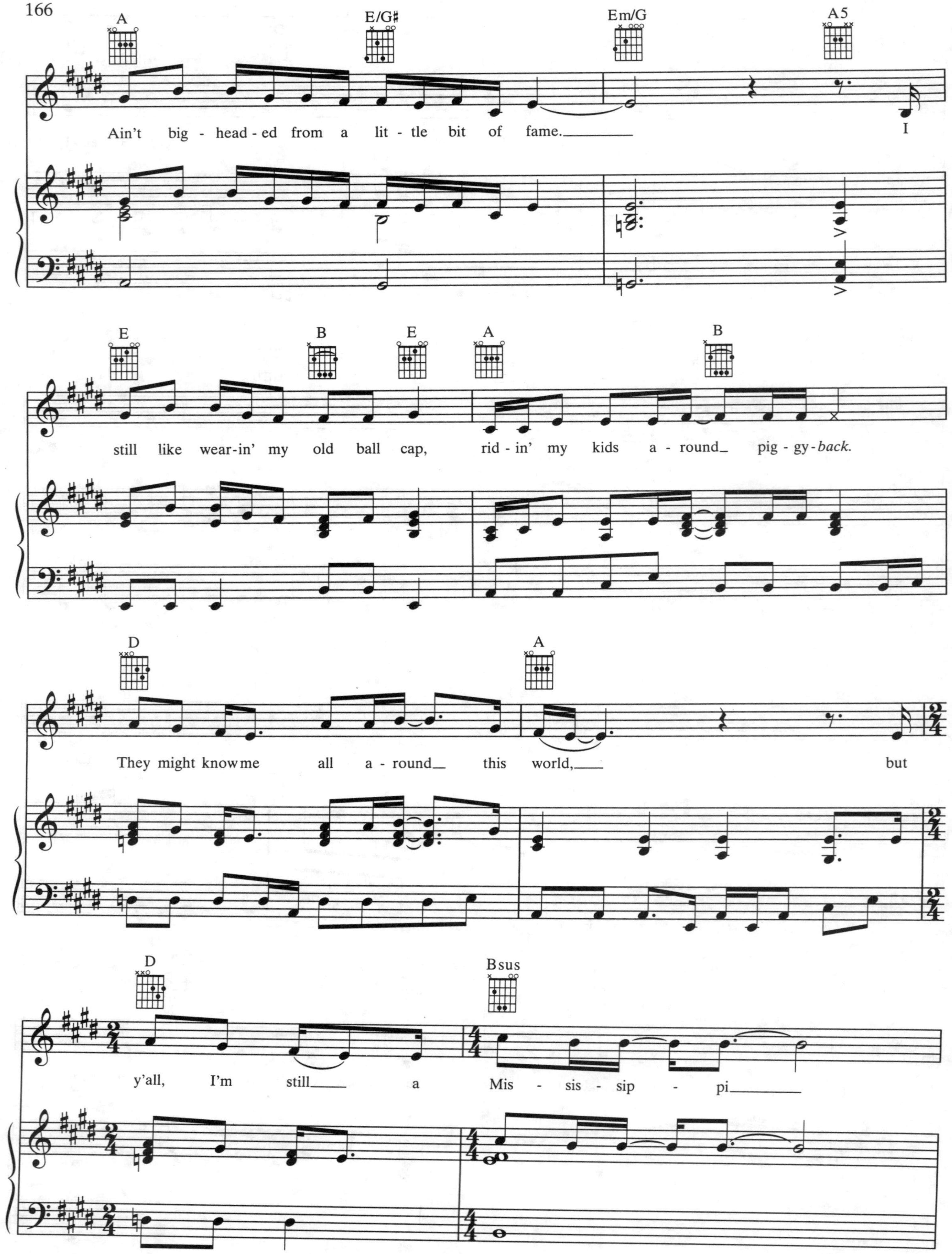
A
E/G♯
Em/G
A5
Ain't big - head - ed from a lit - tle bit of fame.
I
E
B
E
A
B
still like wear-in' my old ball cap,
rid - in' my kids a - round pig - gy - back.
D
A
They might know me all a - round this world,
but
D
Bsus
y'all, I'm still a Mis - sis - sip - pi

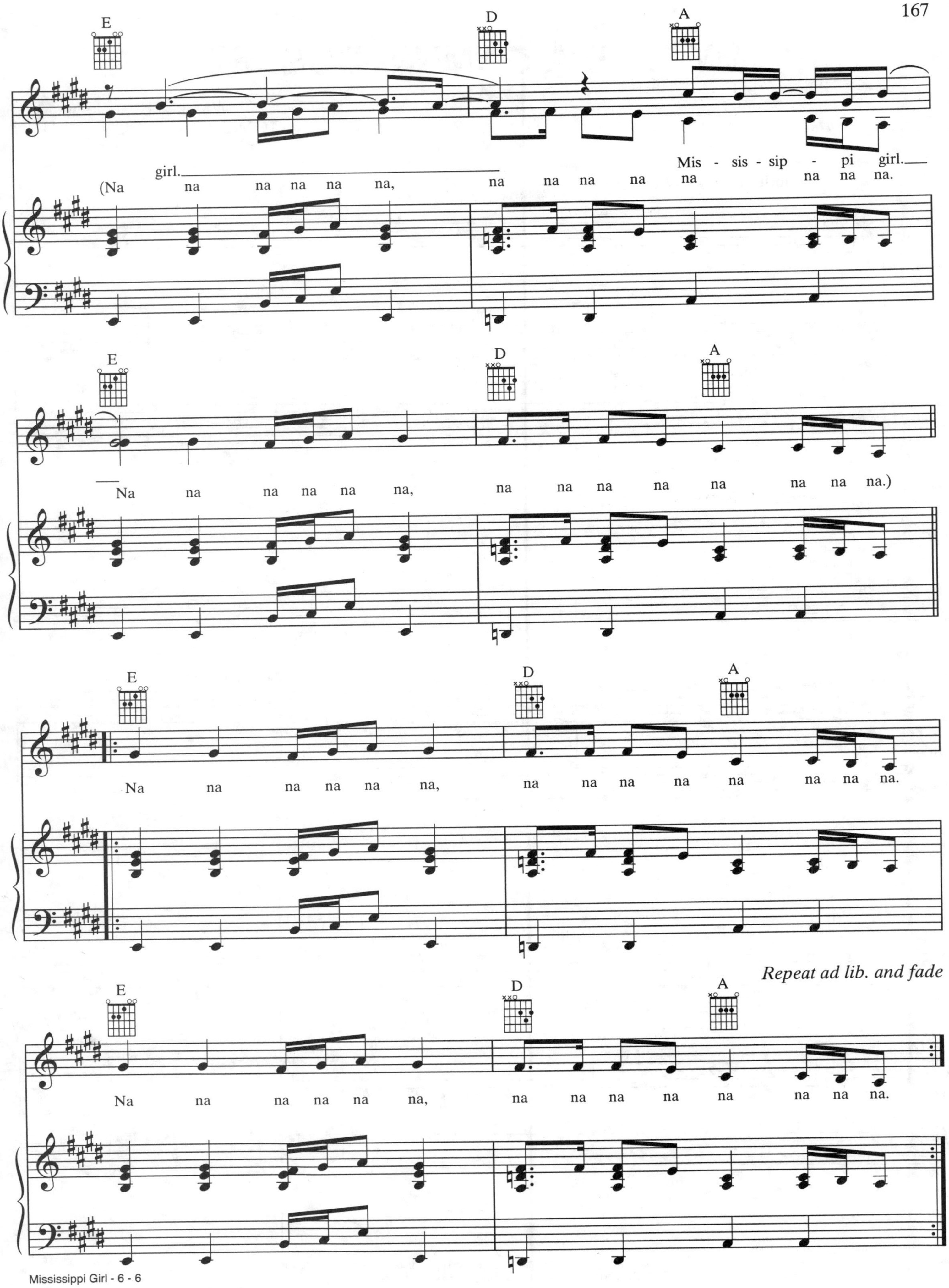
E
D
A
girl.
Mis - sis - sip - pi girl.
(Na na na na na na, na na na na na na na na.
E
D
A
Na na na na na na, na na na na na na na na.)
E
D
A
Na na na na na na, na na na na na na na na.
Repeat ad lib. and fade
E
D
A
Na na na na na na, na na na na na na na na.

MY GIVE A DAMN'S BUSTED

Words and Music by
TOM SHAPIRO, TONY MARTIN
and JOE DIFFIE

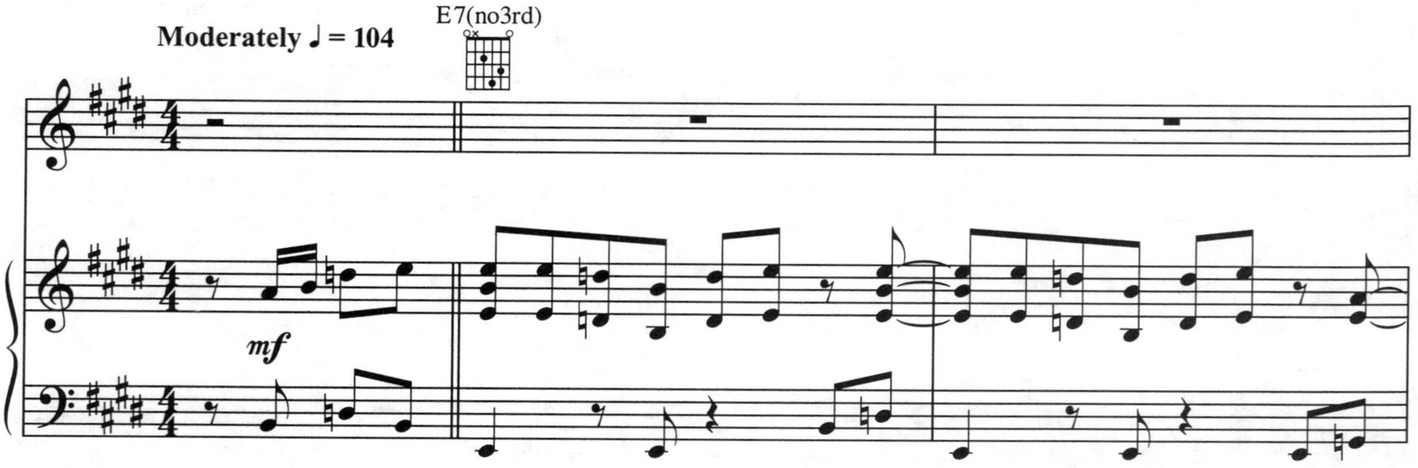

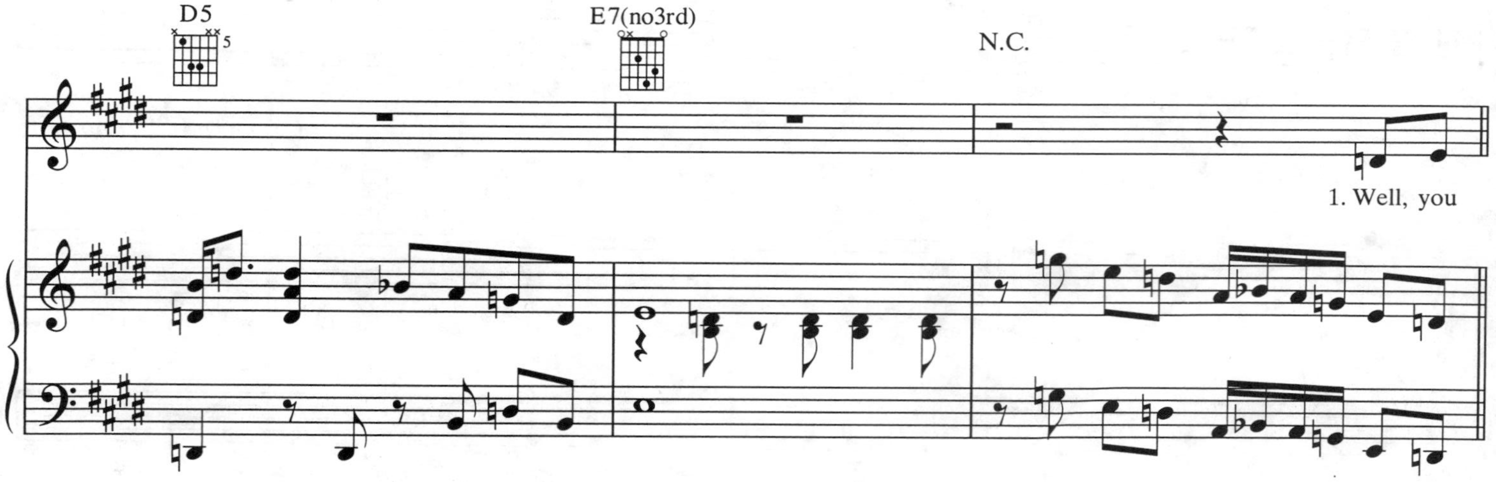

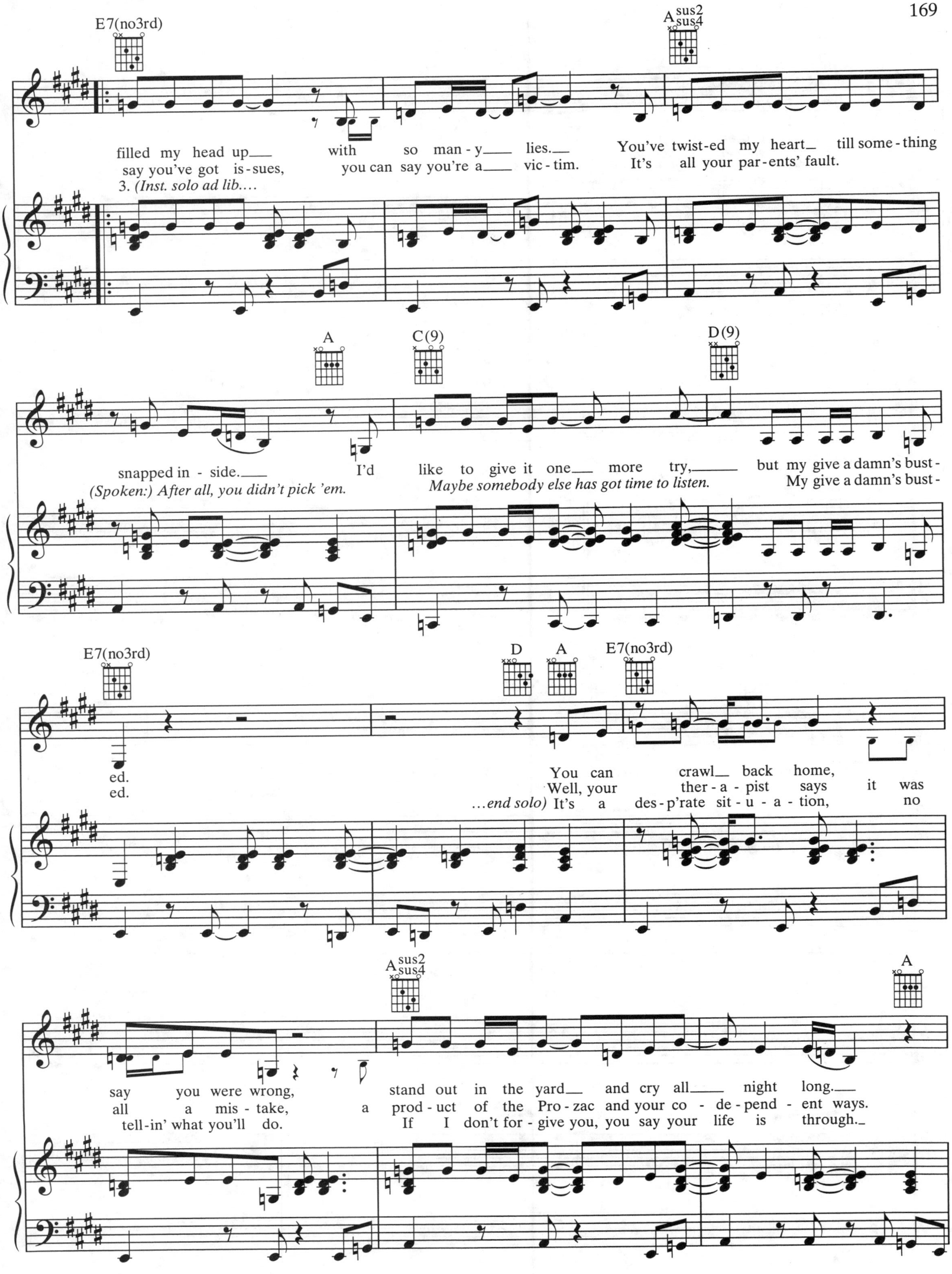
E7(no3rd)
Asus2 sus4
filled my head up__ with so man-y__ lies.__ You've twist-ed my heart__ till some-thing
say you've got is-sues, you can say you're a__ vic-tim. It's all your par-ents' fault.
3. (Inst. solo ad lib....
A
C(9)
D(9)
snapped in - side.__ I'd like to give it one__ more try,__ but my give a damn's bust-
(Spoken:) After all, you didn't pick 'em. Maybe somebody else has got time to listen. My give a damn's bust-
E7(no3rd)
D
A
E7(no3rd)
ed. You can crawl__ back home,
ed. Well, your ther-a-pist says it was
...end solo) It's a des-p'rate sit-u-a-tion, no
Asus2 sus4
A
say you were wrong, stand out in the yard__ and cry all__ night long.__
all a mis-take, a prod-uct of the Pro-zac and your co-de-pend-ent ways.
tell-in' what you'll do. If I don't for-give you, you say your life is through.__

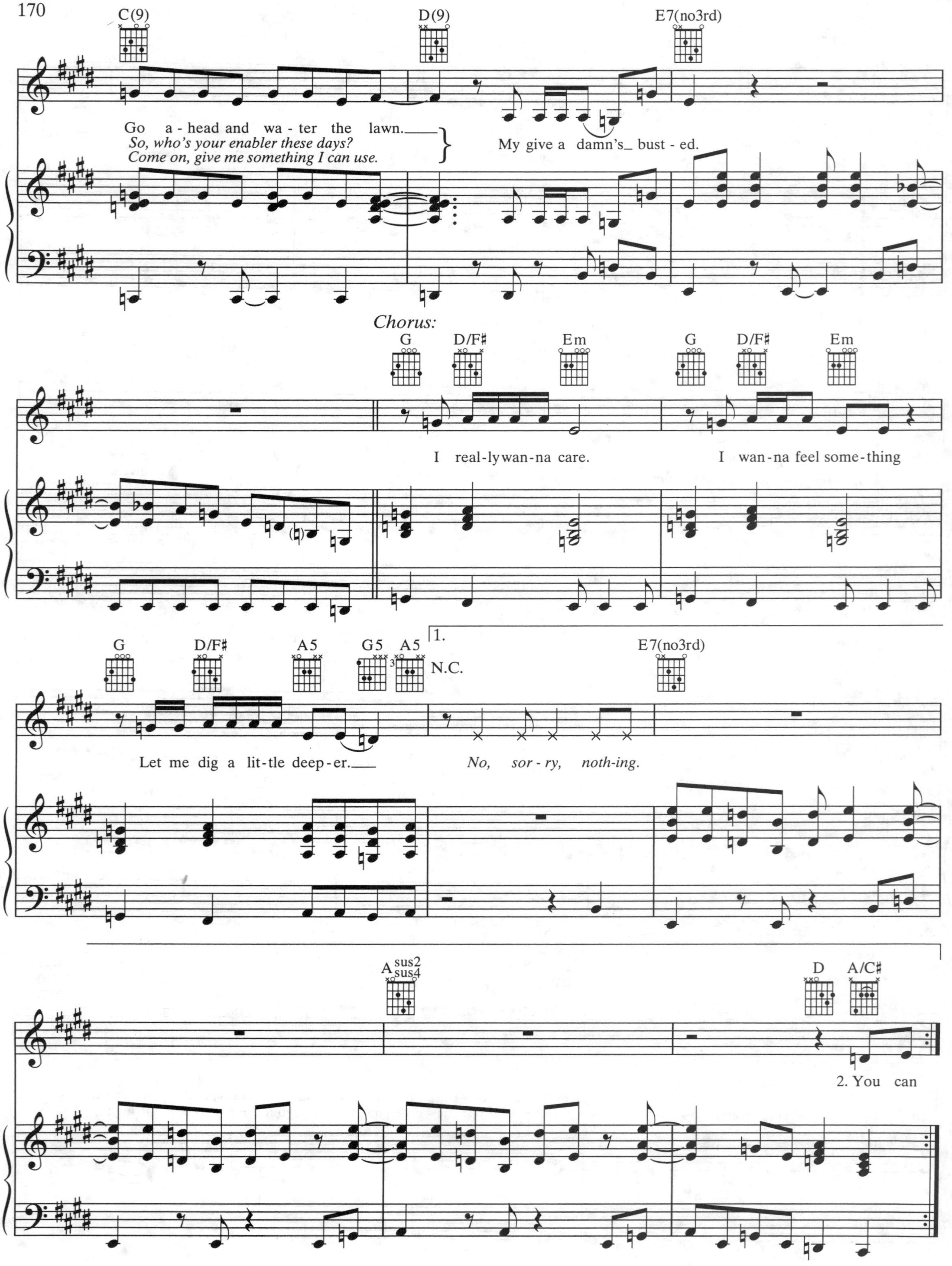
C(9)
D(9)
E7(no3rd)
Go a - head and wa - ter the lawn.
So, who's your enabler these days?
Come on, give me something I can use.
My give a damn's_ bust - ed.
Chorus:
G
D/F♯
Em
I real-lywan-na care.
I wan-na feel some-thing
A5
G5
N.C.
1.
Let me dig a lit-tle deep-er.
No, sor-ry, noth-ing.
A sus2 sus4
D
A/C♯
2. You can

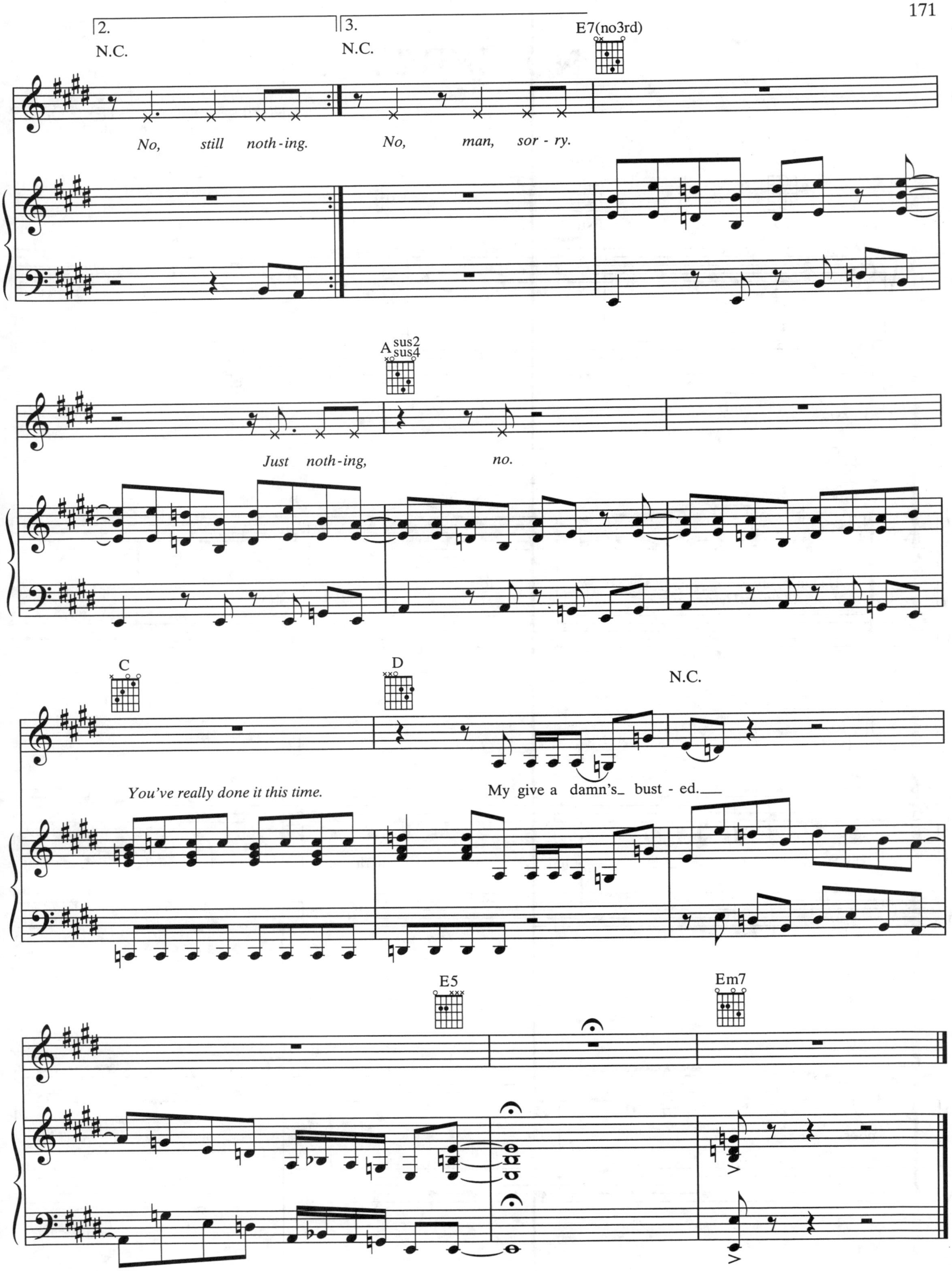
2.
N.C.
3.
N.C.
E7(no3rd)
No, still noth-ing.
No, man, sor - ry.
A sus2 sus4
Just noth-ing,
no.
C
D
N.C.
You've really done it this time.
My give a damn's_ bust - ed.__
E5
Em7

NO MERCY

Words and Music by
DENNIS MORGAN, STEVE DAVIS
and TODD CERNEY

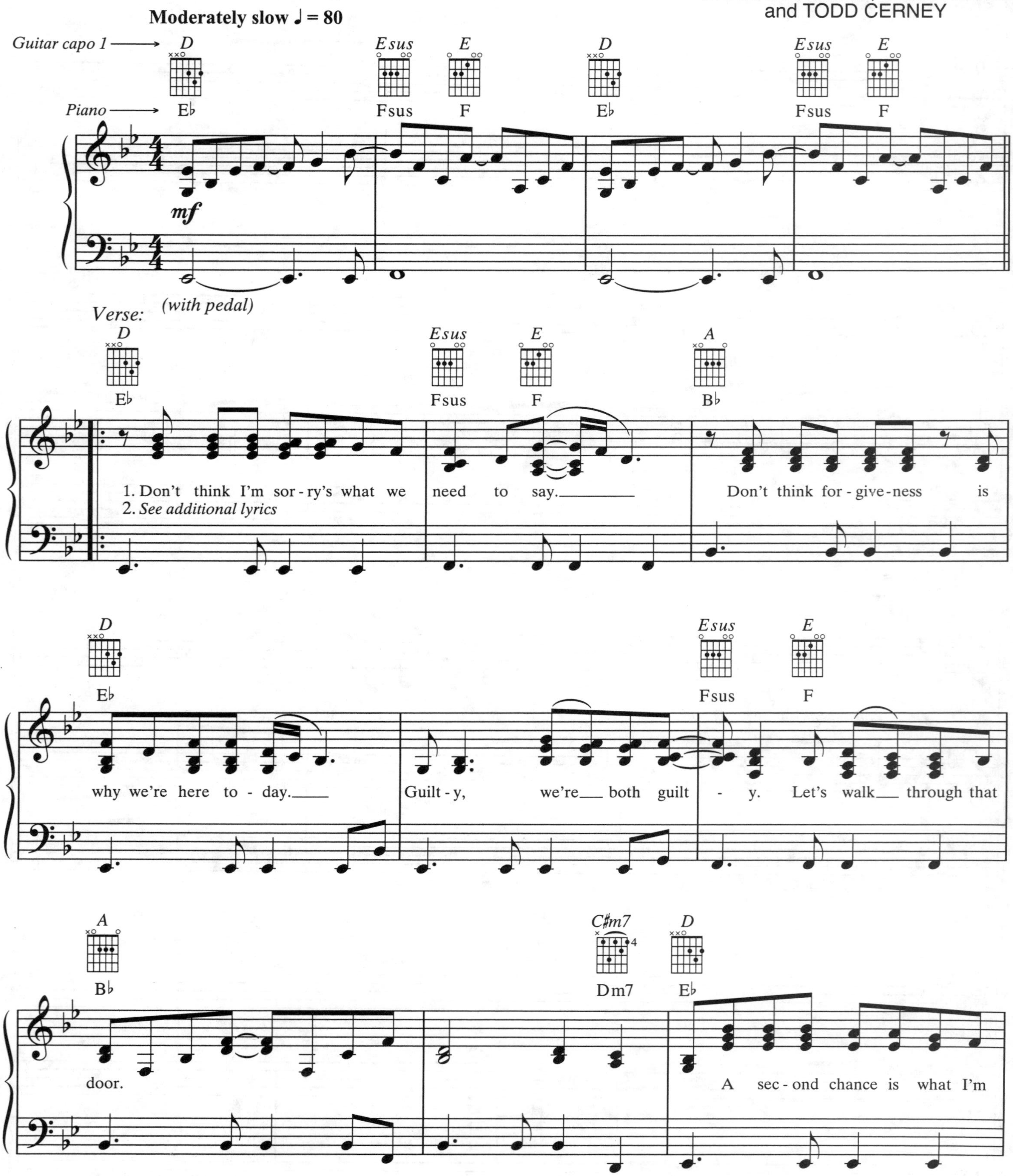

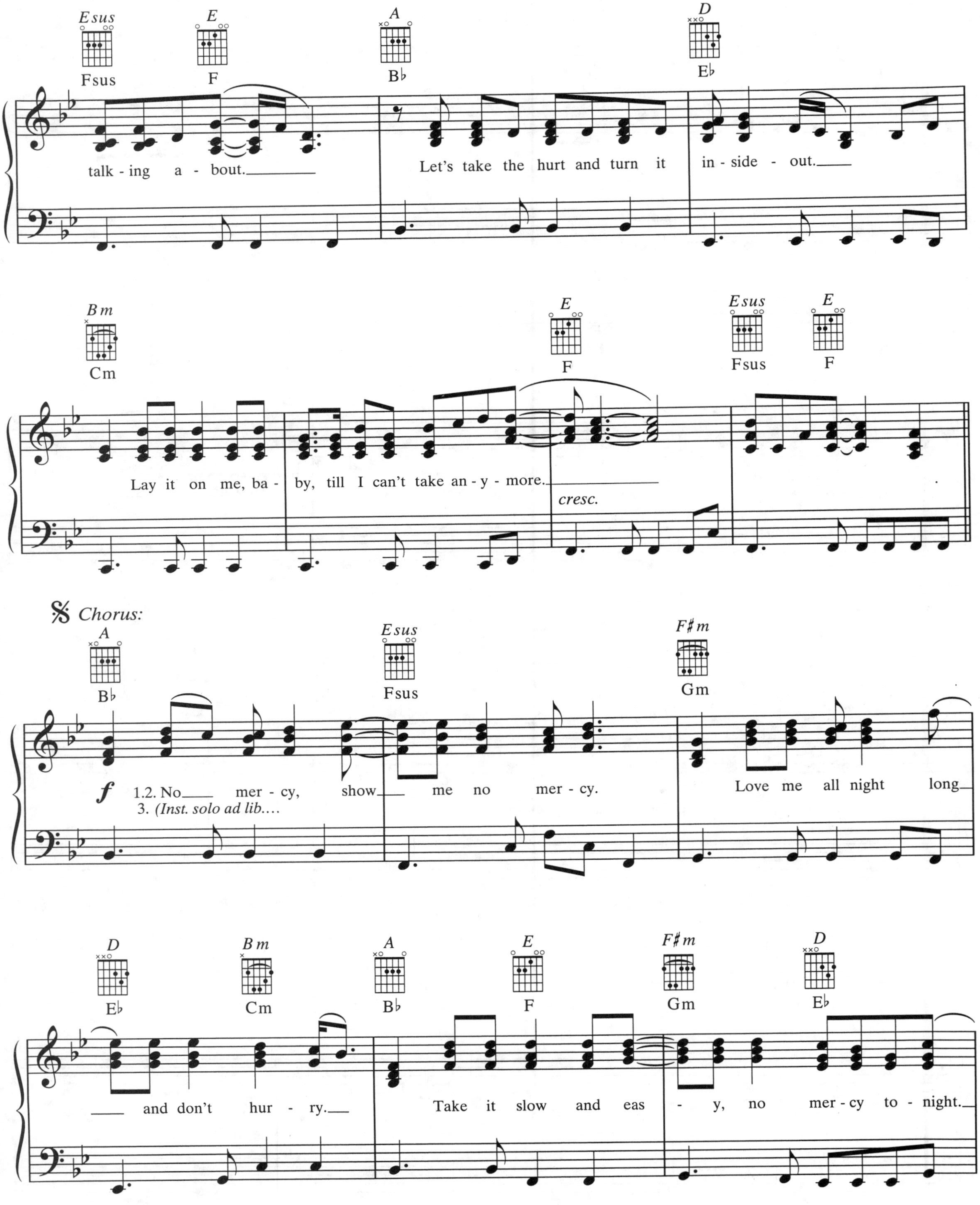
Esus
E
A
D
Fsus
F
B♭
E♭
talk - ing a - bout.
Let's take the hurt and turn it
in - side - out.
Bm
E
Esus
E
Cm
F
Fsus
F
Lay it on me, ba - by, till I can't take an - y - more.
cresc.
Chorus:
A
Esus
F♯m
B♭
Fsus
Gm
f
1.2. No mer - cy, show me no mer - cy.
3. (Inst. solo ad lib....
Love me all night long
D
Bm
A
E
F♯m
D
E♭
Cm
B♭
F
Gm
E♭
and don't hur - ry.
Take it slow and eas - y, no mer - cy to - night.

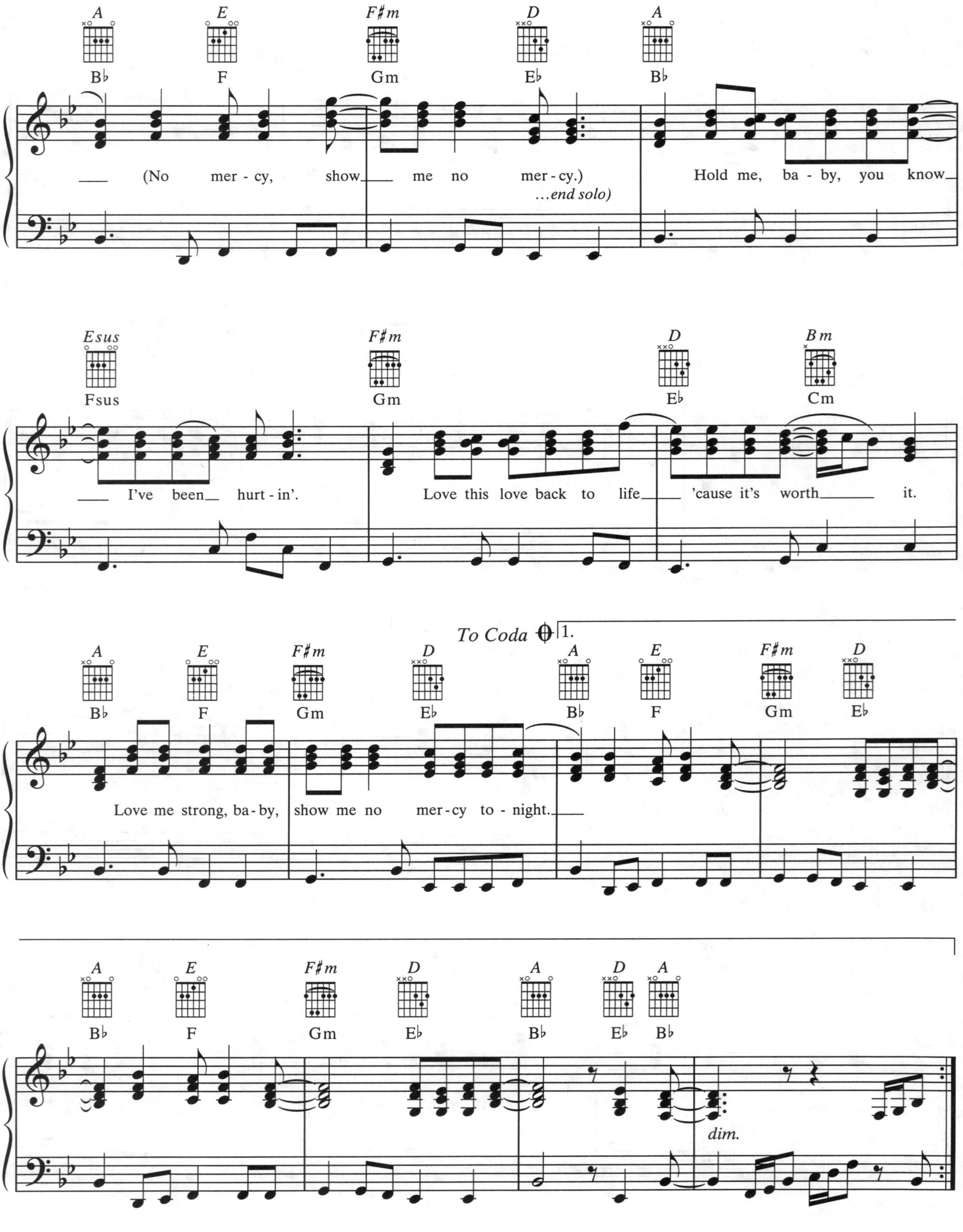
A E F♯m D A
B♭ F Gm E♭ B♭
(No mer - cy, show me no mer - cy.)
...end solo)
Hold me, ba - by, you know
Esus F♯m D Bm
Fsus Gm E♭ Cm
I've been hurt - in'.
Love this love back to life 'cause it's worth it.
To Coda
1.
A E F♯m D A E F♯m D
B♭ F Gm E♭ B♭ F Gm E♭
Love me strong, ba - by, show me no mer - cy to - night.
A E F♯m D A D A
B♭ F Gm E♭ B♭ E♭ B♭
dim.

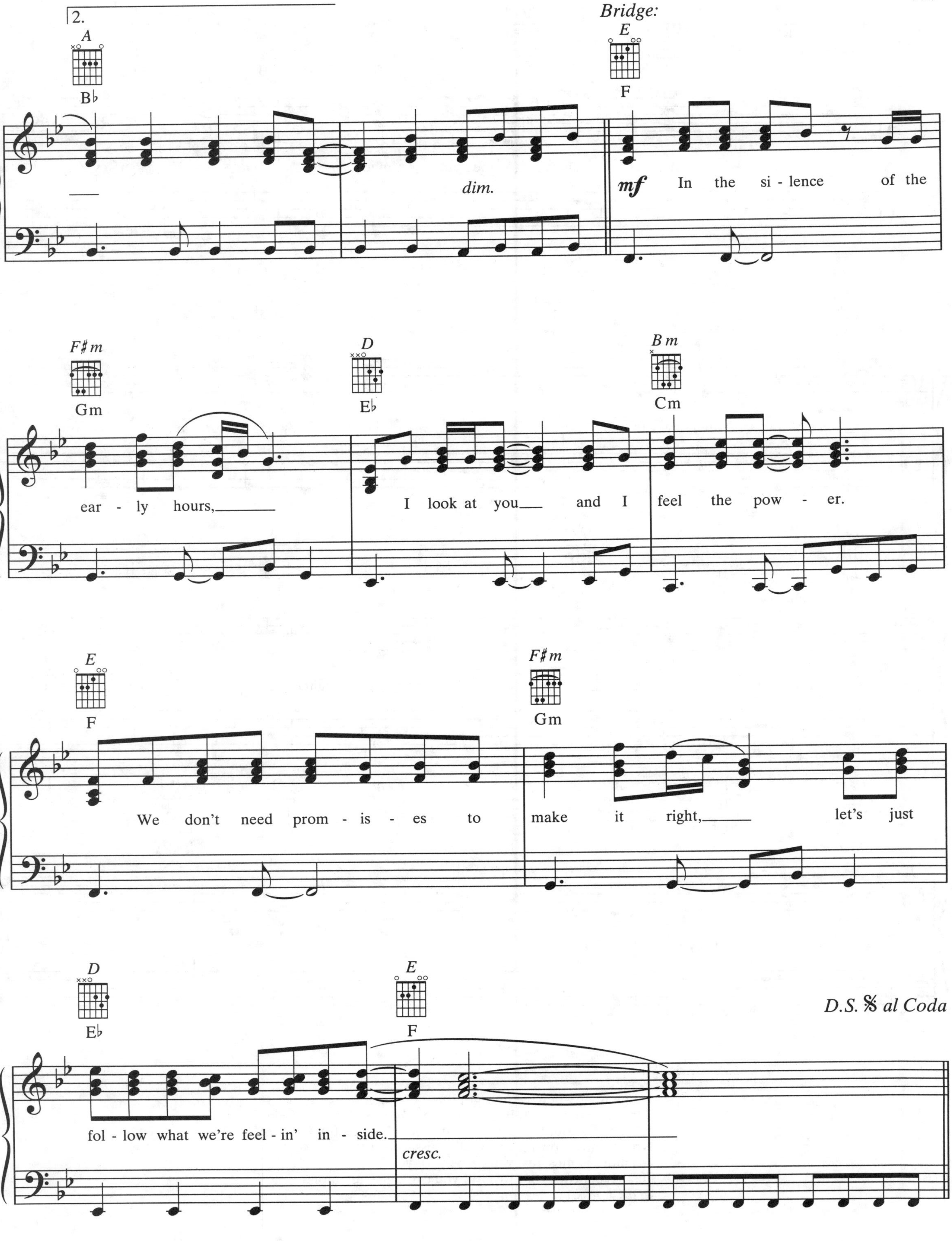
2.
A
B♭
dim.
Bridge:
E
F
mf
In the si - lence of the
F♯m
Gm
ear - ly hours,
D
E♭
I look at you and I
Bm
Cm
feel the pow - er.
E
F
We don't need prom - is - es to
F♯m
Gm
make it right, let's just
D
E♭
fol - low what we're feel - in' in - side.
E
F
cresc.
D.S. 𝄋 al Coda

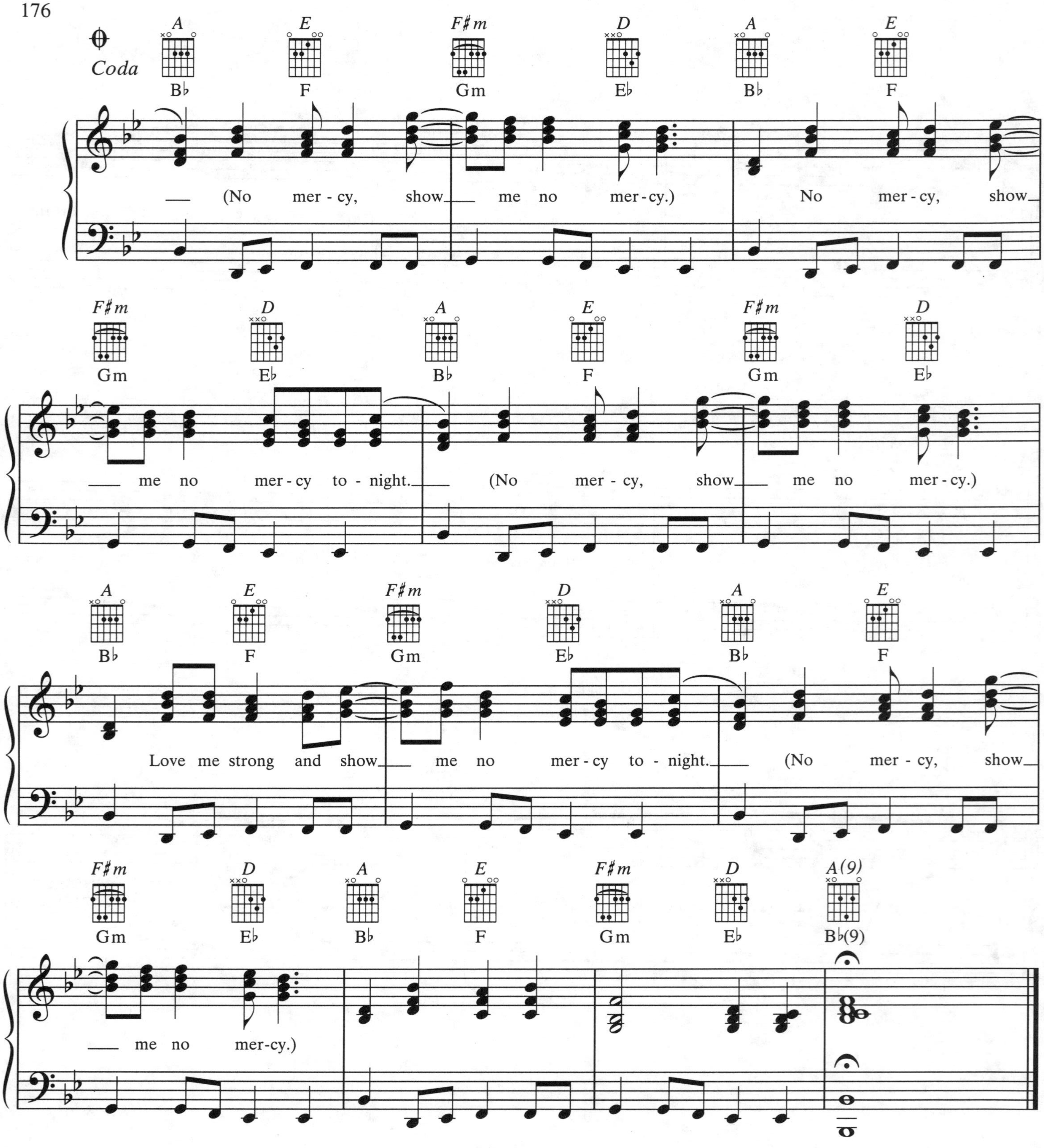

Verse 2:
Remember when we thought that bein' apart
Would be the best thing for both our hearts?
It's a prison out there when you're livin' alone, for sure.
Now I know how much I really missed you.
No more games, just wanna be with you.
Just give me all your love till you can't give anymore.
(*To Chorus:*)

NOBODY GONNA TELL ME WHAT TO DO

Words and Music by
TIM NICHOLS, CRAIG WISEMAN
and TONY MULLINS

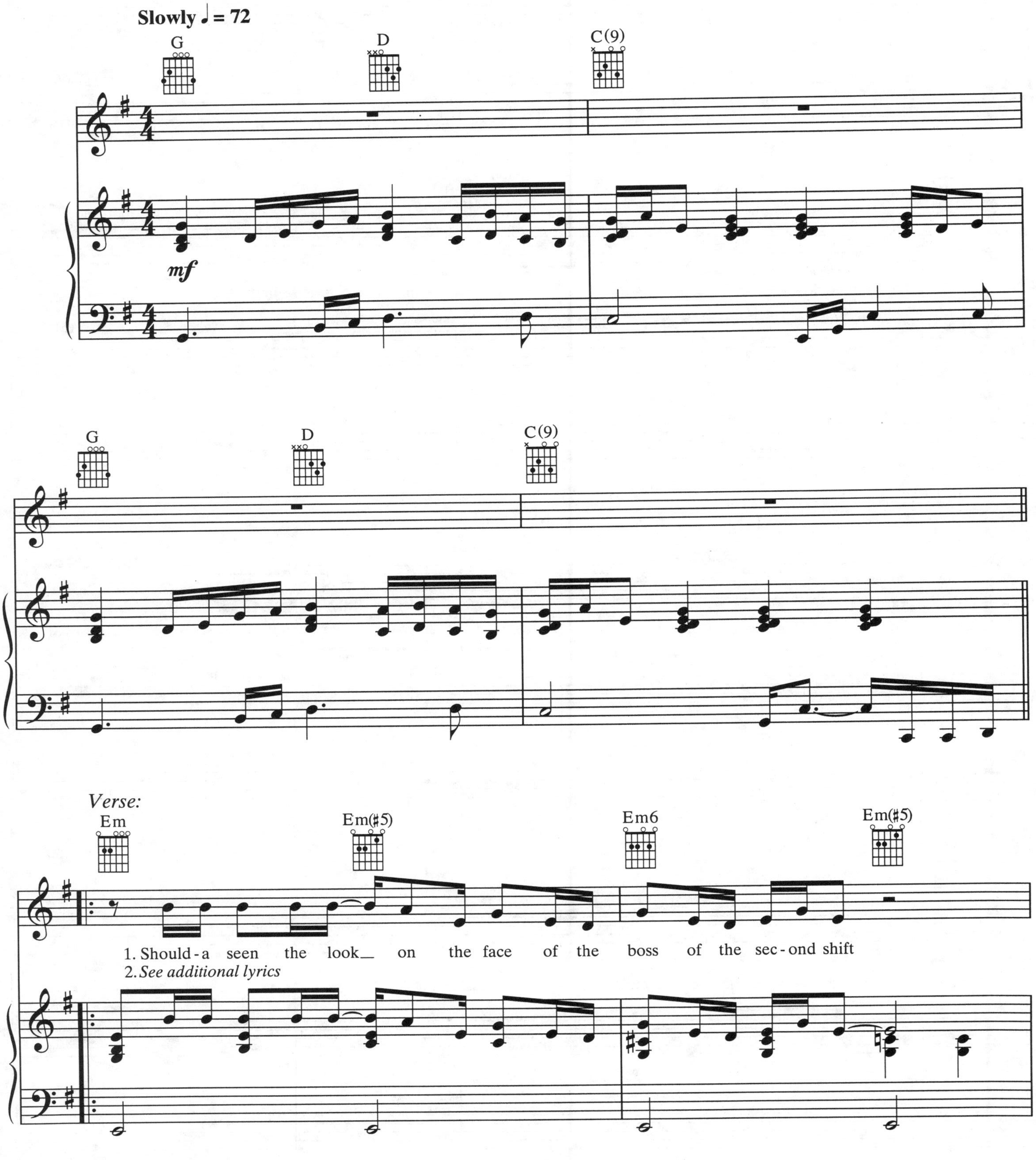

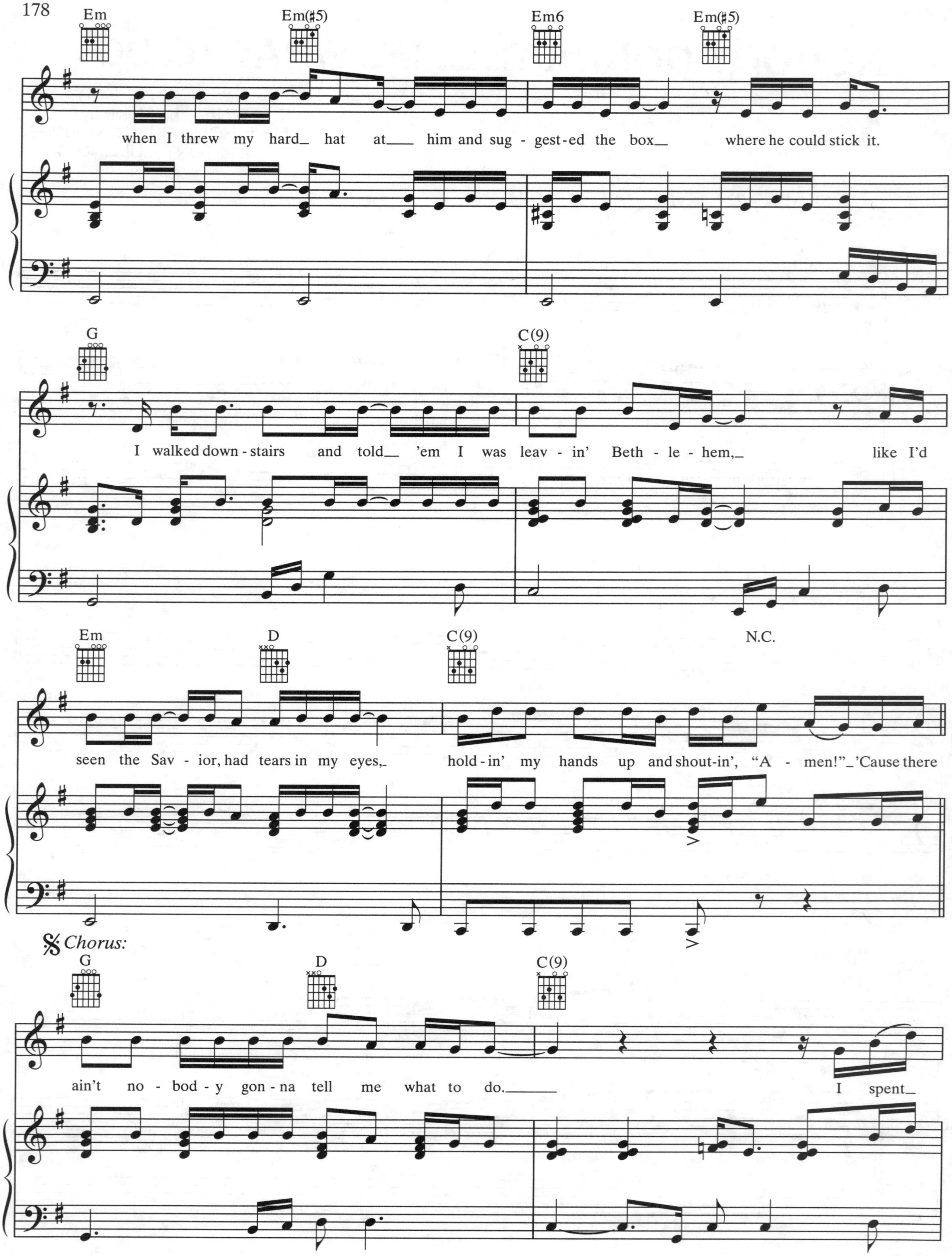
Em
Em(♯5)
Em6
Em(♯5)
when I threw my hard_ hat at___ him and sug - gest-ed the box__ where he could stick it.
G
C(9)
I walked down - stairs and told__ 'em I was leav - in' Beth - le - hem,_ like I'd
Em
D
C(9)
N.C.
seen the Sav - ior, had tears in my eyes,_ hold - in' my hands up and shout-in', "A - men!"_'Cause there
𝄋 Chorus:
G
D
C(9)
ain't no - bod - y gon - na tell me what to do.______ I spent_

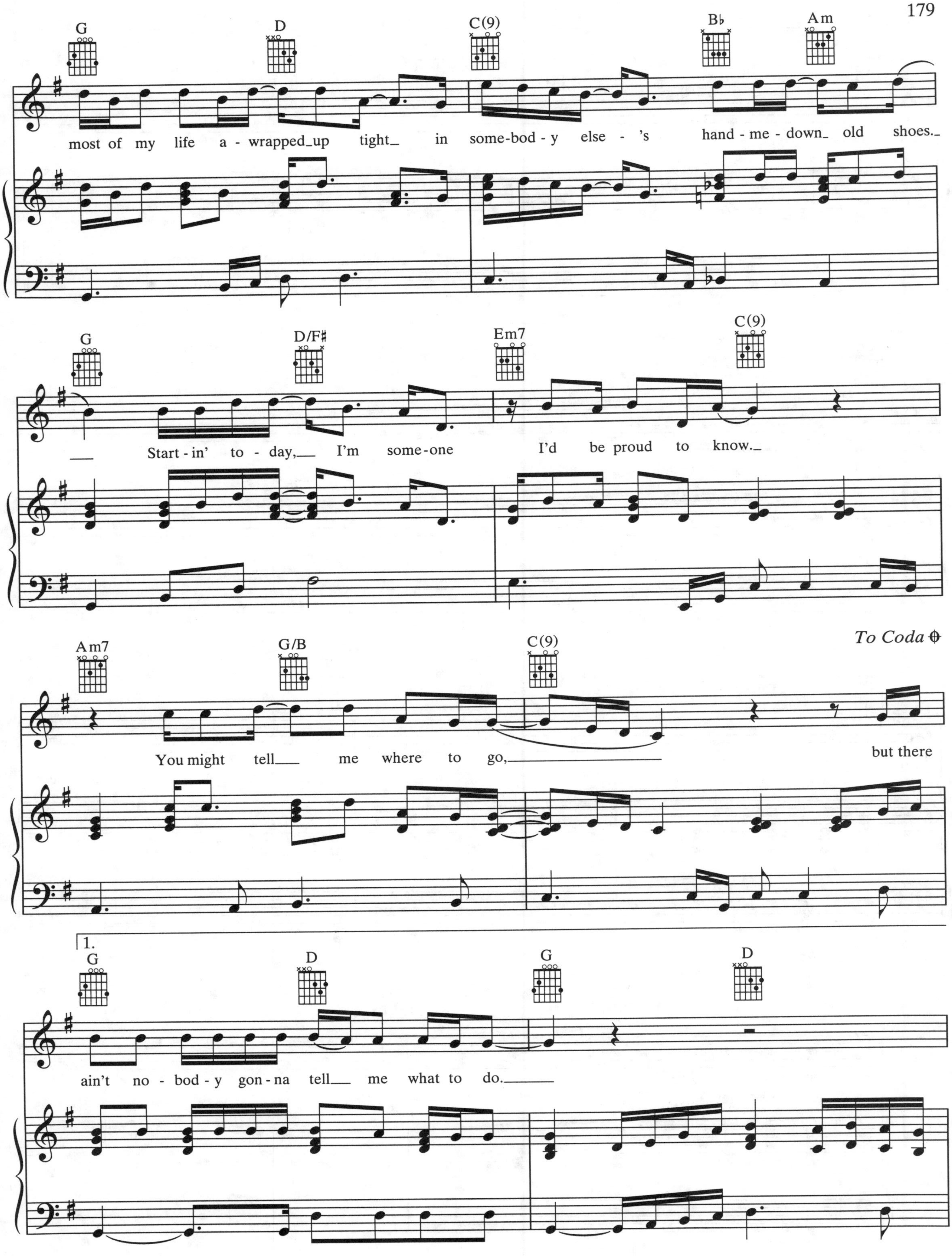
G
D
C(9)
B♭
Am
most of my life a - wrapped_up tight_ in some-bod - y else - 's hand - me - down_ old shoes._
G
D/F♯
Em7
C(9)
Start - in' to - day,_ I'm some-one I'd be proud to know._
To Coda
Am7
G/B
C(9)
You might tell_ me where to go,_ but there
1.
G
D
G
D
ain't no - bod - y gon - na tell_ me what to do._

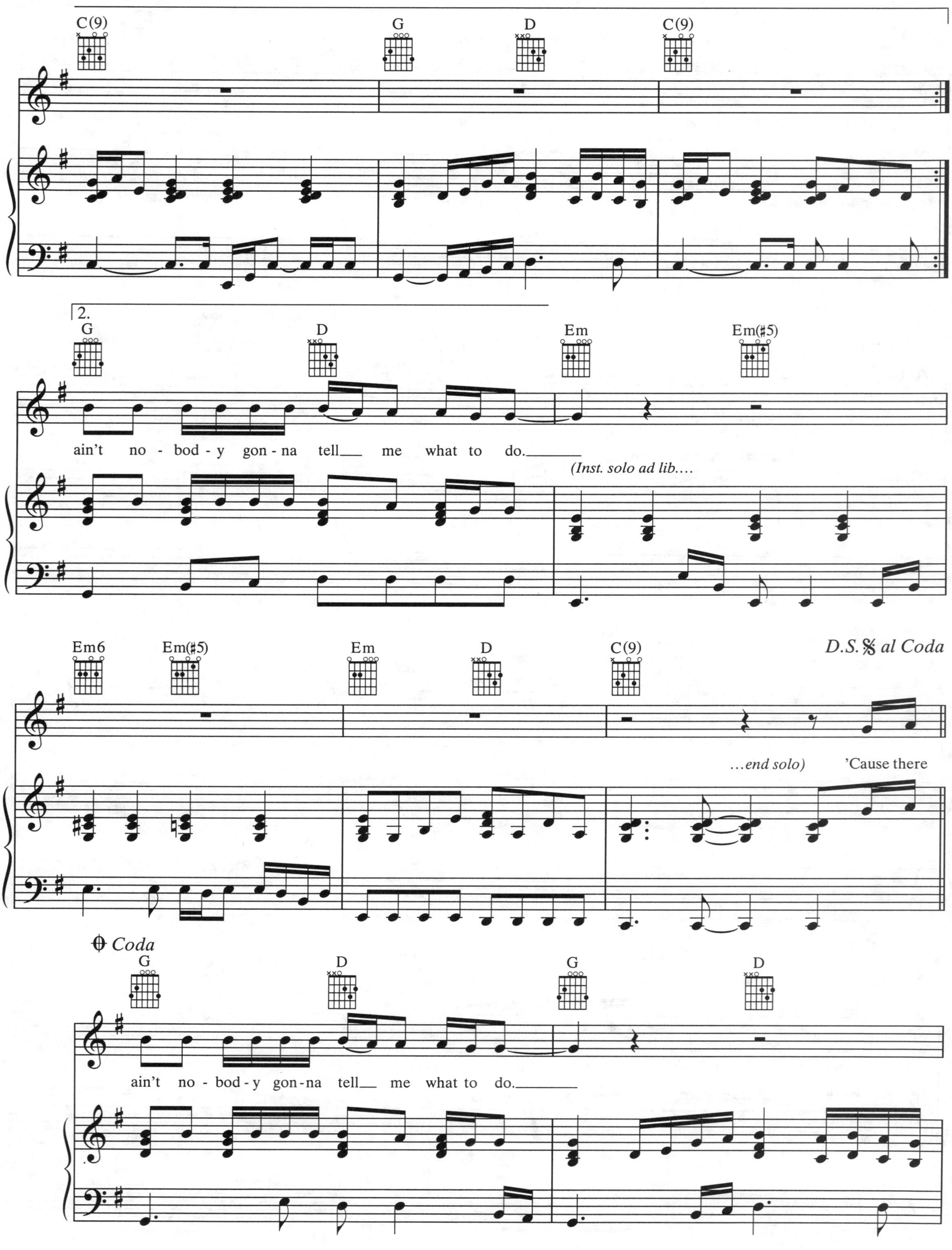
C(9)
G
D
C(9)
2.
G
D
Em
Em(♯5)
ain't no - bod - y gon - na tell__ me what to do.______
(Inst. solo ad lib....
Em6
Em(♯5)
Em
D
C(9)
D.S. 𝄋 al Coda
...end solo)
'Cause there
𝄌 Coda
G
D
G
D
ain't no - bod - y gon - na tell__ me what to do.______

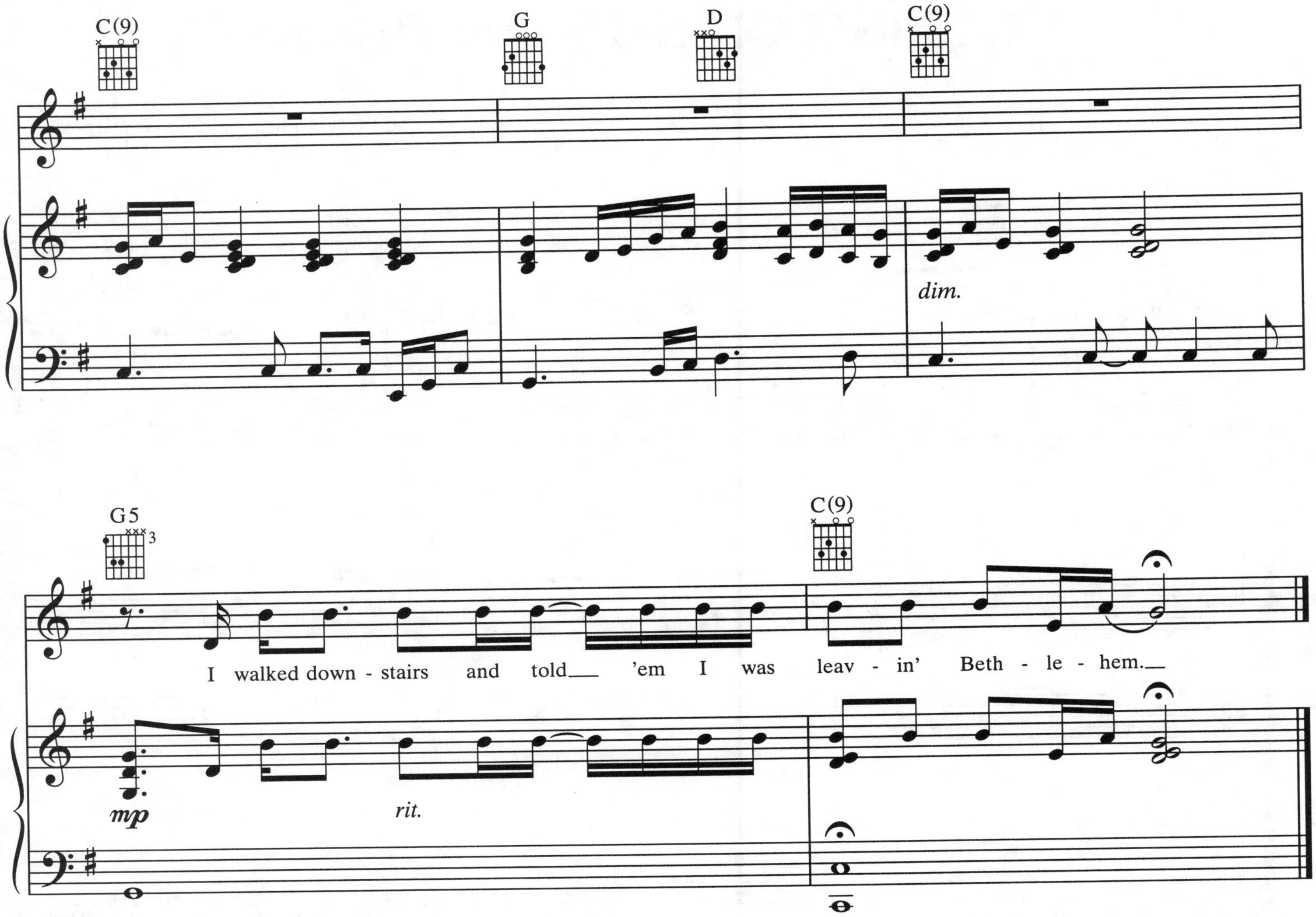

Verse 2:
We buried Daddy just last week at the church that saved his soul.
Man, he dreamed of pilot's wings,
Spent his whole life diggin' coal.
I got a guitar under my bed, but I've been too scared to fly.
But that's enough of that stuff, I'm packin' up my truck.
They can just kiss my butt good-bye.
(To Chorus:)

NOTHING ON BUT THE RADIO

Words and Music by
BYRON HILL, ODIE BLACKMON
and BRICE LONG

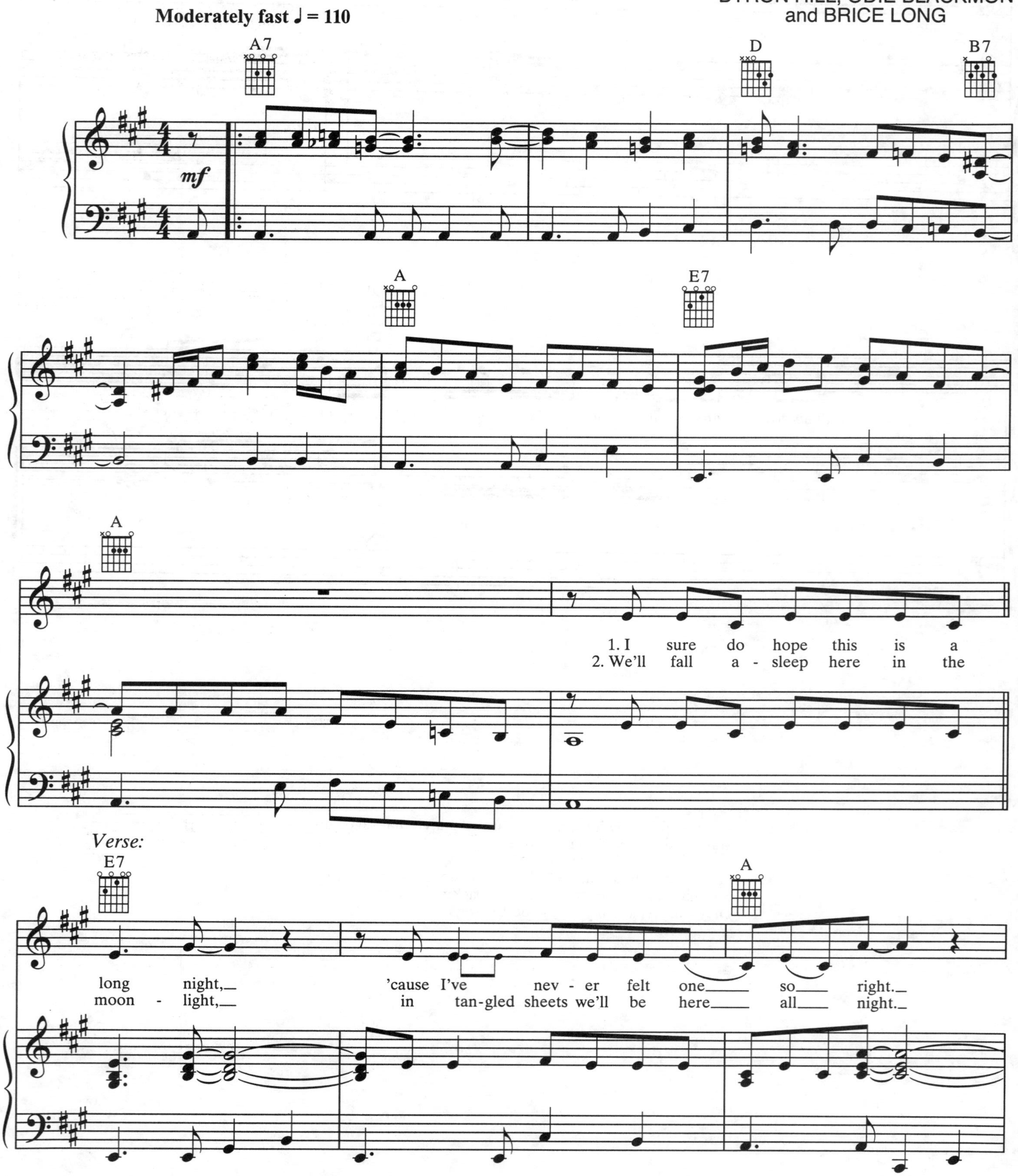

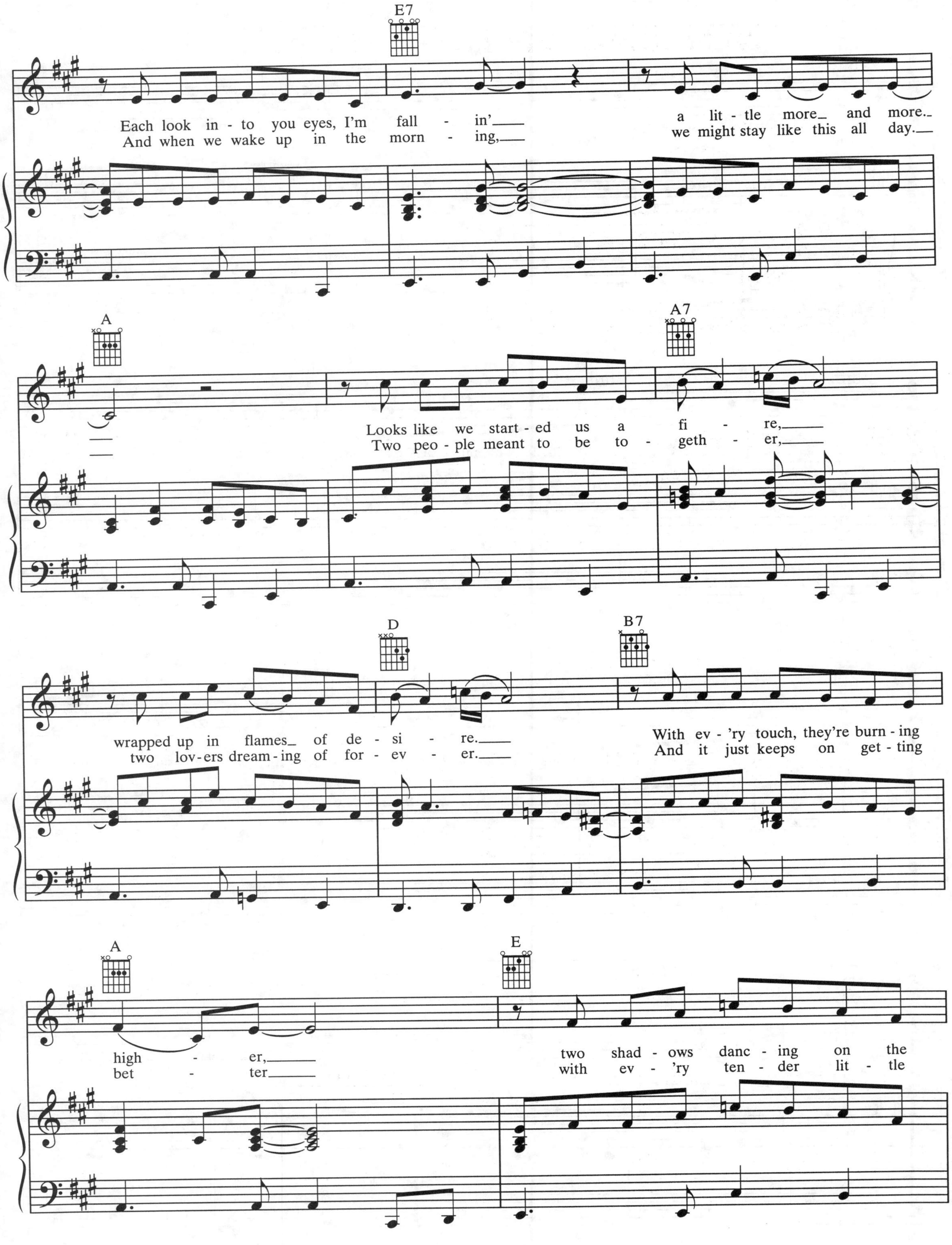
E7
Each look in - to you eyes, I'm fall - in'
a lit - tle more and more.
And when we wake up in the morn - ing,
we might stay like this all day.
A
A7
Looks like we start - ed us a fi - re,
Two peo - ple meant to be to - geth - er,
D
B7
wrapped up in flames of de - si - re.
two lov - ers dream - ing of for - ev - er.
With ev - 'ry touch, they're burn - ing
And it just keeps on get - ting
A
E
high - er,
bet - ter
two shad - ows danc - ing on the
with ev - 'ry ten - der lit - tle

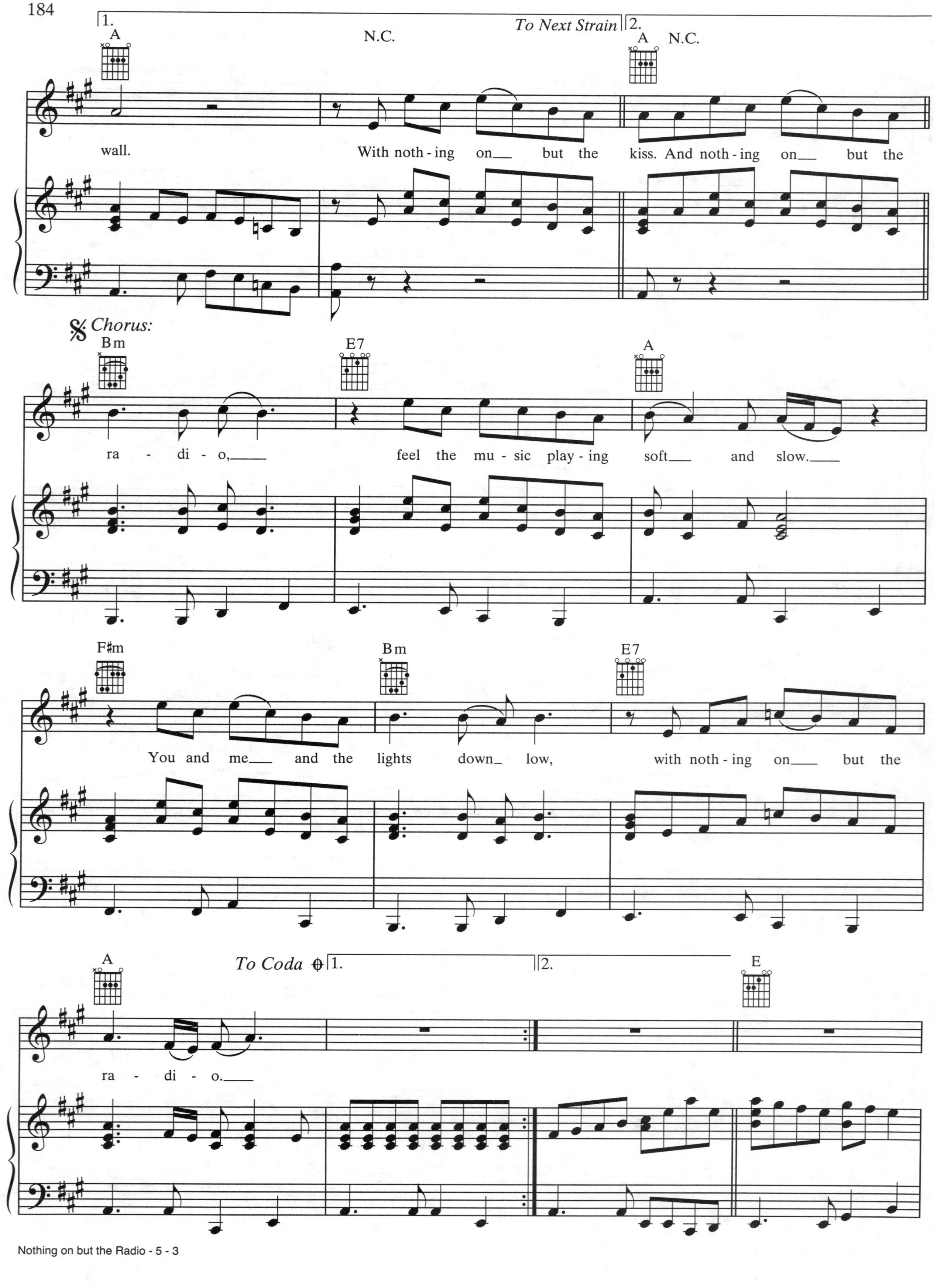
1.
A
N.C.
To Next Strain
2.
A N.C.
wall. With noth - ing on__ but the kiss. And noth - ing on__ but the
Chorus:
Bm
E7
A
ra - di - o,___ feel the mu - sic play - ing soft__ and slow.___
F♯m
Bm
E7
You and me__ and the lights down_ low, with noth - ing on___ but the
A
To Coda
1.
2.
E
ra - di - o.___

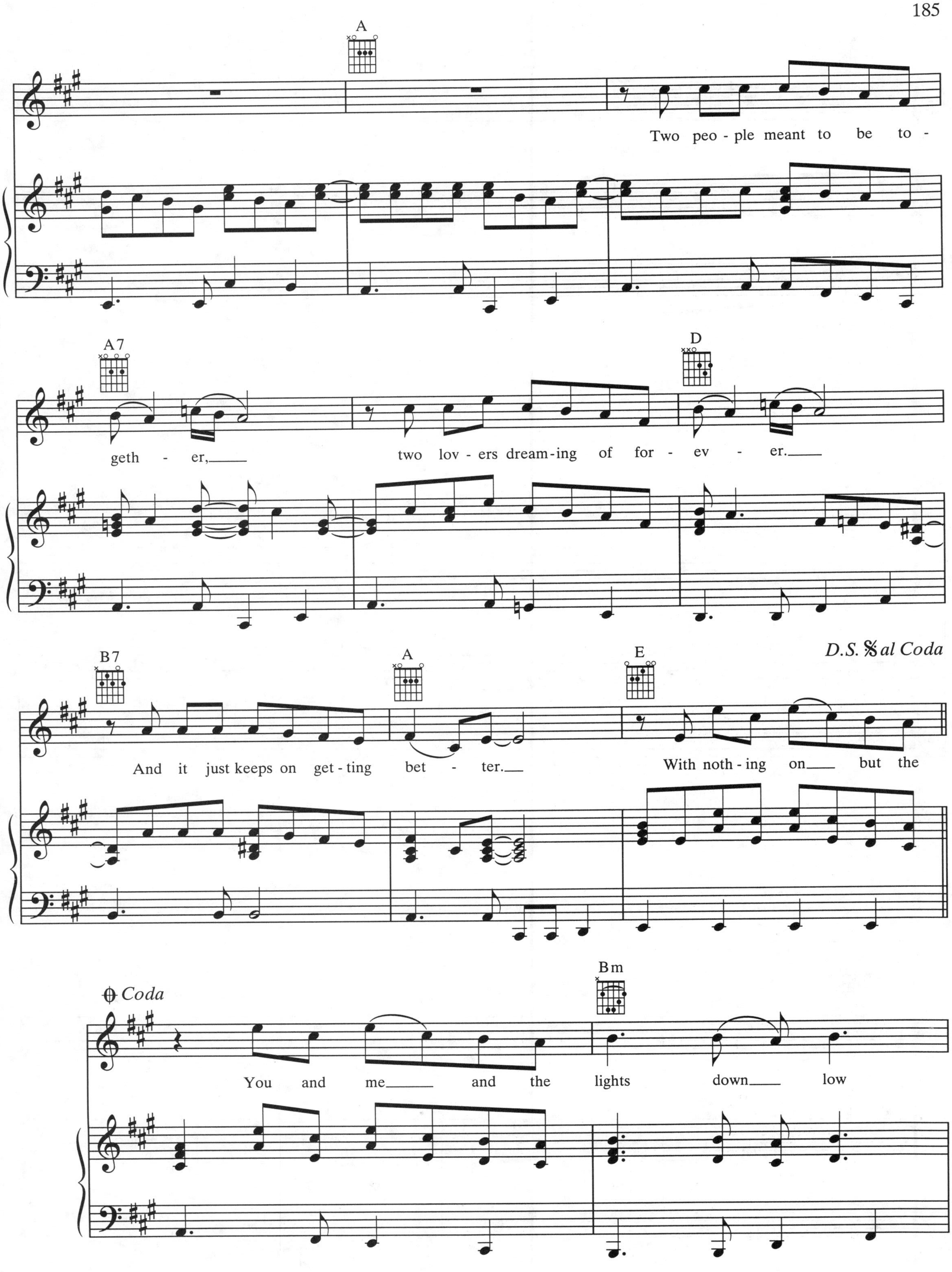
A
Two peo - ple meant to be to -
A7
geth - er,
two lov - ers dream - ing of for - ev - er.
D
D.S. 𝄋 al Coda
B7
And it just keeps on get - ting bet - ter.
A
E
With noth - ing on but the
Coda
You and me and the lights down low
Bm

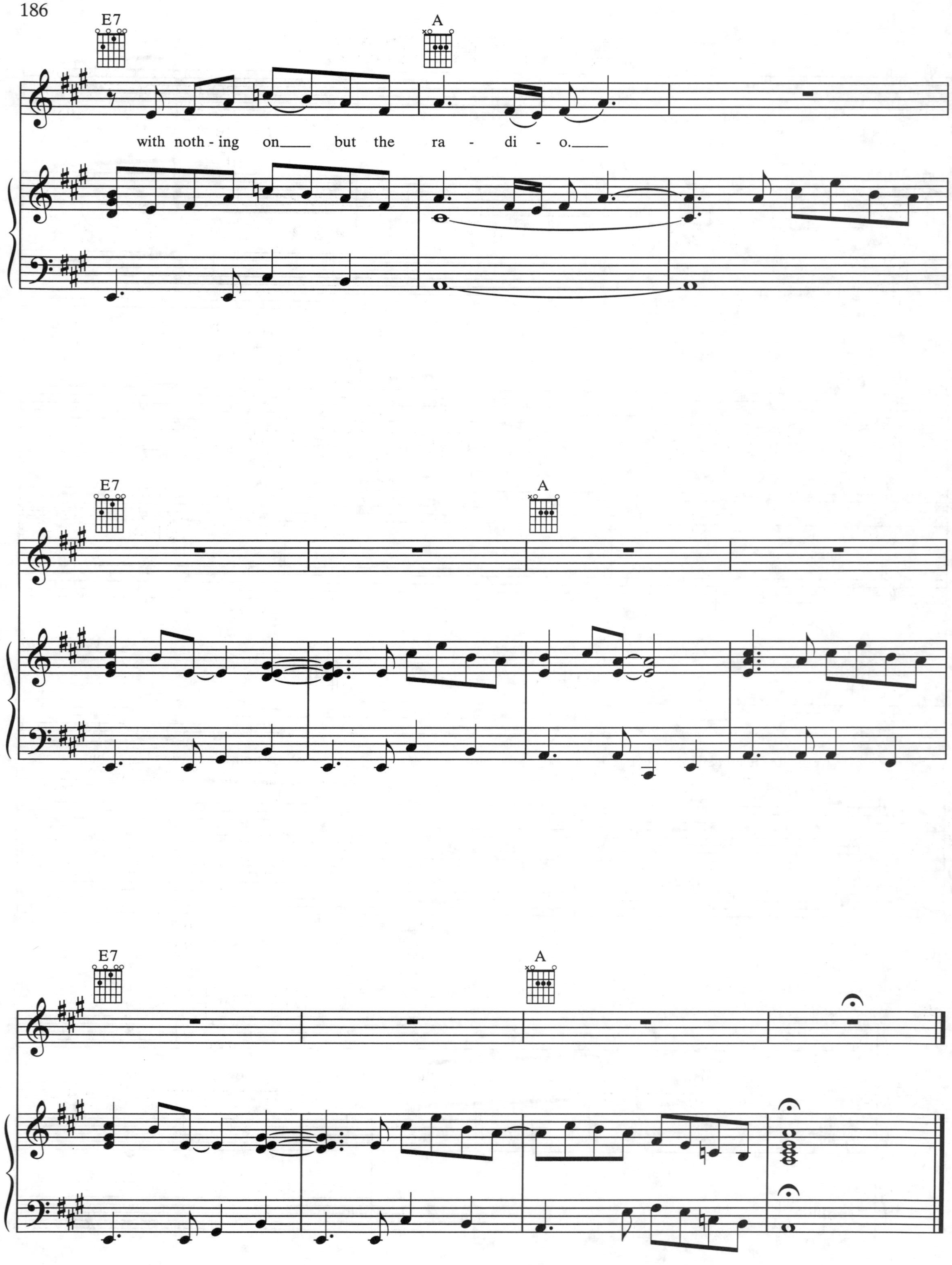
E7
A
with noth - ing on___ but the ra - di - o.___
E7
A
E7
A

ONE MORE DAY

Words and Music by
BOBBY TOMBERLIN and
STEVEN DALE JONES

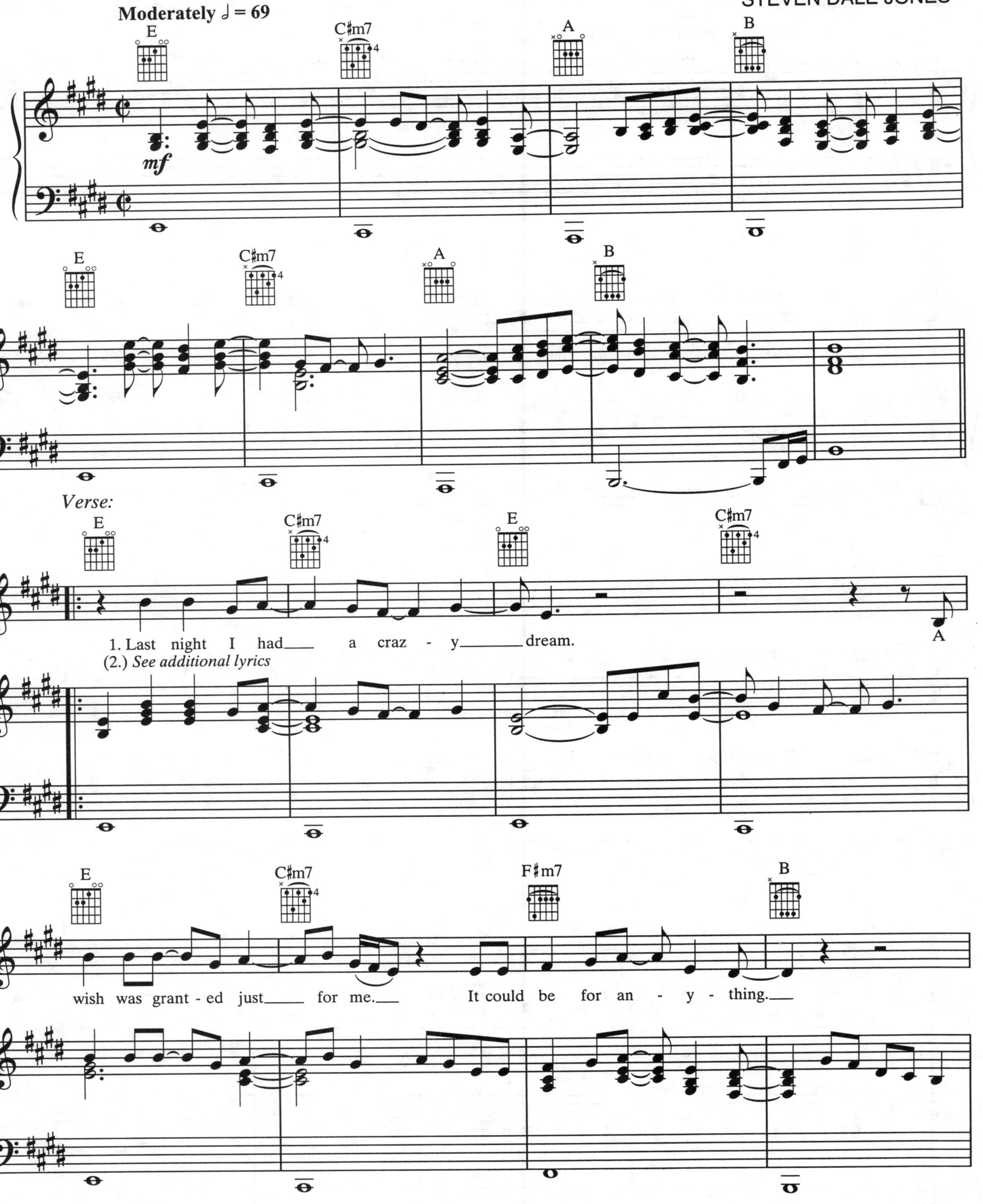

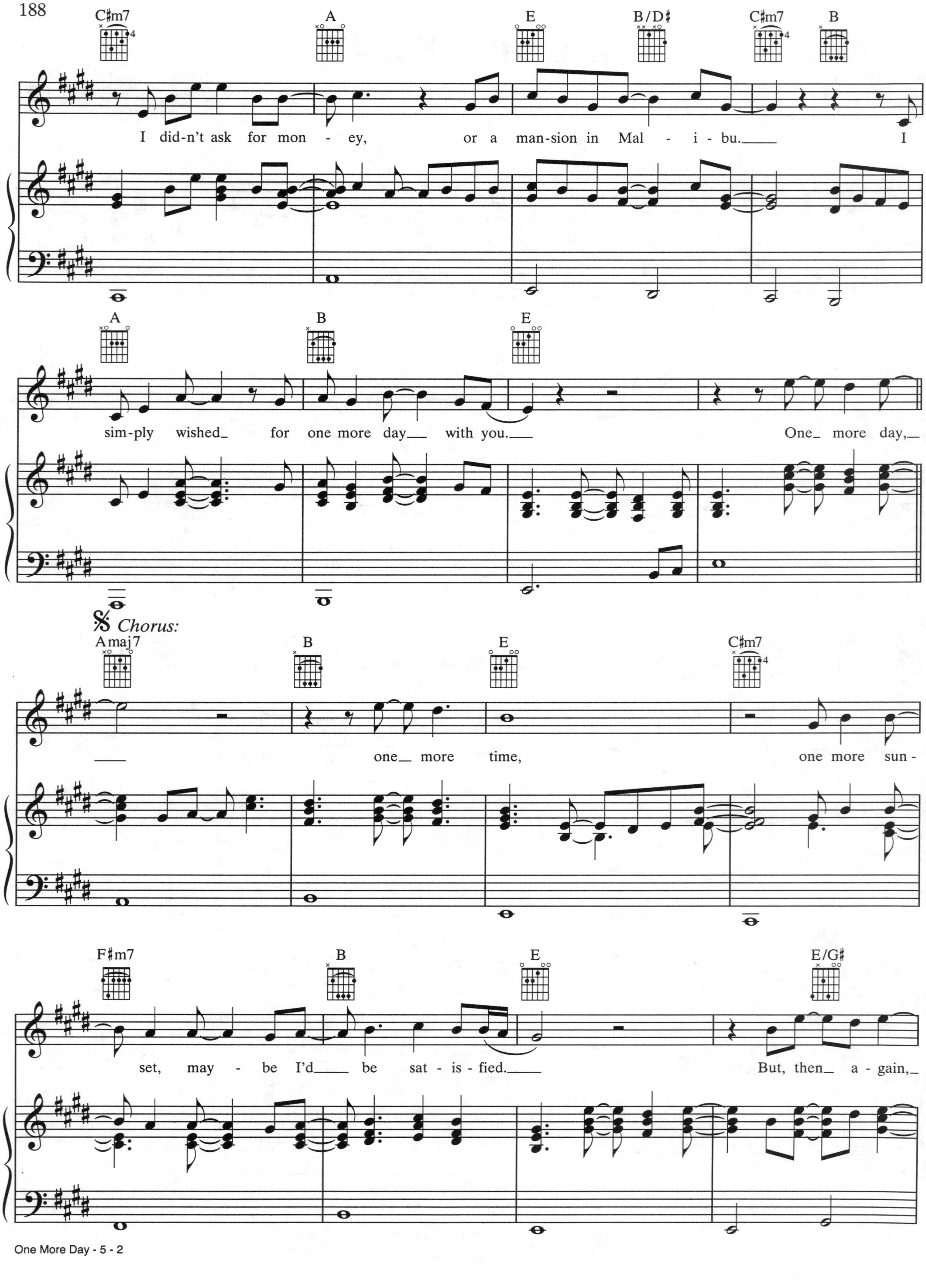
C♯m7
A
E
B/D♯
C♯m7
B
I did-n't ask for mon - ey, or a man-sion in Mal - i - bu.___ I
A
B
E
sim-ply wished_ for one more day__ with you.___ One_ more day,_
𝄋 Chorus:
Amaj7
B
E
C♯m7
___ one_ more time, one more sun -
F♯m7
B
E
E/G♯
set, may - be I'd___ be sat - is - fied.___ But, then_ a - gain,_

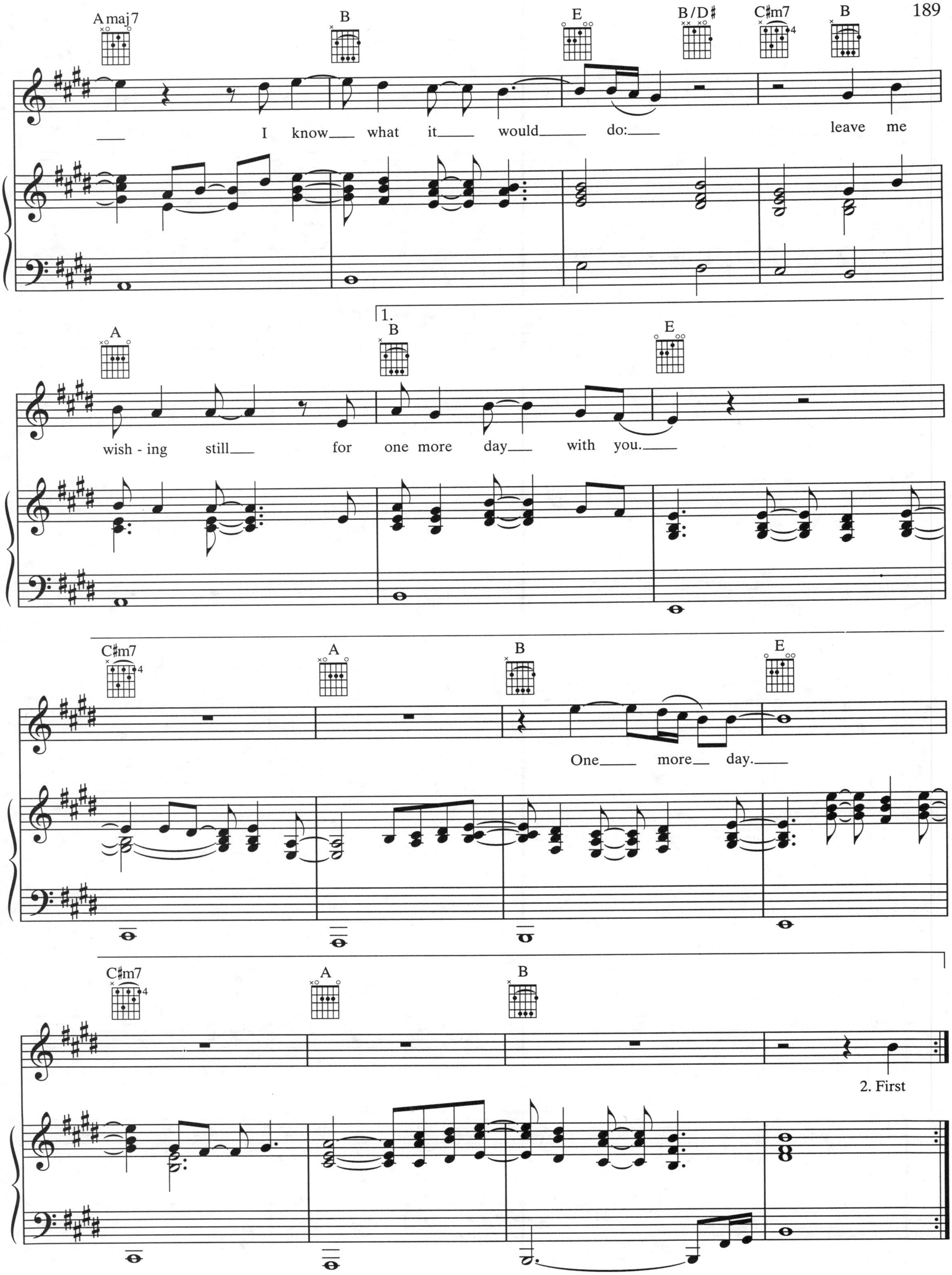
A maj7
B
E
B/D♯
C♯m7
B
I know what it would do:
leave me
A
1.
B
E
wish - ing still for one more day with you.
C♯m7
A
B
E
One more day.
C♯m7
A
B
2. First

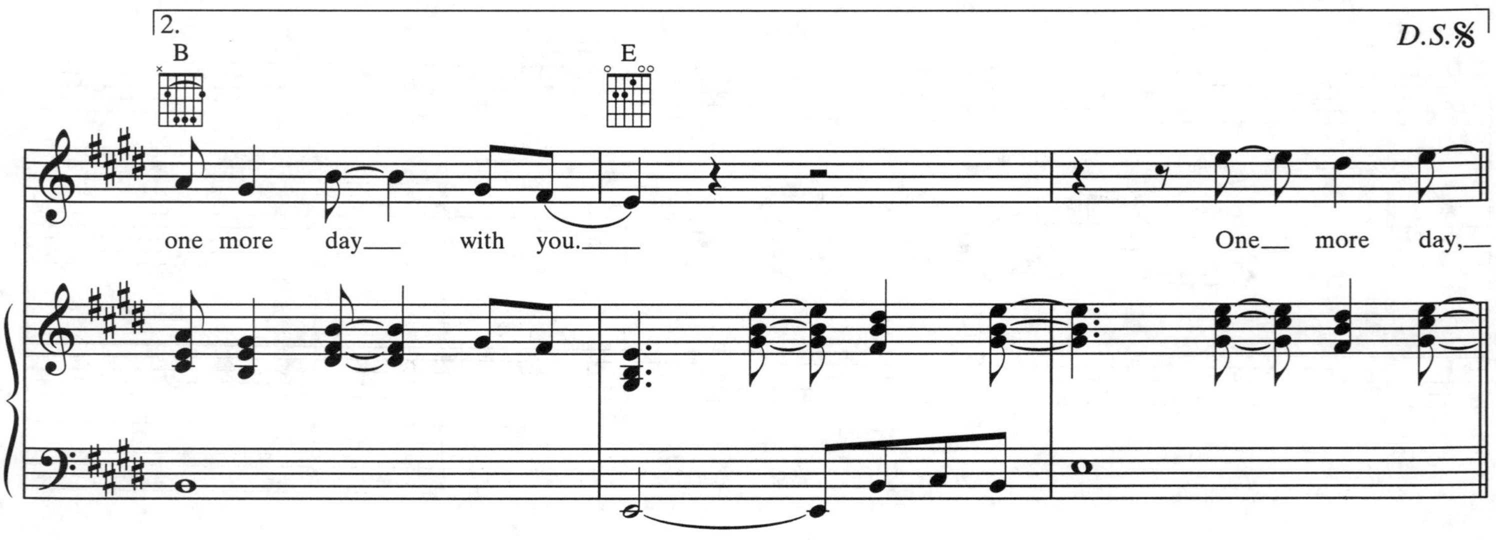
2.
B
E
D.S.𝄋
one more day___ with you.___
One___ more day,___

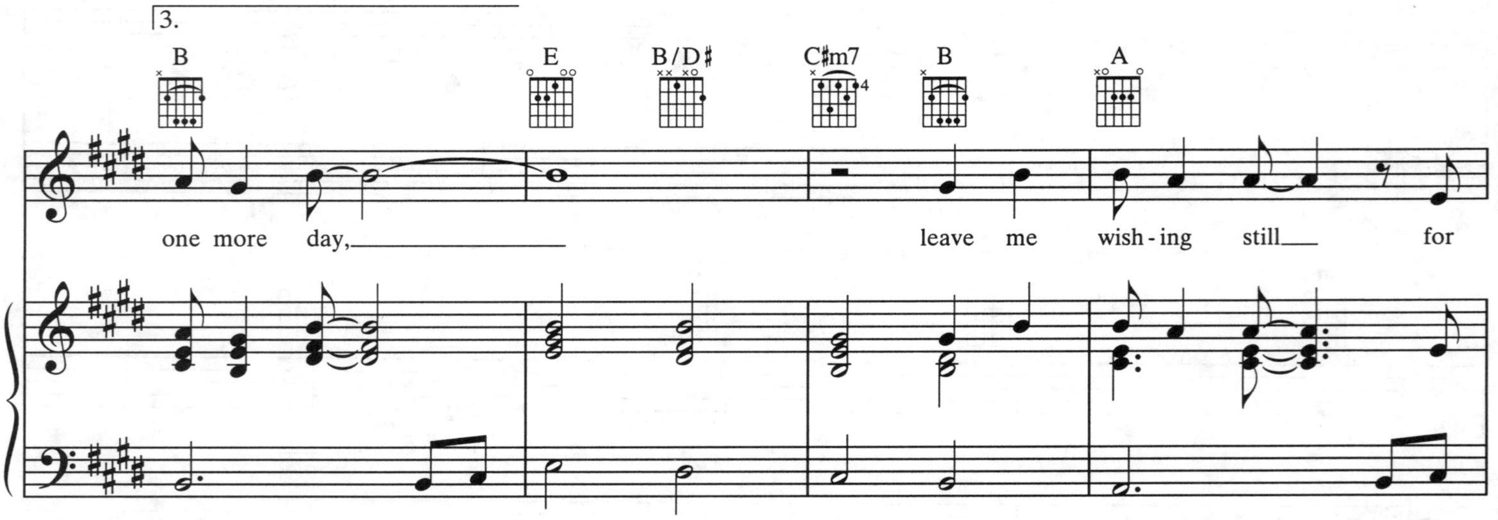
3.
B
E
B/D♯
C♯m7
B
A
one more day,___
leave me wish-ing still___ for

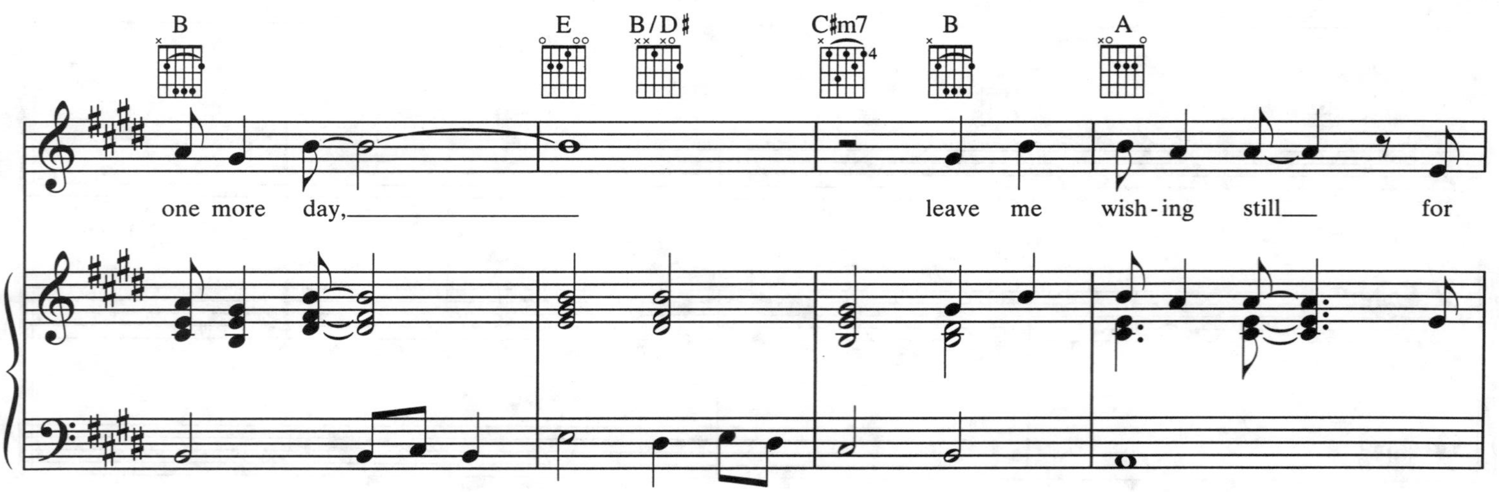
B
E
B/D♯
C♯m7
B
A
one more day,___
leave me wish-ing still___ for

Verse 2:
First thing I'd do is pray for time to crawl.
I'd unplug the telephone and keep the TV off.
I'd hold you every second, say a million "I love yous."
That's what I'd do with one more night with you.
(To Chorus:)

POUR ME

Words and Music by
HEIDI KAY NEWFIELD, IRA LEE DEAN,
BRYAN KEITH BURNS, SAMMY HARP
and RORY WATERS BEIGHLEY

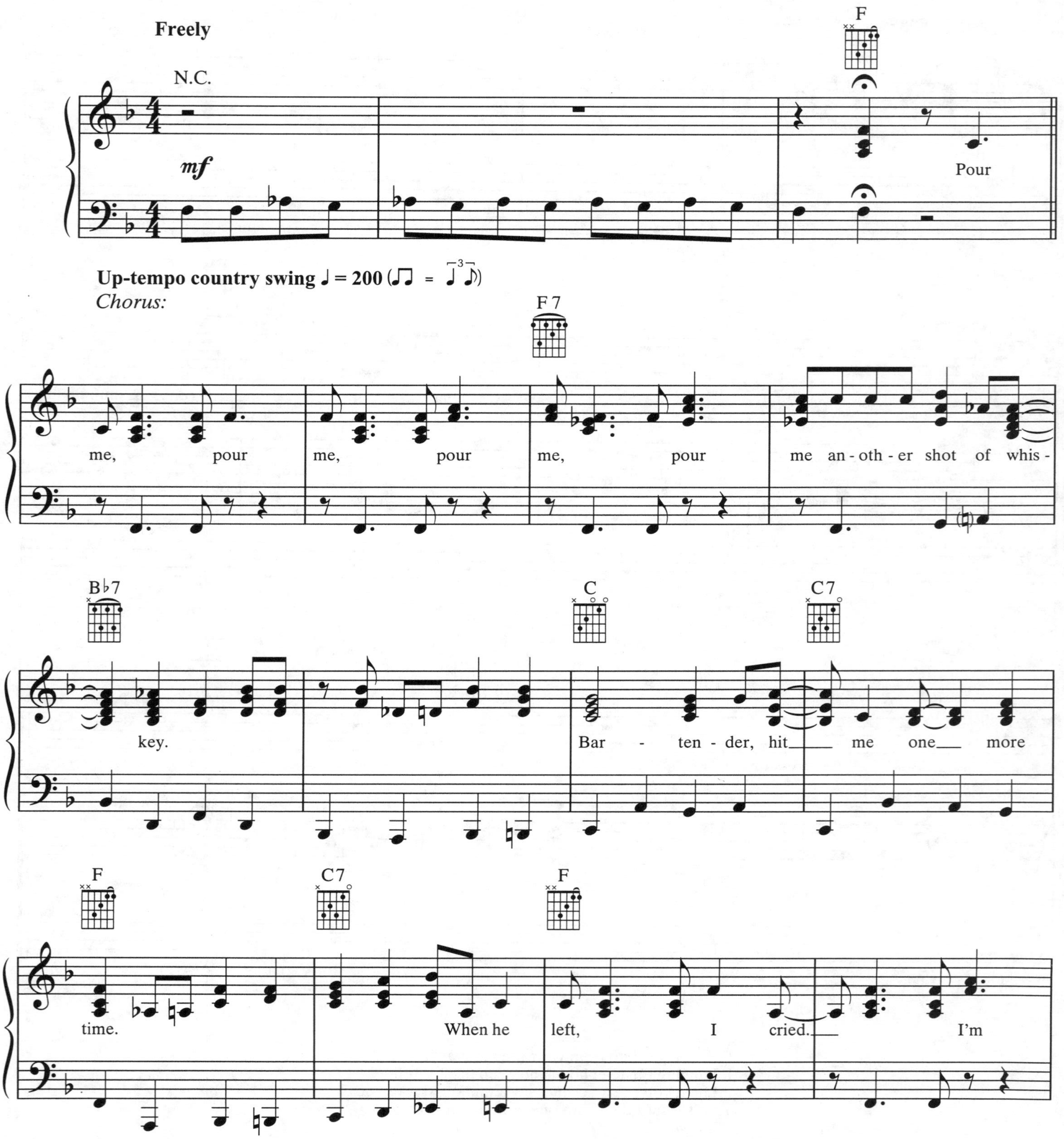

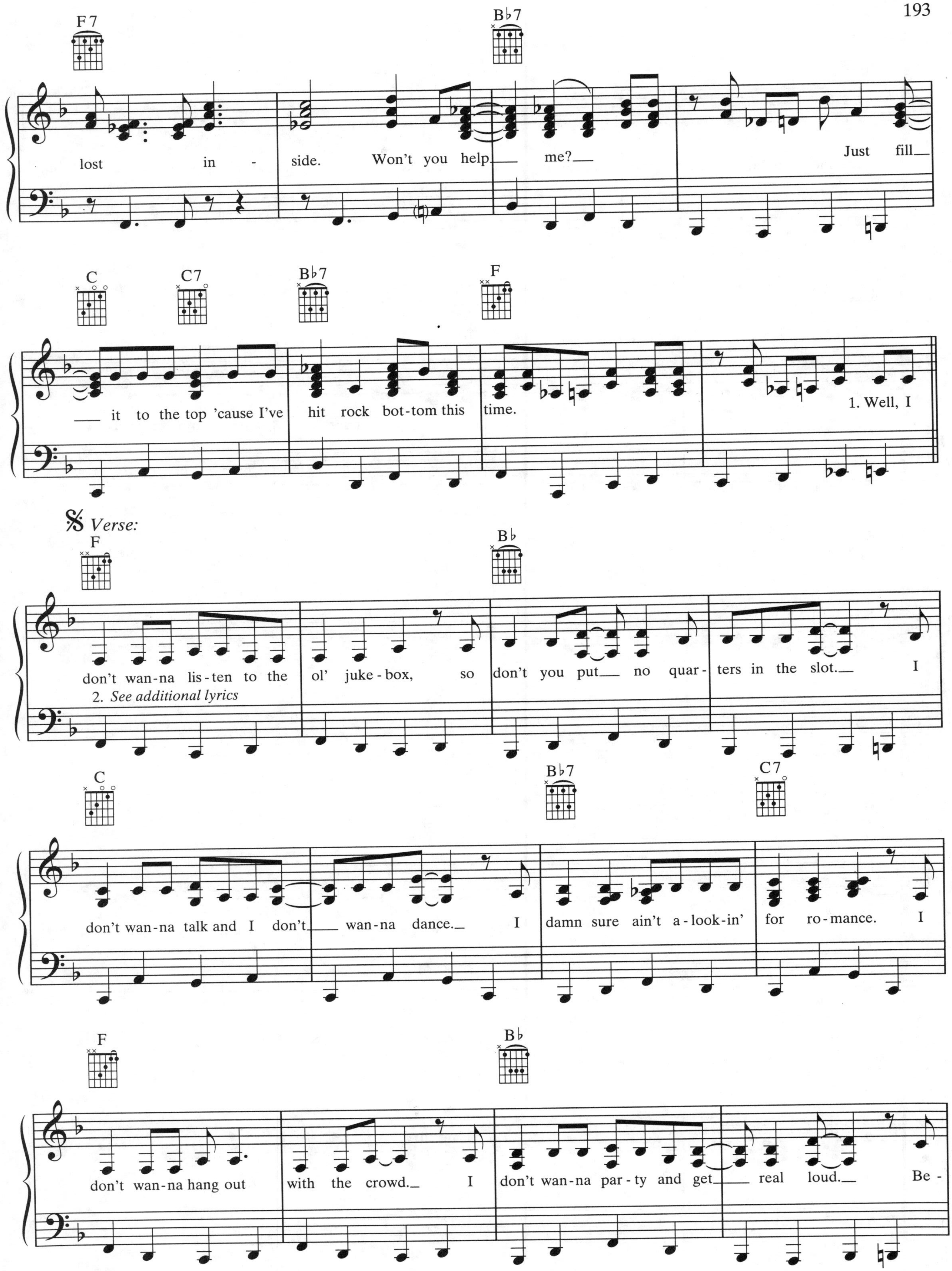
F7
B♭7
lost in - side. Won't you help__ me?__ Just fill__
C
C7
B♭7
F
__ it to the top 'cause I've hit rock bot-tom this time. 1. Well, I
Verse:
F
B♭
don't wan-na lis-ten to the ol' juke-box, so don't you put__ no quar-ters in the slot.__ I
2. See additional lyrics
C
B♭7
C7
don't wan-na talk and I don't__ wan-na dance.__ I damn sure ain't a-look-in' for ro-mance. I
F
B♭
don't wan-na hang out with the crowd.__ I don't wan-na par-ty and get__ real loud.__ Be -

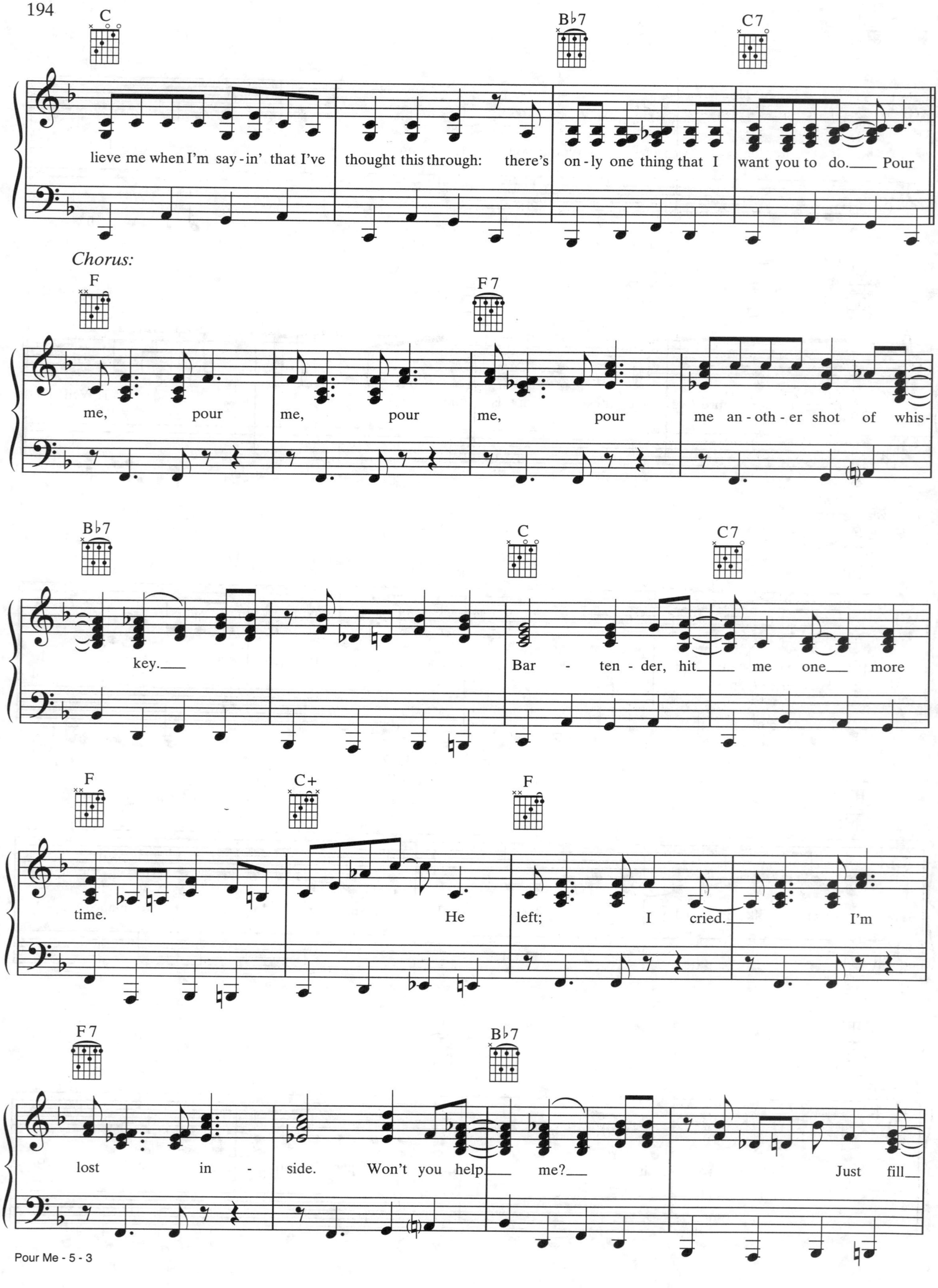
C
B♭7
C7
lieve me when I'm say-in' that I've thought this through: there's on-ly one thing that I want you to do.___ Pour
Chorus:
F
F7
me, pour me, pour me, pour me an-oth-er shot of whis-
B♭7
C
C7
key.___ Bar - ten-der, hit___ me one___ more
F
C+
F
time. He left; I cried.___ I'm
F7
B♭7
lost in - side. Won't you help___ me?___ Just fill___

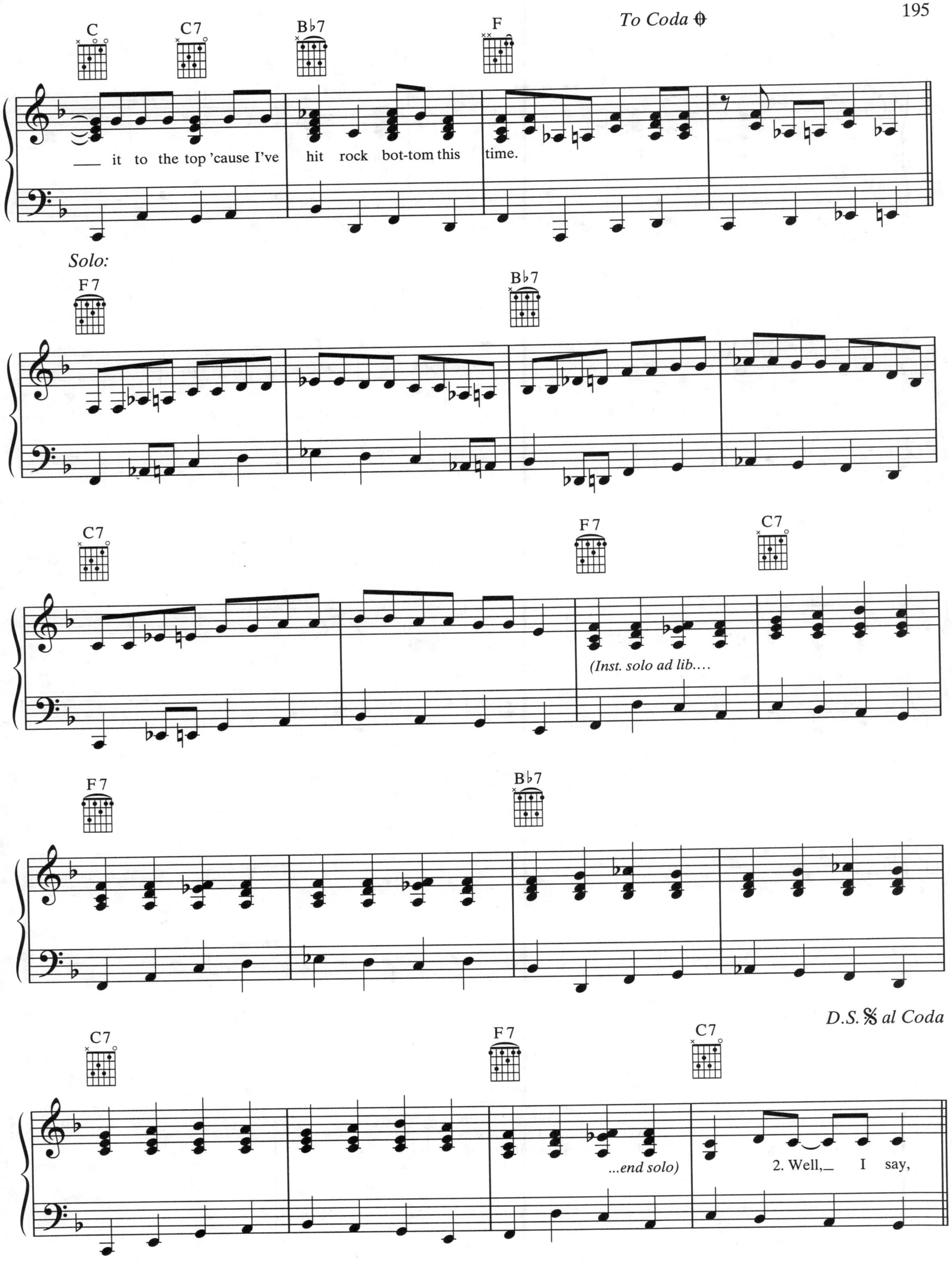
To Coda ⊕
C
C7
B♭7
F
___ it to the top 'cause I've
hit rock bot-tom this
time.
Solo:
F7
B♭7
C7
F7
C7
(Inst. solo ad lib....
F7
B♭7
D.S. 𝄋 al Coda
C7
F7
C7
...end solo)
2. Well,_ I say,

Verse 2:
Well, I say, here's my story; it's sad but it's true.
There's so many things that I never knew.
He loved to party and he loved to dance.
He loved to get loud every time he had the chance.
I always thought he was a simple-minded Okie.
Well, little did I know he was the king of karaoke.
He was everything that a man should be.
My problem was that he wasn't with me.
(To Chorus:)

SAVE A HORSE
(RIDE A COWBOY)

Words and Music by
JOHN RICH and KENNY ALPHIN

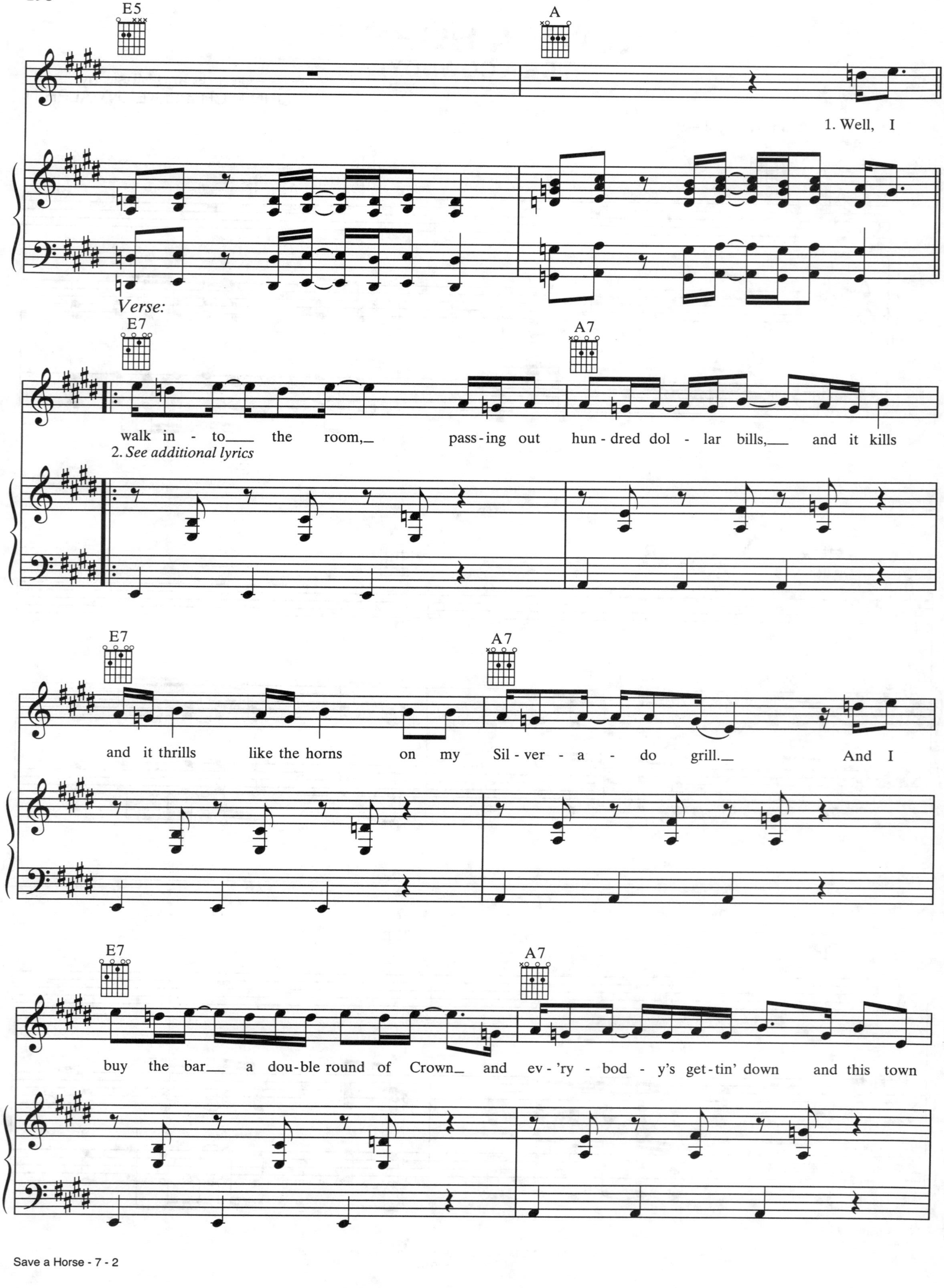
E5
A
1. Well, I
Verse:
E7
A7
walk in - to the room, pass-ing out hun - dred dol - lar bills, and it kills
2. See additional lyrics
E7
A7
and it thrills like the horns on my Sil - ver - a - do grill. And I
E7
A7
buy the bar a dou-ble round of Crown and ev - 'ry - bod - y's get-tin' down and this town

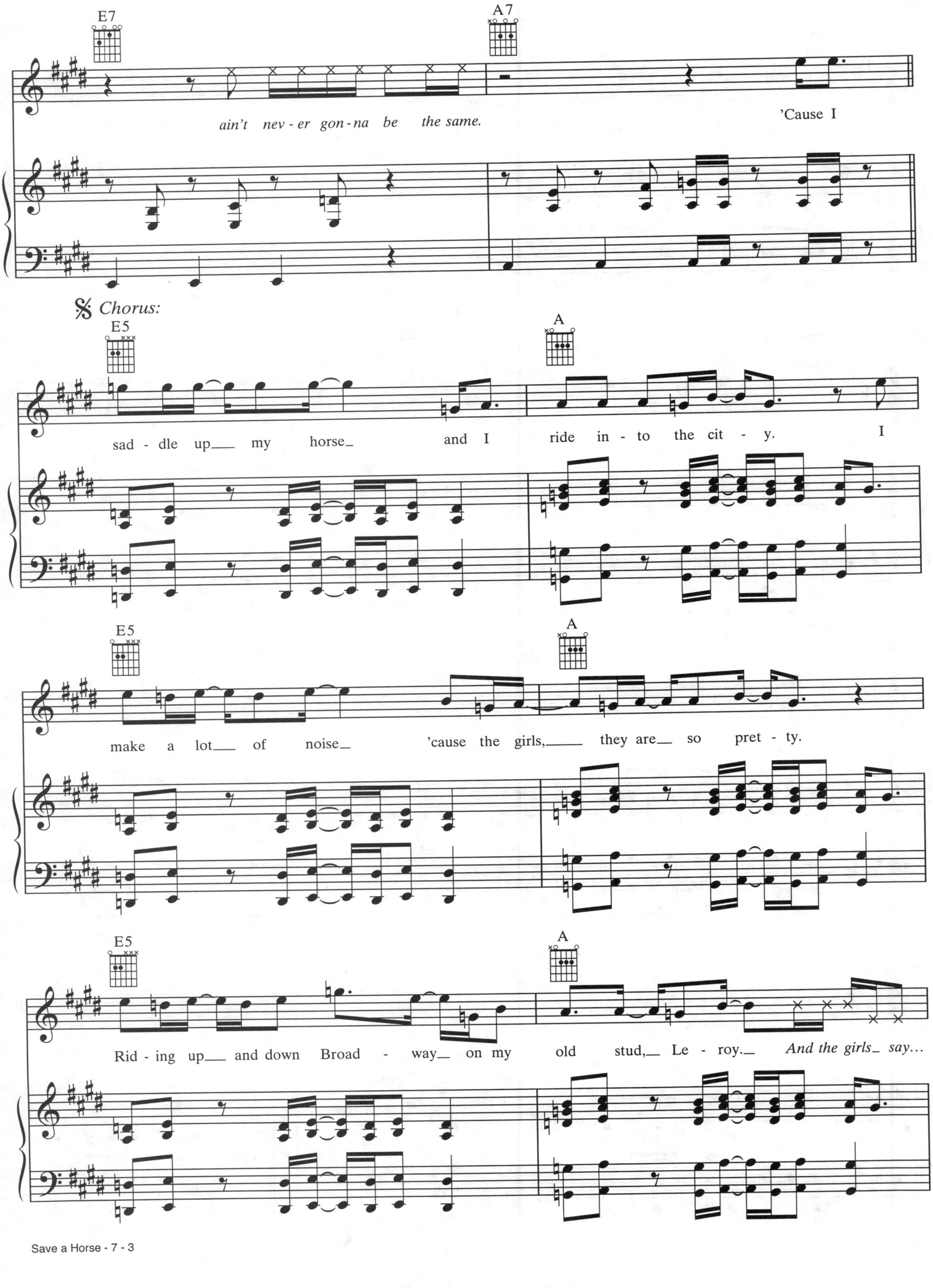
E7
A7
ain't nev-er gon-na be the same.
'Cause I
Chorus:
E5
A
sad-dle up__ my horse__ and I ride in-to the cit-y. I
E5
A
make a lot__ of noise__ 'cause the girls,____ they are__ so pret-ty.
E5
A
Rid-ing up__ and down Broad-way__ on my old stud,__ Le-roy.__ And the girls__ say...

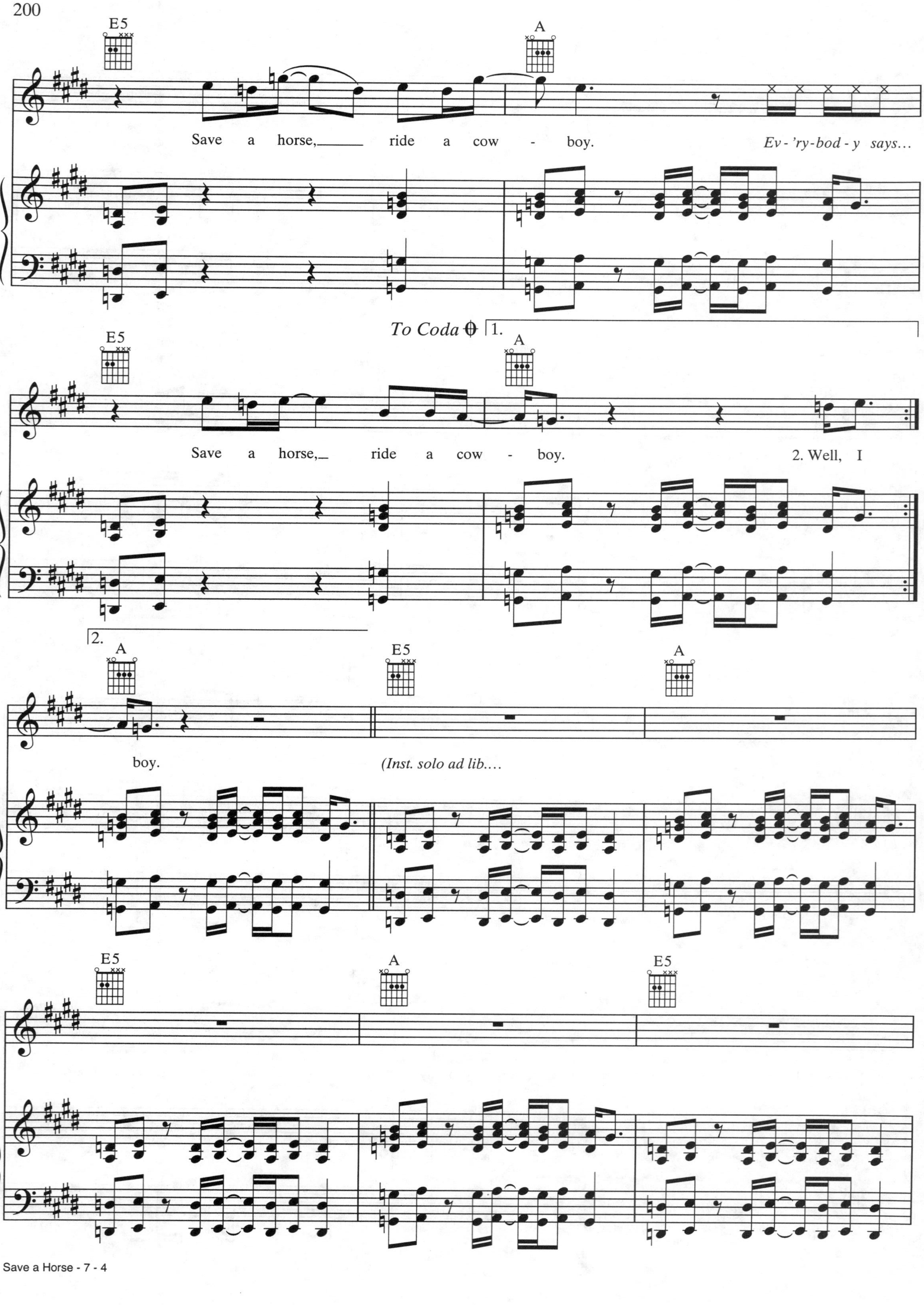
E5
A
Save a horse,___ ride a cow - boy.
Ev - 'ry-bod - y says...
To Coda
1.
E5
A
Save a horse,_ ride a cow - boy.
2. Well, I
2.
A
E5
A
boy.
(Inst. solo ad lib....
E5
A
E5

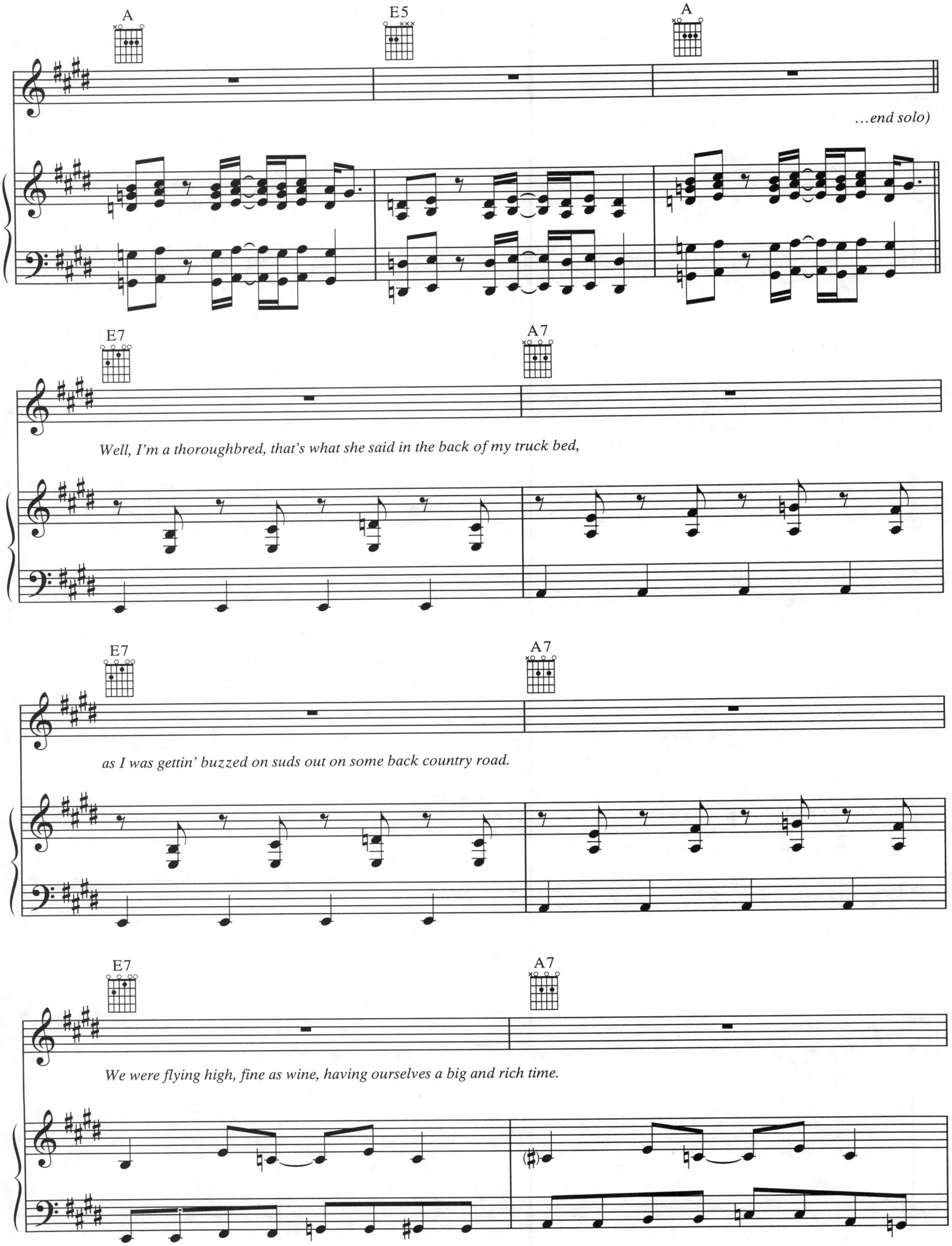
A
E5
A
...end solo)
E7
A7
Well, I'm a thoroughbred, that's what she said in the back of my truck bed,
E7
A7
as I was gettin' buzzed on suds out on some back country road.
E7
A7
We were flying high, fine as wine, having ourselves a big and rich time.

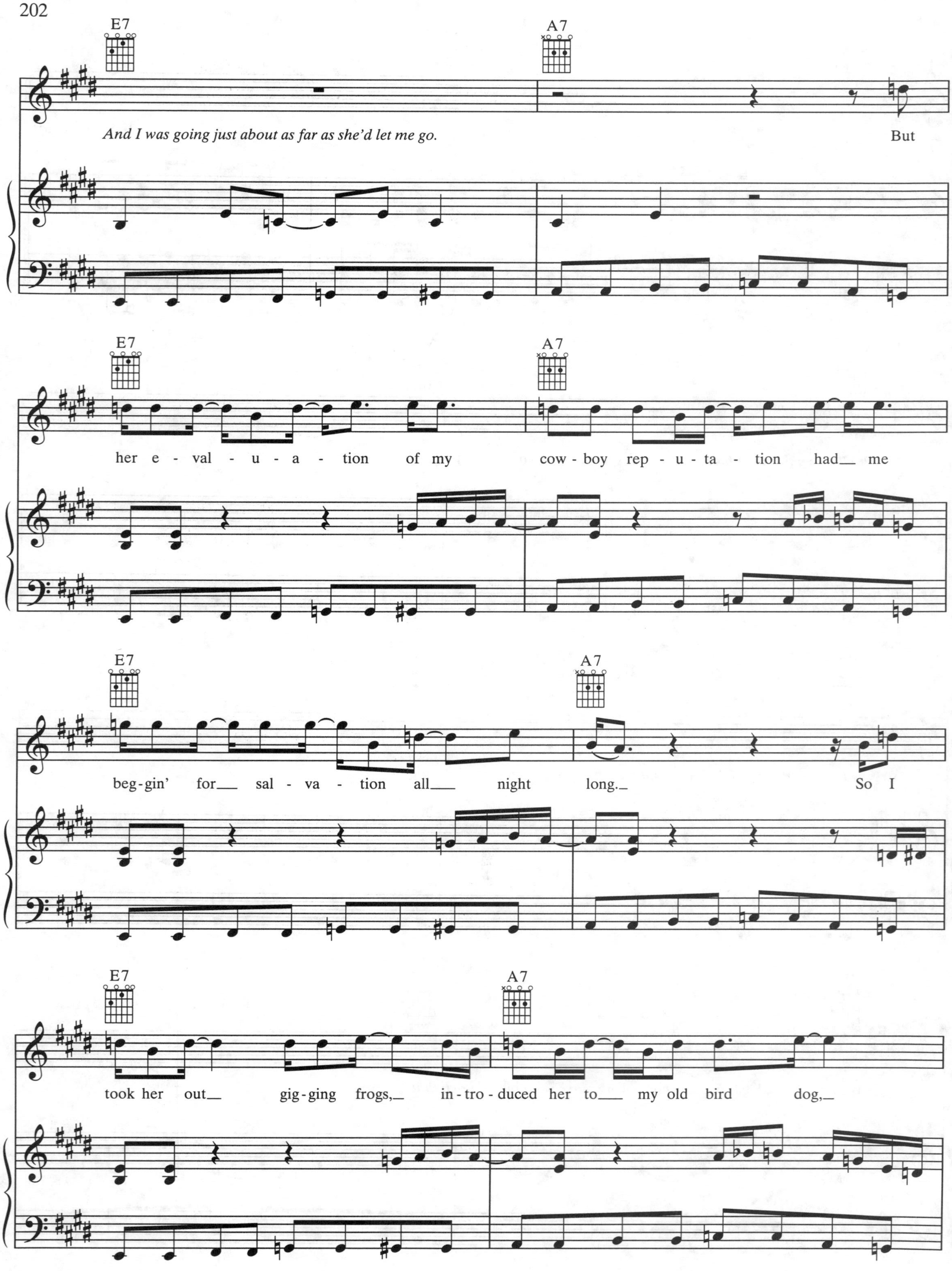
E7
A7
And I was going just about as far as she'd let me go.
But
E7
A7
her e - val - u - a - tion of my cow - boy rep - u - ta - tion had__ me
E7
A7
beg - gin' for__ sal - va - tion all__ night long.__
So I
E7
A7
took her out__ gig - ging frogs,__ in - tro - duced her to__ my old bird dog,__

Verse 2:
Well, I don't give a dang about nothing.
I'm singing and bling-blinging
While the girls are drinking longnecks down.
And I wouldn't trade old Leroy
Or my Chevrolet for your Escalade,
Or your freak parade.
I'm the only John Wayne left in this town.
And I…
(To Chorus:)

REDNECK WOMAN

Words and Music by
JOHN RICH and GRETCHEN WILSON

*Original recording in key of F♯.

I can't swig that sweet cham-pagne. I'd rath-er drink beer all night in a tav -
C7
ern, or in a hon-ky-tonk, or on a four-wheel-drive tail - gate.
G
I've got post - ers on my wall of Sky-nyrd, Kid and Strait. Some
D7
peo-ple look down on me, but I don't give a rip. I

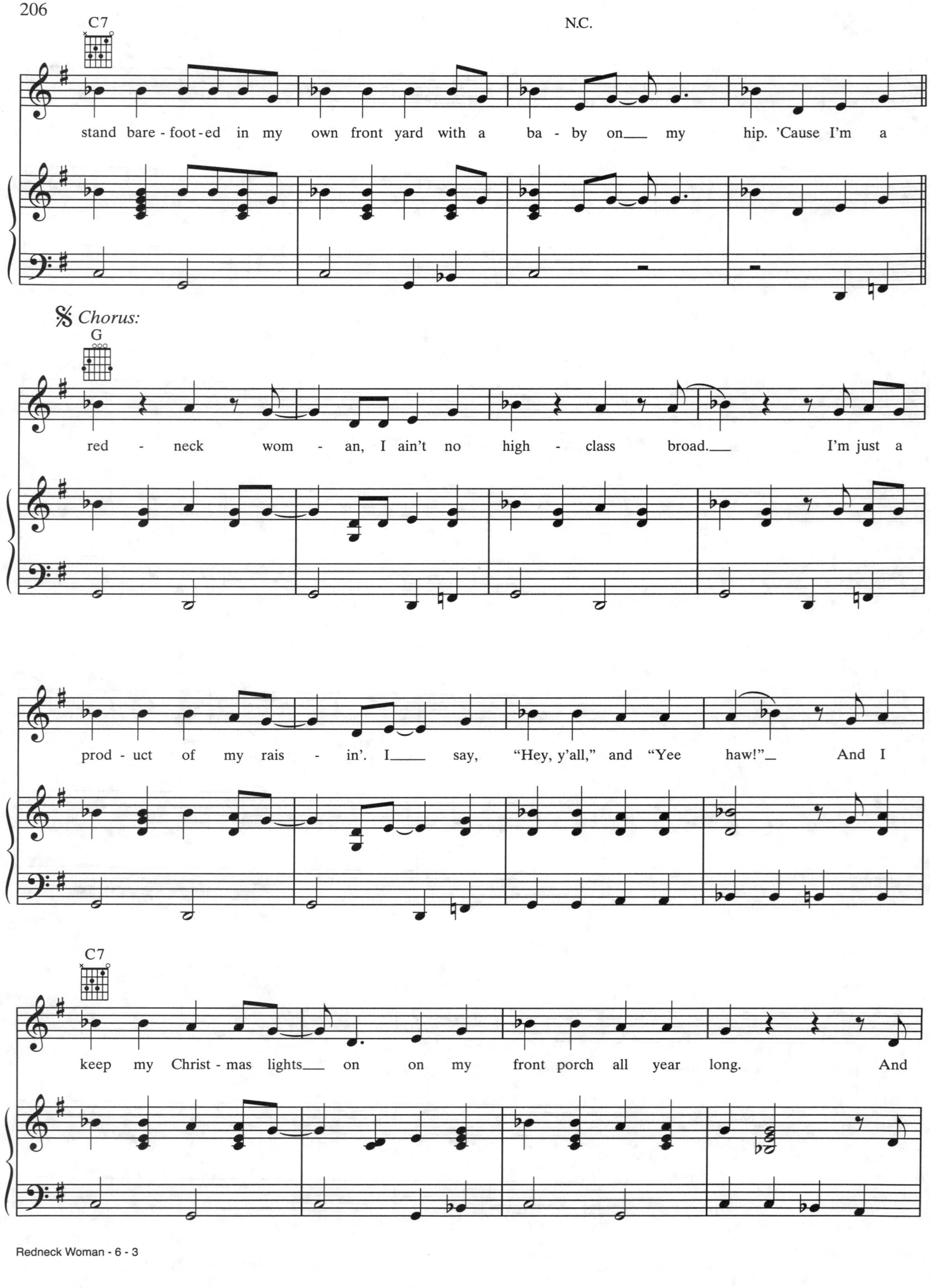
C7
N.C.
stand bare - foot - ed in my own front yard with a ba - by on___ my hip. 'Cause I'm a
Chorus:
G
red - neck wom - an, I ain't no high - class broad.___ I'm just a
prod - uct of my rais - in'. I___ say, "Hey, y'all," and "Yee haw!"_ And I
C7
keep my Christ - mas lights___ on on my front porch all year long. And

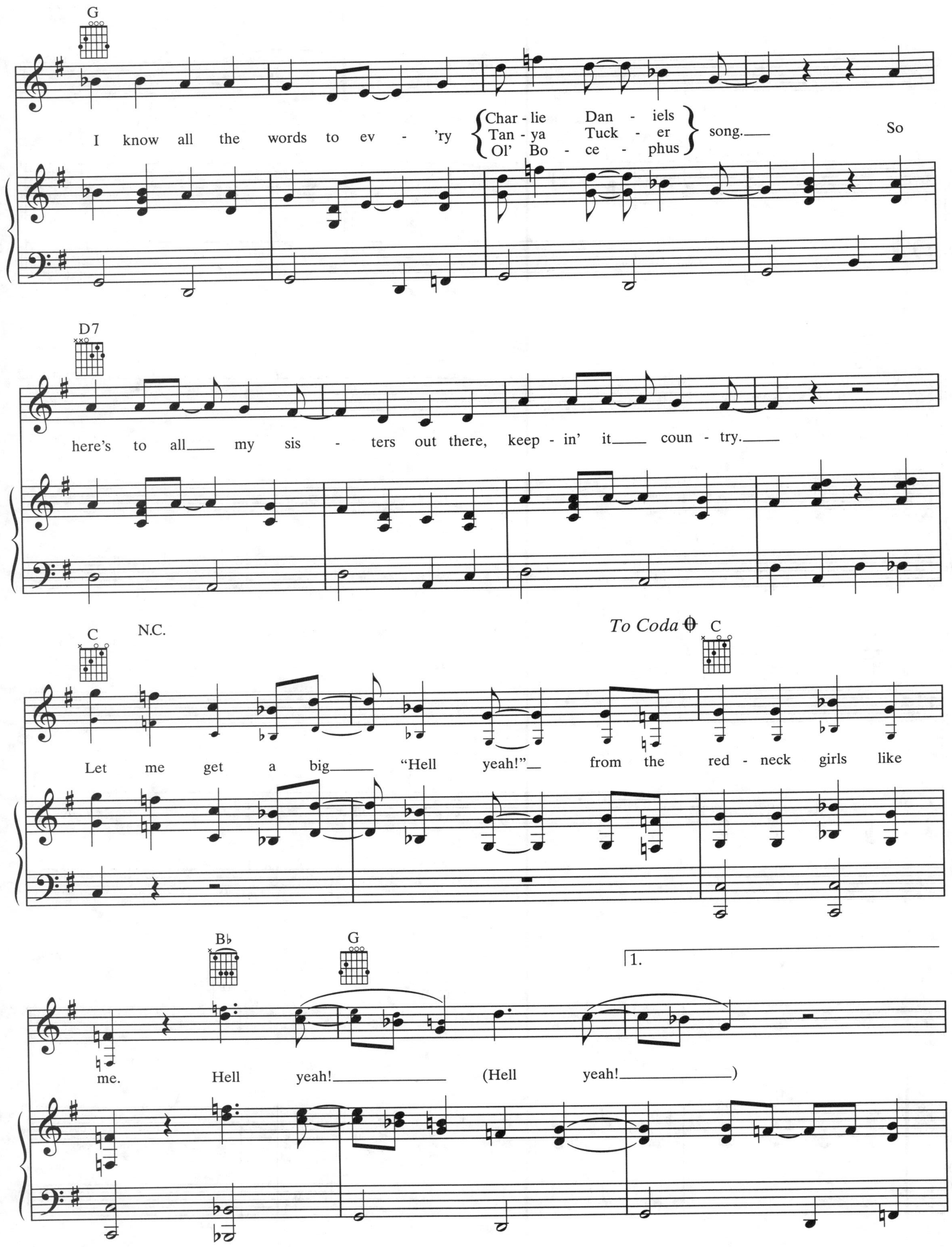
G
I know all the words to ev - 'ry
Char - lie Dan - iels
Tan - ya Tuck - er
Ol' Bo - ce - phus
song. So
D7
here's to all my sis - ters out there, keep - in' it coun - try.
C
N.C.
Let me get a big "Hell yeah!" from the red - neck girls like
To Coda
C
B♭
G
1.
me. Hell yeah! (Hell yeah!)

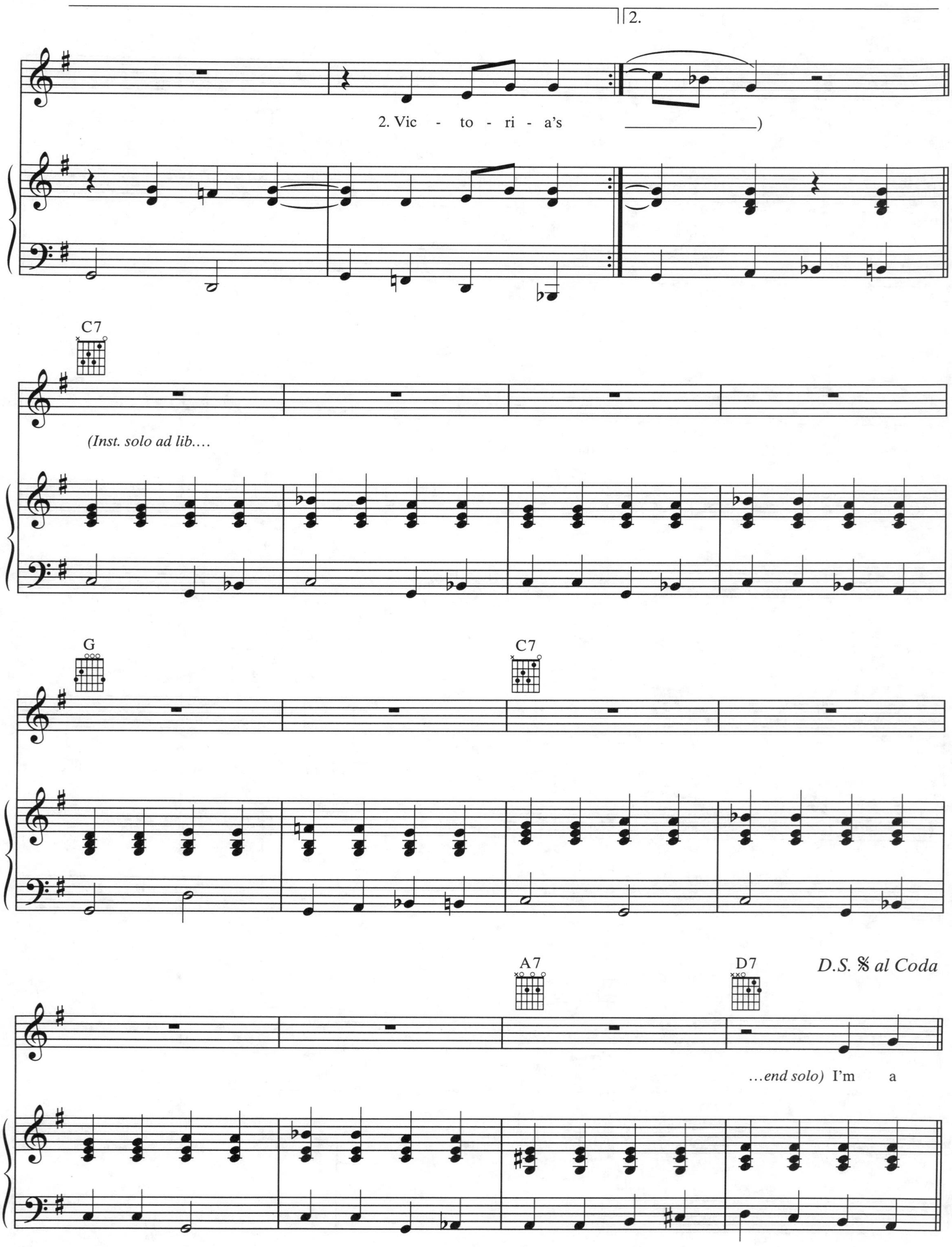
2.
2. Vic - to - ri - a's ________)
C7
(Inst. solo ad lib.…
G
C7
A7
D7
D.S. 𝄋 al Coda
…end solo) I'm a

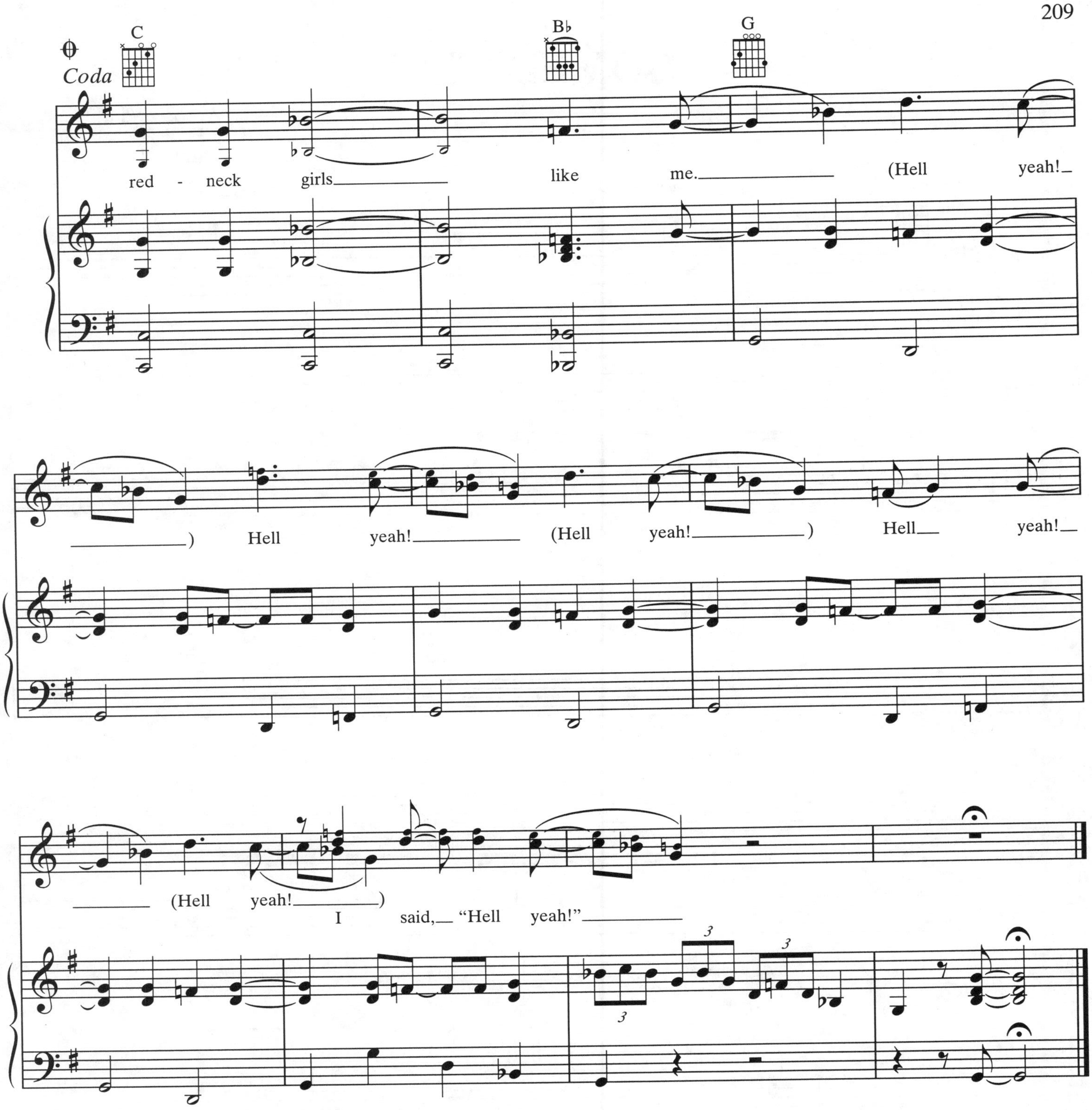

Verse 2:
Victoria's Secret,
Well, their stuff's real nice.
Oh, but I can buy the same damn thing
On a Wal-Mart shelf, half price
And still look sexy,
Just as sexy as those models on TV.
No, I don't need no designer tag
To make my man want me.
You might think I'm trashy,
A little too hard-core,
But in my neck of the woods,
I'm just the girl next door.
(To Chorus:)

SOMEBODY

Words and Music by
DAVE BERG, SAM TATE
and ANNIE TATE

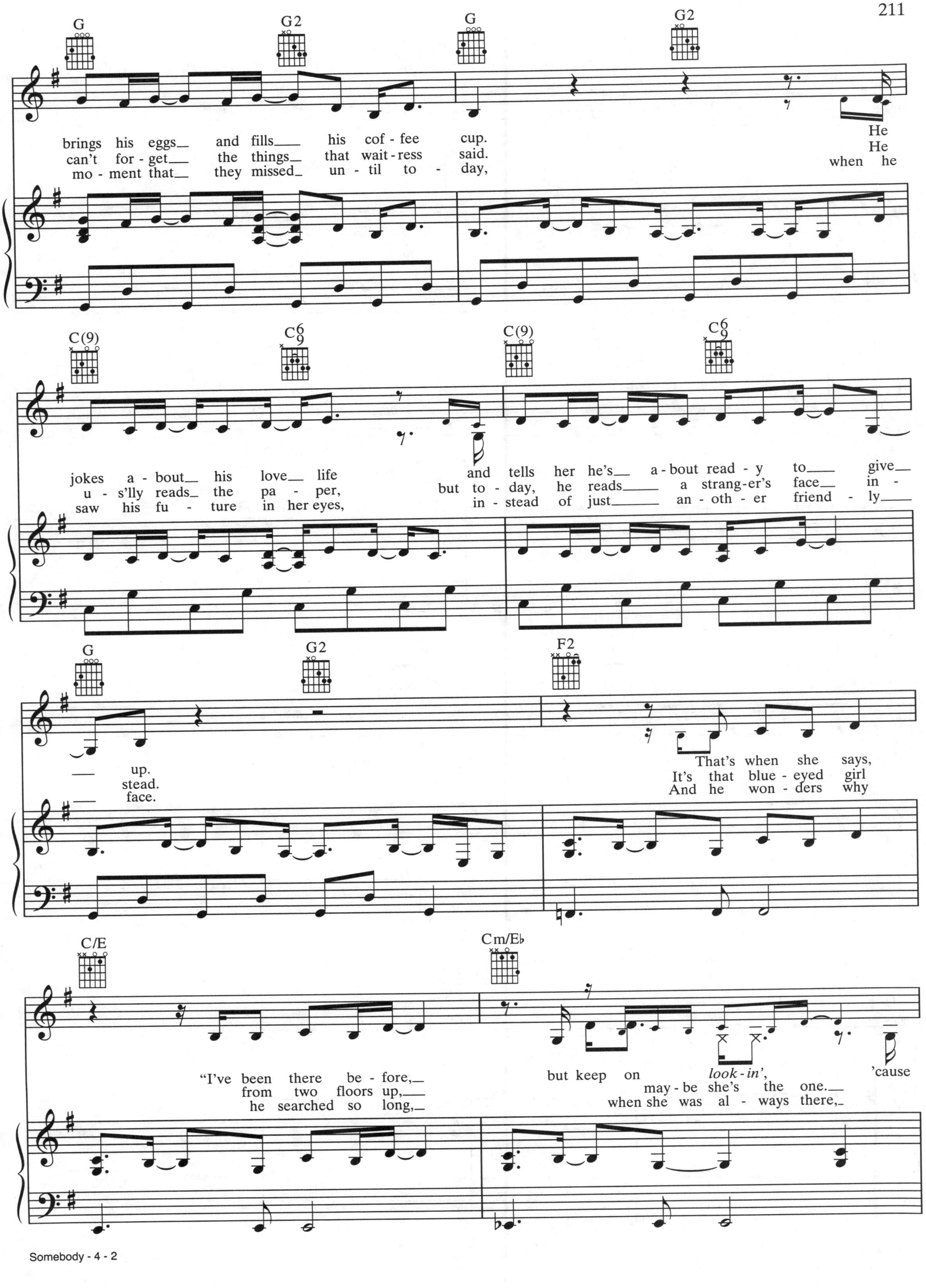
G
G2
G
G2
brings his eggs and fills his cof - fee cup.
can't for - get the things that wait - ress said.
mo - ment that they missed un - til to - day,
He
He
when he
C(9)
C6/9
C(9)
C6/9
jokes a - bout his love life
u - s'lly reads the pa - per,
saw his fu - ture in her eyes,
and tells her he's a - bout read - y to give
but to - day, he reads a strang - er's face in -
in - stead of just an - oth - er friend - ly
G
G2
F2
up.
stead.
face.
That's when she says,
It's that blue - eyed girl
And he won - ders why
C/E
Cm/E♭
"I've been there be - fore,
from two floors up,
he searched so long,
but keep on look - in',
may - be she's the one.
when she was al - ways there,
'cause

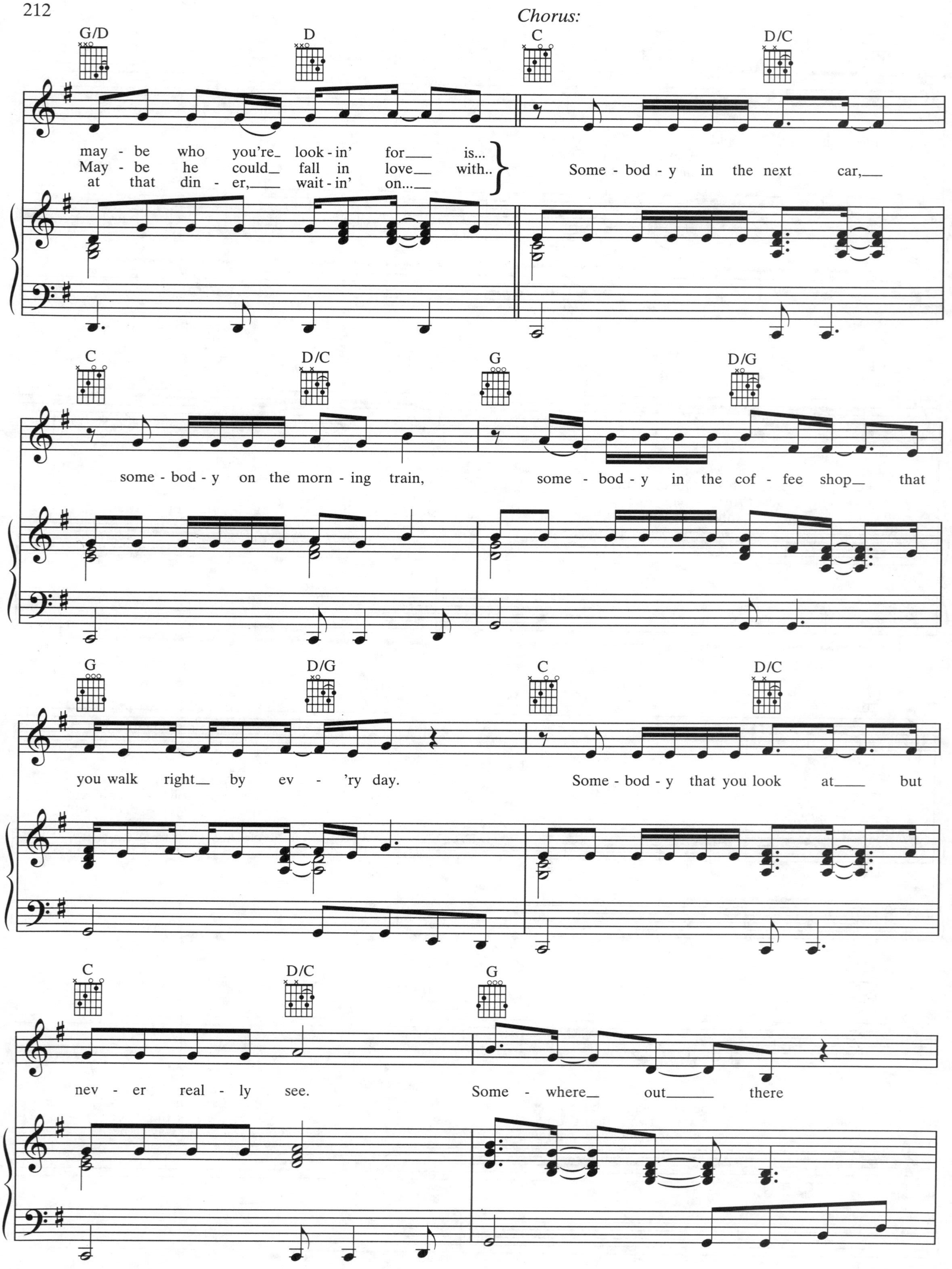
Chorus:
G/D
D
C
D/C
may - be who you're look - in' for is...
May - be he could fall in love with..
at that din - er, wait - in' on...
Some - bod - y in the next car,
C
D/C
G
D/G
some - bod - y on the morn - ing train,
some - bod - y in the cof - fee shop that
G
D/G
C
D/C
you walk right by ev - 'ry day.
Some - bod - y that you look at but
C
D/C
G
nev - er real - ly see.
Some - where out there

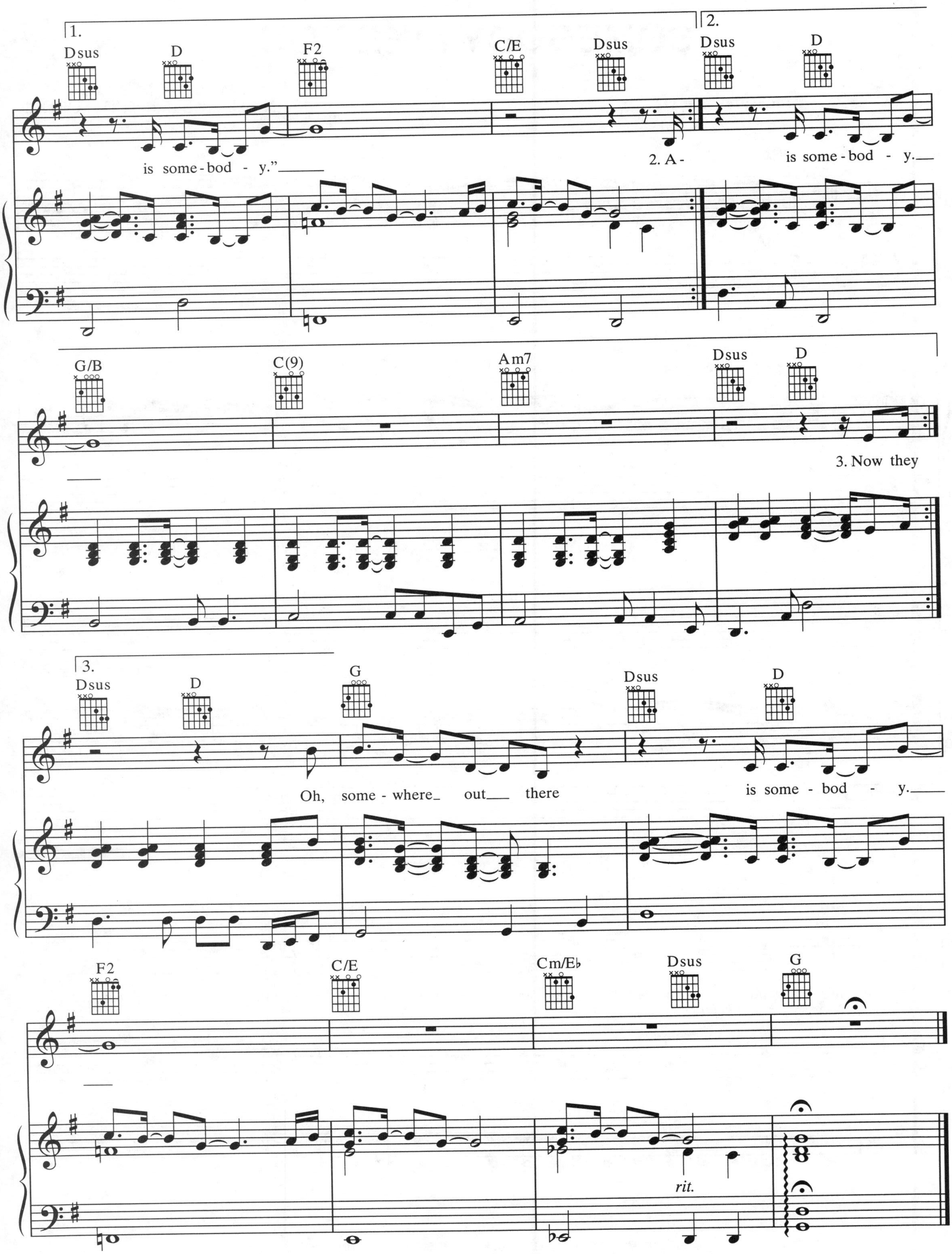
1.
Dsus
D
F2
C/E
Dsus
2.
Dsus
D
is some-bod - y."
2. A-
is some-bod - y.
G/B
C(9)
Am7
Dsus
D
3. Now they
3.
Dsus
D
G
Dsus
D
Oh, some - where out there
is some - bod - y.
F2
C/E
Cm/E♭
Dsus
G
rit.

SOMEBODY LIKE YOU

Words and Music by
JOHN SHANKS and KEITH URBAN

Moderately ♩ = 112

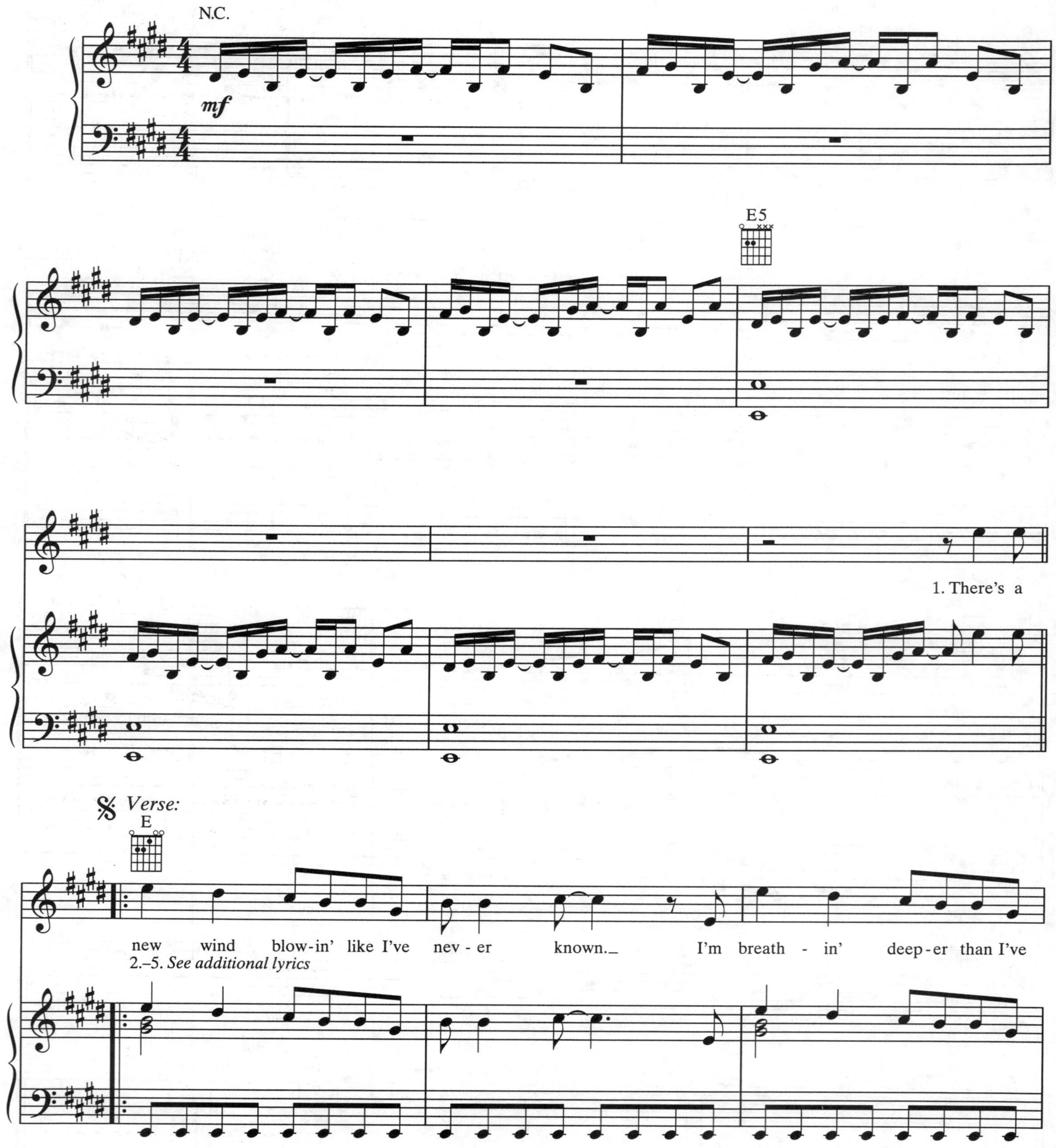

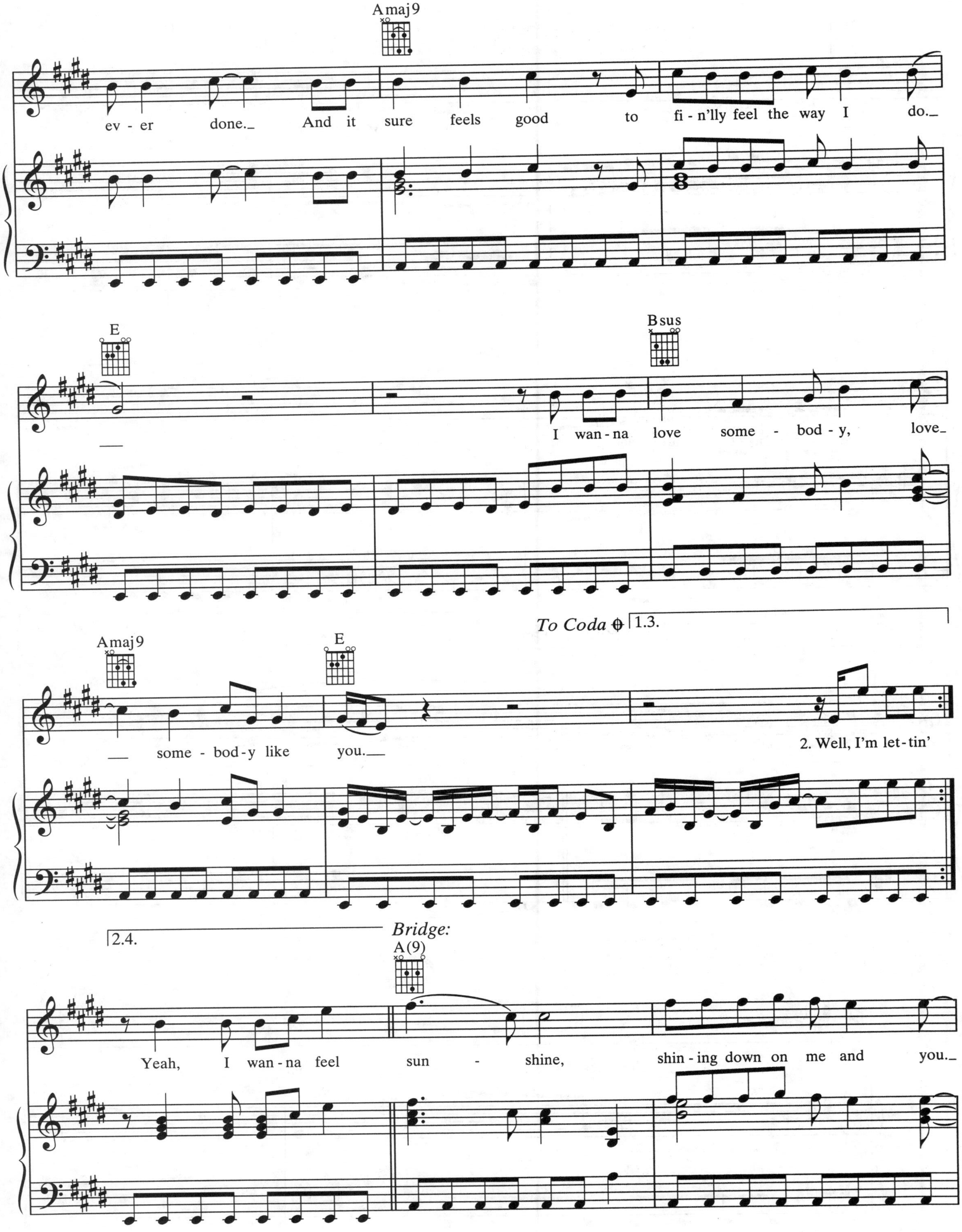
Amaj9
ev - er done._ And it sure feels good to fi - n'lly feel the way I do._
E
Bsus
I wan - na love some - bod - y, love._
To Coda
1.3.
Amaj9
E
some - bod - y like you._
2. Well, I'm let - tin'
2.4.
Bridge:
A(9)
Yeah, I wan - na feel sun - shine, shin - ing down on me and you._

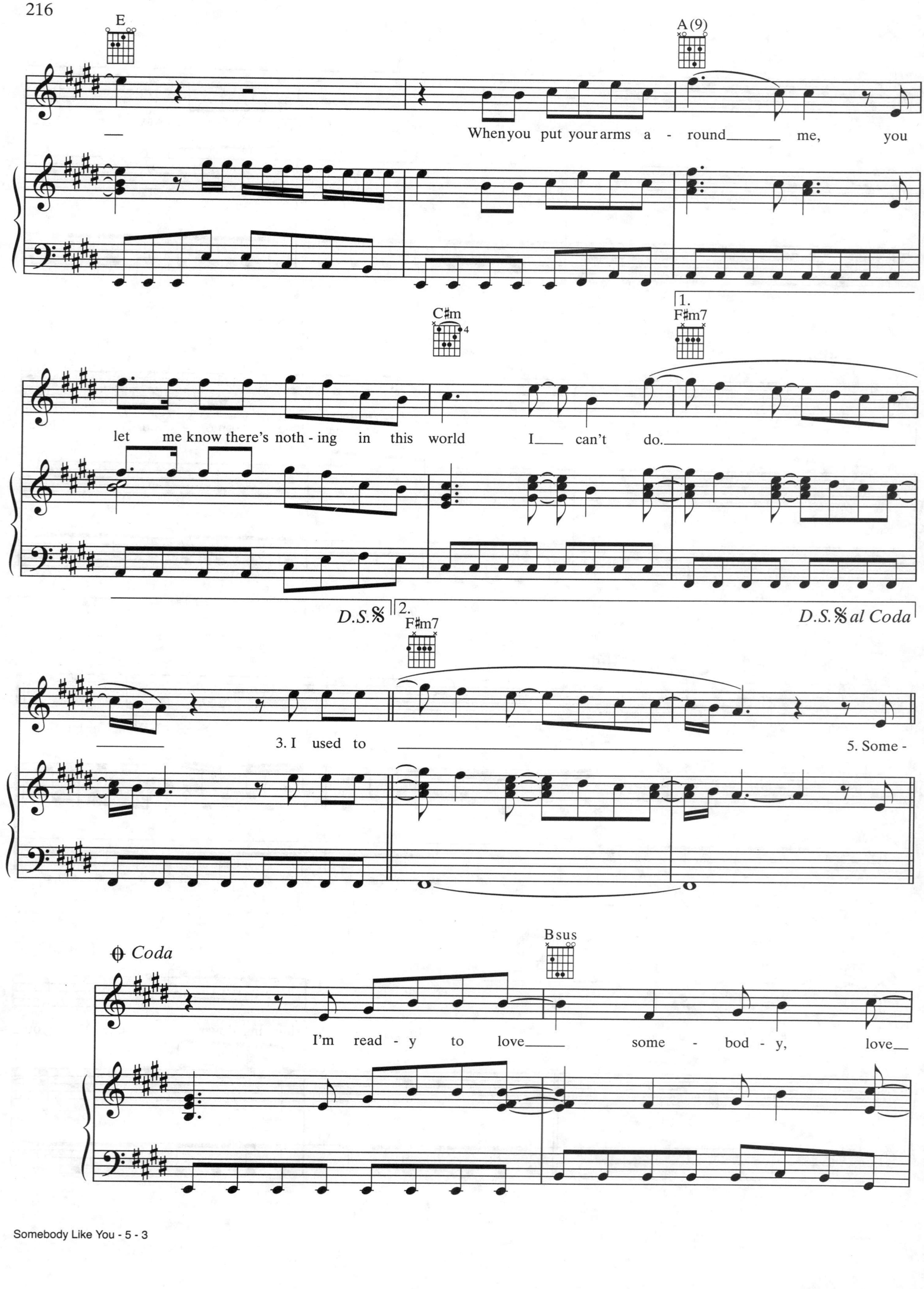
E
A (9)
When you put your arms a - round ___ me, you
C♯m
1.
F♯m7
let me know there's noth - ing in this world I ___ can't do. ___
D.S.𝄋
2.
F♯m7
D.S.𝄋 al Coda
3. I used to ___
5. Some -
𝄌 Coda
Bsus
I'm read - y to love ___ some - bod - y, love ___

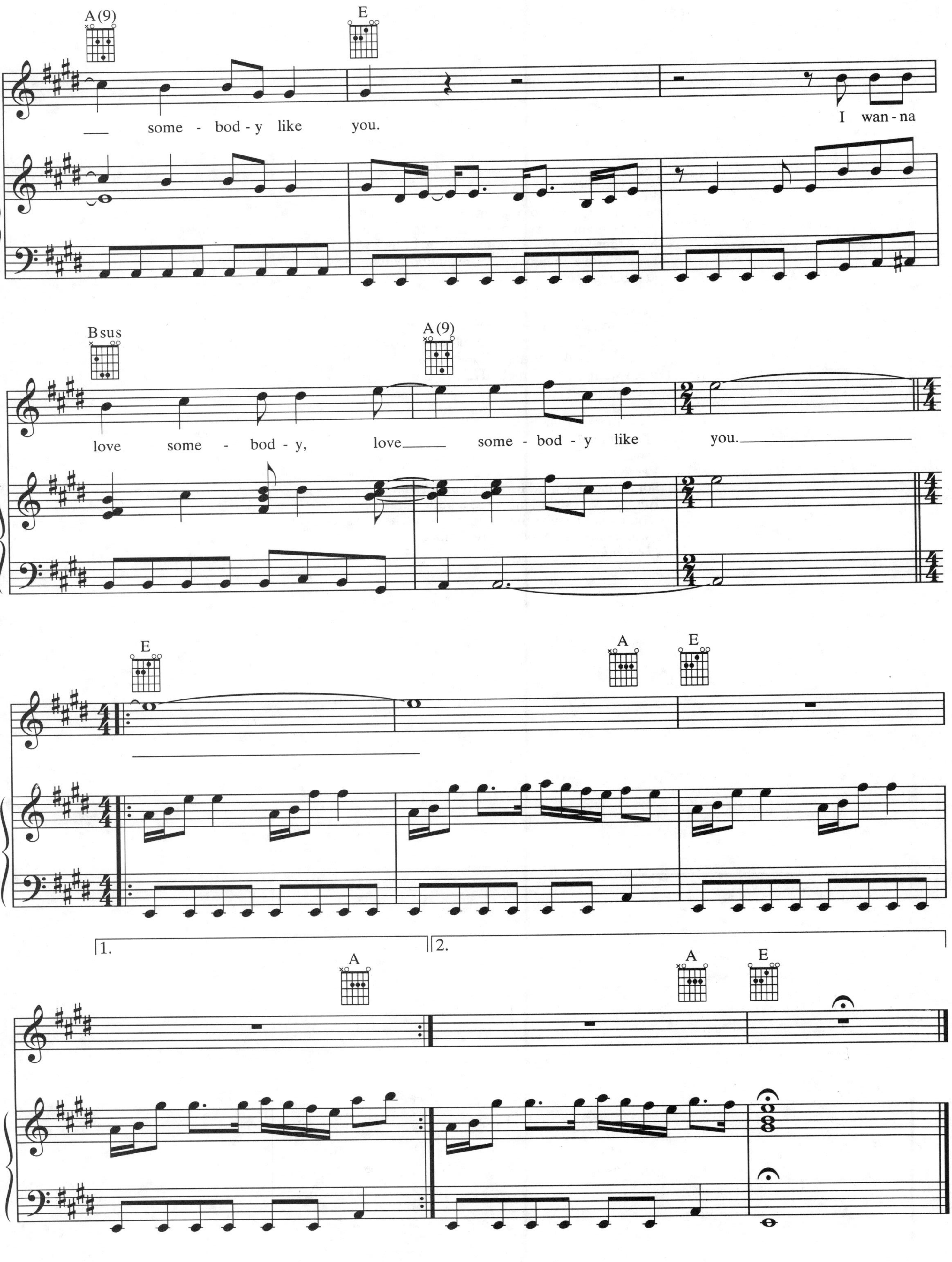
A(9)
E
some - bod - y like you.
I wan - na
Bsus
A(9)
love some - bod - y, love some - bod - y like you.
E
A
E
1.
2.
A
A
E

Verse 2:
Well, I'm letting go of all my lonely yesterdays
And forgiving myself for the mistakes I've made.
Now there's just one thing, the only thing I wanna do.
I wanna love somebody, love somebody like you.
(To Bridge:)

Verse 3:
I used to run in circles, goin' nowhere fast.
I'd take one step forward, end up two steps back.
I couldn't walk a straight line even if I wanted to,
But I wanna love somebody, love somebody like you.

Verse 4:
Instrumental solo
(To Bridge:)

Verse 5:
Sometimes it's hard for me to understand,
But you're teachin' me to be a better man.
Don't want to take this life for granted like I used to do.
I wanna love somebody, love somebody like you.
(To Coda)

WHEN I THINK ABOUT ANGELS

Words and Music by
ROXIE DEAN, SONNY TILLIS
and JAMIE O'NEAL

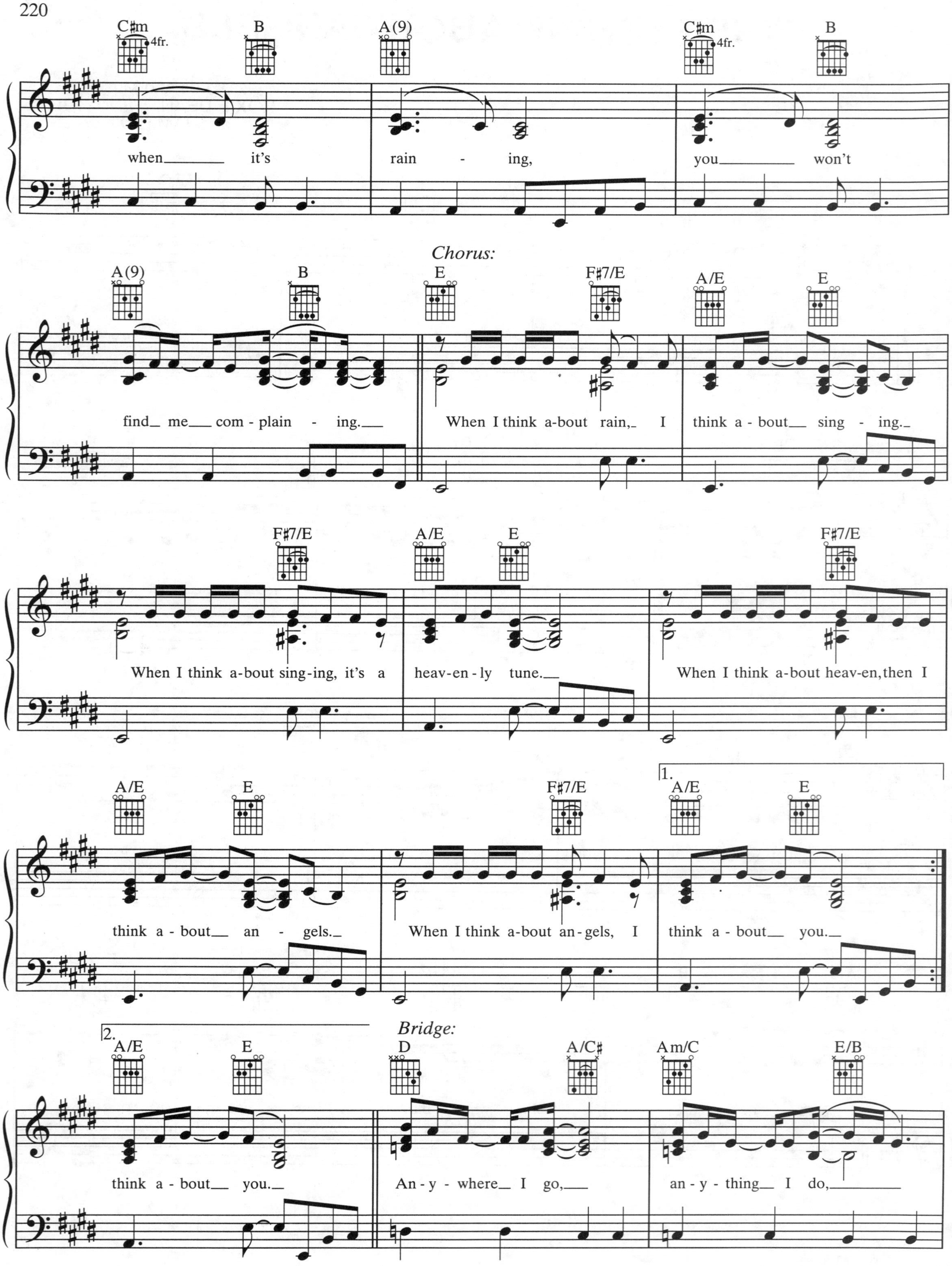
C♯m
4fr.
B
A(9)
when___ it's
rain - ing,
you___ won't
Chorus:
E
F♯7/E
A/E
find_ me_ com - plain - ing._
When I think a-bout rain,_ I
think a - bout_ sing - ing._
When I think a-bout sing-ing, it's a
heav-en-ly tune._
When I think a-bout heav-en, then I
think a - bout_ an - gels._
When I think a-bout an-gels, I
1.
think a - bout_ you._
2.
Bridge:
D
A/C♯
Am/C
E/B
think a - bout_ you._
An-y - where_ I go,_
an-y - thing_ I do,___

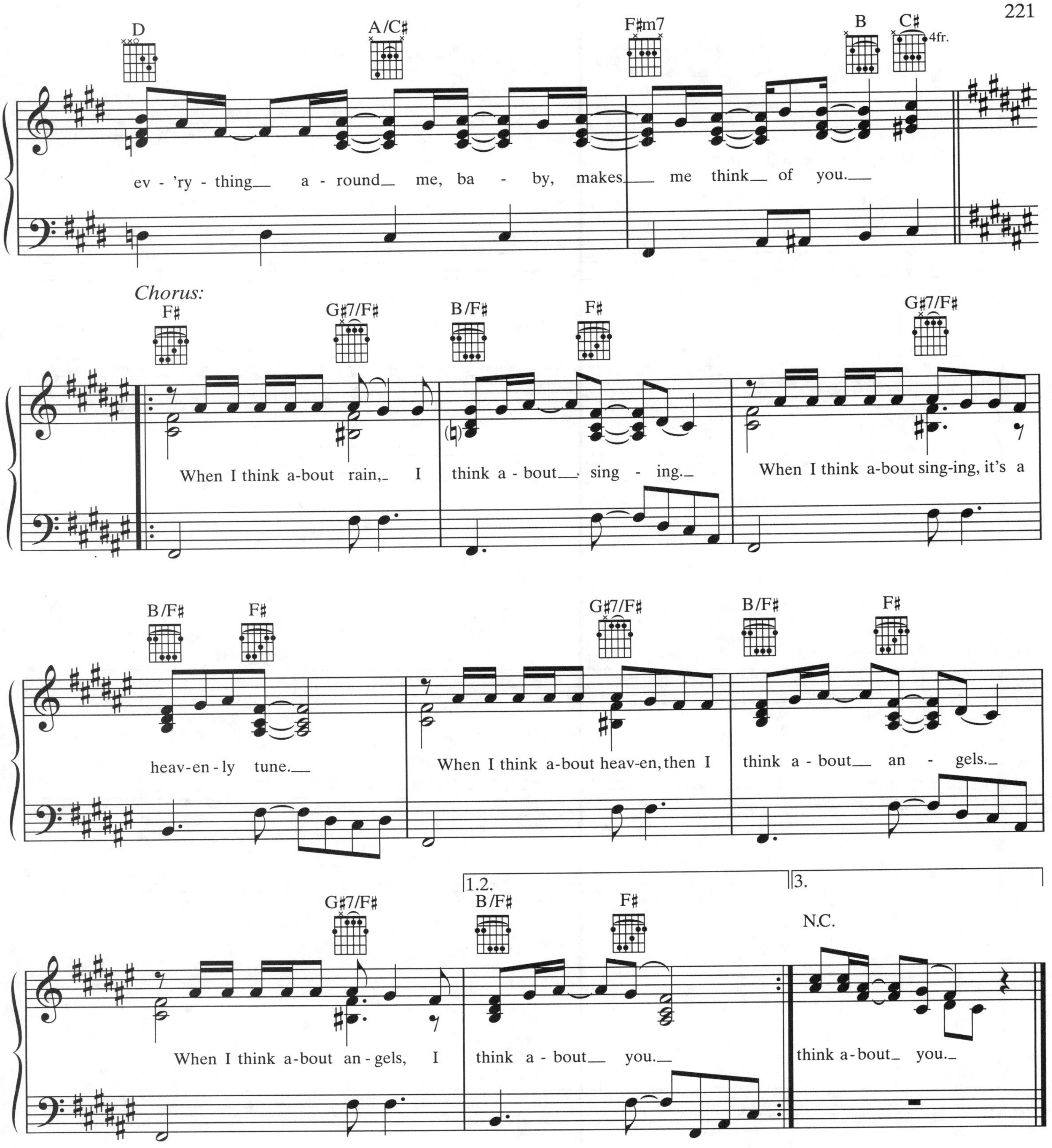

Verse 2:
The taste of sugar sure reminds me of your kiss.
I like the way they both linger on my lips.
Kisses remind me of a field of butterflies.
Must be the way the heart is fluttering inside.
Beautiful distraction,
You make every thought a chain reaction.
(To Chorus:)

SUDS IN THE BUCKET

Words and Music by
BILLY MONTANA and JENAI

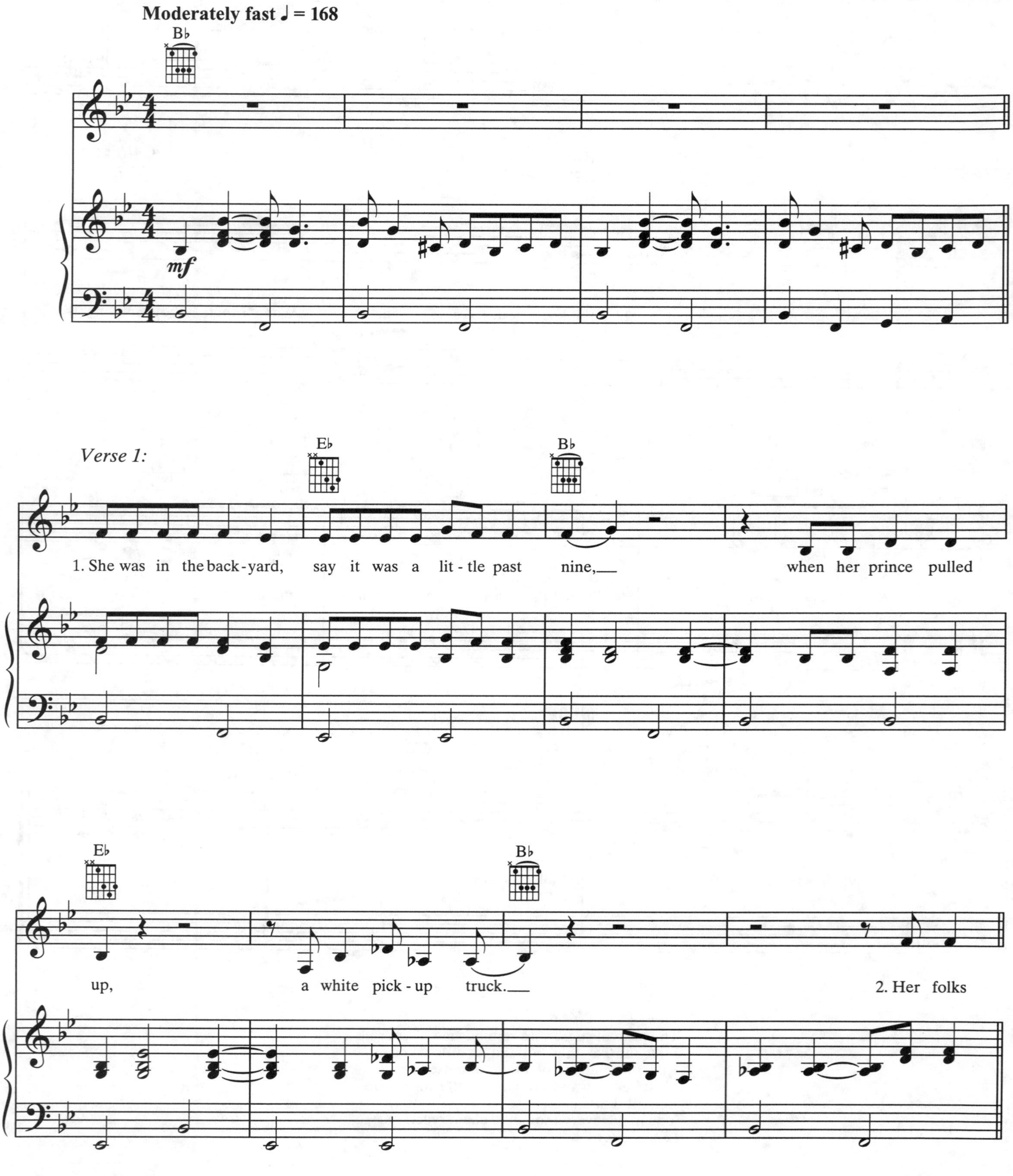

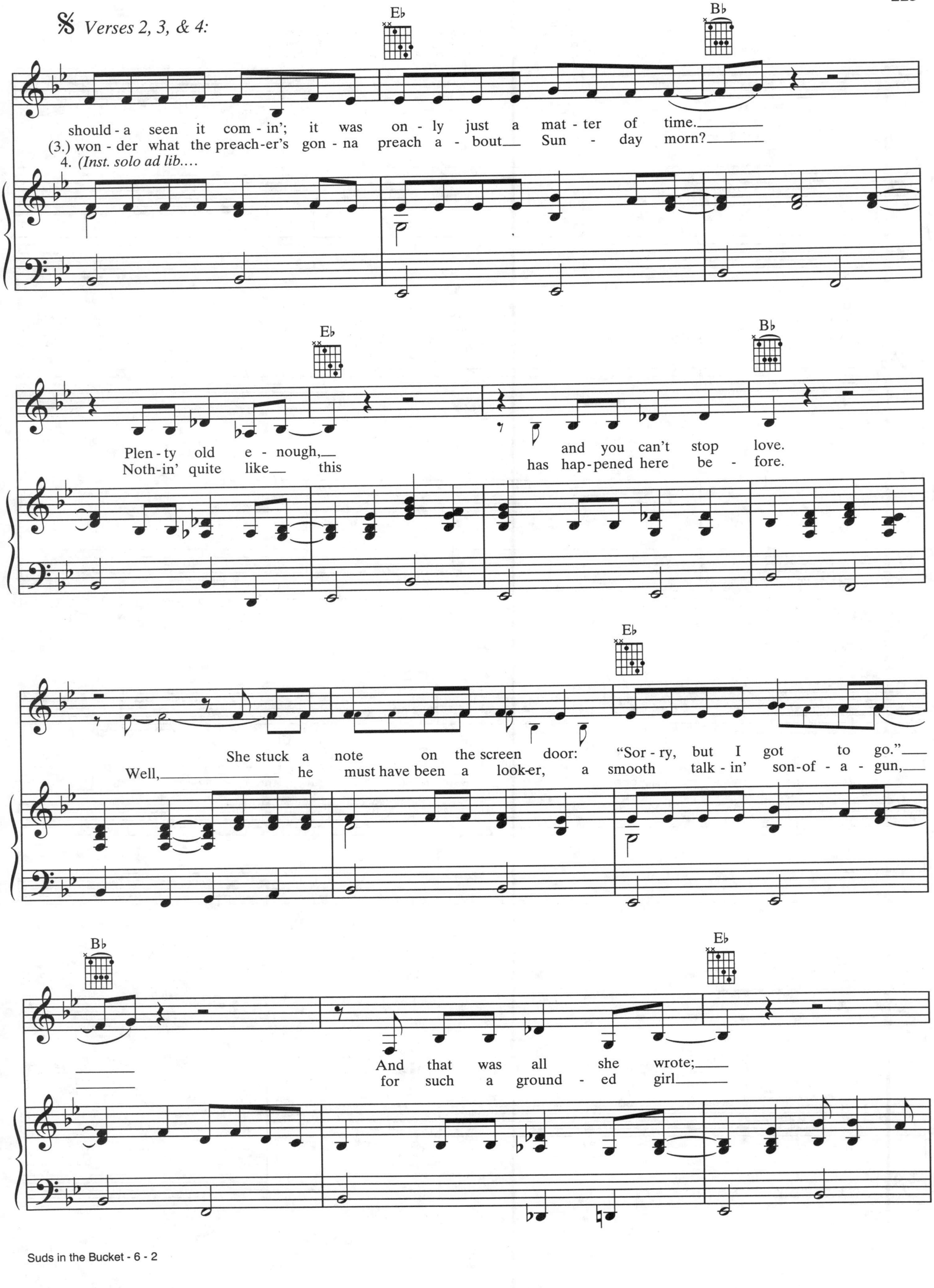
𝄋 Verses 2, 3, & 4:
E♭
B♭
should - a seen it com - in'; it was on - ly just a mat - ter of time.
(3.) won - der what the preach-er's gon - na preach a - bout Sun - day morn?
4. (Inst. solo ad lib....
E♭
B♭
Plen - ty old e - nough, and you can't stop love.
Noth - in' quite like this has hap - pened here be - fore.
E♭
She stuck a note on the screen door: "Sor - ry, but I got to go."
Well, he must have been a look-er, a smooth talk - in' son-of - a - gun,
B♭
E♭
And that was all she wrote;
for such a ground - ed girl

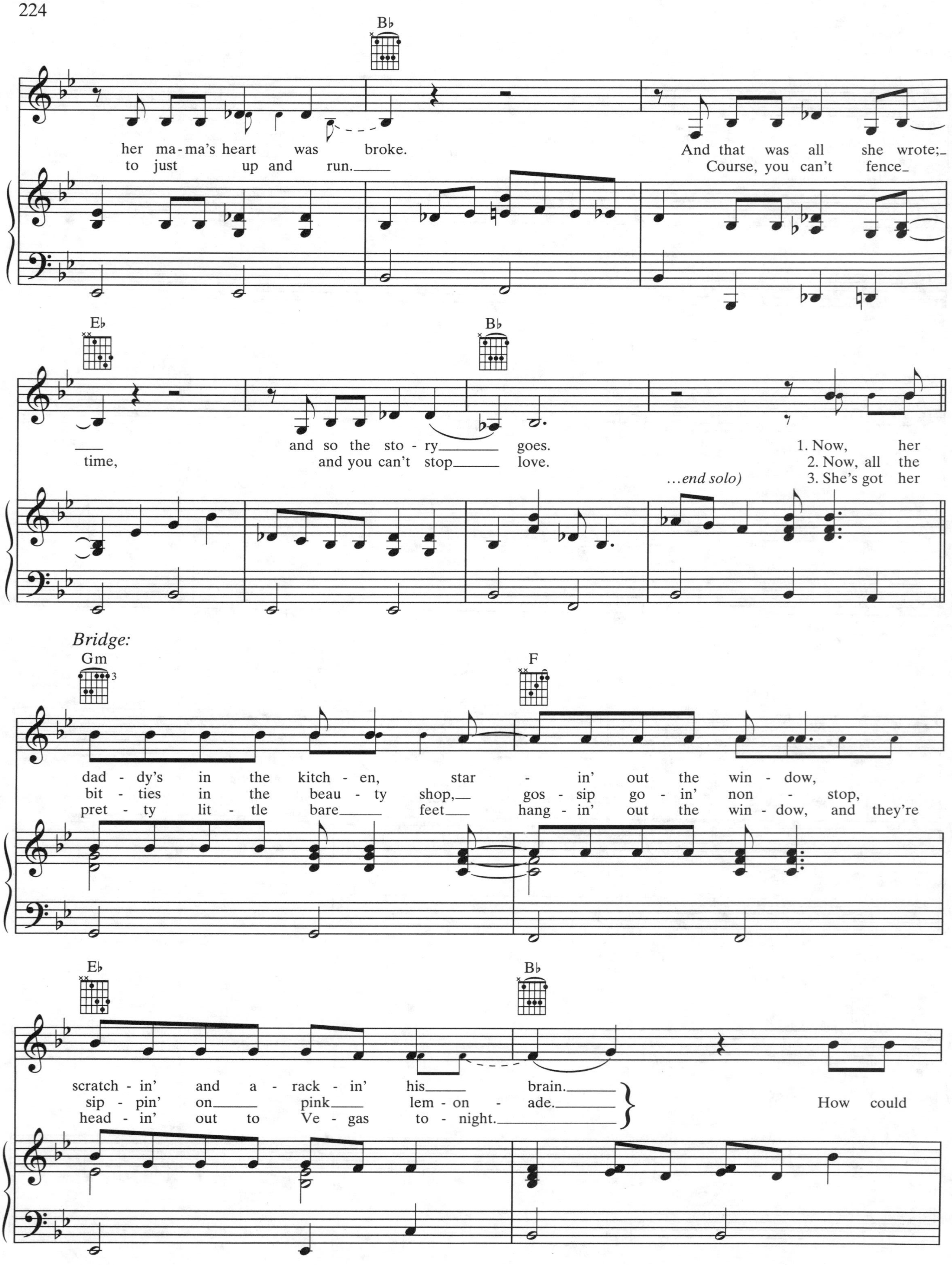
B♭
her ma-ma's heart was broke.
to just up and run.
And that was all she wrote;
Course, you can't fence
E♭
B♭
and so the sto - ry goes.
time, and you can't stop love.
1. Now, her
2. Now, all the
…end solo)
3. She's got her
Bridge:
Gm
F
dad - dy's in the kitch - en, star - in' out the win - dow,
bit - ties in the beau - ty shop, gos - sip go - in' non - stop,
pret - ty lit - tle bare feet hang - in' out the win - dow, and they're
E♭
B♭
scratch - in' and a - rack - in' his brain.
sip - pin' on pink lem - on - ade.
head - in' out to Ve - gas to - night.
How could

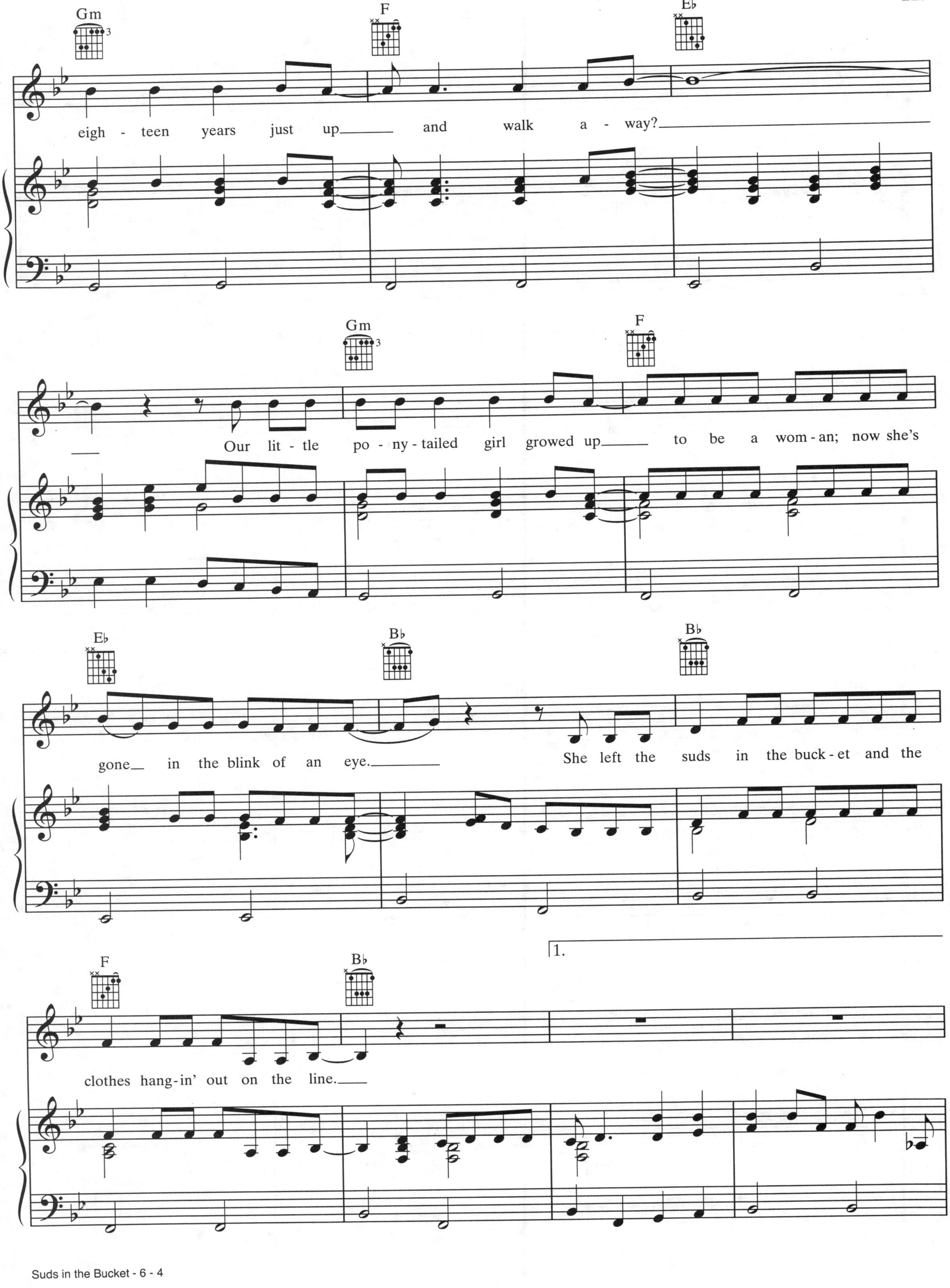
Gm
F
E♭
eigh - teen years just up___ and walk a - way?___
Gm
F
___ Our lit - tle po - ny - tailed girl growed up___ to be a wom - an; now she's
E♭
B♭
B♭
gone___ in the blink of an eye.___ She left the suds in the buck - et and the
1.
F
B♭
clothes hang - in' out on the line.___

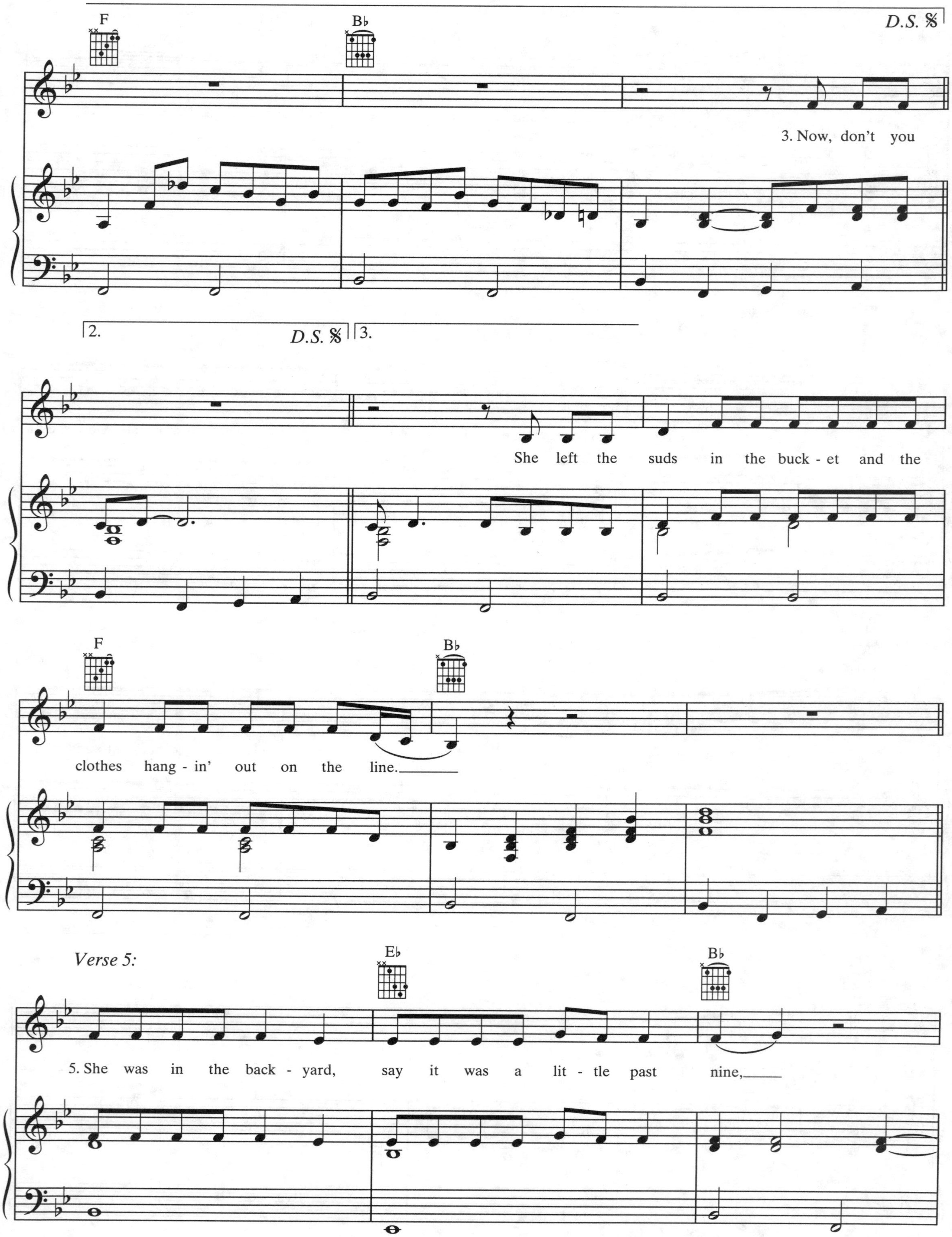
F
B♭
D.S. 𝄋
3. Now, don't you
2.
D.S. 𝄋
3.
She left the suds in the buck - et and the
F
B♭
clothes hang - in' out on the line.
Verse 5:
E♭
B♭
5. She was in the back - yard, say it was a lit - tle past nine,

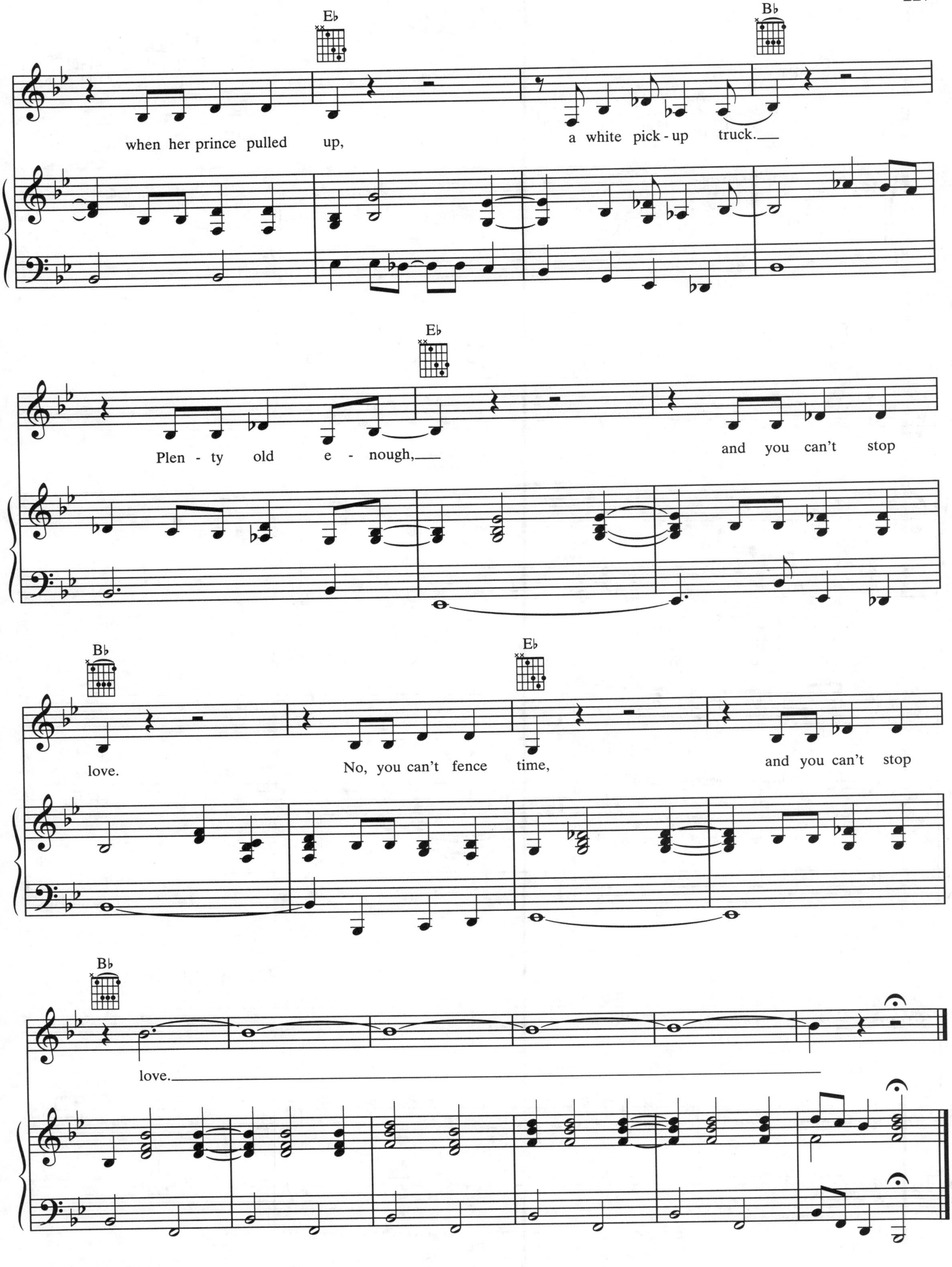

E♭
B♭
when her prince pulled up,
a white pick-up truck.
E♭
Plen - ty old e - nough,
and you can't stop
B♭
E♭
love.
No, you can't fence time,
and you can't stop
B♭
love.

TEXAS

Words and Music by
PHILLIP B. WHITE
and STEVEN DALE JONES

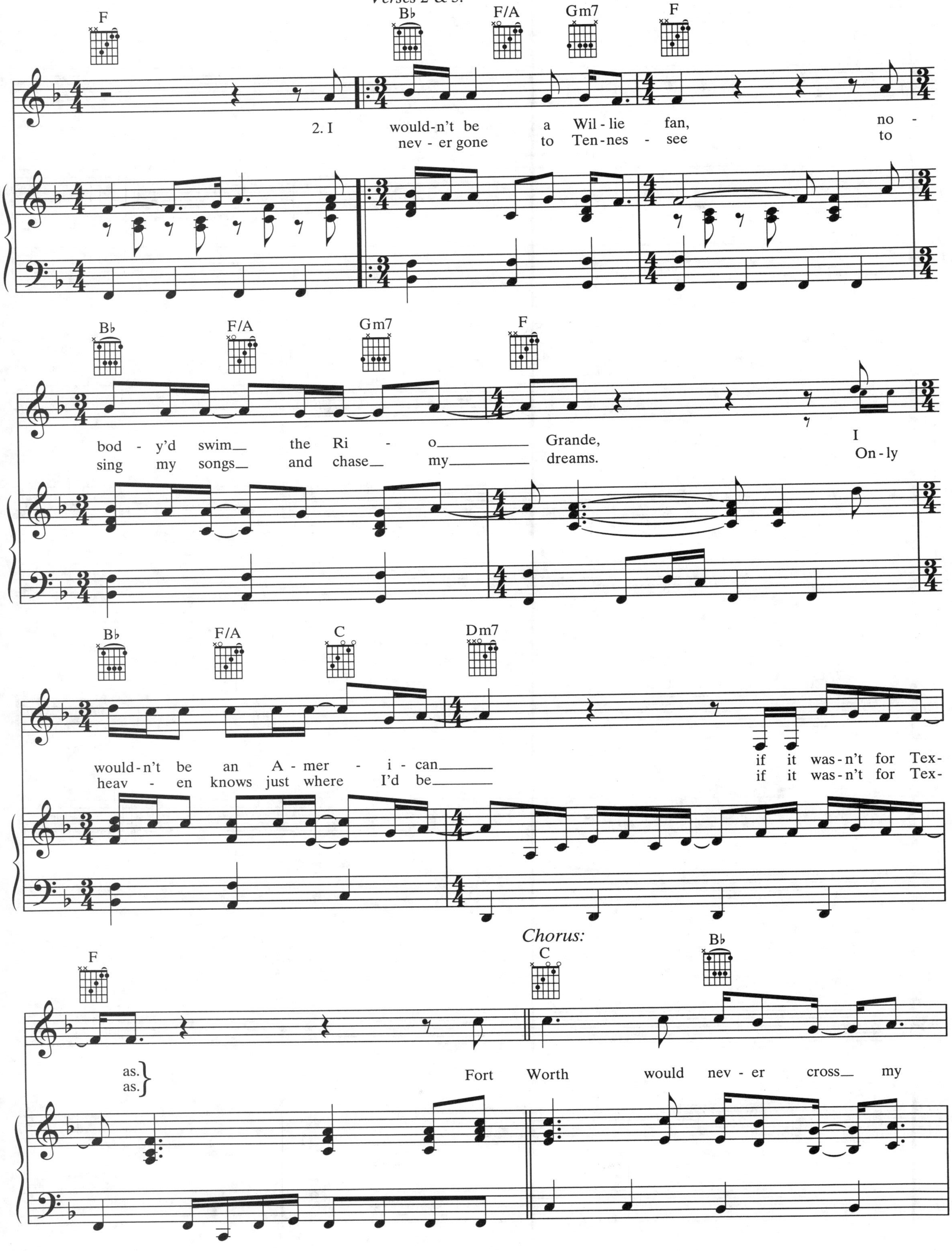
Verses 2 & 3:
F
Bb
F/A
Gm7
F
2. I would-n't be a Wil-lie fan, no-
nev-er gone to Ten-nes-see to
Bb
F/A
Gm7
F
bod-y'd swim the Ri-o Grande, I
sing my songs and chase my dreams. On-ly
Bb
F/A
C
Dm7
would-n't be an A-mer-i-can if it was-n't for Tex-
heav-en knows just where I'd be if it was-n't for Tex-
Chorus:
F
C
Bb
as.
as.
Fort Worth would nev-er cross my

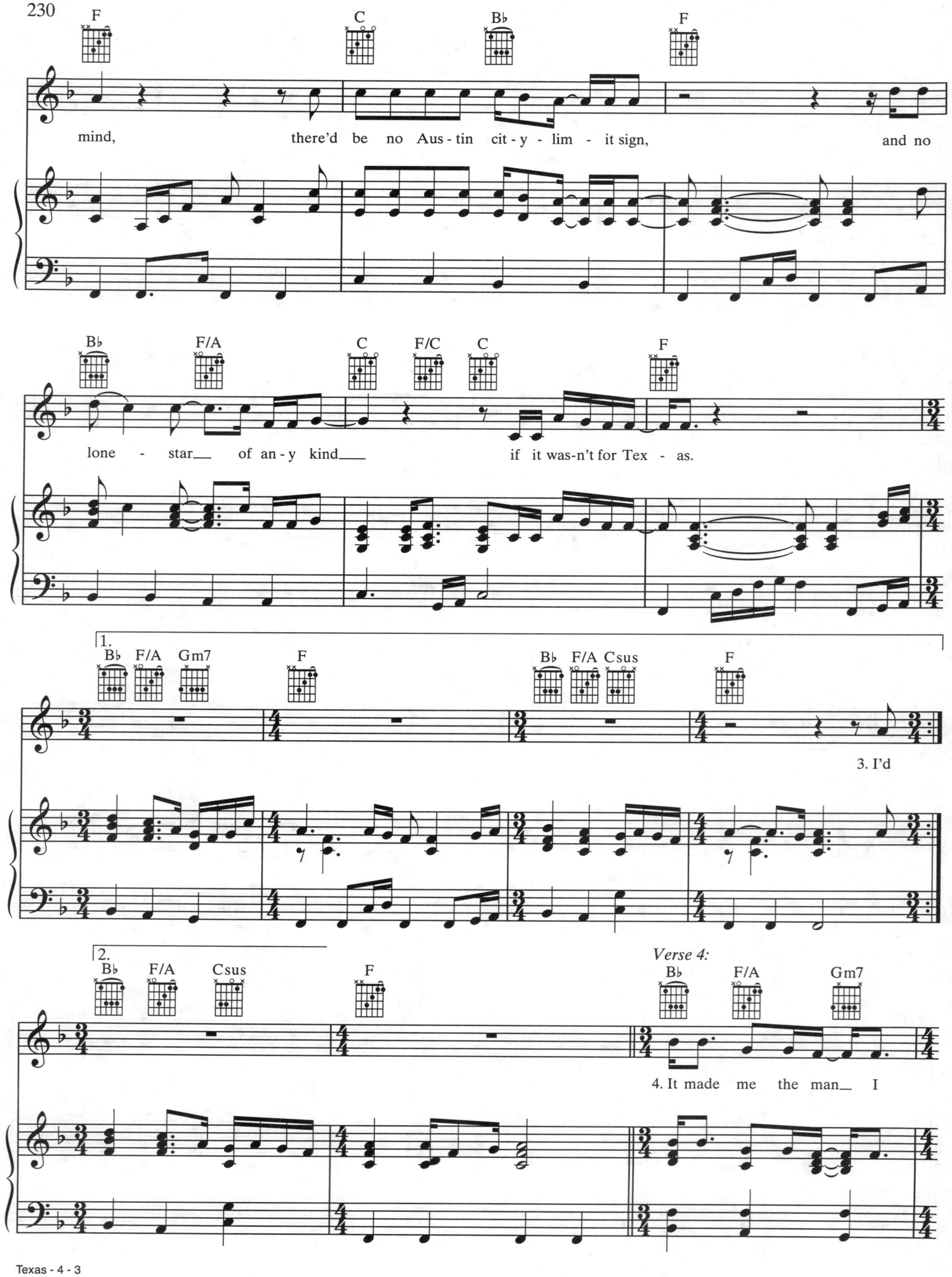
F C B♭ F
mind, there'd be no Aus-tin cit-y-lim-it sign, and no
B♭ F/A C F/C C F
lone-star of an-y kind if it was-n't for Tex-as.
1.
B♭ F/A Gm7 F B♭ F/A Csus F
3. I'd
2.
B♭ F/A Csus F
Verse 4:
B♭ F/A Gm7
4. It made me the man I

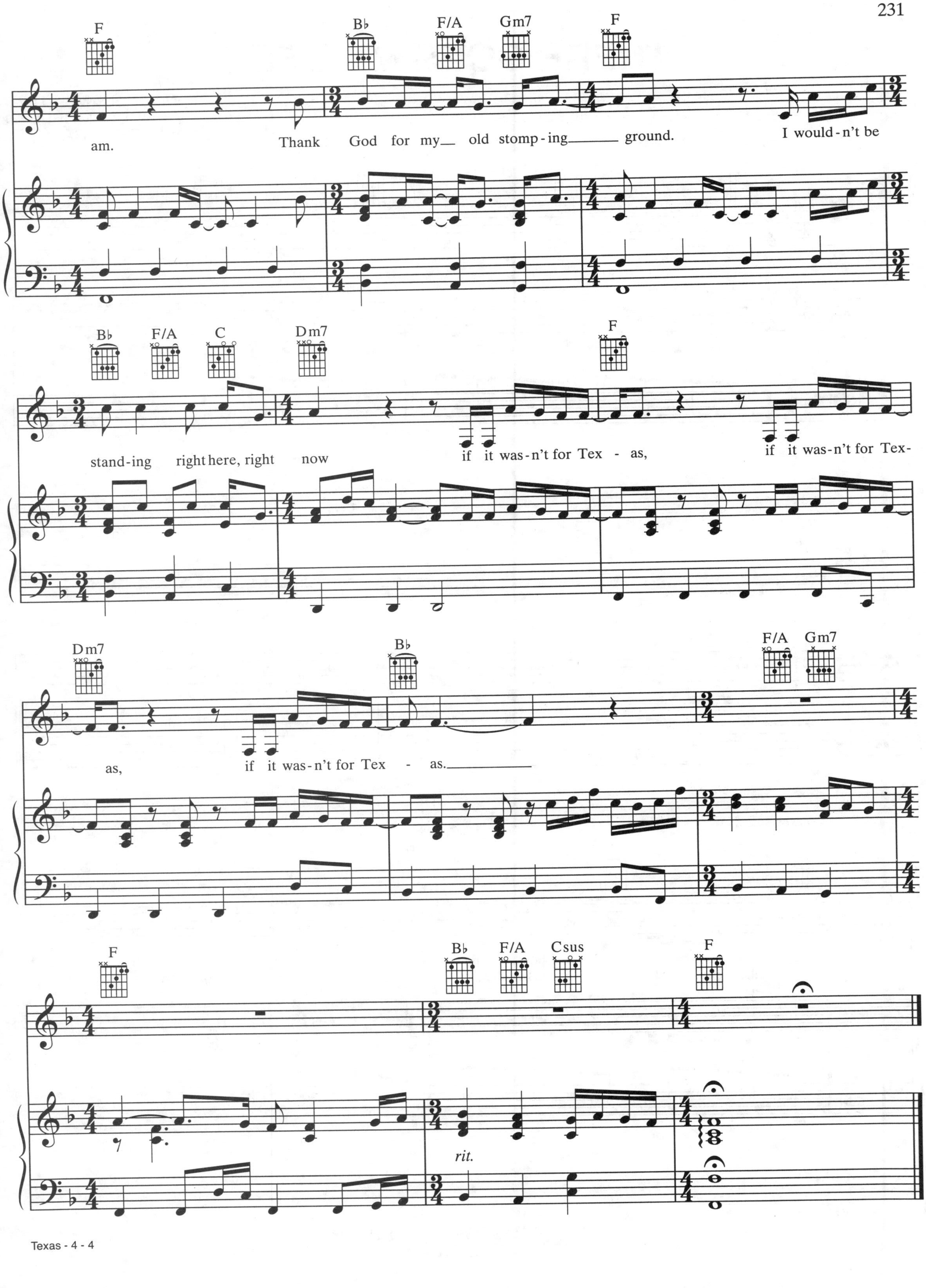
F
B♭
F/A
Gm7
F
am. Thank God for my old stomp-ing ground. I would-n't be
B♭
F/A
C
Dm7
F
stand-ing right here, right now if it was-n't for Tex - as, if it was-n't for Tex-
Dm7
B♭
F/A
Gm7
as, if it was-n't for Tex - as.
F
B♭
F/A
Csus
F
rit.

THERE GOES MY LIFE

Words and Music by
WENDELL MOBLEY
and NEIL THRASHER

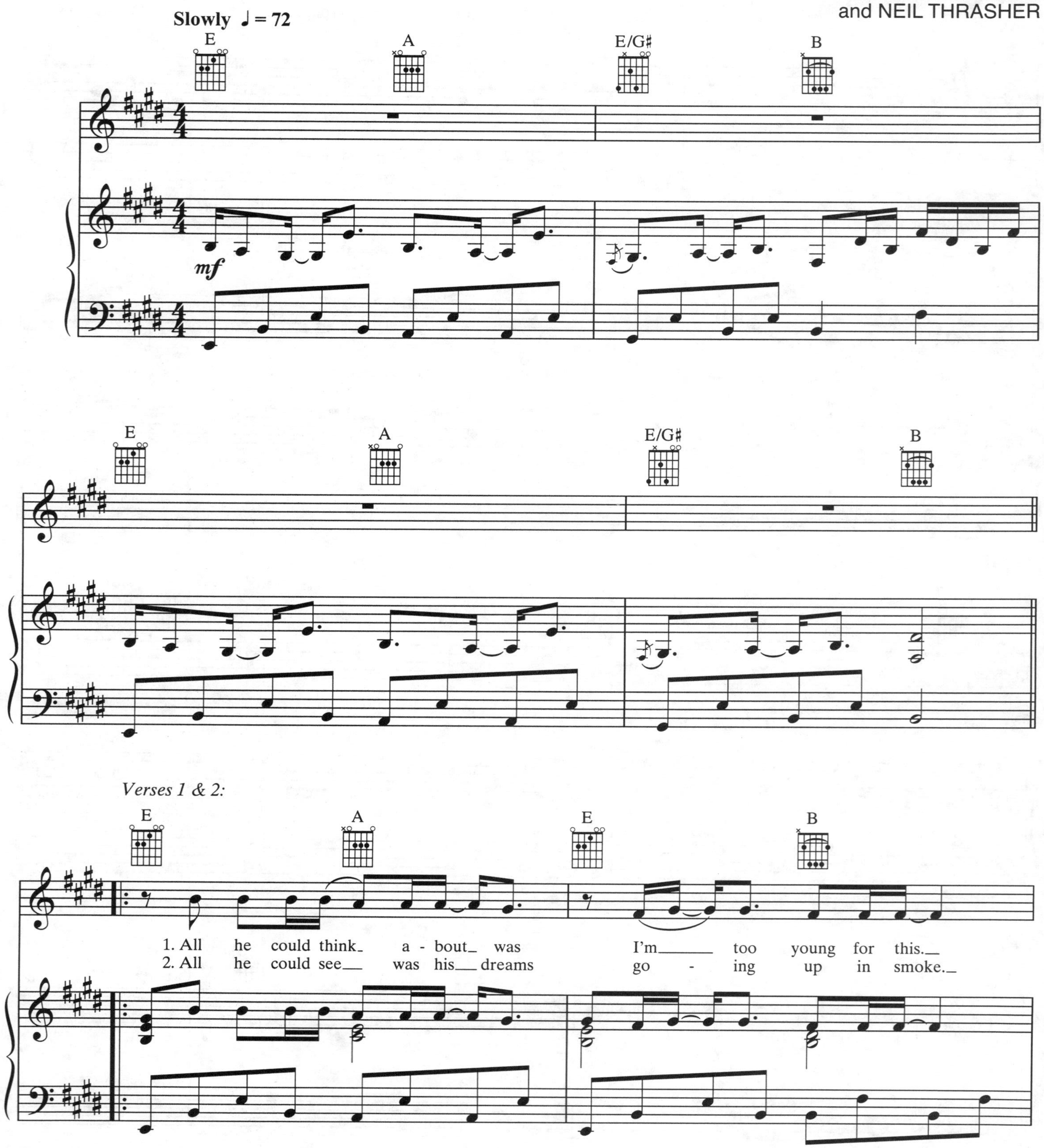

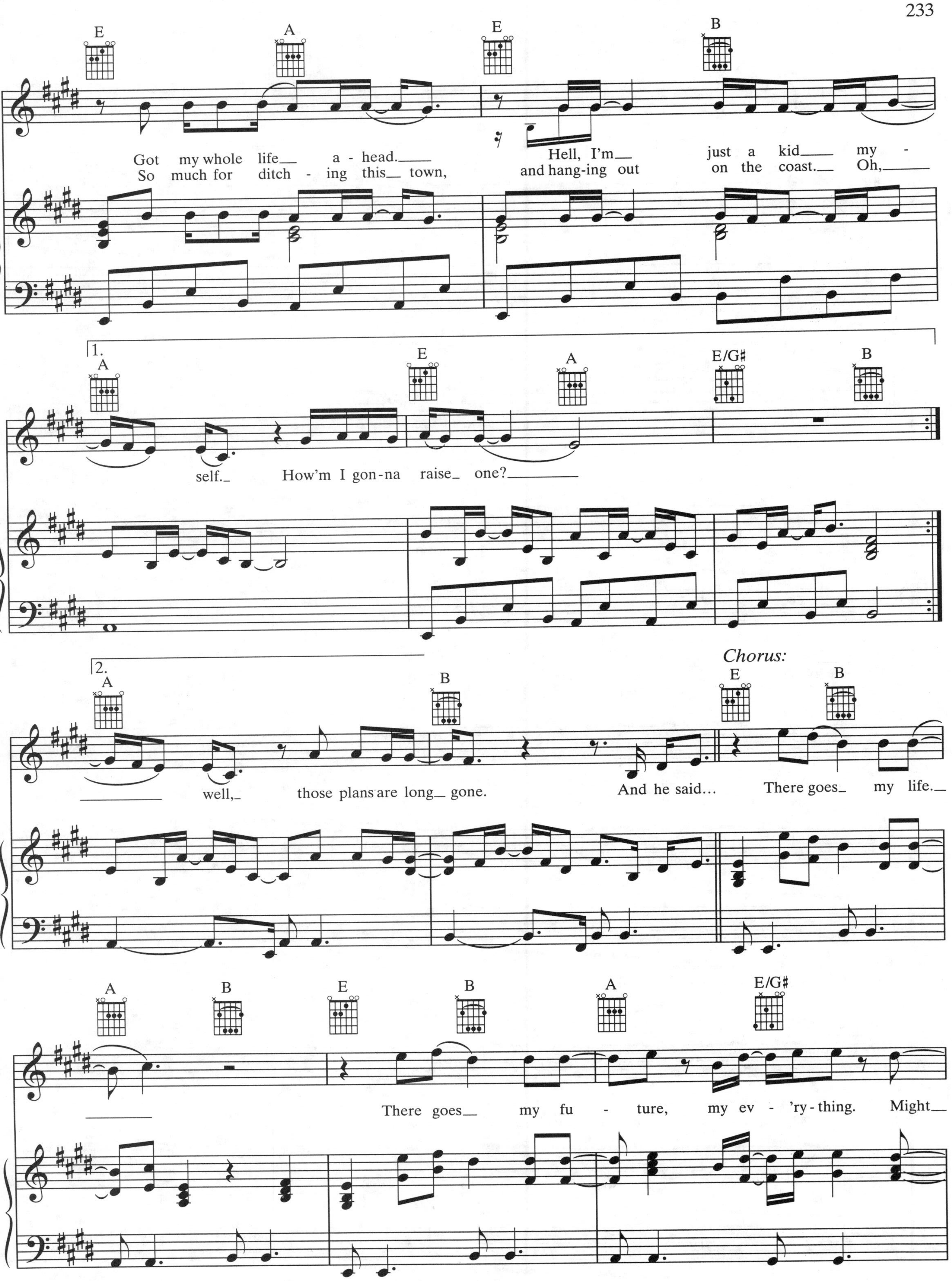
E
A
E
B
Got my whole life a - head.
So much for ditch - ing this town,
Hell, I'm
and hang-ing out
just a kid my -
on the coast. Oh,
1.
A
E
A
E/G#
B
self.
How'm I gon-na raise one?
2.
A
B
well,
those plans are long gone.
And he said...
Chorus:
E
B
There goes my life.
A
B
E
B
A
E/G#
There goes my fu - ture, my ev - 'ry-thing. Might

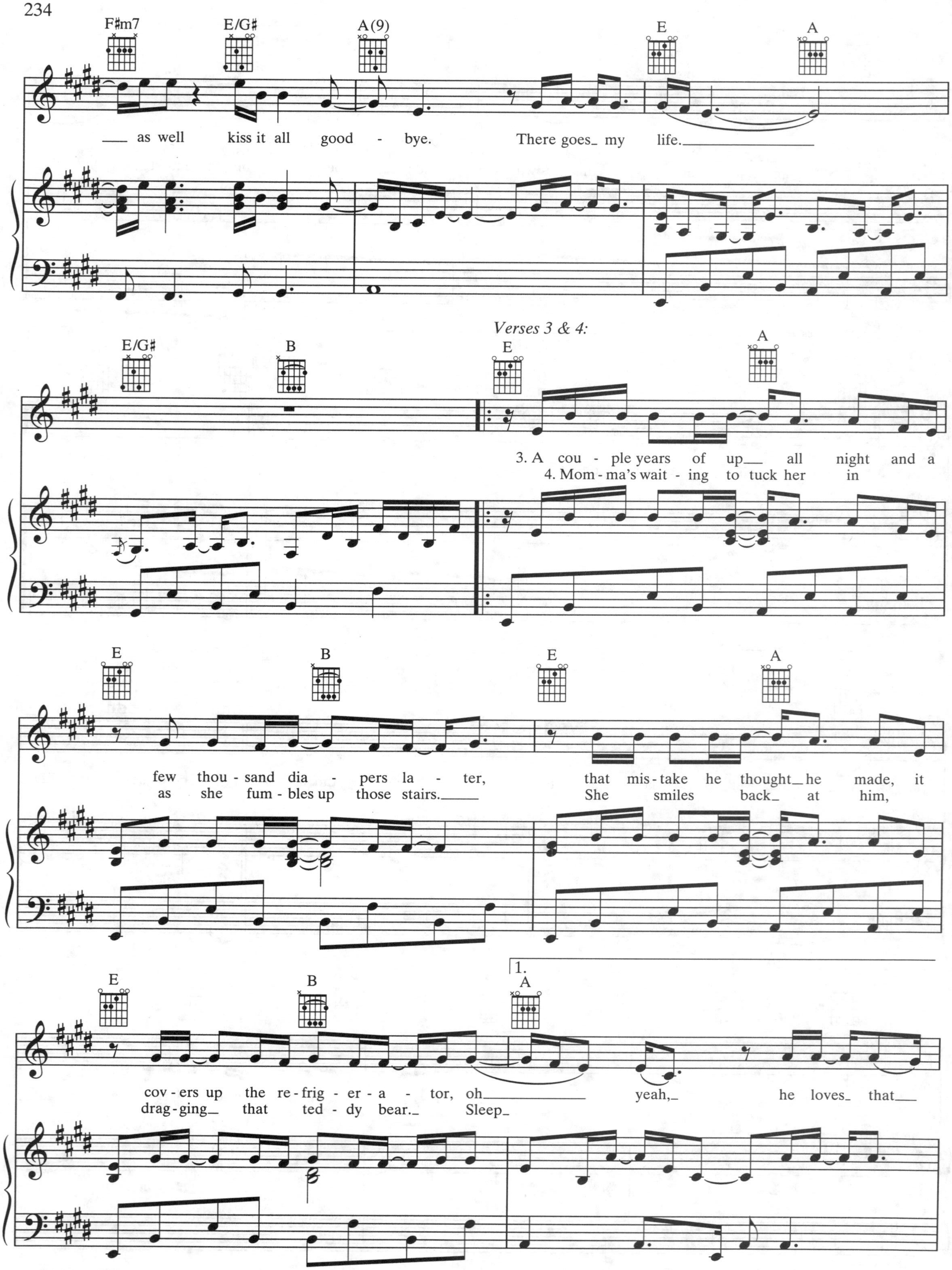
F♯m7
E/G♯
A (9)
E
A
— as well kiss it all good - bye. There goes_ my life.
E/G♯
B
Verses 3 & 4:
E
A
3. A cou - ple years of up_ all night and a
4. Mom - ma's wait - ing to tuck her in
E
B
E
A
few thou - sand dia - pers la - ter, that mis - take he thought_ he made, it
as she fum - bles up those stairs._ She smiles back_ at him,
E
B
1.
A
cov - ers up the re - frig - er - a - tor, oh_ yeah,_ he loves_ that_
drag - ging_ that ted - dy bear._ Sleep_

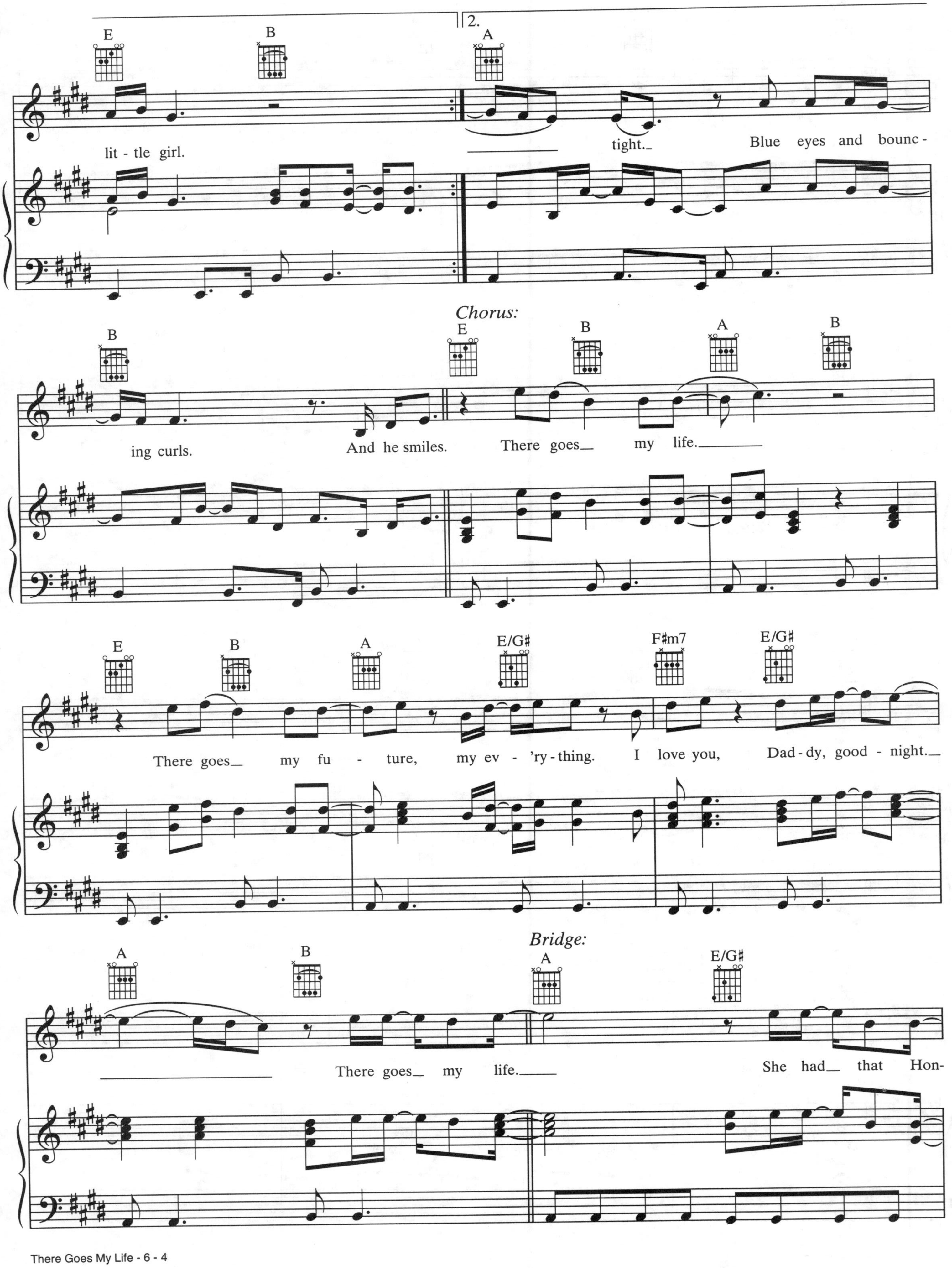
2.
E
B
A
lit - tle girl.
tight.
Blue eyes and bounc -
Chorus:
B
E
B
A
B
ing curls.
And he smiles.
There goes my life.
E
B
A
E/G♯
F♯m7
E/G♯
There goes my fu - ture, my ev - 'ry - thing.
I love you, Dad - dy, good - night.
Bridge:
A
B
A
E/G♯
There goes my life.
She had that Hon-

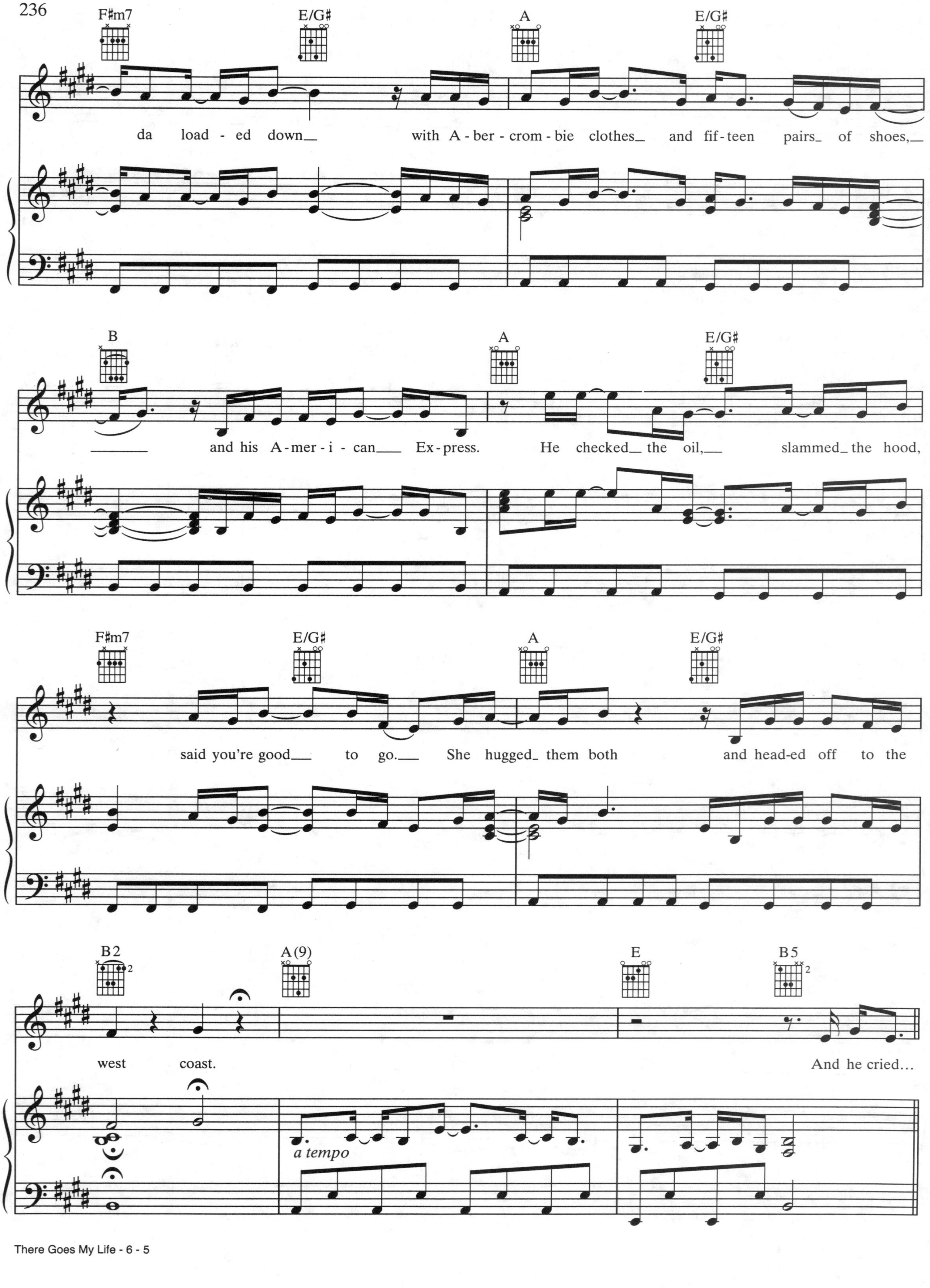
F♯m7
E/G♯
A
E/G♯
da load - ed down_ with A - ber - crom - bie clothes_ and fif - teen pairs_ of shoes,_
B
A
E/G♯
_ and his A - mer - i - can_ Ex - press. He checked_ the oil,_ slammed_ the hood,
F♯m7
E/G♯
A
E/G♯
said you're good_ to go._ She hugged_ them both and head-ed off to the
B2
A(9)
E
B5
west coast. And he cried...
a tempo

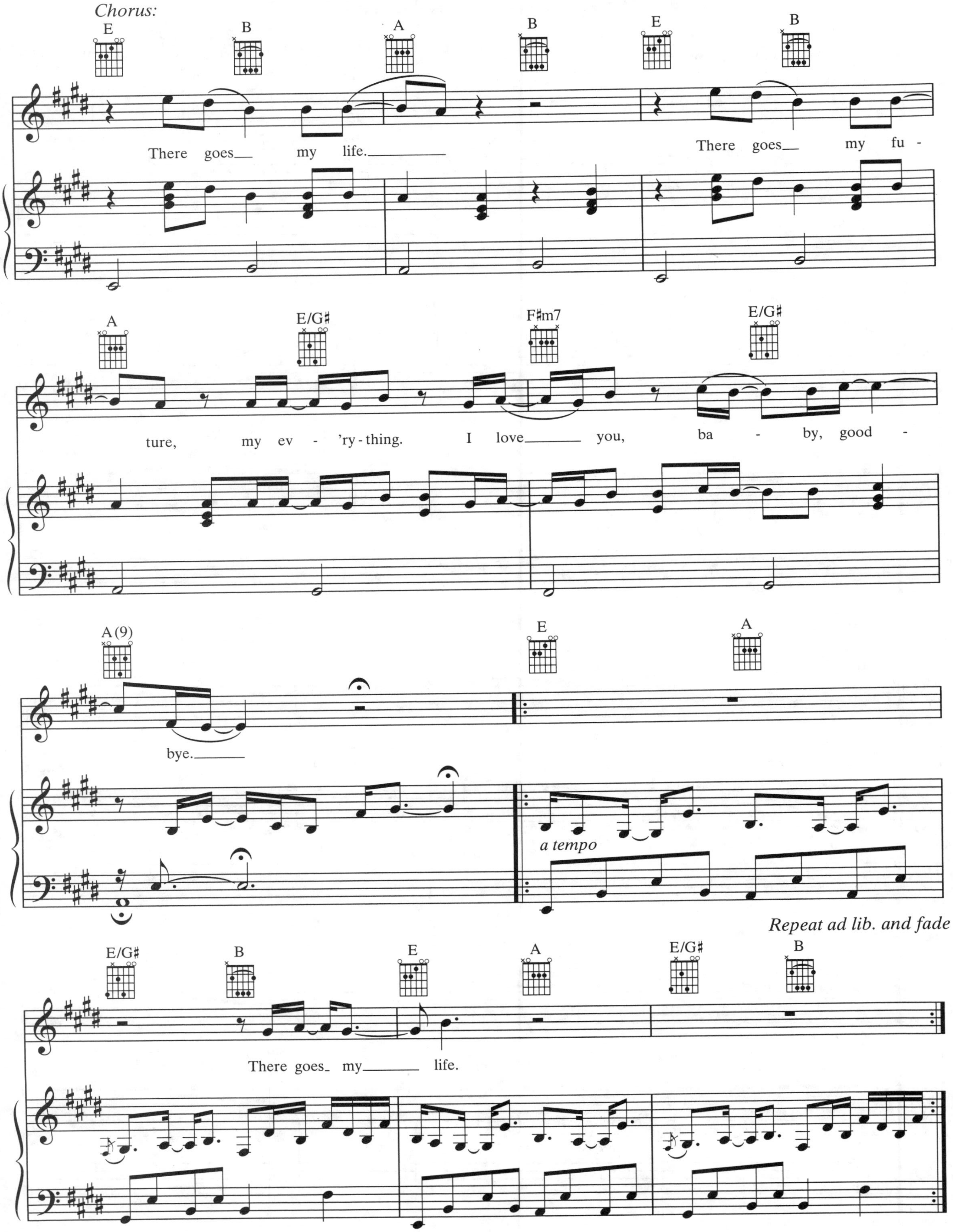

Chorus:
E
B
A
B
E
B
There goes my life.
There goes my fu-
A
E/G♯
F♯m7
E/G♯
ture, my ev-'ry-thing. I love you, ba-by, good-
A(9)
E
A
bye.
a tempo
Repeat ad lib. and fade
E/G♯
B
E
A
E/G♯
B
There goes my life.

TOUGH LITTLE BOYS

Words and Music by
HARLEY ALLEN and DONALD SAMPSON

Moderately slow ♩ = 84

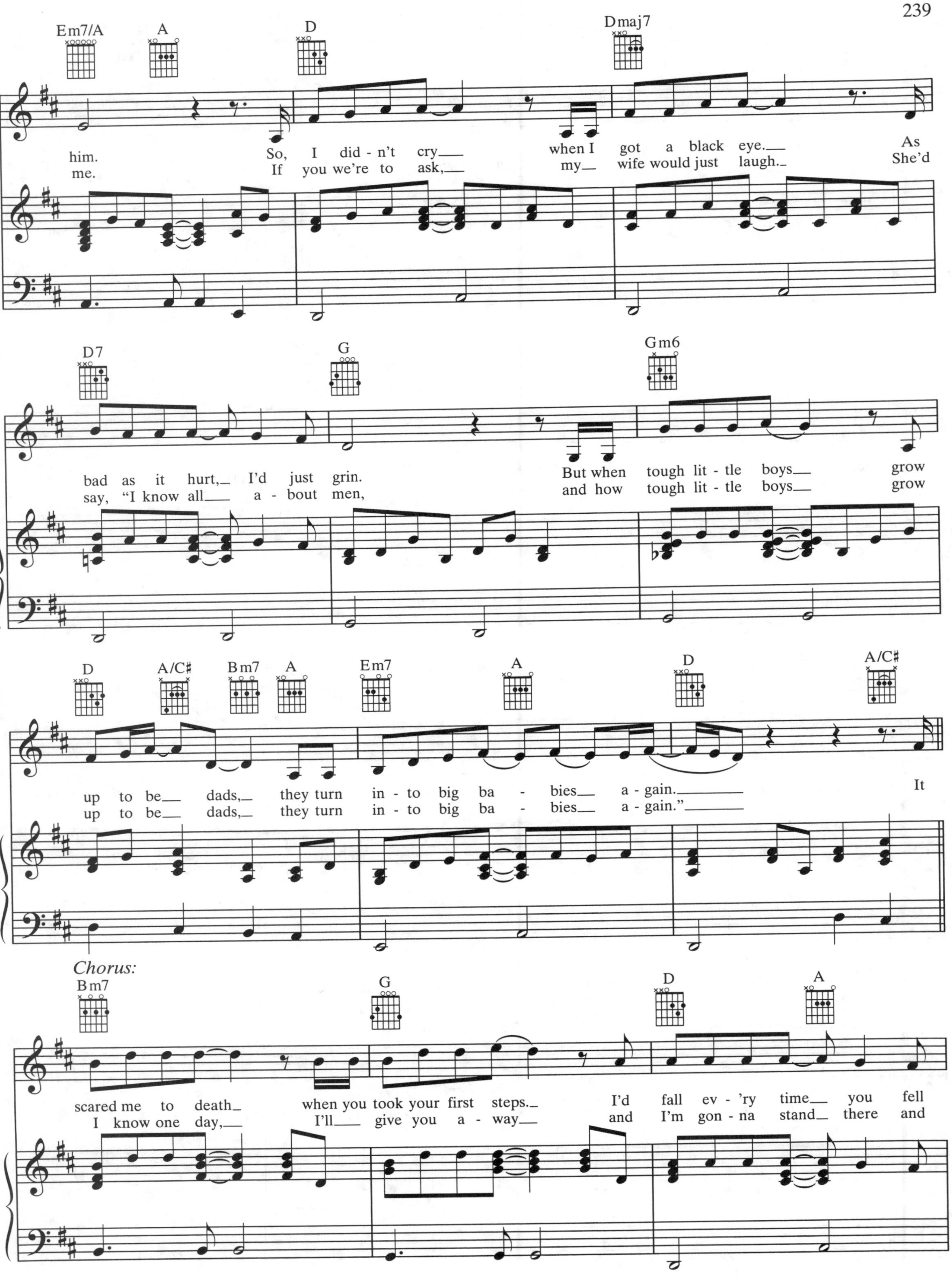
Em7/A
A
D
Dmaj7
him.
me.
So, I did - n't cry___ when I got a black eye.___ As
If you we're to ask,___ my___ wife would just laugh._ She'd
D7
G
Gm6
bad as it hurt,_ I'd just grin. But when tough lit - tle boys___ grow
say, "I know all___ a - bout men, and how tough lit - tle boys___ grow
D
A/C♯
Bm7
A
Em7
up to be___ dads,_ they turn in - to big ba - bies___ a - gain.______ It
up to be___ dads,_ they turn in - to big ba - bies___ a - gain."______
Chorus:
Bm7
G
scared me to death_ when you took your first steps._ I'd fall ev - 'ry time___ you fell
I know one day,___ I'll___ give you a - way___ and I'm gon - na stand_ there and

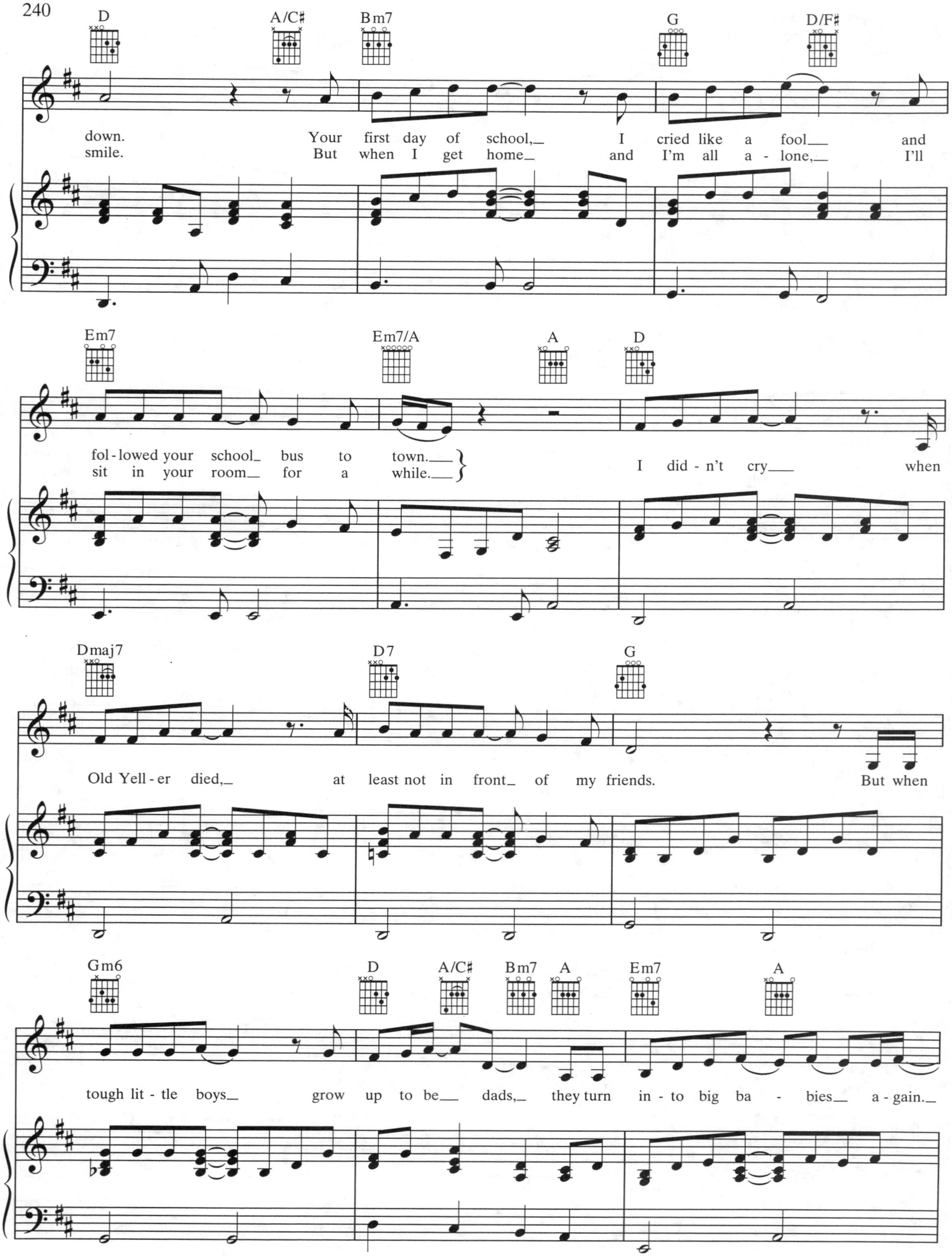
D A/C♯ Bm7 G D/F♯
down. Your first day of school,_ I cried like a fool_ and
smile. But when I get home_ and I'm all a-lone,_ I'll
Em7 Em7/A A D
fol-lowed your school_ bus to town._
sit in your room_ for a while._
I did-n't cry_ when
Dmaj7 D7 G
Old Yell-er died,_ at least not in front_ of my friends. But when
Gm6 D A/C♯ Bm7 A Em7 A
tough lit-tle boys_ grow up to be_ dads,_ they turn in-to big ba-bies_ a-gain._

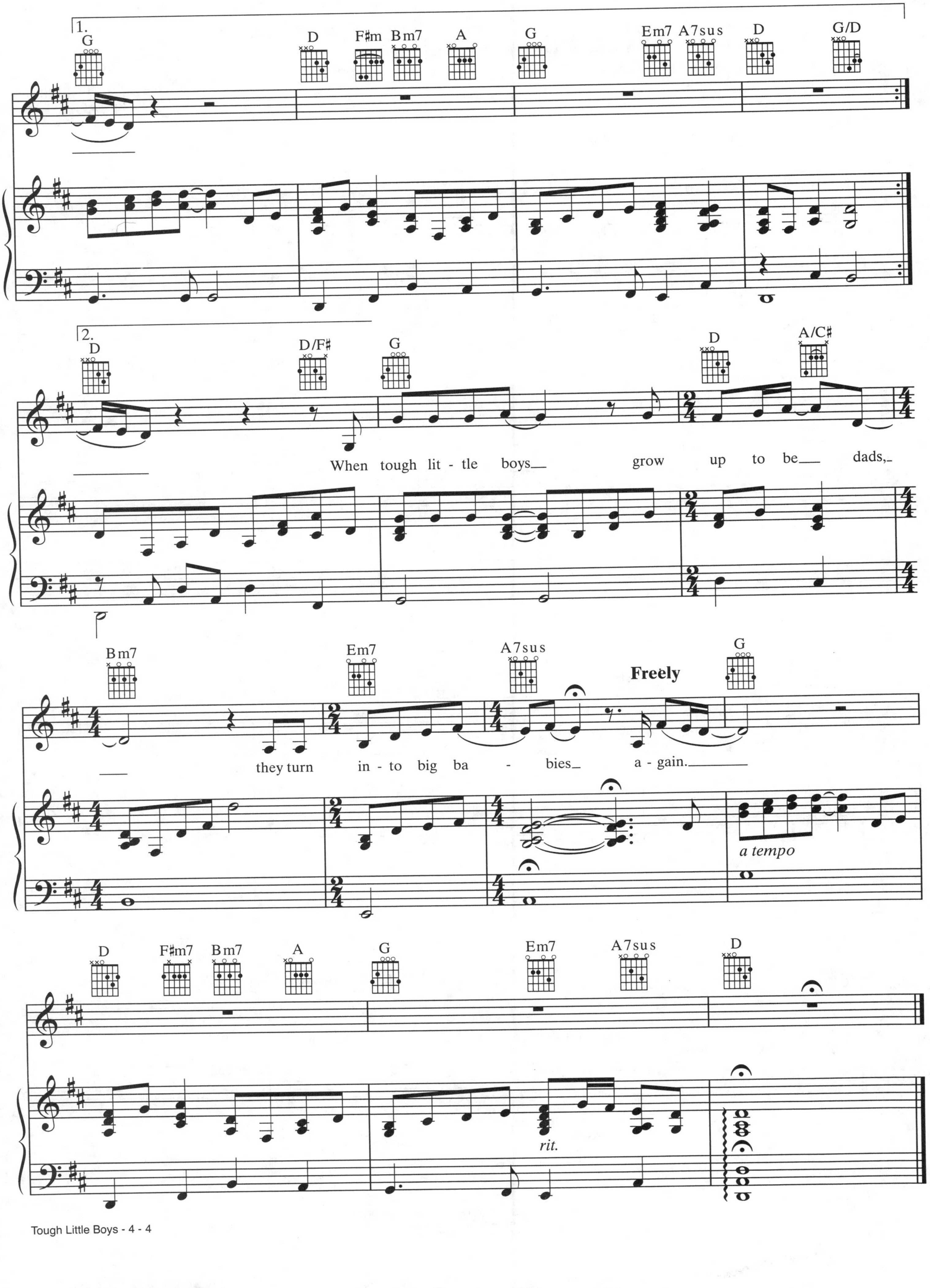
1.
G
D
F♯m
Bm7
A
G
Em7
A7sus
D
G/D
2.
D
D/F♯
G
D
A/C♯
When tough lit - tle boys grow up to be dads,
Bm7
Em7
A7sus
Freely
G
they turn in - to big ba - bies a - gain.
a tempo
D
F♯m7
Bm7
A
G
Em7
A7sus
D
rit.

WHERE I COME FROM

Words and Music by
ALAN JACKSON

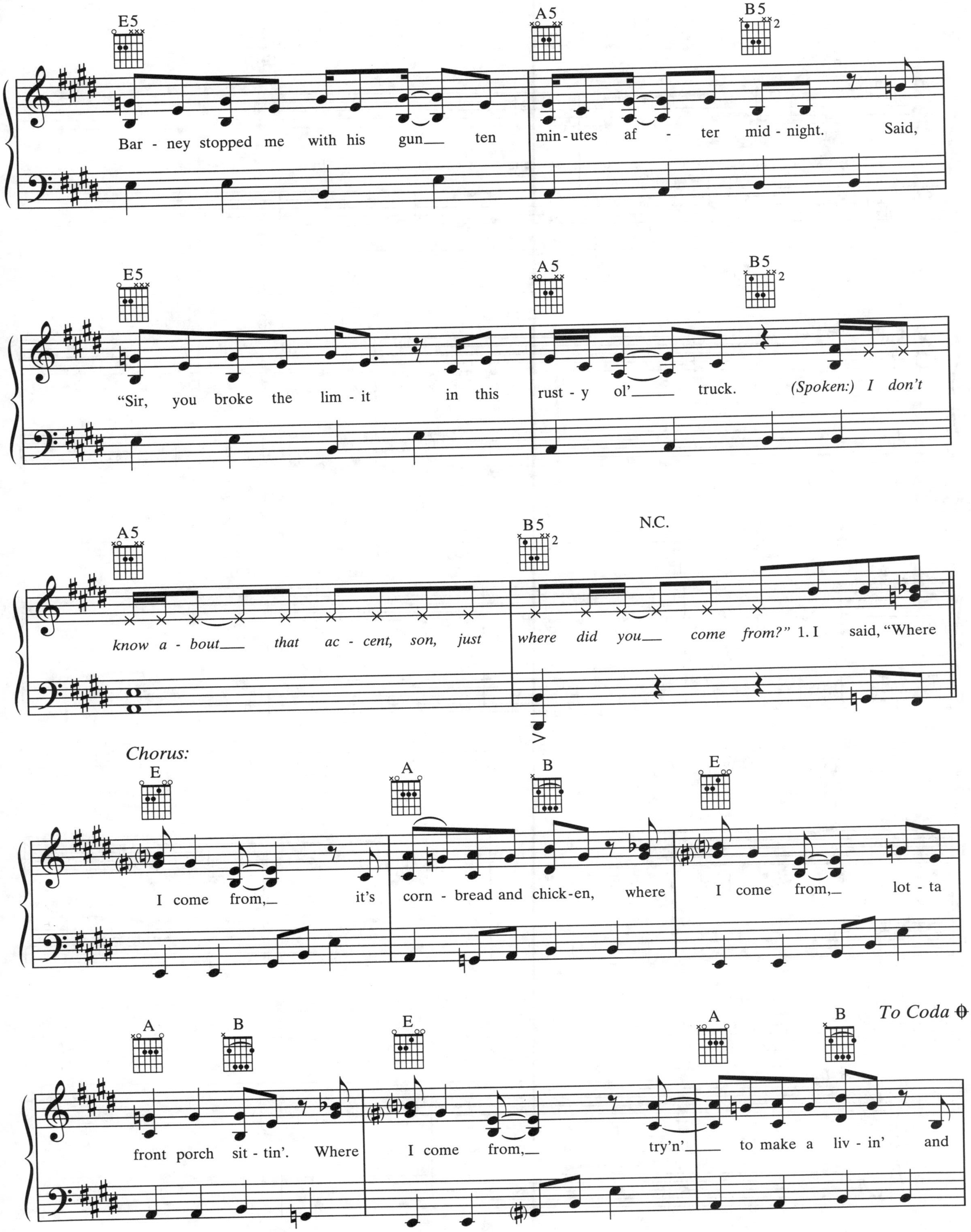
E5
A5
B5
Bar - ney stopped me with his gun__ ten
min - utes af - ter mid - night. Said,
E5
A5
B5
"Sir, you broke the lim - it in this
rust - y ol'__ truck. (Spoken:) I don't
A5
B5
N.C.
know a - bout__ that ac - cent, son, just
where did you__ come from?" 1. I said, "Where
Chorus:
E
A
B
E
I come from,__ it's
corn - bread and chick - en, where
I come from,__ lot - ta
A
B
E
A
B
To Coda
front porch sit - tin'. Where
I come from,__
try'n'__ to make a liv - in' and

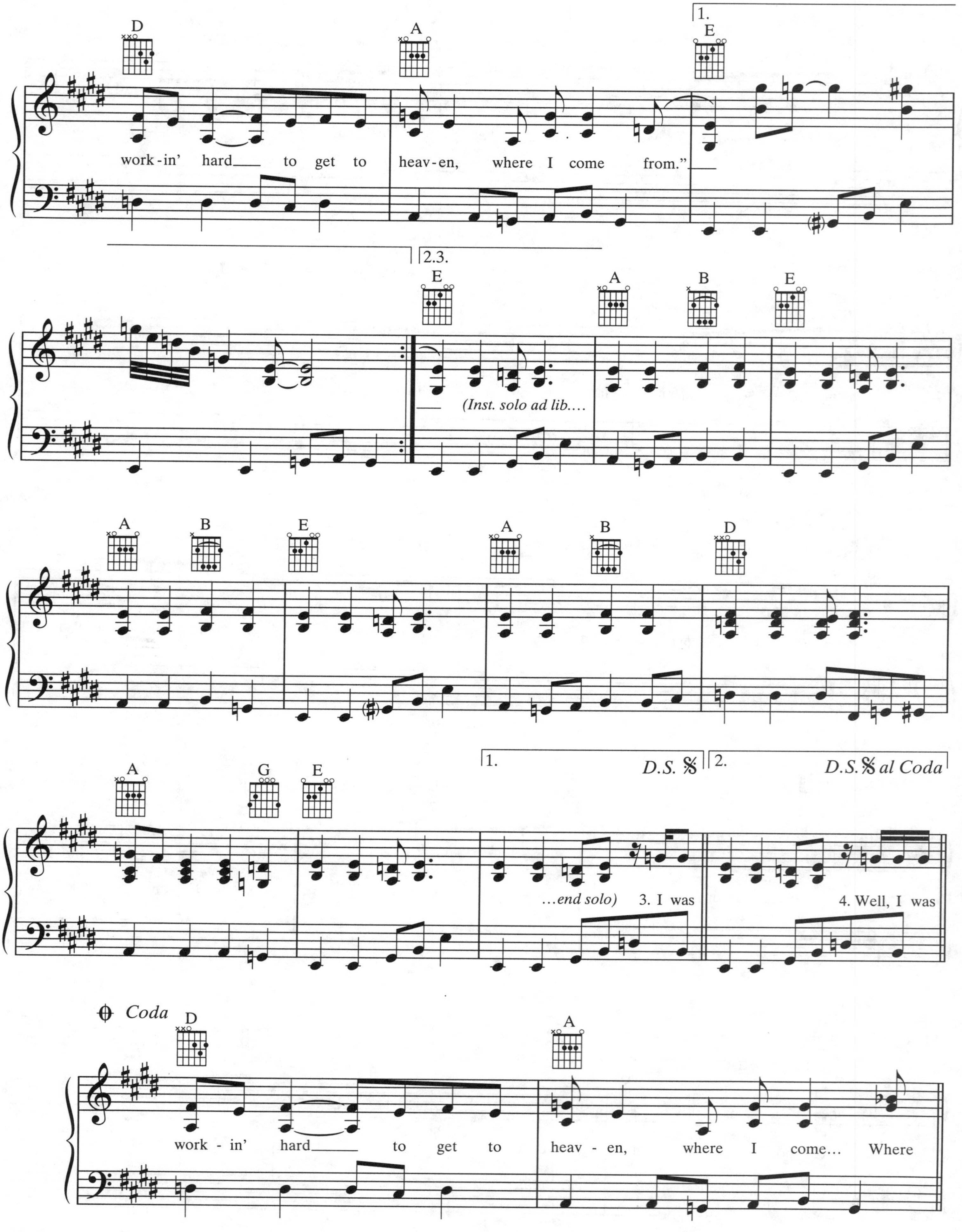
D
A
1.
E
work-in' hard___ to get to heav-en, where I come from."___
2.3.
E
A
B
E
(Inst. solo ad lib....
A
B
E
A
B
D
1.
D.S. 𝄋
2.
D.S. 𝄋 al Coda
A
G
E
...end solo) 3. I was
4. Well, I was
𝄌 Coda
D
A
work - in' hard___ to get to heav - en, where I come... Where

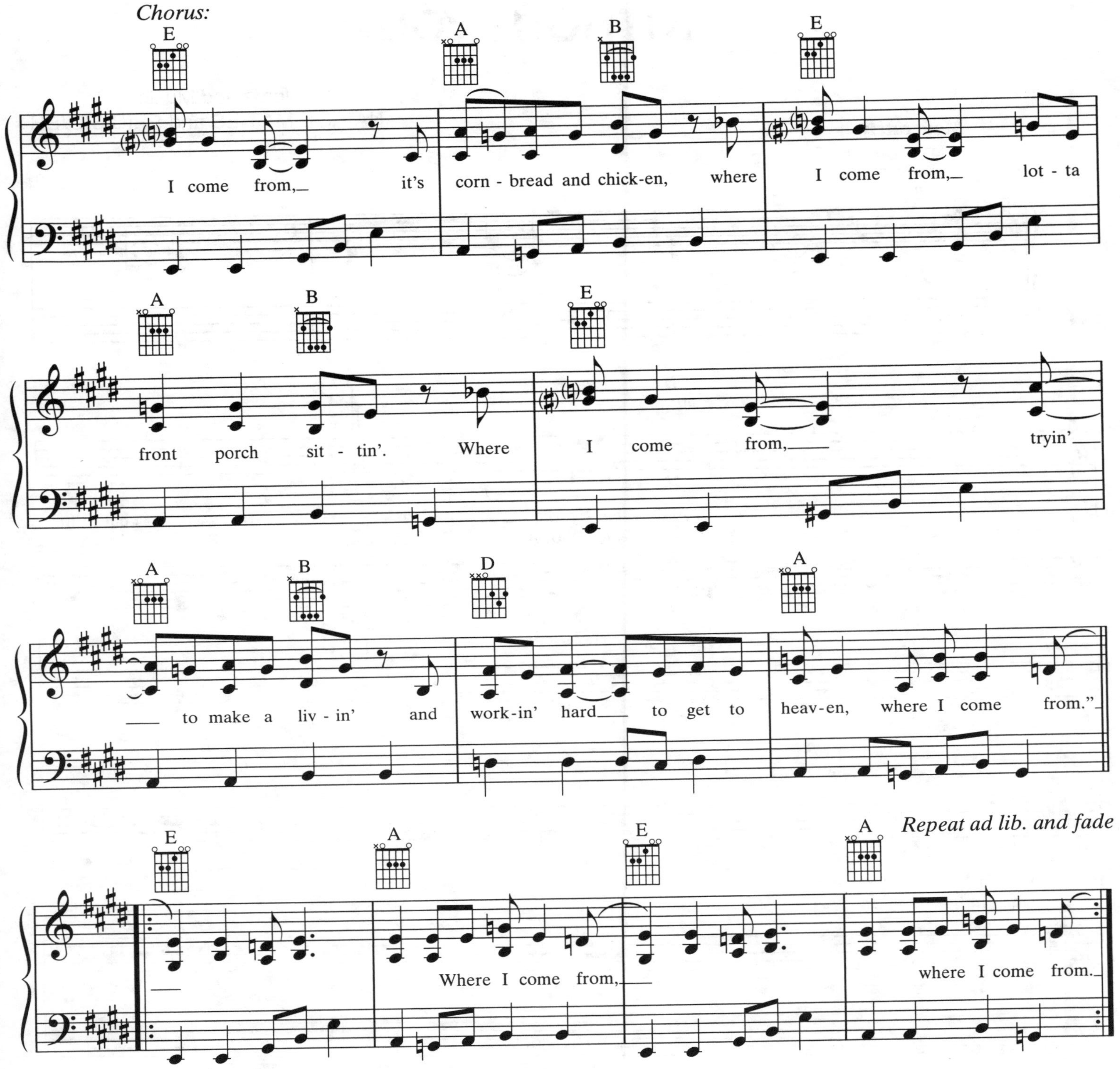

Verse 2:
Well, I was south of Detroit City,
I pulled in the country kitchen
To try their brand of barbecue.
The sign said "finger-lickin'."
Well, I paid the tab and the lady asked me
How'd I like my biscuit.
"I'll be honest with you, ma'am,
It ain't like Mama fixed it."
(To Chorus:)

Verse 3:
I was chasin' sun on 101
Somewhere around Ventura.
I lost a universal joint and I had to use my finger.
This tall lady stopped and asked
If I had plans for dinner.
Said, "No thanks, ma'am, back home
We like the girls that sing soprano."
(To Chorus:)

Verse 4:
Well, I was headed home on 65
Somewhere around Kentucky.
The CB rang for a bobtail rig
That's rollin' on like thunder.
Well, I answered him and he asked me,
"Aren't you from out in Tulsa?"
"Naw, but you might have seen me there,
I just dropped a load of salsa."
(To Chorus:)

WITHOUT YOU

Words and Music by
NATALIE MAINES and ERIC SILVER

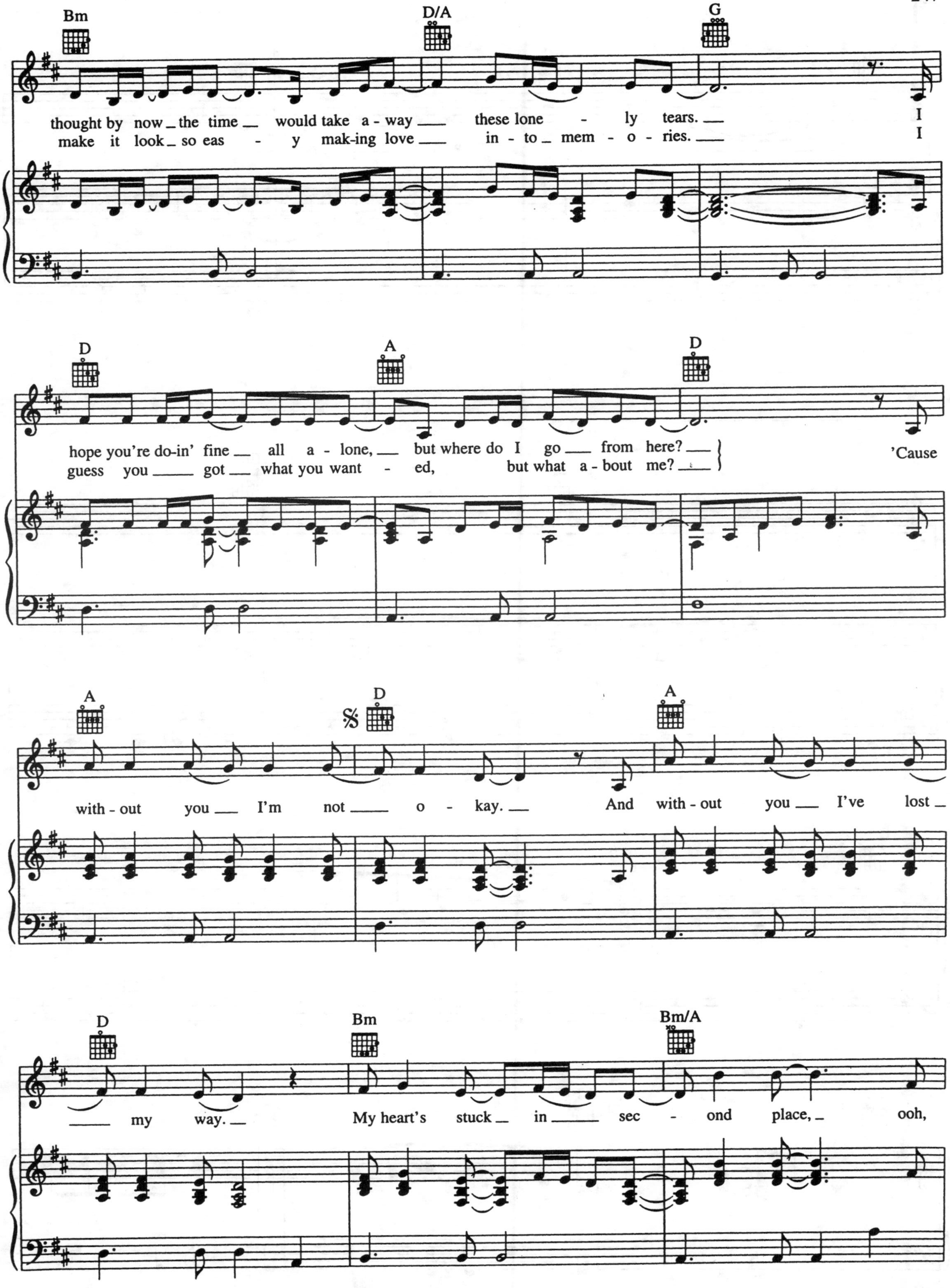
Bm
D/A
G
thought by now the time would take a-way these lone - ly tears. I
make it look so eas - y mak-ing love in-to mem - o - ries. I
D
A
D
hope you're do-in' fine all a - lone, but where do I go from here?
guess you got what you want - ed, but what a - bout me?
'Cause
A
D
A
with-out you I'm not o - kay. And with-out you I've lost
D
Bm
Bm/A
my way. My heart's stuck in sec - ond place, ooh,

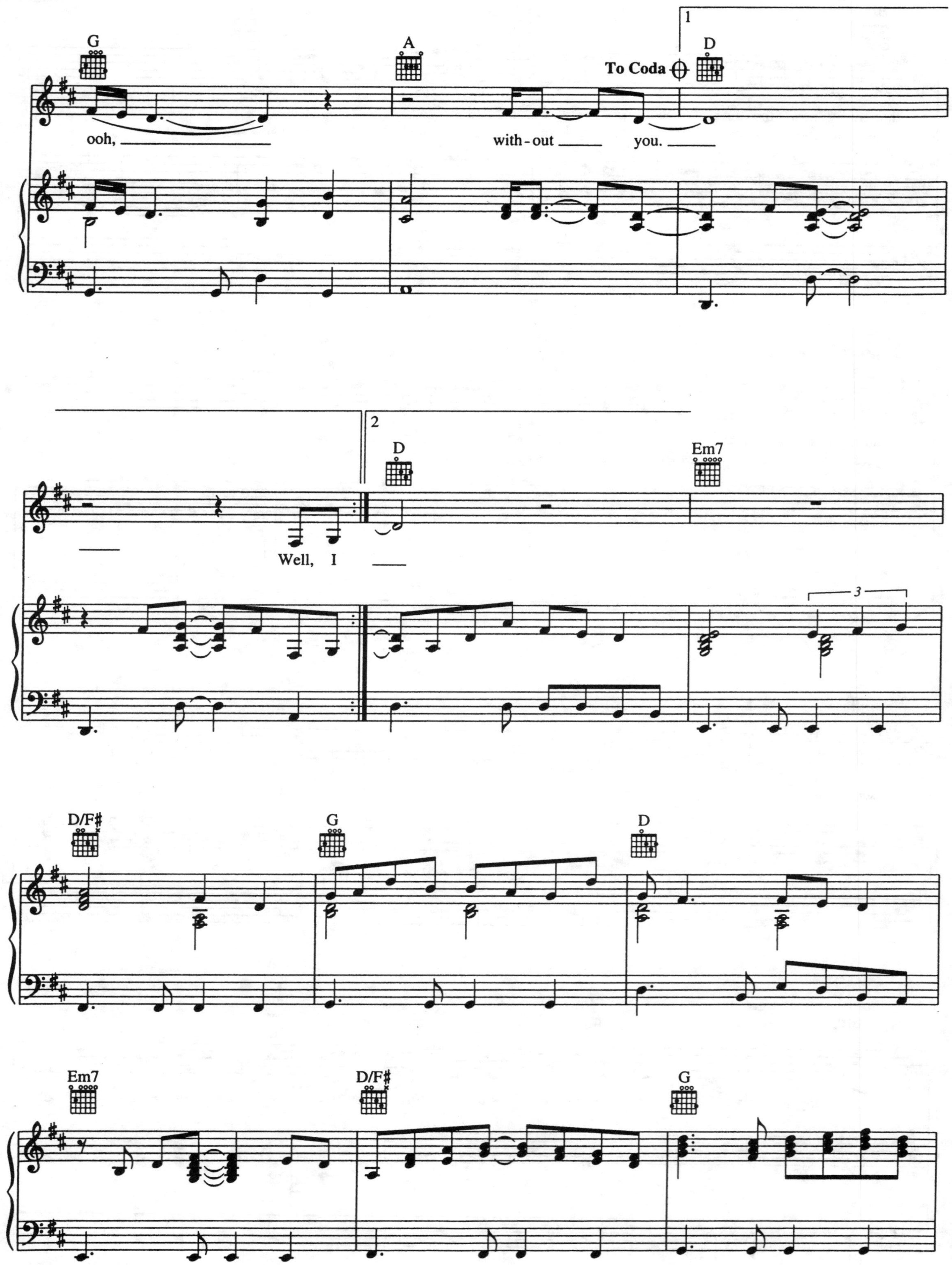

1
2
G
A
To Coda
D
ooh,
with - out
you.
Well, I
D
Em7
3
D/F#
G
D
Em7
D/F#
G

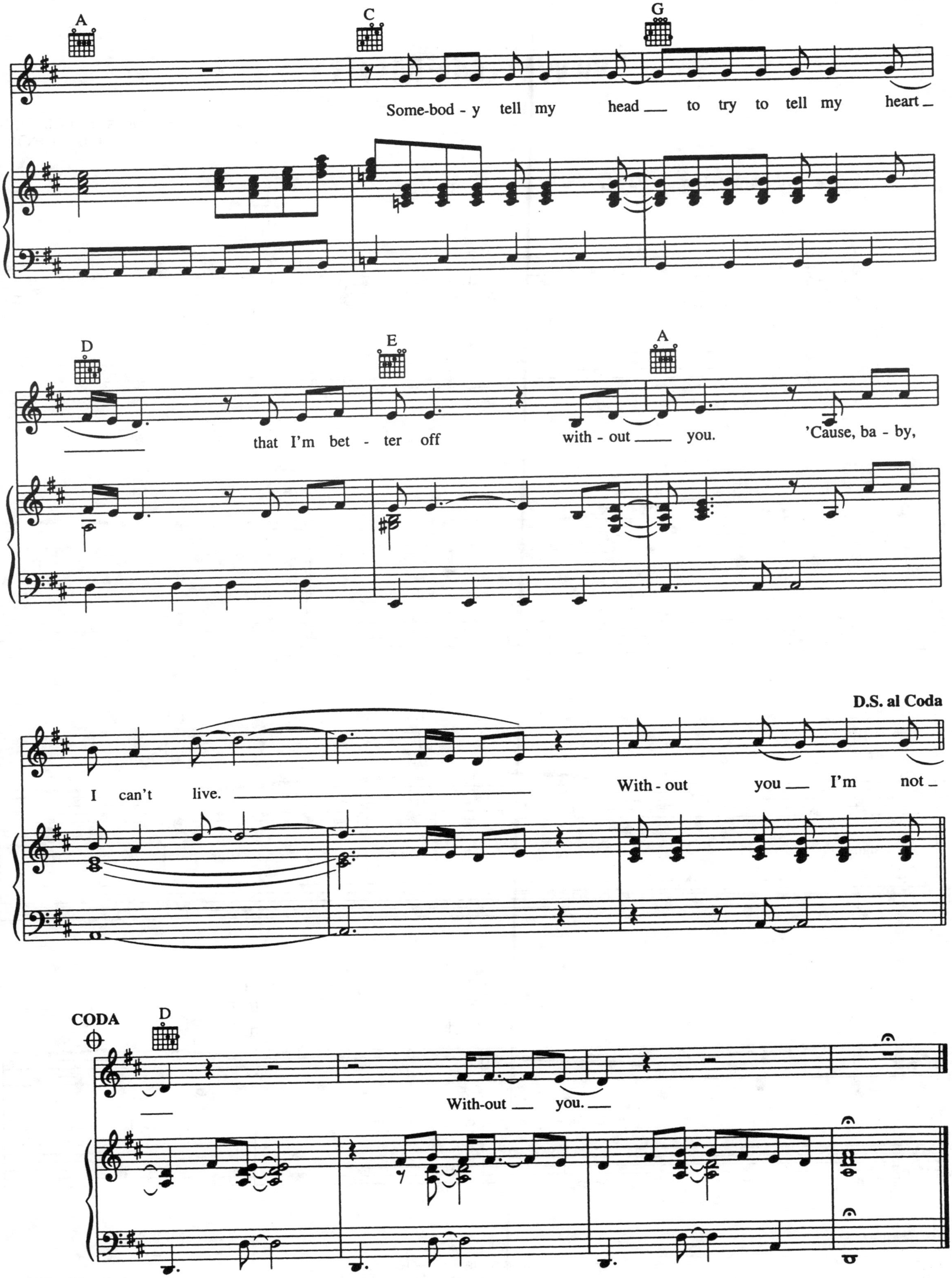
A
C
G
Some-bod - y tell my head to try to tell my heart
D
E
A
that I'm bet - ter off with - out you. 'Cause, ba - by,
D.S. al Coda
I can't live. With - out you I'm not
CODA
D
With-out you.

WWW.MEMORY

Words and Music by
ALAN JACKSON

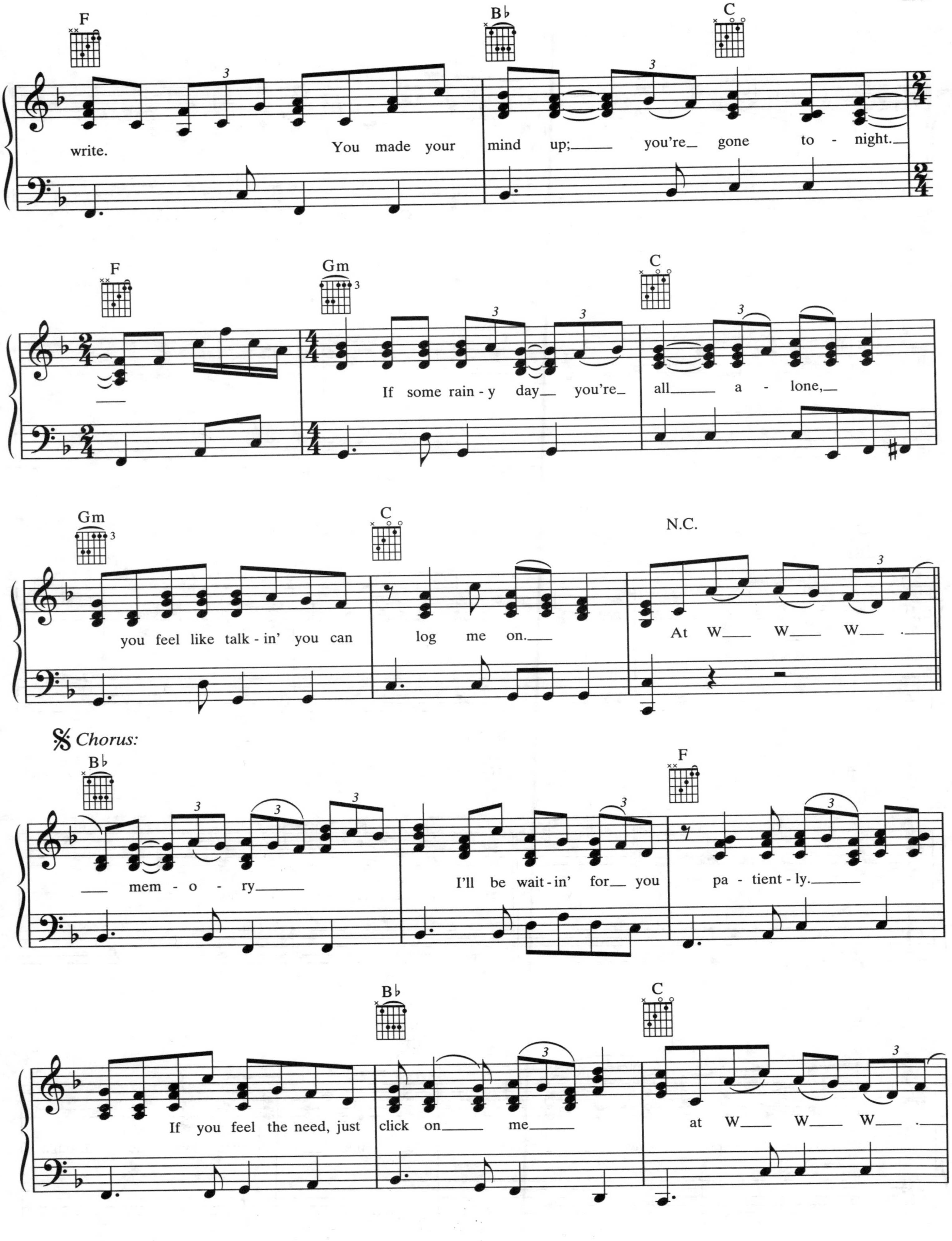
F
B♭
C
write. You made your mind up; you're gone to - night.
F
Gm
C
If some rain - y day you're all a - lone,
Gm
C
N.C.
you feel like talk - in' you can log me on. At W W W.
Chorus:
B♭
F
mem - o - ry I'll be wait - in' for you pa - tient - ly.
B♭
C
If you feel the need, just click on me at W W W.

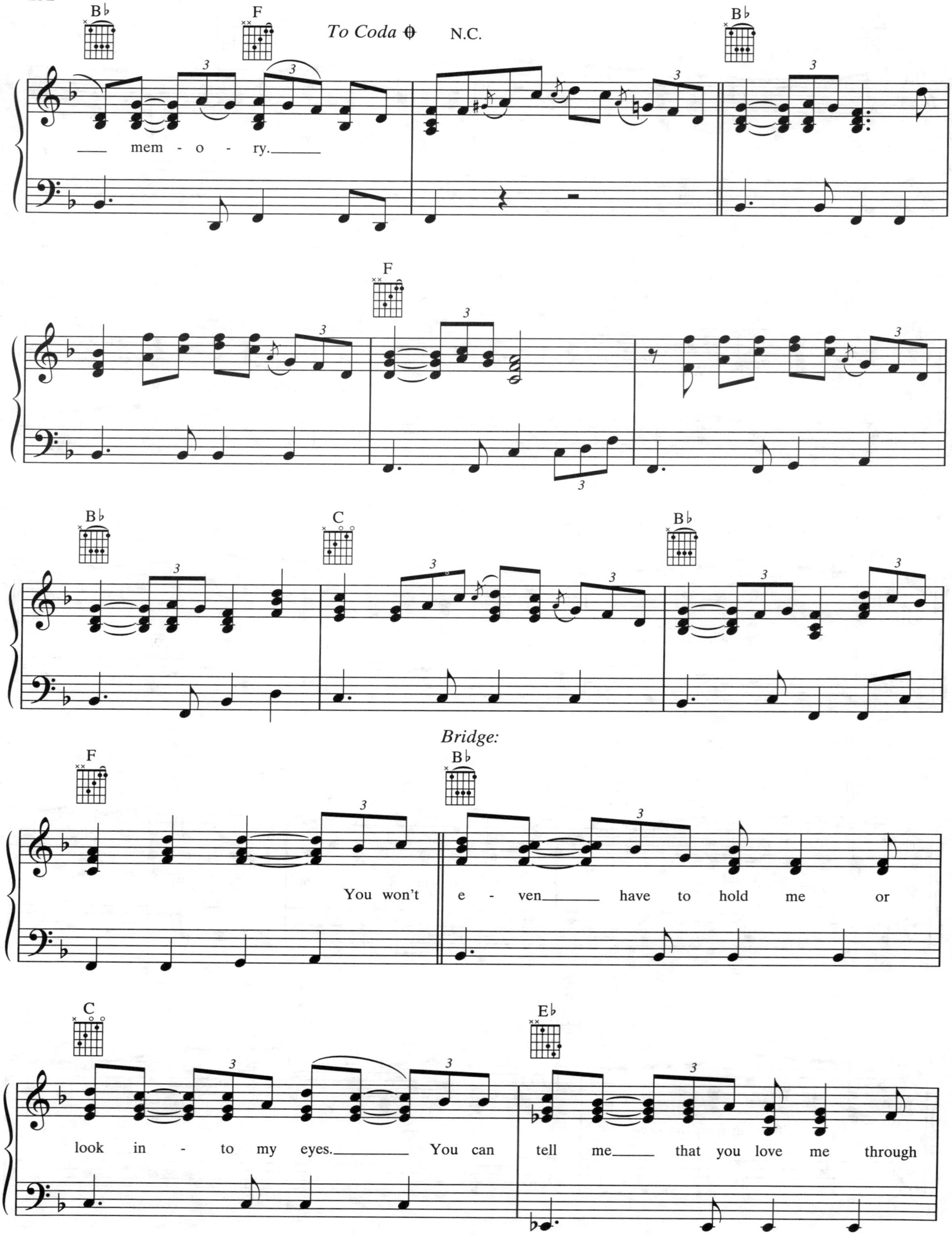
B♭
F
To Coda ⊕
N.C.
B♭
— mem - o - ry. —
F
B♭
C
B♭
Bridge:
F
B♭
You won't e - ven — have to hold me or
C
E♭
look in - to my eyes. — You can tell me — that you love me through

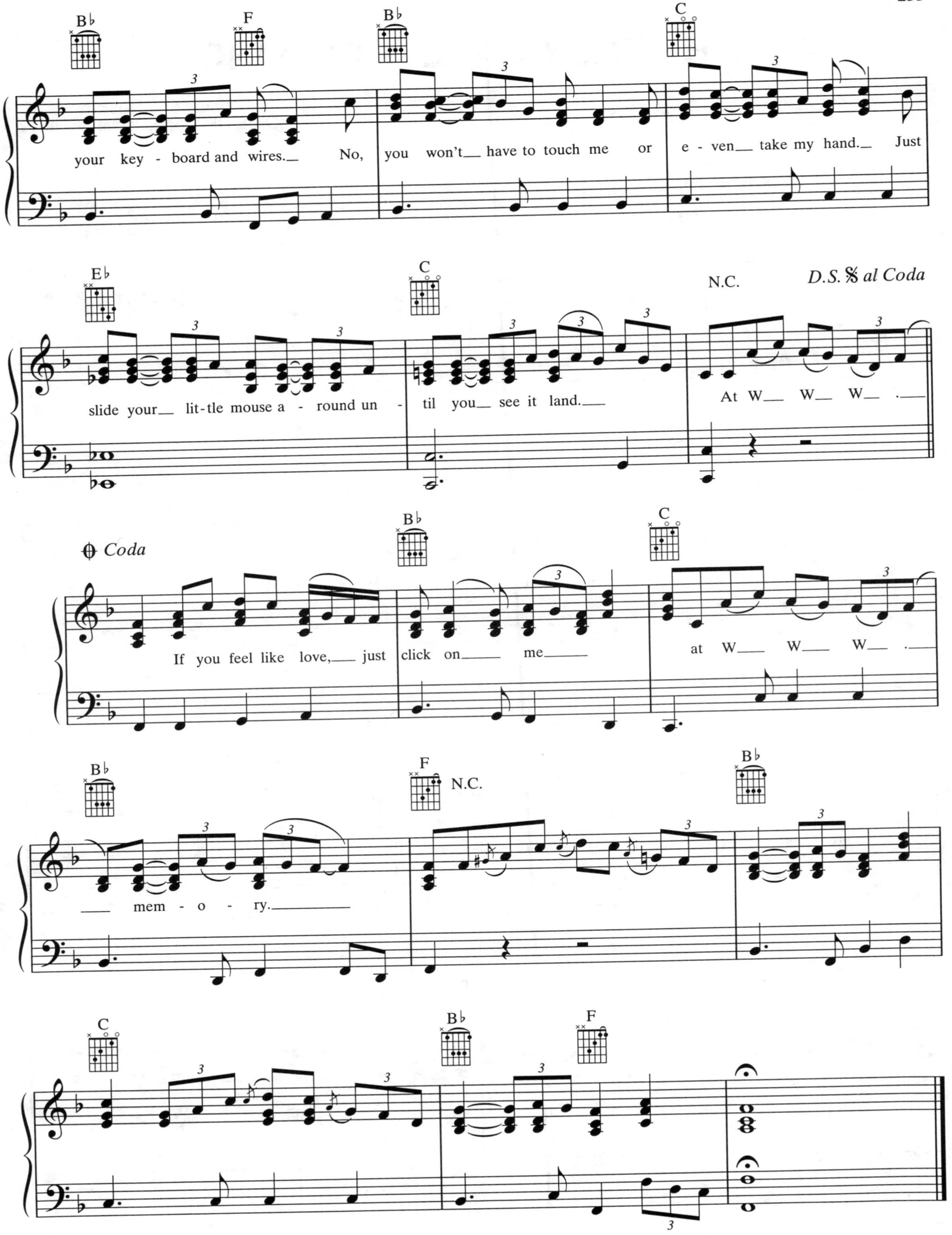
B♭
F
B♭
C
your key - board and wires.__ No, you won't__ have to touch me or e - ven__ take my hand.__ Just
E♭
C
N.C.
D.S. 𝄋 al Coda
slide your__ lit-tle mouse a - round un - til you__ see it land.__ At W__ W__ W__ .__
Coda
B♭
C
If you feel like love,__ just click on__ me__ at W__ W__ W__ .
B♭
F
N.C.
B♭
__ mem - o - ry.__
C
B♭
F

WHY THEY CALL IT FALLING

Words and Music by
ROXIE DEAN and DON SCHLITZ

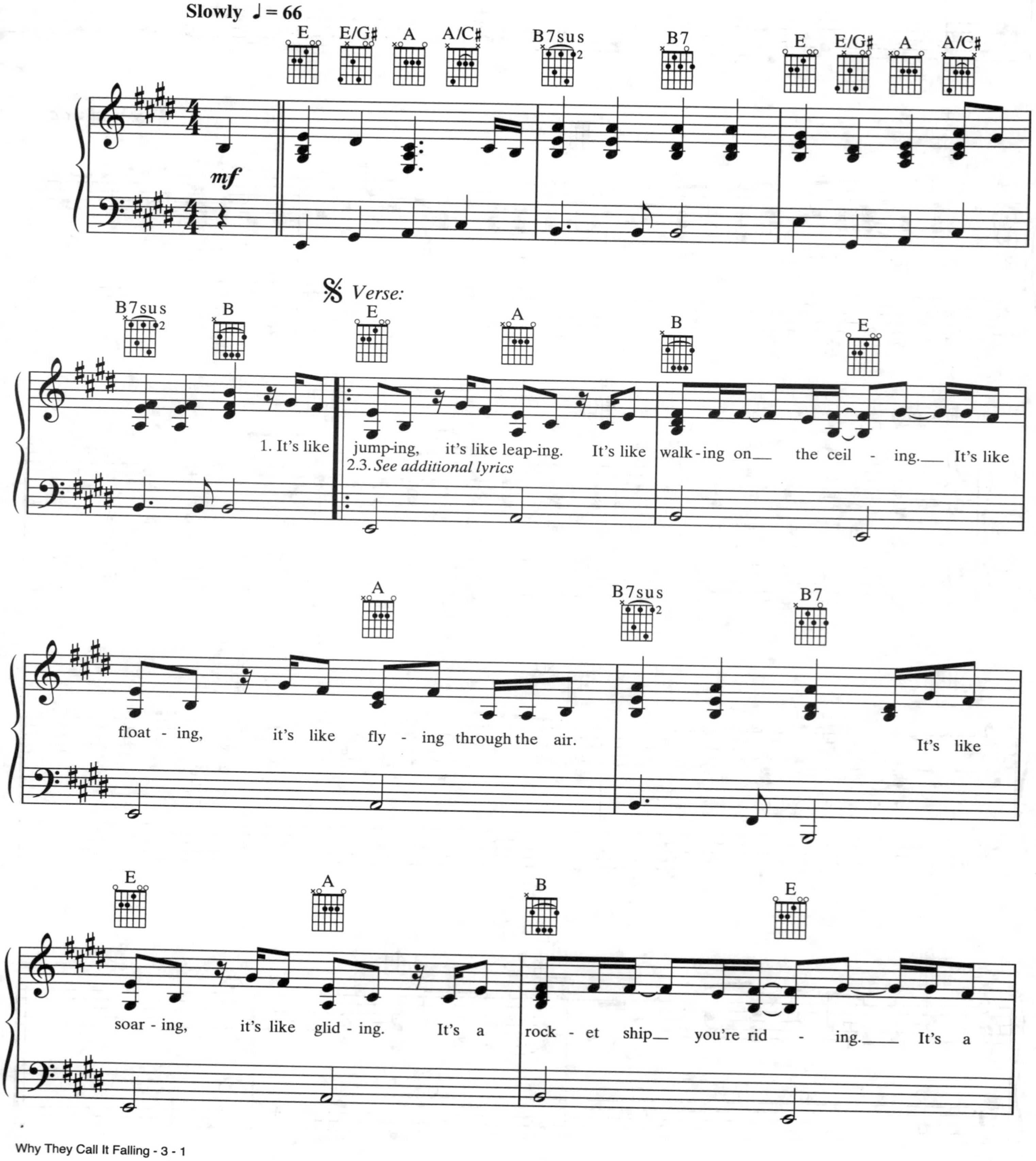

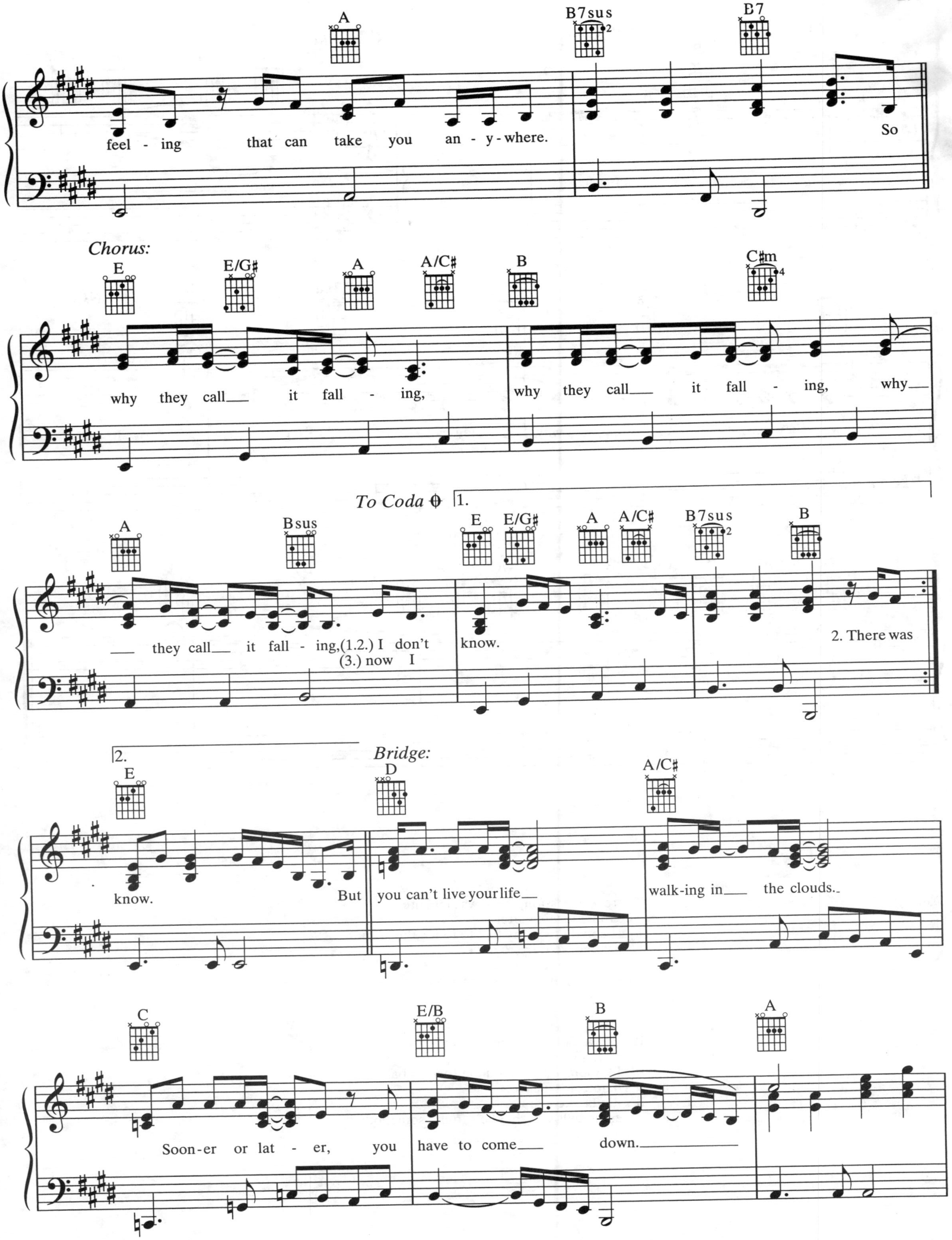
A
B7sus
B7
feel - ing that can take you an - y - where.
So
Chorus:
E
E/G♯
A
A/C♯
B
C♯m
why they call it fall - ing,
why they call it fall - ing, why
To Coda
1.
A
Bsus
E
E/G♯
A
A/C♯
B7sus
B
they call it fall - ing, (1.2.) I don't
(3.) now I
know.
2. There was
2.
Bridge:
E
D
A/C♯
know.
But
you can't live your life
walk-ing in the clouds.
C
E/B
B
A
Soon-er or lat - er, you
have to come down.

Verse 2:
There was passion, there was laughter
The first morning after.
I just couldn't get my feet to touch the ground.
Everytime we were together
We talked about forever.
I was certain it was heaven we had found.
(To Chorus:)

Verse 3:
It's like a knife through the heart
When it all comes apart.
It's like someone takes a pin to your balloon.
It's a hole, it's a cave,
It's kinda like a grave
When he tells you that he's found somebody new.
(To Chorus:)